Handbook of Distributed Sensor Networks

Volume II

Handbook of Distributed Sensor Networks
Volume II

Edited by **Marvin Heather**

CLANRYE INTERNATIONAL

New Jersey

Published by Clanrye International,
55 Van Reypen Street,
Jersey City, NJ 07306, USA
www.clanryeinternational.com

Handbook of Distributed Sensor Networks: Volume II
Edited by Marvin Heather

© 2015 Clanrye International

International Standard Book Number: 978-1-63240-267-7 (Hardback)

Contents

Preface

Distributed Sensor Networks is a concept which provides a smart communication, located in a network, with the potential to handle applications that iterate according to the user's requirement. Due to the recently developed technical advancements in the field, distributed sensor networks are gradually becoming an important part of human life. They are a big challenge for researchers these days, in terms of designing of algorithms and protocols. If the central node fails when a centralized architecture is applied in a sensor network, the entire network collapses. This problem can only be avoided by using distributed control architecture. There are numerous advantages of using distributed sensor networks, a crucial one being that it provides nodes with backup in case the central node fails, especially when better collection of data is priority.

Popular advanced techniques applied in sensor networks are localization algorithms in large-scale underwater acoustic sensor networks, mobility aware energy efficient congestion control in mobile wireless sensor network, continuous probabilistic skyline queries for uncertain moving objects in road network, fractal cross-layer service with integration and interaction in internet of things, etc.

Some of the chapters discussed in this book are provided with a close discussion of different applications such as load balanced routing for wireless multi-hop network applications and node placement analysis for overlay networks in iot applications. Several other technical aspects of the distributed sensor networks are elucidated.

I hope that this book will help engineers and researchers in the field of networking as well as computer technologies. Lastly, I wish to thank all the contributors and my family for all the support they provided for the completion of this project.

Editor

A Priority-Based CSMA/CA Mechanism to Support Deadline-Aware Scheduling in Home Automation Applications Using IEEE 802.15.4

Mario Collotta, Gianfranco Scatà, and Giovanni Pau

Facoltà di Ingegneria, Architettura e delle Scienze Motorie, Università degli Studi di Enna—Kore Cittadella Universitaria, 94100 Enna, Italy

Correspondence should be addressed to Gianfranco Scatà; gianfranco.scata@unikore.it

Academic Editor: Danny Hughes

The wireless sensor networks (WSNs) are characterized by several small nodes able to perform measurements on one or more parameters and to communicate with each other through several protocols. Most of home automation networks (depending on the specific application) are mainly characterized by periodic traffic flows. In soft real-time contexts, the main problem is represented by the efficient allocation of guaranteed time slots (GTSs) for periodic traffic flows transmission in IEEE 802.15.4 networks. Moreover, it is important to ensure adequate performance for those embedded devices competing for the access to the medium through the carrier sense multiple access/collision avoidance algorithm (CSMA/CA). The main aim of this paper is to show a new approach for network flows scheduling in home automation applications based on IEEE 802.15.4 wireless sensor networks. This work addresses several advantages due to the introduction of rate monotonic (RM) for guaranteed time slots (GTSs) allocation combined with priority-based CSMA/CA for latencies reduction on transmission attempts as clearly demonstrated by obtained results.

1. Introduction

In order to provide a detailed introduction to the issue, this section will be divided into three subsections. Section 1.1 specifically deals with wireless sensor networks for home automation systems, explaining the reasons which led to the choice of the IEEE 802.15.4 protocol. In Section 1.2, a general overview of the IEEE 802.15.4 protocol will be shown, placing emphasis on how it supports real-time communication using the guaranteed time slots mechanism. Finally, Section 1.3 will discuss the main motivations and aims of this research work.

1.1. Wireless Sensor Networks in Home Automation Systems. Wireless sensor networks are widely used in several application areas including data processing [1], industry [2–5] home automation [6–8], and road monitoring [9, 10] thanks to several characteristics like flexibility, adaptability, and scalability [11]. An automated house is the integration of embedded devices with other nonautomated systems such as lighting, heating, and air conditioning in order to realize

smart applications for home control. The main aim of this integration is to provide greater comfort, safety, optimizing and the energy consumption. Wireless sensor networks are fundamental in home automation applications whose main requirements are quality of service (QoS) and real-time constraints satisfaction [12]. Most of the domotic systems, currently available on the market, use wired networks through different communication protocols like Ethernet [13], X-10 [14], Modbus [15], or Powerline [16]. Although their functionality and reliability have been proven over the years, some important disadvantages must be considered. For example, Powerline and X-10 use the existing power line but suffer of high error rates on poor quality lines affected by noise. Modbus and Ethernet require cables for both power and data transmission. This can be expensive in terms of implementation and maintenance costs as well as being aesthetically not very functional. WSNs represent the obvious solution to these problems because they consist of several low cost and low power devices. There are several protocols available for sensor networks like Bluetooth and

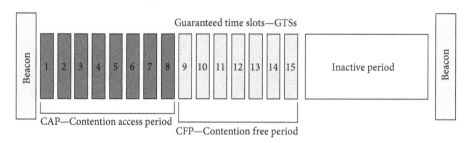

FIGURE 1: IEEE 802.15.4 MAC superframe structure.

IEEE 802.15.4 [17]. Through Bluetooth it is possible to connect up to seven active devices for each piconet and it uses frequency hopping (FH) and time division multiplexing (TDM) in order to regulate transmissions. Moreover, it is characterized by high power consumption. As a consequence, the IEEE 802.15.4 standard protocol is more appropriate for home automation applications.

1.2. The IEEE 802.15.4 Protocol. The IEEE 802.15.4 standard provides the physical (PHY) layer and medium access control (MAC) sublayer specifications for low data rate (up to 250 kbps in ISM frequencies, 2.4 GHz) wireless connectivity. According to the IEEE 802.15.4 standard protocol, a wireless sensor network can optionally operate in beacon-enabled mode (the more suitable for real-time traffic flows management). In this case, the time axis is divided into a sequence of superframes, each one delimited by special signaling packets (beacons). The beacons are transmitted by the PAN coordinator and are responsible for the synchronization of all network devices. In this operating mode, the superframe is divided into time slots and contains a contention access period (CAP) in which the multiple accesses to the channel are managed through the CSMA/CA algorithm. The superframe also provides a contention free period (CFP), in which certain stations can obtain access to the medium without collisions (in FIFO order) in special guaranteed time slots (GTSs), and an inactive period in which the radio interface can be put in a low energy consumption status in order to improve energy savings. Figure 1 shows the IEEE 802.15.4 superframe structure.

1.3. Motivations and Main Aim. The use of wireless technologies in home automation networks needs the study and the implementation of new scheduling and QoS [18, 19] management mechanisms in order to meet real-time constraints. In fact, considering the IEEE 802.15.4 protocol, in contention access period the access to the medium is variable and unpredictable due to the backoff mechanism. In this work, we propose an approach based on the combined use of rate monotonic (RM) [20], for GTSs allocation in the contention free period, and a variation of the CSMA/CA algorithm for channel accesses management in the CAP based on traffic flows classification. The proposed approach can help in the development of home automation applications characterized, as known, by soft real-time constraints. The main aim of this work is to reduce the waiting time during

access attempts to the radio channel of embedded devices improving, at the same time, network performance of home automated environments. Results, obtained through several measurement campaigns, show how differentiating traffic flows makes it possible to effectively improve performance in terms of throughput/workload (Th/Wl) on each embedded device and, in general, on the whole network. The paper is organized as follows. Section 2 reports the main literature works about approaches to improve IEEE 802.15.4 networks performance. Section 3 shows the considered network architecture, the proposed approach, and a probabilistic analysis about relationship between network throughput and the probability of each node to find the radio channel free. Section 4 proposes a test-bed scenario showing obtained results, while Section 5 summarizes the paper reporting conclusions.

2. Related Works

The IEEE 802.15.4 wireless sensor networks have been studied by researchers which evaluated several aspects. In order to cover the main issues, the related works section has been organized by topic areas. Our main aim is to take stock of the current situation about the various aspects of the issue object of this work and then to propose our improvements.

2.1. Home Automation Networks Applications Based on the IEEE 802.15.4 Standard Protocol. In the literature, there are several works focused on home and building automation, and many of them use the IEEE 802.15.4 standard protocol for wireless connectivity of sensor nodes. In [21], the deployment of wireless sensor networks and wireless systems applied to home and building automation systems is analyzed. Authors propose an in-house deterministic code based on 3D ray launching in order to analyze the effect of the indoor topology and morphology in the operation of wireless links within different realistic scenarios. Several simulations were performed in order to obtain performance parameters, such as RSSI (received signal strength indication) and PER (packet error rate). Simulation results show that the analysis of the topology of the wireless sensor network has a strong impact on complex indoor scenarios. The use of adequate radio-planning strategies, through the application of deterministic techniques in the planning phase, leads to optimal wireless network deployments in terms of capacity, quality of service, and energy consumption. The purpose of [22] is to

A Priority-Based CSMA/CA Mechanism to Support Deadline-Aware Scheduling in Home Automation
Applications Using IEEE 802.15.4

3

demonstrate the use of IEEE 802.15.4 to provide real-time environmental information to a smart home simulator. In this work, the simulator itself and a brief technical introduction of the IEEE 802.15.4 standard are presented. Moreover, the authors analyze the reliability of IEEE 802.15.4 in a real home automation application. In fact, authors came to the conclusion that the IEEE 802.15.4 standard is very reliable and easy to implement in home wireless network scenarios thanks to the versatility and scalability of the protocol. In addition, an analysis on exposure levels to electromagnetic fields is provided. Using the IEEE 802.15.4 protocol, the exposure levels of electromagnetic radiation are very low, about 600 times lower than an ordinary cell phone. The authors of [23] describe the IEEE 802.15.4/ZigBee communication protocol, and they present its potential deployment in smart home environments. Some examples of prototype applications, in home security and automation using a ZigBee-based wireless sensor network, are presented. The authors made a comparison between the designed ZigBee-based wireless smart home system and other existing systems in market. A careful analysis on wireless architecture shows that sensors and communication devices, used for the deployment in smart home, are not required to have a high speed in communication capacities. The authors show how using the ZigBee network technology, as wireless communication standard, makes it possible to satisfy home automation networks requirements, because IEEE 802.15.4 allows to obtain robust mesh networks and complete interoperability. Instead, more studies are needed to limit the energy consumptions of devices, to improve the network scheduling mechanism, and to validate the coexistence of multiple protocols.

2.2. Energy Saving IEEE 802.15.4 Applications in Home Automation Networks. The need of smart energy management in home environments, for sustainable energy efficiency and monetary savings, is analyzed in several works. The authors of [24] provide a comprehensive summary of the state of the art in home area communications and networking technologies for energy management. The analysis shows that there are several wireless standards for home area networks, including IEEE 802.15.4, and, accordingly, the system designers choose the wireless technology that best fits their application. Moreover, the authors point out on the challenges dealing with the design of energy management systems, in terms of accuracy, compatibility, low power cost, and integration, in order to provide the guidelines for standardized and more user-friendly smart energy home automation systems. Energy management is also examined in [25]. This work introduces a novel home-energy control system design, based on ZigBee devices, that provides intelligent services for users. The authors implement the proposed system and demonstrate its potentiality using a real test bed. After an accurate analysis, the paper clearly shows that smart home control systems can provide significant cost savings in home environment applications. In this work, a specific dissertation about lighting energy reduction is done. In fact, by using an automated control system it could be possible to turn lights off based on several factors such as available daylight or time

of day. Therefore, the use of wireless connections rather than wired networks involves several benefits in terms of flexibility and money savings. In order to meet home automation networks requirements, several aspects of the IEEE 802.15.4 medium access control (MAC) in contention access period (CAP), contention free period (CFP), and the overall cross period, respectively, are analyzed in [26]. An extensive discussion focuses on a variety of adaptive real-time protocols based on IEEE 802.15.4 and on many problems of wireless networks like high latency, system complexity, implementation overhead, and, mainly, great energy consumption. The authors come to the conclusion that the requirements of all aspects usually cannot be satisfied simultaneously. However, the network efficiency can be significantly improved optimizing the original specifications and dynamically adjusting the IEEE 802.15.4 protocol parameters. A home automation network architecture for energy management inside smart grid environments is presented in [27]. In order to achieve smart grid potential, the authors aim to resolve the problem of interoperability among different communications technologies deployed in the grid. The authors propose a framework for end-to-end interoperability in home and building area networks. This framework includes the 6LoWPAN protocol in order to simplify the use of IPv6 and ZigBee application profiles. The authors also focus on other issues, including interference mitigation and load scheduling, and they propose a solution to them. They propose a priority contention algorithm for high priority messages management, while, at the same time, the proposed approach uses a compression and scheduling mechanism in order to increase the efficiency of transferred data. Moreover, a frequency-agility-based interference mitigation algorithm is proposed in order to guarantee the performance of network protocols coexistence.

2.3. GTS Mechanism in Home Automation Networks. Wireless technologies in home automation applications need the development of new scheduling mechanisms in order to meet real-time constraints. A scheduling scheme, whose main aim is to obtain optimal parameters regarding the IEEE 802.15.4 frame and subframes in home automation networks, is presented in [28]. The proposed approach uses guaranteed time slots (GTSs) for transmission of real-time periodic traffic flows, since they can guarantee time constraints using the periodic delivery of beacon frames as provided by the IEEE 802.15.4 protocol. The authors consider a set of nodes requirements in an IEEE 802.15.4 network in order to define the beacon interval considering the required periods and the duty cycles. Moreover, the active subframe duration is chosen according to required bandwidths and to ensure energy saving. The authors show results in terms of throughput for different frame and subframes lengths. Numerical results show that frame and subframe duration and GTS's schedule can be determined in order to ensure an efficient use of the network resources. Several works on the GTS aim at increasing utilization and reducing the waste of bandwidth. Anyhow, using IEEE 802.15.4 standard protocol, the GTS does not guarantee the reliable transmission in multihop networks. For this reason, GTS mechanism is also analyzed in

[29] where authors propose and implement a multihop GTS mechanism for reliable transmission in multihop networks. After a discussion on the reliable transmission in multihop networks, the authors present simulations results. In fact, several simulations have been carried out through NS-2 simulator, and results show that low end-to-end delay and high delivery ratio can be checked. Therefore, thanks to these features, the proposed mechanism is especially suitable for delivering time-sensitive data. In [30], a preliminary solution for the transmission of real-time time-triggered traffic over the IEEE 802.15.4 standard in a home automation environment with real-time requirements is shown. Authors define the design solutions focusing on GTSs transmission and reception for time-triggered traffic with real-time requirements. The proposed approach can be useful for infrastructure-to-vehicle and vehicle-to-vehicle communications and home automation applications supporting life monitoring. The authors focus their future works in peer-to-peer topology because, in this case, a device can communicate with any other device and, furthermore, several coordinators may exist. The peer-to-peer topology has the advantage of increased coverage area but it involves increased message latency and nodes synchronization.

2.4. Coexistence of IEEE 802.15.4 with Other Communication Protocols in Home Automation Networks. Several works in the literature analyze the coexistence of IEEE 802.15.4 with other networks protocols in home automation applications. In [31], a tunneling solution that allows running KNX/EIB over IEEE 802.15.4 links is presented. The authors analyze wireless sensor and actuator networks as an alternative to wired solutions in the home and building automation domain because several technologies that fulfill the specific requirements of this class of wireless networks have reached commercial status. The approach proposed by authors emulates the properties of the KNX/EIB wired medium via wireless communication, over an IEEE 802.15.4 network, allowing a seamless extension. Moreover, this novel architecture provides a basic level of communications security using a shared key through standard IEEE 802.15.4 security mechanism. As future works, the authors aim to a better evaluation of proposed approach performance, in terms of the effects of contention occurring on the tunneling medium. The use of 6LoWPAN and IEEE 802.15.4 protocols has been presented in [27], while 6LoWPAN, IPv6, and IEEE 802.15.4 protocols are also used in [32]. The authors propose a prototypical implementation of a home automation network that uses IPv6 over 6LoWPAN to control home applications. The proposed implementation is based on an embedded web server which, connected over a low-power IEEE 802.15.4 network, provides the ability to remotely open and close an electric door lock. Through this architecture, it is also possible to control other electronic consumer devices such as heating, air conditioning, lighting systems, and many others. The use of the proposed approach can offer many benefits for energy conservation, and, at the same time, it can involve new usage patterns in home automation applications, such as assisted living or smart grids. In [33] the development

process of a smart home network is presented based on IEEE 802.15.4/ZigBee technology with the combination of SAANet, a smart home appliance communication protocol. The SAANet protocol aims at solving the data recognition between different types of devices because most of ZigBee devices profiles were not built completely. Therefore, the combination of ZigBee and SAANet protocols can be a solution to solve several problems. The integration between the two protocols has been successfully applied in order to achieve a supervisory home control system. The approach proposed by authors implements the functions of entrance control, temperature and humid sensing, and appliance control. A methodology to measure and avoid WiFi interference while deploying and installing ZigBee-based products in a home automation architecture is introduced in [34]. A detailed analysis shows that ZigBee products can successfully withstand interference from microwave ovens and Bluetooth devices but they are still vulnerable to high load WiFi traffic. Anyhow, the authors come to the conclusion that ZigBee can coexist with WiFi in a typical home environment if several preventative measures are taken into account. The recommendations to avoid WiFi interference, that authors derived experimentally, are to place WiFi router no closer than 5 meters of window shutters, and, moreover, it would be appropriate to use a frequency offset of at least 20 MHz between ZigBee and WiFi. However, other factors, such as traffic type, might also affect the performance of a system under WiFi interference. In future works, the authors focus on a more thorough study, taking into account these factors and using real user traffic instead of synthetically generated traffic.

3. The Proposed Approach

In this work, a two-tiered architecture in home automation environment (Figure 2) is shown. The first tier is characterized by a WSN in which devices are organized in home cells (HCs). Each HC is managed by a PAN coordinator that provides several modules.

(i) Ethernet module: it is the interface through which it is possible to establish a wired connection between each home cell and the real-time Ethernet backbone.

(ii) The IEEE 802.15.4 module through which the PAN coordinator receives and processes data detected by its home devices (HDs).

(iii) Scheduling module: this module is a quality of service (QoS) manager for real-time (RT) communications and dynamically decides transmission priorities of HDs using an approach based on rate monotonic (RM) and priority-based CSMA/CA (PB).

As already said, main system devices are home devices (HDs) and PAN coordinators. Each HD sends data acquired to its PAN coordinator and can be either an IEEE 802.15.4 reduced function device (RFD) or a full function device (FFD) in a clustered network. This paper addresses several advantages in the use of a novel intracell scheduling approach combined with the use of CSMA/CA-PB. The PAN coordinators are

A Priority-Based CSMA/CA Mechanism to Support Deadline-Aware Scheduling in Home Automation
Applications Using IEEE 802.15.4

5

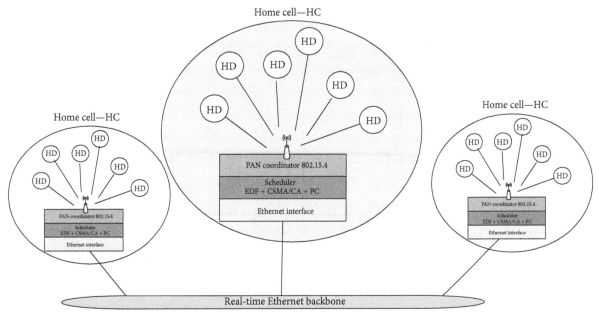

FIGURE 2: Network scenario.

responsible for data transmission of their associated nodes and for scheduling traffic decisions within their respective home cells.

The intracell scheduling in this architecture is realized through the preallocation of guaranteed time slots to devices involved in transmissions of periodic messages through the RM scheduling algorithm [20]. The GTS list contains the addresses of all devices interested to transmit. Each device will wait its turn according to its address position in the GTS List and then it will transmit using its allocated GTS. In case of high workloads or high number of nodes, it is possible to use the CSMA/CA-PB. The use of GTSs, allocated with RM, guarantees a deterministic allocation of slots. Consider

    (i) a set of messages M_i, each one with relative deadline (d_i) equal to the period (T_i);

    (ii) online scheduling;

    (iii) nonpreemption.

Rate monotonic and earliest deadline first (EDF) [20] produce the same schedule. Under these assumptions, we could also use the EDF algorithm. Figure 3 demonstrates how 7 messages, each with $d_i = T_i$ and a certain computational time (C_i), as described by Table 1, can indifferently be scheduled using RM or EDF.

It is important to remind that in case of RM algorithm, the schedulability is guaranteed if

$$\left(\sum_{i=1}^{n}\frac{C_i}{T_i}\right) \le 0,68. \tag{1}$$

Otherwise, in case of EDF algorithm, the schedulability is guaranteed if

$$\left(\sum_{i=1}^{n}\frac{C_i}{T_i}\right) \le 1. \tag{2}$$

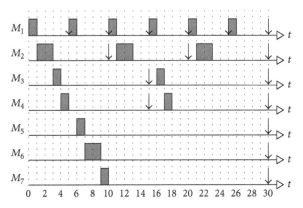

FIGURE 3: Set of messages scheduled at the same way with EDF and RM.

TABLE 1: Scheduling parameters.

	$d_i = T_i$	C_i	U_i
M_1	5	1	0.2
M_2	10	2	0.2
M_3	15	1	0.06
M_4	15	1	0.06
M_5	30	1	0.03
M_6	30	2	0.06
M_7	30	1	0.03

It is also possible to have a guarantee about messages schedulability, in accordance with deadlines, through the known Jeffay's theorem [20]. A set of periodic requests (messages) is scheduled using a nonpreemptive algorithm if two conditions are met. The first equation (1) relates to system utilization (in terms of bandwidth, as we are dealing with the transmission of packets), whereas the second equation (2) refers to the system demand.

Theorem 1. *A system can schedule a set of periodic requests using nonpreemptive EDF algorithm if Jeffay's conditions ((2) and (3)) are met:*

$$U_{tot} = U_P + U_S = \left(\sum_{i=1}^{n} \frac{C_i}{T_i} + U_S \right) \leq 1, \qquad (3)$$

$$1 < i \leq n; \quad \forall L, T_1 < L < T_n : L \geq C_i + \sum_{j=1}^{i-1} \left\lfloor \frac{L-1}{T_j} \right\rfloor C_j. \qquad (4)$$

The periodic traffic flows are represented by a set of periodic variables $\tau p = \{p1, p2, \ldots, pn\}$, where $p_i = (C_i, T_i)$, sorted in a nondecreasing order by period (i.e., for any pair of variables p_i and p_j, if $i > j$ then $T_i \geq T_j$), and C_i is the transmission time for a periodic traffic flow generated by ith wireless node.

Equation (3) relates to the system utilization (in terms of bandwidth, as we are dealing with the transmission of packets), whereas (4) refers to the system demand. Equation (3) defines that total bandwidth utilization must not exceed 1; U_P is the utilization factor for periodic traffic while US is the utilization factor for sporadic and aperiodic traffic flows (i.e., server utilization). The inequality in (3) refers to a least upper bound on bandwidth demand that can be achieved in an interval of length L. This interval starts when the periodic variable is invoked and ends before the relative deadline. Then, a set of variables is schedulable if the demand in the interval L is less than or equal to the length of the interval. In this paper, we choose to work according to slotted CSMA/CA as provided by the standard. Scheduling management through preallocated GTS can be considered efficient. The RM + CSMA/CA-PB approach, proposed in this paper, guarantees the access to the medium for periodic transmissions providing a division into three priority classes for all transmission regulated by CSMA/CA in contention access period: high priority, medium priority, and low priority. The three priority classes have been created modifying two standard parameters.

(i) CW (contention window): it is the contention window length, in other words, the number of backoff periods during which it is necessary to listen to the channel before the transmission.

(ii) BE (backoff exponent): it is the variable that determines the number of backoff periods the device shall wait before channel access attempts.

The number of waiting periods (CW) is a random number inside the range $[0, 2^{BE}-1]$ where macMinBE < BE < macMaxBE.

In home automation environments, the coexistence of different traffic types must be taken into account. In order to define the priority class, BE and CW variables of the CSMA/CA have been used. BE has been considered as a variable in the range $1 \leq BE \leq 3$. Considering that in each beacon interval, with n preallocated slots for GTS ($0 \leq n \leq 7$),

TABLE 2: Priorities classification.

	CW	macMinBE–macMaxBE
High priority	1	0-1
Medium priority	1-2	1-2
Low priority	2	2-3
Standard	2	3–5

it is possible to use up to 15-n slots for the CSMA/CA. As a consequence, it has been possible to define three priority classes as shown in Table 2.

These values must be set on each HC's node in order to define the priority of each device. The choice of contention window and backoff exponential determines nodes transmission frequency. High-priority nodes will listen to the channel more frequently and with higher probability of transmission success. Clearly, this approach does not resolve the nondeterminism of the wireless channel but significantly reduces latencies of nodes involved in the contention access to the channel.

3.1. Probabilistic Analysis of IEEE 802.15.4 Transmissions through CSMA/CA-PB. Another aspect considered and proposed through this paper concerns the relationship between the probability that a station finds the channel free and the network throughput varying CW and BE parameters. As already proposed by several works in the literature [35–37], the CSMA/CA algorithm can be modeled through an M/G/1 queue. Consider

(i) n: the number of nodes associated to a PAN coordinator;

(ii) N: the total number of network nodes (associated and not);

(iii) λ: packets generation rate (according to a poisson process);

(iv) T_{TX}: the fixed packet transmission time;

(v) Wl: network workload;

(vi) T_{turn}: turnaround time;

(vii) T_{ACK}: transmission time for ACK packet;

(viii) σ: backoff slot duration.

The probability (α) of channel busy during the contention window CW, the packet loss probability P_{loss}, and the average delay $E[D_{HOL}]$ are given by the nonlinear equations system:

$$\alpha = \frac{(n-1)(1-P_{loss}) \, \text{Wl} \cdot (CW + T_{TX} + 2T_{turn} + T_{ACK})}{(1/\lambda) + \text{Wl} + E[D_{HoL}]},$$

$$P_{loss} = \alpha^{N+1},$$

A Priority-Based CSMA/CA Mechanism to Support Deadline-Aware Scheduling in Home Automation
Applications Using IEEE 802.15.4

7

$$E\left[D_{\text{HoL}}\right] = \sum_{v=0}^{N} \alpha^{v}\left(1-\alpha\right)\left\{\sum_{i=0}^{v}\frac{W_{i}-1}{2}\sigma + (v+1)\,\text{CW}\right\}$$

$$+ \alpha^{N+1}\left\{\sum_{i=0}^{N}\frac{W_{i}-1}{2}\sigma + (N+1)\,\text{CW}\right\}. \tag{5}$$

The equations previously expressed in the variables α, P_{loss}, and $E\left[D_{\text{HOL}}\right]$ can be numerically solved in order to obtain the value α of busy channel probability, from which afterwards it is possible to obtain the throughput value according to

$$\text{TH} = \frac{n\left(1-P_{\text{loss}}\right)\text{Wl}\cdot T_{\text{TX}}}{(1/\lambda) + \text{Wl}\cdot\left(E\left[D_{\text{HoL}}\right] + T_{\text{TX}} + 2T_{\text{turn}} + T_{\text{ACK}}\right)}. \tag{6}$$

The term $(E[D_{\text{HoL}}] + T_{\text{TX}} + 2T_{\text{turn}} + T_{\text{ACK}})$ represents the waiting period in an M/G/1 queuing system. Figure 4 analyzes system's performance in terms of transmission probability behavior varying the number of nodes in the network.

It is easily observable that the transmission probability of low priority nodes is slightly better than the standard, while medium and high priority nodes have a higher transmission probability.

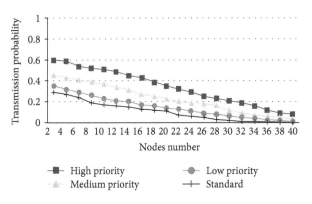

Transmission probability versus nodes number

- ■ High priority
- ● Low priority
- ▲ Medium priority
- + Standard

FIGURE 4: Transmission probability estimation.

TABLE 3: Nodes priorities classification cases.

Nodes number	Priority	Case 1		Case 2		Case 3		Case 4	
		CW	BE	CW	BE	CW	BE	CW	BE
2	High	1	1	1	2	1	1	1	2
3	Medium	1	2	1	2	2	2	2	2
4	Low	2	3	2	3	2	3	2	3

4. Performance Evaluation

Performance of our approach has been tested through a real experimental scenario implemented using IRIS MTS300 [38] and MTS300 boards from Crossbow/Memsic and taking into account requirements of an IEEE 802.15.4 network described in [39]. Tests have been conducted on a star topology network with 9 RFD devices (HD) and a gateway (PAN coordinator). In particular, 3 "high priority" nodes, 2 "medium priority" nodes, and 4 "low priority" nodes have been considered as shown in Figure 5.

Varying CW and BE parameters, 4 case analyses have been identified, as better explained through Table 3.

Case 1. Consider the following:

(i) high priority nodes $\rightarrow$ CW = 1, BE = 1;

(ii) medium priority nodes $\rightarrow$ CW = 1, BE = 2;

(iii) low priority nodes $\rightarrow$ CW = 2, BE = 3.

Figures 6 and 7 show performance obtained in Case 1. Figure 6 shows how higher priority nodes are characterized by throughput/workload (Th/Wl) values higher than nodes with lower priority. On average, high priority nodes obtain better performance with the use of CSMA/CA-PB than the standard. This is due to the fact that they have higher probability to transmit. In other words, they have a high reduction of waiting times during radio channel accesses

attempts. On the contrary, lower and medium priority nodes measure values lower than the standard because for them CW = 2 and BE = 3. Figure 7 shows improvements in terms of Th/Wl obtained by each priority class. In general, total network Th/Wl is better than the standard but Th/Wl measured by all low priority nodes is lower.

Case 2. Consider the following:

(i) high priority nodes $\rightarrow$ CW = 1, BE = 2;

(ii) medium priority nodes $\rightarrow$ CW = 1, BE = 2;

(iii) low priority nodes $\rightarrow$ CW = 2, BE = 3.

Figures 8 and 9 show performance obtained in Case 2. Figure 8 shows Th/Wl values measured on each node. Even in this case, higher priority nodes reach throughput/workload (Th/Wl) values higher than nodes with lower priority. But, it is possible also to see that even medium priority nodes obtain better performance through our approach. At the same time, differences in results, between CSMA/CA-PB and the standard, decrease also for low priority nodes. Figure 9 shows improvements in terms of Th/Wl classified for priority classes. Using a priority classification of traffic flows, the obtained Th/Wl of the whole network is higher than the standard and, in this case, even the Th/Wl measured by all low priority nodes is better than the standard.

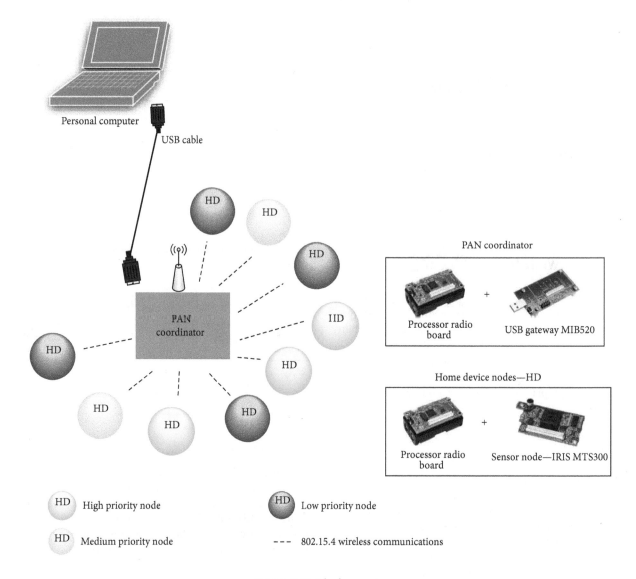

FIGURE 5: Test-bed scenario.

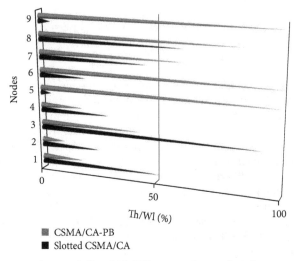

■ CSMA/CA-PB
■ Slotted CSMA/CA

FIGURE 6: Case 1: Th/Wl measured on each node.

Case 3. Consider the following:

    (i) high priority nodes → CW = 1, BE = 1;

    (ii) medium priority nodes → CW = 2, BE = 2;

    (iii) low priority nodes → CW = 2, BE = 3.

Figures 10 and 11 show performance obtained in Case 3. Figure 10 shows Th/Wl values measured on each node. Even in this case, higher priority nodes reach throughput/workload (Th/Wl) values higher than nodes with lower priority. Just nodes 1 and 3 measure the worst performance than the standard. This is due to the fact that the traffic flows classification, based on priorities, supports a more frequent transmission of messages with higher priority, resulting in a slight increase of waiting times for some nodes having medium or low priority. Figure 11 shows improvements in terms of Th/Wl classified for priority classes. Results clearly

A Priority-Based CSMA/CA Mechanism to Support Deadline-Aware Scheduling in Home Automation
Applications Using IEEE 802.15.4

9

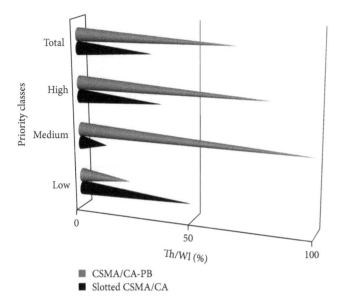

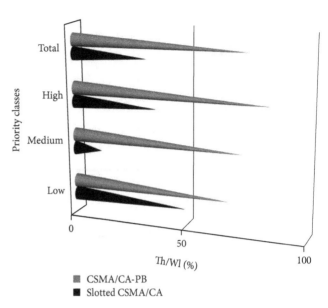

FIGURE 7: Case 1: Th/Wl results for priority classes.

FIGURE 9: Case 2: Th/Wl results for priority classes.

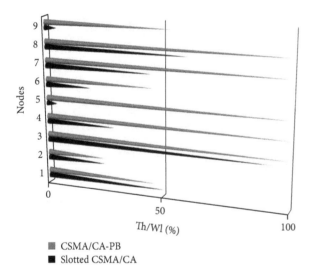

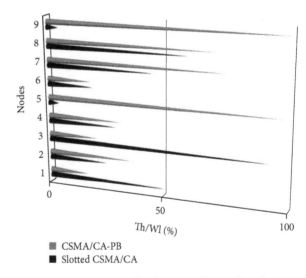

FIGURE 8: Case 2: Th/Wl measured on each node.

FIGURE 10: Case 3: Th/Wl measured on each node.

show how, using the proposed algorithm, the Th/Wl ratio of the whole network is higher than Th/Wl obtained using the standard algorithm. As already explained in Figure 10, the Th/Wl obtained by all low priority nodes is lower than the standard because they can transmit with lower frequency.

Case 4. Consider the following:

(i) high priority nodes → CW = 1, BE = 2;

(ii) medium priority nodes → CW = 2, BE = 2;

(iii) low priority nodes → CW = 2, BE = 3.

Finally, Figures 12 and 13 show performance obtained in Case 4. In particular, Figure 12 shows Th/Wl values measured on each node. Even in this case, higher priority

nodes reach throughput/workload (Th/Wl) values higher than nodes with lower priority. This case study produced best performance results. In fact, just node 3 obtained the worst performance, and generally, even low priority nodes obtained better performance than the standard algorithm, as it is possible to see through Figure 13.

5. Conclusions

In this paper, a novel scheduling mechanism for periodic traffic flows management has been proposed in order to support the development of home-automated networks. The main aim is to reduce latencies of channel access attempts of network embedded devices in home automation applications. This new approach, called rate monotonic + CSMA/CA-PB,

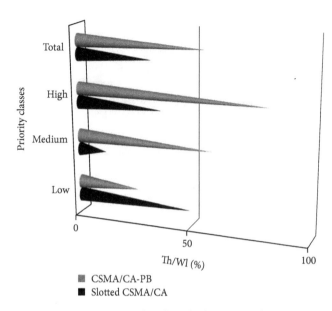

FIGURE 11: Case 3: Th/Wl results for priority classes.

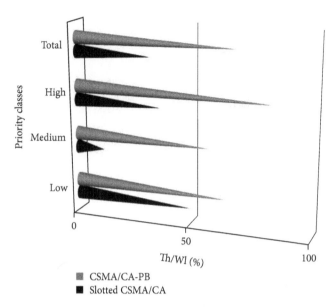

FIGURE 13: Case 4: Th/Wl results for priority classes.

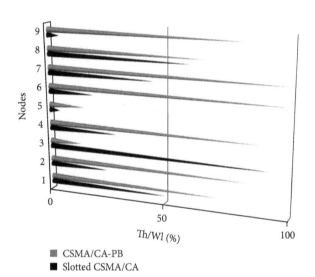

FIGURE 12: Case 4: Th/Wl measured on each node.

provides the preallocation of guaranteed time slots (GTSs) through the rate monotonic algorithm for those devices which want to transmit periodic messages. As known, the standard algorithm provides a FIFO allocation of GTSs. Moreover, this approach reduces waiting times of nodes competing for the medium access using the CSMA/CA in contention access period through a priority classification of network traffic flows. An experimental real scenario, based on the IEEE 802.15.4 standard protocol, has been deployed in order to demonstrate benefits introduced by this approach. Varying the contention window (CW) and the backoff Exponential (BE) parameters, it has been possible to produce a traffic flows classification based on priorities. Obtained results show how high priority nodes will reach better performance than those with lower priority. Measured

performances are generally better than the IEEE 802.15.4 standard that does not differentiate network traffic flows.

References

[1] Z. Ruyan, L. Huifang, H. Shijun, and W. Dongyun, "Data processing and node management in wireless sensor network," in *Proceedings of the 1st International Symposium on Computer Network and Multimedia Technology (CNMT '09)*, pp. 1–4, December 2009.

[2] M. Collotta, G. Pau, V. M. Salerno, and G. Scatà, "A fuzzy based algorithm to manage power consumption in industrial wireless sensor networks," in *Proceedings of the 9th IEEE International Conference on Industrial Informatics (INDIN '11)*, pp. 151–156, 2011.

[3] M. Collotta, L. Gentile, G. Pau, and G. Scatà, "A dynamic algorithm to improve industrial wireless sensor networks management," in *Proceedings of the 38th Annual Conference of IEEE Industrial Electronics (IECON '12)*, pp. 2802–2807, 2012.

[4] V. C. Gungor and G. P. Hancke, "Industrial wireless sensor networks: challenges, design principles, and technical approaches," *IEEE Transactions on Industrial Electronics*, vol. 56, no. 10, pp. 4258–4265, 2009.

[5] M. Collotta, L. Lo Bello, and O. Mirabella, "An innovative frequency hopping management mechanism for Bluetooth-based industrial networks," in *Proceedings of the 5th International Symposium on Industrial Embedded Systems (SIES '10)*, pp. 45–50, July 2010.

[6] M. Collotta, V. Conti, G. Pau, G. Scatà, and S. Vitabile, "Fuzzy techniques for access and data management in home automation environments," *Journal of Mobile Multimedia*, vol. 8, no. 3, pp. 181–203, 2012.

[7] Y. Li, J. Maorong, G. Zhenru, Z. Weiping, and G. Tao, "Design of home automation system based on ZigBee wireless sensor network," in *Proceedings of the 1st International Conference on Information Science and Engineering (ICISE '09)*, pp. 2610–2613, December 2009.

A Priority-Based CSMA/CA Mechanism to Support Deadline-Aware Scheduling in Home Automation
Applications Using IEEE 802.15.4

11

[8] M. Collotta, G. Nicolosi, E. Toscano, and O. Mirabella, "A ZigBee-based network for home heating control," in *Proceedings of the 34th Annual Conference of IEEE Industrial Electronics (IECON '08)*, pp. 2724–2729, November 2008.

[9] A. Pascale, M. Nicoli, F. Deflorio, B. Dalla Chiara, and U. Spagnolini, "Wireless sensor networks for traffic management and road safety," *IET Intelligent Transport Systems*, vol. 6, no. 1, pp. 67–77, 2012.

[10] M. Collotta, G. Pau, V. M. Salerno, and G. Scatà, "A novel road monitoring approach using wireless sensor networks," in *Proceedings of the 6th International Conference on Complex, Intelligent and Software Intensive Systems (CISIS '12)*, pp. 376–381, 2012.

[11] L. Yong-Min, W. Shu-Ci, and N. Xiao-Hong, "The architetcure and characteristics of wireless sensor network," in *Proceedings of the International Conference on Computer Technology and Development (ICCTD '09)*, vol. 1, pp. 561–565, 2009.

[12] S. Vitabile, V. Conti, M. Collotta et al., "A real-time network architecture for biometric data delivery in Ambient Intelligence," *Journal of Ambient Intelligence and Humanized Computing*, 2012.

[13] IEEE Standard for Information technology—Telecommunications and information exchange between systems—Local and metropolitan area networks—Specific requirements Part 3: Carrier Sense Multiple Access with Collision Detection (CSMA/CD) Access Method and Physical Layer Specifications.

[14] J. She Jin, J. Jin, Y. Hui Wang, K. Zhao, and J. Jun Hu, "Development of remote-controlled home automation system with wireless sensor network," in *Proceedings of the 5th IEEE International Symposium on Embedded Computing (SEC '08)*, pp. 169–173, Beijing, China, October 2008.

[15] L. Yanfei, W. Cheng, Y. Chengbo, and Q. Xiaojun, "Research on ZigBee wireless sensors network based on ModBus protocol," in *Proceedings of the International Forum on Information Technology and Applications (IFITA '09)*, vol. 1, pp. 487–490, May 2009.

[16] C. Jin and T. Kuntz, "Smart home networking: combining wireless and powerline networking," in *Proceedings of the 7th International Conference on Wireless Communications and Mobile Computing (IWCMC '11)*, pp. 1276–1281, 2011.

[17] "802.15.4: Wireless Medium Access Control (MAC) and Physical Layer (PHY) Specifications for Low-Rate Wireless Personal Area Networks (LR-WPANs)"—June 2006 IEEE standard for information technology. Part 15.4.

[18] M. Collotta, G. Pau, V. M. Salerno, and G. Scatà, "A distributed load balancing approach for industrial IEEE 802.11 wireless networks," in *Proceedings of IEEE Conference on Emerging Technologies & Factory Automation (ETFA '12)*, pp. 1–4, 2012.

[19] M. Collotta, L. Lo Bello, E. Toscano, and O. Mirabella, "Dynamic load balancing techniques for flexible wireless industrial networks," in *Proceedings of the 36th Annual Conference on IEEE Industrial Electronics Society (IECON '10)*, pp. 1329–11334, 2010.

[20] G. C. Buttazzo, *Hard Real-Time Computing Systems—Predictable Scheduling Algorithms and Applications*, Springer, 3rd edition, 2011.

[21] J. A. Nazabal, P. L. Iturri, L. Azpilicueta, F. Falcone, and C. F. Valdivielso, "Performance analysis of IEEE 802.15.4 compliant wireless devices for heterogeneous indoor home automation environments," *International Journal of Antennas and Propagation*, vol. 2012, Article ID 176383, 14 pages, 2012.

[22] C. A. M. Bolzani, C. Montagnoli, and M. L. Netto, "Domotics over IEEE 802.15.4—a spread spectrum home automation application," in *Proceedings of the 9th IEEE International Symposium on Spread Spectrum Techniques and Applications (ISSSTA '06)*, pp. 396–400, August 2006.

[23] M. A. B. Sarijari, R. A. Rashid, M. R. A. Rahim, and N. H. Mahalin, "Wireless home security and automation system utilizing ZigBee based multi-hop communication," in *Proceedings of the 6th IEEE National Conference on Telecommunication Technologies and 2nd IEEE Malaysia Conference on Photonics (NCTT-MCP '08)*, pp. 242–245, August 2008.

[24] A. Kailas, V. Cecchi, and A. Mukherjee, "A survey of communications and networking technologies for energy management in buildings and home Automation," *Journal of Computer Networks and Communications*, vol. 2012, Article ID 932181, 12 pages, 2012.

[25] D. M. Han and J. H. Lim, "Smart home energy management system using IEEE 802.15.4 and ZigBee," *IEEE Transactions on Consumer Electronics*, vol. 56, no. 3, pp. 1403–1410, 2010.

[26] F. Xia, R. Hao, Y. Cao, and L. Xue, "A survey of adaptive and real-time protocols based on IEEE 802.15.4," *International Journal of Distributed Sensor Networks*, vol. 2011, Article ID 212737, 11 pages, 2011.

[27] P. Yi, A. Iwayemi, and C. Zhou, "Building automation networks for smart grids," *International Journal of Digital Multimedia Broadcasting*, vol. 2011, Article ID 926363, 12 pages, 2011.

[28] H. Seok Kim, J. H. Song, and S. Lee, "Energy-efficient traffic scheduling in IEEE 802.15.4 for home automation networks," *IEEE Transactions on Consumer Electronics*, vol. 53, no. 2, pp. 369–374, 2007.

[29] W. Choi and S. Lee, "A novel GTS mechanism for reliable multihop transmission in the IEEE 802.15.4 Network," *International Journal of Distributed Sensor Networks*, vol. 2012, Article ID 796426, 10 pages, 2012.

[30] N. Ferreira and J. A. Fonseca, "Using time-triggered communications over IEEE 802.15.4," in *Proceedings of the 12th IEEE International Conference on Emerging Technologies and Factory Automation (ETFA '07)*, pp. 1384–1387, September 2007.

[31] C. Reinisch, W. Kastner, G. Neugschwandtner, and W. Granzer, "Wireless technologies in home and building automation," in *Proceedings of the 5th IEEE International Conference on Industrial Informatics (INDIN '07)*, vol. 1, pp. 93–98, June 2007.

[32] B. M. Dorge and T. Scheffler, "Using IPv6 and 6LoWPAN for home automation networks," in *Proceedings of IEEE International Conference on Consumer Electronics—Berlin (ICCE '11)*, pp. 44–47, September 2011.

[33] Y.-P. Tsou, J.-W. Hsieh, C.-T. Lin, and C.-Y. Chen, "Building a remote supervisory control network system for smart home applications," in *Proceedings of the IEEE International Conference on Systems, Man and Cybernetics ((SMC '06)*, vol. 3, pp. 1826–1830, October 2006.

[34] F. Dominguez, A. Touhafi, J. Tiete, and K. Steenhaut, "Coexistence with WiFi for a home automation ZigBee product," in *Proceedings of the 19th IEEE Symposium on Communications and Vehicular Technology in the Benelux (SCVT '12)*, pp. 1 6, 2012.

[35] T. Ok Kim, J. Soo Park, H. Jin Chong, K. Jae Kim, and B. Dae Choi, "Performance analysis of IEEE 802.15.4 non-beacon mode with the unslotted CSMA/CA," *IEEE Communications Letters*, vol. 12, no. 4, pp. 238–240, 2008.

[36] Z. Chen, C. Lin, H. Wen, and H. Yin, "An analytical model for evaluating IEEE 802.15.4 CSMA/CA protocol in low-rate

wireless application," in *Proceedings of the 21st International Conference on Advanced Information Networking and Applications Workshops (AINAW '07)*, vol. 2, pp. 899–904, May 2007.

[37] J. He, Z. Tang, H.-H. Chen, and Q. Zhang, "An accurate and scalable analytical model for IEEE 802.15.4 slotted CSMA/CA networks," *IEEE Transactions on Wireless Communications*, vol. 8, no. 1, pp. 440–448, 2009.

[38] http://www.memsic.com/support/documentation/wireless-sensor-networks/category/7-datasheets.html?download=135%-3Airis.

[39] M. Collotta, L. Lo Bello, and E. Toscano, "A proposal towards flexible wireless communication in factory automation based on the IEEE 802.15.4 protocol," in *Proceedings of IEEE Conference on Emerging Technologies & Factory Automation (ETFA '09)*, pp. 1–4, September 2009.

2

The RSU Access Problem Based on Evolutionary Game Theory for VANET

Di Wu,[1] Yan Ling,[1] Hongsong Zhu,[2] and Jie Liang[3]

[1] School of Computer Science and Engineering, Dalian University of Technology, Dalian 116023, China
[2] State Key Laboratory of Information Security, Institute of Information Engineering, Chinese Academy of Sciences, Beijing 100093, China
[3] School of Engineering Science, Simon Fraser University, Burnaby, BC, Canada V5A1S6

Correspondence should be addressed to Yan Ling; lingyan321.love@163.com

Academic Editor: Limin Sun

We identify some challenges in RSU access problem. There are two main problems in V2R communication. (1) It is difficult to maintain the end-to-end connection between vehicles and RSU due to the high mobility of vehicles. (2) The limited RSU bandwidth resources lead to the vehicles' disorderly competition behavior, which will give rise to multiple RSUs having overlap area environment where RSU access becomes crucial for increasing vehicles' throughput. Focusing on the problems mentioned above, the RSU access question in the paper is formulated as a dynamic evolutionary game for studying the competition of vehicles in the single community and among multiple communities to share the limited bandwidth in the available RSUs, and the evolutionary equilibrium evolutionary stable strategy (ESS) is considered to be the solution to this game. Simulation results based on a realistic vehicular traffic model demonstrate the evolution process of the game and how the ESS can affect the network performance.

1. Introduction

Vehicle ad hoc network (VANET) is a special case of mobile ad hoc network. The motions of vehicles are restricted to a geographical pattern. Further, the communication patterns of VANET include vehicle to vehicle (V2V) and vehicle to road side unit (V2R). RSU is referred to as road side unit, which is a wireless transceivers and receivers and has the characters of data storage, computing power, and router. In recent years, V2R communication has received considerable attentions [1–4]. In this paper, we mainly research the RSU access problem.

When vehicles drive through RSU, it will ask the RSU for service requirements. However in VANET, (1) it is difficult to maintain the end-to-end connection between vehicles and RSU due to the high mobility of vehicles; (2) the limited RSU bandwidth resources lead to the vehicles' disorderly competition behavior, which may reduce the network throughput; (3) due to the uneven distribution of vehicles, RSU's load may become diversification, which will lead to the load imbalance of RSU. In order to solve the problems above and achieve good network throughput, one question needs to be addressed: in the highly dynamic network, when and which RSU should be accessed. Focusing on the problem, the paper puts forward evolutionary game theory.

Game theory provides a mathematical modeling for the study of competition strategies in a game where players have conflicting benefits or goals and consider the rivals' strategy to make their own strategy [5, 6]. Evolutionary game theory describes game models in which players choose their strategies through a trial-and-error process in which they learn over time that some strategies work better than others [7, 8]. In this paper, we analyze the RSU access problem under the framework of game theory as the vehicles are noncooperative and competitive and need to consider the strategy of other vehicles to make their own strategy. In addition, vehicles are controlled by bounded rational entities, such as human or organization [9], and the traditional game theory assumed that the players are perfectly rational, so we adopt the evolutionary game theory to analyze the access problem.

The research scene includes multiple vehicles versus two RSUs and multiple vehicles versus multiple RSUs. We divide the vehicles into different populations according to the strategies. The two RSU's scene belongs to a single-community evolutionary game as all vehicles' strategy set is the same, while the multiple RSU's scene belongs to multiple communities evolutionary game as vehicles in different populations have different strategies. The payoff function of our model is the difference of the throughput and the cost. In our paper, the cost contains two aspects: bandwidth occupation cost and handoff cost. The Nash equilibrium is evolutionarily stable strategy (ESS), that is, the probability of vehicles access to RSU. In order to ensure the accuracy and reliability of research results, the paper adopted the traffic flow simulator VanetMobiSim to generate the real vehicle moving track. The simulation results demonstrate the evolution process of the game and how the ESS can affect the network performance.

The main contributions of this paper can be summarized as follows.

(1) An evolutionary game-theoretic approach is presented to solve the RSU access problem in VANET. In particular, the replicator dynamics is quoted to investigate the dynamics of vehicle behavior and solution.

(2) Under two RSU's scene and multiple RSU's scene, the paper sets up single-community and multiple-community evolutionary game models to analyze the dynamic evolutionary process and the effect on network performance.

The rest of this paper is organized as the following. Section 2 reviewed problem description. In Section 3, we introduced the related work. Section 4 formalized the system model, which includes single-community and multiple-community evolutionary game models. The numerical experiments were performed in Section 5. Finally, we draw our conclusions in Section 6.

In the paper, we also use the terms "population" and "species" to refer to the VANET community.

2. Problem Definition

In VANET, vehicles have no Internet access and arrive randomly in VANET; vehicles have to access to RSU if they want to obtain the Internet services.

RSU broadcasts the beacon messages to vehicles periodically when the vehicle lies in the coverage area of an RSU, from which the vehicle can get the current state information of the RSU and the network. For simplicity, we assume that RSU's transmission range is equal, and we divide the road into different areas according to the RSUs' coverage area, which is defined as $S = \{S_1, S_2, \ldots, S_K\}$. As shown in Figure 1, the road is divided into four areas $S = \{S_1, S_2, S_3, S_4\}$. In different areas, vehicles can access different RSUs. Vehicle requests services from RSU when driving through RSU, and it can get the service profit from RSUs, while it also incurs a cost in requesting for RSU, where the cost can be the price that vehicles spend on RSUs' bandwidth, buffer size, and

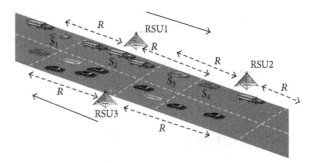

FIGURE 1: The RSU's access scene.

other resource. Besides, when vehicles drive from an RSU to another, the vehicles have to pay for the handoff cost. The payoff function of vehicles is

$$F = Q_i^j - P_i^j - h_i^j, \tag{1}$$

where Q_i^j is the achievable throughput of vehicle i got from RSU j

$$Q_i^j = \delta * \left(T_i^j - t^j\right) * c_i^j * N^j \tag{2}$$

T_i^j is the time when vehicle i is driving in the coverage area of RSU j

$$T_i^j = \frac{R^j}{v_i}. \tag{3}$$

t^j represents the communicate delay when vehicles communication with RSU j

$$t^j = \frac{N^j}{f_s}. \tag{4}$$

P_i^j stands for the resource cost

$$P_i^j = \beta * N^j * \alpha_i * \frac{l_i}{c_i^j}, \tag{5}$$

where l_i/c_i^j is the time that vehicle i should communicate with RSU j if it wants to finish its request. α_i is the importance index of vehicle i's request file. If $\alpha_i > 2$, the request file is urgent, such as emergency information, $1 < \alpha_i < 2$ means that the request is less important, such as road information, and the request is video and audio streams if $\alpha_i < 1$.

c_i^j is the transmission rate of vehicle i

$$c_i^j = w^j * \log_2\left(1 + \frac{S/N}{N^j * \overline{(d_i^j)^r}}\right). \tag{6}$$

h_i^j is the handoff cost

$$h_i^j = \varphi * t_{\text{left}} * T_{\text{left}}, \tag{7}$$

where t_{left} is the request files that have finished and T_{left} is the distance that vehicles have driven in RSU's coverage. Detailed parameters are listed in Table 1.

TABLE 1: The parameters.

Symbol	Semantics
N^j	The total number of vehicles in the coverage area of RSU j
R^j	The transmission radius of RSU j
v_i	The speed of vehicle i
l_i	The request file length of vehicle i
S/N	The signal-to-noise ratio
d_i^j	The distance between vehicle i and RSU j
w^j	The link bandwidth of RSU j
f_s^j	The communication frequency of RSU j
γ	The path loss exponent
Φ, β, δ	The weighting coefficient

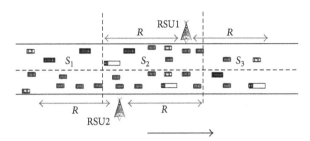

FIGURE 2: The two RSUs' scene.

3. Related Work

A number of previous results have been reported on the RSU access problems. In [10], a distributed association algorithm according to the number of mobile users (MUs) associated with APs was introduced. Besides, reference [11] built a game model according to the potential link rate and the number of WSs access to RSU, which can ensure that each WS gets achievable throughput. Reference [12] presented a new load balancing technique by controlling the size of WLANs (i.e., APs' coverage range) to ensure the load balancing among APs. As we know, vehicles in VANET are highly mobile and the network typology changes dynamically, which demonstrated that the approaches ignore VANET's mobile properties. Besides, these approaches only consider the profit of RSU but vehicles and the papers above all assumed that the players are perfectly rational, which did not fit the realities that human and organizations and other players are bounded rationality. In a word, these methods were not applicable for VANET.

In recent years, evolutionary game theory has been used in wireless network in many fields. Reference [13] that showed the evolutionary game is used to obtain the forward probability of nodes in two-hop DTN and analyze the stability of ESS. In [14], the authors presented two algorithms, namely, population evolution and reinforcement-learning algorithms, for network selection and formulated the game to model the competition among populations of users in the different service areas in heterogeneous wireless networks. Reference [15] presented a model based on evolutionary game theory (EGT) in which it demonstrated that the model was able to encourage selfish nodes to cooperate and forward packets from others with only one period of punishment if nodes are sufficiently patient. As we know, the traditional game theory has been used in VANET for some applications [16–18]; however, the evolutionary game theory's applications in VANET are growing due to the following reasons. (1) The evolutionary equilibrium of evolutionary game is a refined solution, which ensures stability (i.e., population of players will not change their chosen strategies over time). (2) An evolutionary game changes their strategies slowly to achieve the solution eventually, and the traditional game makes decisions immediately. (3) The replicator dynamics is useful

for investigating the trajectory of the players' strategies [14]. In our paper, we solve the RSU access problem in VANET by using evolutionary game.

4. Evolutionary Game Model

The evolutionary game for our paper can be described as follows.

(i) Players: the vehicle in the coverage area of RSU is a player of the game.

(ii) Population: the vehicles that have the same strategy set are a population. In different populations, the number of vehicles is defined separately as $N = \{N^1, N^2, \ldots, N^j, \ldots\}$.

(iii) Strategy: the strategy set is $X^j = \{x_0^j, x_1^j, \ldots, x_i^j, \ldots, x_N^j\}$, $i = 1, 2 \ldots, N$, where x_i^j means the access probability that player i chooses RSU j.

(iv) Payoff: the payoff function is $F = Q_i^j - P_i^j - h_i^j$, which is the difference of the throughput of that strategy and the cost. In multiple communities, the payoff of the vehicle depends on not only the strategy played by the number of vehicles from the same population but also other populations that participate to the game.

In this section, we present the evolutionary game model in two RSU's scene and multiple RSU's scene, respectively.

4.1. Two RSUs' Scene. As shown in Figure 2, in two RSU's scene, there is a set of vehicles who want to request services from RSU1 and RSU2. Vehicles can only access RSU2 when they enter S1 and may change its selection when they enter S2. We assume that the vehicle needs to pay for the handover cost if it does not finish its service request while it performs the handoff operation. On the contrary, If the vehicles' requested services have been finished, the handoff cost is zero and vehicles get their strategy based on their location, the file size, service type, and so on. The vehicles in RSU1 and RSU2's coverage area are a single-community evolutionary game, in which all vehicles' strategy set is the same. The payoff matrix is as described in Table 2.

In the game, we let $X := \{(x, x-) \mid x+x- = 1\}$ be the set of probabilities distributions of population i. x and y represent the probabilities of vehicles in population i accessing RSU1 and RSU2, respectively, $1 - x - y$ means vehicles do not

TABLE 2: Two RSUs' payoff matrix.

	RSU1	RSU2	None
RSU1	$\theta^1 - \varphi(P^1 + h^1)$	$\theta^1 - (P^1 + h^1)$	$\theta^1 - (P^1 + h^1)$
RSU2	$\theta^2 - (P^2 + h^2)$	$\theta^2 - \varphi(P^2 + h^2)$	$\theta^2 - (P^2 + h^2)$
None	0	0	0

access any RSUs' probability, and φ is the congestion index. The payoff function is as follows.

The profit of vehicles accessing RSU1 is

$$F(x, 1) = x * \left(\theta^1 - \varphi * \left(P^1 + h^1\right)\right) + y \left(\theta^1 - \left(P^1 + h^1\right)\right)$$
$$+ (1 - x - y) * \left(\theta^1 - \left(P^1 + h^1\right)\right). \tag{8}$$

The profit of vehicles accessing RSU2 is

$$F(y, 2) = x * \left(\theta^2 - \left(P^2 + h^2\right)\right) + y * \left(\theta^2 - \varphi * \left(P^2 + h^2\right)\right)$$
$$+ (1 - x - y) * \left(\theta^2 - \left(P^2 + h^2\right)\right). \tag{9}$$

The payoff of vehicles in population 1 and population 2 which do not choose any RSU is 0.

The average payoff of populations is

$$\overline{F} = x * F(x, 1) + y * F(y, 2) + (1 - x - y) * 0. \tag{10}$$

In a dynamic evolutionary game, an individual from a population, who is able to replicate itself through the process of mutation and selection, is called replicator. In this case, a replicator with a higher payoff can reproduce itself faster. The game is a repeated game, and in each period, a player observes the payoff of other players in the same community. Then, in the next period, the player adopts a strategy that gives a higher payoff. The speed of the vehicle in observing and adapting the RSU access is controlled by the parameter μ.

In the case of single community, the replicator dynamics is:

$$\frac{dx}{dt} = \mu \left[F(x, 1) - \overline{F}\right] * x,$$
$$\frac{dy}{dt} = \mu \left[F(y, 2) - \overline{F}\right] * y. \tag{11}$$

4.2. Multiple RSUs' Scene. Figure 3 depicts the multiple RSUs' scene, in which vehicles in different populations have different strategies. So it is a multiple-community evolutionary game. As shown in Figure 3, area 1 is the overlap area of RSU1 and RSU2, and area 2 is the overlap area of RSU1, RSU2, and RSU3. The set of strategies for the players in area 1 is {RSU1, RSU2}, while that for the players in area 2 is {RSU1 RSU2, RSU3}. Area 1 and area 2 depict a two community evolutionary game. The vehicles in multiple-community evolutionary game will compete with each other

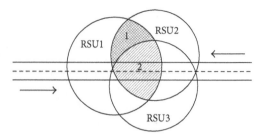

FIGURE 3: Multiple RSUs' scene.

within population and also carry on the competition among the populations. During the evolutionary process, the vehicles adjust their strategies according to their payoff until all the vehicle's strategies maintain stable, and the strategy is ESS at this time.

The payoff function of vehicles in population i accessing RSU j is

$$F_i^j = \theta_i^j - P_i^j - h_i^j. \tag{12}$$

The payoff of vehicles in population i which do not access any RSU is 0.

The average payoff of all populations is

$$\overline{F^i} = \sum_{j=1}^{M} x_j^i * F_j^i. \tag{13}$$

The replicator dynamics of population i is

$$\frac{dx_j^i}{dt} = \mu \left[F_j^j - \overline{F^i}\right] * x_j^i. \tag{14}$$

5. Simulations and Evaluations

VANET is a special network, it has a highly dynamic typology, vehicles are highly mobile, and the motions of vehicles are restricted to a geographical pattern. In order to make the simulation results more realistic, we use VanetMobiSim and Google Earth map tools to simulate traffic track. As shown in Figure 4, the paper chooses Zhongshan district, Dalian, as the simulation area, and the area size is 2.0 km by 2.0 km. VanetMobiSim is a simulation tool which can generate vehicle trajectory. In our simulation, we need to use the VanetMobiSim to get the movement trajectory of vehicles.

We study the access problem through the following two aspects: the evolutionary process of the ESS and the effect of resource cost parameters on network performance. We set the simulation parameters as described in Table 3.

In Figures 4 and 5, the horizontal axis stands for the number of evolution, while the vertical axis stands for the ESS.

Figure 4 demonstrates the influence on ESS along with the vehicle speed, package size changing. In the simulation we set the number of vehicles as 150, the vehicles speed as 15 m/s for Figure 4(a), and the package size as 20 for Figure 4(b). With size increment, the probability that vehicles finish their service within RSU's coverage area decreases, leading to the

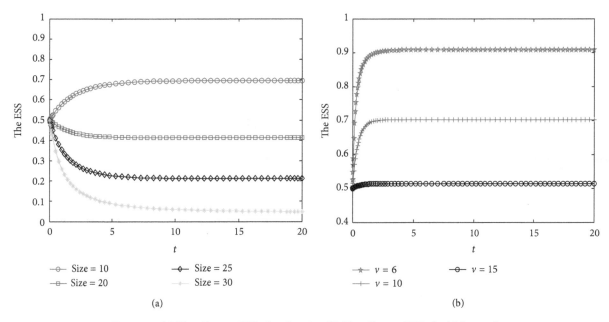

FIGURE 4: (a) The effect on ESS of packet size. (b) The effect on ESS of vehicle speed.

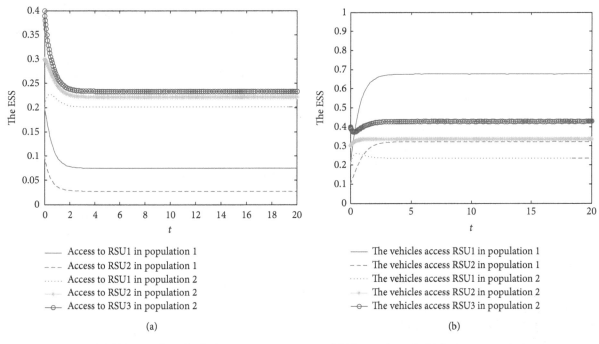

FIGURE 5: (a) The number of vehicles in community is 100. (b) The number of vehicles in community is 70.

decrease in the probability that vehicles access RSU. Similarly, the probability of vehicles accessing to RSU increases if the speed decreases or the number of vehicles having accessed RSU decreases.

Figure 5 shows the influence of N^j, $j = 1, 2$, on ESS in two-community evolutionary game. Figure 5(a) shows the ESS when $N^j = 100$ while Figure 5(a) shows the ESS when $N^j = 70$. As the simulation result demonstrates that the traffic load and the cost of RSU1, RSU2, and RSU3 in population 2 decrease when N^2 reduces, which makes the vehicles in

population 2 would like to access RSU1, RSU2, and RSU3, vehicles in population 1 are also more inclined to access RSU1 and RSU2 as they thought the number of vehicles accessing RSU1 and RSU2 decreases. As shown in Figure 5, the ESS $x = (0.14, 0.06, 0.23, 0.14, 0.06)$ in Figure 5(a) increases to Figure 5(b) $x = (0.68, 0.3, 0.22, 0.33, 0.42)$ if N^2 decreases.

Figure 6 shows the service types' effect on average throughput. The RSU's price increases along with the increase of the request file importance index (a), which makes the number of vehicles accessing RSU decreases. Meanwhile,

TABLE 3: Simulation parameter values.

Parameter	Value
RSU's transmission radius R	1000 m
S/N	30 dB
Bandwidth W	20 MHz
Path loss exponent γ	2
The congestion index φ	1.2
Weight coefficient β	0.15
Weight coefficient δ	0.1
Weight coefficient Φ	0.1

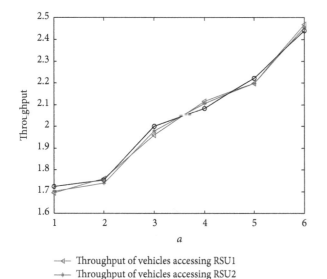

—◁— Throughput of vehicles accessing RSU1
—✳— Throughput of vehicles accessing RSU2
—◯— Throughput of vehicles accessing RSU3

FIGURE 6: The request service type on throughput.

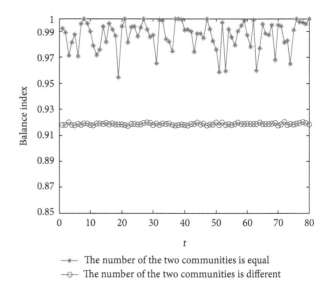

—✳— The number of the two communities is equal
—◯— The number of the two communities is different

FIGURE 7: The effect on balance index of the number of vehicles in community.

been considered to be the stable solution for which all vehicles receive identical payoff from difference RSUs. Detailed analyses have shown the evolutionary process. Besides, in the simulation result we can know that the package size, vehicle speed, and the number of vehicles in community have effects on the ESS, which then affect the network throughput and load balancing.

Due to the limited communication time between vehicles and RSU, in the future work, we can use cooperative download method to improve the network throughput.

Acknowledgments

This work is supported by the Scientific Research Foundation for the Returned Overseas Chinese Scholars, High-Tech 863 Program (no. 2012AA111902) and State Key Program of National Natural Science of China (no. 60933011).

References

[1] M. H. Cheung, F. Hou, V. W. S. Wong, and J. Huang, "Dynamic optimal random access for vehicle-to-roadside communications," in *Proceedings of the IEEE International Conference on Communications (ICC '11)*, June 2011.

[2] O. Trullols-Cruces, M. Fiore, and J. M. Barcelo-Ordinas, "Cooperative download in vehicular environments," *IEEE Transactions on Mobile Computing*, vol. 11, no. 4, pp. 663–678, 2012.

[3] J. Liu, J. Bi, Y. Bian, X. Liu, and Z. Li, "SRelay: a scheme of cooperative downloading based on dynamic slot," in *Proceedings of the IEEE International Conference on Communications (ICC '12)*, pp. 381–386, 2012.

[4] Y. Zhang, J. Zhao, and G. Cao, "On scheduling vehicle-roadside data access," in *Proceedings of the 4th ACM International Workshop on Vehicular Ad Hoc Networks (VANET '07)*, pp. 9–18, September 2007.

[5] A. Mas-Colell, M. D. Whinston, and J. R. Green, *Microeconomic Theory*, Oxford University Press, 1995.

the average bandwidth which the RSU assigned to vehicles increases as the population did not change, which makes the average throughput increase.

Figure 7 represents the load balancing of RSUs. RSU's pricing and the average bandwidth maintain stable when the number of vehicles in communities is the same, which makes the traffic load balancing; RSU's traffic load retained around 0.99. The number changing leads to the changing of RSU's pricing and the probability of accessing RSU, so the RSU's balance index decreased to 0.92.

6. Conclusions

In this paper, we have set up an evolutionary game model to formulate the competition among vehicles in the same community and different communities with bounded rationality in VANET for RSU access problem. We have investigated the dynamic evolutionary process of ESS when vehicles drive through RSU. A vehicle accesses RSU based on its payoff, which is a function of throughput and cost. The dynamics of RSU access has been mathematically modeled by the replicator dynamics that describes the adaptation in proportions of vehicles accessing different RSUs. The ESS has

[6] R. J. Aumann, *Handbook of Game Theory With Economic Applications*, Elsevier, Amsterdam, The Netherlands, 1994.

[7] J. Weibull, *The Evolutionary Game Theory*, Shanghai People's Publishing House, 2006.

[8] F. Vega-Redondo, *Evolution, Games, and Economic Behaviour*, Oxford University Press, Oxford, UK, 1996.

[9] A. Chaintreau, P. Hui, J. Crowcroft, C. Diot, R. Gass, and J. Scott, "Impact of human mobility on the design of opportunistic forwarding algorithms," in *Proceedings of the 25th Conference on Computing and Communication (INFOCOM '06)*, Barcelona, Spain, 2006.

[10] Y. Fukuda, A. Fujiwara, M. Tsuru, and Y. Oie, "Analysis of access point selection strategy in wireless LAN," in *Proceedings of the VTC*, pp. 2532–2536, 2005.

[11] L.-H. Yen, J.-J. Li, and C.-M. Lin, "Stability and fairness of AP selection games in IEEE 802.11 access networks," *IEEE Transactions on Vehicular Technology*, vol. 60, no. 3, pp. 1150–1160, 2011.

[12] Y. Bejerano and S.-J. Han, "Cell breathing techniques for load balancing in wireless LANs," *IEEE Transactions on Mobile Computing*, vol. 8, no. 6, pp. 735–749, 2009.

[13] R. El-Azouzi, F. De Pellegrini, and V. Kamble, "Evolutionary forwarding games in delay tolerant networks," in *Proceedings of the 8th International Symposium on Modeling and Optimization in Mobile, Ad Hoc, and Wireless Networks (WiOpt '10)*, pp. 76–84, June 2010.

[14] D. Niyato and E. Hossain, "Dynamics of network selection in heterogeneous wireless networks: an evolutionary game approach," *IEEE Transactions on Vehicular Technology*, vol. 58, no. 4, pp. 2008–2017, 2009.

[15] C. A. Kamhoua, N. Pissinou, J. Miller, and S. K. Makki, "Mitigating routing misbehavior in multi-hop networks using evolutionary game theory," in *Proceedings of the IEEE Globecom Workshops (GC '10)*, pp. 1957–1962, December 2010.

[16] T. Chen, L. Zhu, F. Wu, and S. Zhong, "Stimulating cooperation in vehicular ad hoc networks: a coalitional game theoretic approach," *IEEE Transactions on Vehicular Technology*, vol. 60, no. 2, pp. 566–579, 2011.

[17] W. Wang, F. Xie, and M. Chatterjee, "Small-scale and large-scale routing in vehicular ad hoc networks," *IEEE Transactions on Vehicular Technology*, vol. 58, no. 9, pp. 5200–5213, 2009.

[18] S. Bitam and A. Mellouk, "QoS swarm bee routing protocol for vehicular ad hoc networks," in *Proceedings of the IEEE International Conference on Communications (ICC '11)*, pp. 1–5, June 2011.

3

Optimal Planning of Distributed Sensor Layouts for Collaborative Surveillance

Thomas A. Wettergren and Russell Costa

Naval Undersea Warfare Center, 1176 Howell Street, Newport, RI 02841, USA

Correspondence should be addressed to Thomas A. Wettergren; t.a.wettergren@ieee.org

Academic Editor: Nadjib Achir

The use of a spatially distributed set of sensors has become a cost-effective approach to achieve surveillance coverage against moving targets. As more sensors are utilized in a collaborative manner, the optimal placement of sensors becomes critical to achieve the most efficient coverage. In this paper, we develop a numerical optimization approach to place distributed sets of sensors to perform surveillance against moving targets over extended areas. In particular, we develop a genetic algorithm solution to find spatial sensor density functions that maximize effectiveness against moving targets, where the surveillance performance of individual sensors is dependent on their absolute position in the region as well as their relative position to both the expected target(s) and any asset that is being protected. The density function representation of optimal sensor locations is shown to provide a computationally efficient method for determining sensor asset location planning. We illustrate the effective performance of this method on numerical examples based on problems of general area surveillance and risk-based surveillance in protection of an asset.

1. Introduction

Target surveillance in large areas is a difficult problem with many challenges; however, due to its importance for military operations it is one that has been studied extensively [1]. In the future, the importance of this problem will only grow as technical advances worldwide create more numerous and capable adversaries. This challenge has created more areas of the world where surveillance assets (sensors) must operate to achieve mission goals of varying scales. The descriptor "large area" is relative to the sensing capability of available (individual) sensors deployed in a specific region against specified targets of interest. A surveillance problem is deemed large area if the sensing capability of an individual sensor is small relative to the area to be searched (covered), in a fixed time scale. For example, problems can be defined in hours, days, weeks, and so forth, depending on tactical mission, and ultimately this will determine scale such as number of required sensors. Military surveillance problems may take the form of covering a bounded region against any intruders (the coverage problem), or may be more specific to covering

a region around an asset of interest in order to protect the asset. In both of these situations, the selection of the best from a limited predefined set of surveillance configuration options is the standard practice [2].

Advances in sensor technology have made distributed sensor networks [3–5] a viable candidate technology for performing the military surveillance mission. In order for distributed sensor networks to achieve reasonable surveillance goals, some forms of collaboration must exist amongst the sensors. Historically, this collaboration has been managed in one of two ways. One method has been to partition the search region in such a way so that individual sensors are responsible for their own portion of the region of interest. This partitioning is done *a priori* using algorithms or human judgment to attempt to optimally split up the search effort among available sensors. The collaboration in this approach is limited to occasional reports (amongst sensors or to a central authority) which lead to suboptimal surveillance performance. The other common approach is to again partition the space, but with the emphasis on post processing of detection events. This approach focuses on the reactionary part of the problem (i.e., conditional on the presence and initial detection of a target) and thus, once again is suboptimal in its use of collaboration among sensors. In this work a methodology is developed to plan deployment of distributed sensors which includes a functional dependence on collaboration, as well as an explicit dependence on spatial variation in sensor performance.

With recent technological improvements in automation and communications networking capabilities, there has been an increase in the utilization of collaboration among sensors to perform target surveillance over large areas [6]. The focus of these studies for distributed sensor surveillance has been to spread out a number of sensors and use the spatial distribution of the individual sensors to cover a larger area (much larger than the coverage of any individual sensor) to monitor against intruders [7, 8]. These studies have been primarily for use in networks of sensors that are simple and autonomous in nature but have led to a fresh look at distributed surveillance particularly in the form of postdetection data fusion [9]. Other advances have used sensor repositioning after deployment to improve coverage, such as the use of virtual force algorithms [10] to move randomly deployed sensors to improve the coverage of the sensor network. While related, the problem of sensor network detection and classification algorithm design [11, 12] follows from the positioning of the sensors. We hold that the optimal placement of sensors will benefit from any further improvements gained from the detection and classification process. Similarly, the ability of the surveillance system to track any target of interest is critical to mission performance. Previous efforts in sensor network configuration have examined the positioning of sensors for target tracking applications [13], and it is well recognized that the target tracking performance of adaptively managed sensor networks is heavily dependent on the spatial deployment pattern [14]. In contrast to those efforts, the current paper is focused on the prior problem of maximizing the ability of gaining the initial detection for the surveillance application alone.

In this paper, we optimize distributed sensor configurations to achieve optimal surveillance performance. We utilize objectives based on a prescribed level of collaboration among sensors such that optimization of these objectives results in sensor placement that is optimal with respect to collaboration as well as individual sensor performance. This approach scales well with the number of sensors and, thus, is applicable to the large scale sensor network topologies down to the tactical scales more commonly found in current surveillance (search) problems. It is this latter scale that is the focus of this paper. In this distributed sensing objective, the sensors independently perform target detection and target detection decisions are made by comparing multiple non-collocated detections to check for kinematic consistency, as a form of target classification. If the individual detections are consistent (in spatiotemporal relation) with the anticipated target behavior, then the multiple detections corroborate and the collaborative sensors declare a target present.

The motivation of this work is to utilize a collaboration framework in a formal manner so that with modern computing resources, tactical decision aids can be developed to facilitate the command decisions with respect to collaborative sensors. With the formulation of a numerical objective, more target hypotheses can be considered than notional examination on which current approaches rely. To improve the performance of such a distributed sensor surveillance system, we consider the problem of determining the optimal layout of a group of sensors. Rather than optimizing all of the parameters of a system design, we focus instead on the key component of optimizing the opportunities for multiple sensor detections over time. Such opportunities are a critical first step in the many approaches to collaborative sensing. We consider this optimization of geometrical opportunities for collaboration as a fundamental goal of sensor layout planning, and secondary goals that are particular to a specific form of collaboration are beyond our scope. Our goal is the development of a computationally efficient numerical method that accounts for the geometric and environmental complexity of the problem, while maintaining enough generality to be useful in a variety of scenarios.

In the following, we refer generically to the platform that performs the sensing function as a "sensor," with the implied interpretation that all sensors have an underlying platform that holds them, be it a large manned asset or simply the device's housing. Thus a sensor may be as large as a manned radar or sonar platform, or as small as a simple proximity measurement device. The characterization of these devices, for our application, is given by their expected detection performance against the target of interest, which is presumed to be known from a prior model.

Given a fixed number of sensors, an expected distribution of target behavior, and a model of the sensors' detection performance in the region of interest, we develop an optimization framework that provides a sensor layout (set of sensor positions) for optimal surveillance protection of a region of interest under varying levels of collaboration. In particular, we consider three surveillance problems: (1) the detection of targets that are transiting throughout the region (typical area surveillance), (2) the detection of targets in the region that are far enough away from a high-valued unit (HVU) to provide reaction, and (3) the detection of objects that are weighted by their relative risk to the HVU. In the next section, we provide a mathematical model that accounts for all three of these distributed sensor surveillance problems. This common model has forms for both the cases of independent and of collaborative sensing and, thus provides a framework to study the implications of collaboration in the optimal positioning of sensors. The following develops a genetic algorithm-based optimization framework for optimizing sensor placement under this model. Finally, we conclude with some examples of the optimization to provide a comparison of the sensor layout patterns for various scenarios.

2. Mathematical Model of Distributed Surveillance

A crucial element in utilizing mathematical modeling to find practical solutions to problems such as optimal placement of distributed sensors (distributed assets) is in the formulation and numerical representation of the underlying objective. The formulation of the objective should be an accurate model of the problem that captures all parametric dependencies. In particular, any dependence on tactical parameters such as target behaviors and environmental characteristics requires a method that allows these parameters to be accounted for with varying levels of uncertainty. The numerical calculation of this objective should be a suitable approximation while being as efficient as possible to allow practical use in optimization approaches. The approach we follow is to model all of these dependencies in an integral formulation of expected performance over the search space. This integral form is then integrated with respect to any particular spatial distribution of sensors to arrive at probabilities representing expected surveillance field performance.

The first component in this model of distributed surveillance is the model for target motion (behavior). This model should allow varying levels of constraints on target motion to be of general use in a wide variety of problems. The model developed in this paper assumes the target motion to be Markovian in nature, such that its behavior can be decomposed into a sequence of short time behaviors. This assumption implies that the target motion path $\mathbf{y}(t)$ is effectively modeled by the sequence of intervals $\{[t_0, t_1), [t_1, t_2), \ldots\}$ and the path on the ith interval is $\mathbf{y}_i(t)$. The union of the collection of paths gives the total target path

$$\mathbf{y}(t) = \{\mathbf{y}_i(t) : t_i \le t < t_{i+1}\}, \tag{1}$$

where each path $\mathbf{y}_i(t) = \mathbf{y}_{\tau,i} + v_i \cdot (t - t_i) \cdot [\cos(\theta_i), \sin(\theta_i)]^T$ represents a path of constant velocity target motion v_i in direction θ_i. Furthermore, each interval has motion parameters $\mathbf{p}_i = (\mathbf{y}_{\tau,i}, v_i, \theta_i)$ which are sampled from known distributions, and the specific values are only dependent on the previous time step, $\mathbf{p}_{i+1} = f(\mathbf{p}_i)$, as opposed to depending on the entire history (this is the Markov assumption). This Markov motion model is regularly assumed in modeling nonreactive targets [15] and is the basis of many Monte Carlo simulation approaches to target modeling [16]. We utilize the model to limit our analysis to optimizing the performance over a fixed, finite time step, where the motion of the target follows constant velocity during the interval of interest and the probability distributions of the motion parameters are all known *a priori*.

For a given interval $[t_i, t_{i+1})$, the probability of collaborative detection is a function of the random variables that describe target motion, as well as the location of the sensing assets and their detection performance. Consider a single given target motion track over this chosen interval. Assume that all of the sensors and the entire target track are contained within the surveillance region $\mathscr{S} \subseteq \mathbb{R}^2$ (we assume the region is large enough that edge effects are negligible). The probability of detecting this track by N_D individual sensor detections (the probability of successfully surveilling the track) is written as [17]

$$P_{ST}(N_D \ge k) = 1 - \exp(-NP_D\phi) \sum_{m=0}^{k-1} \frac{(NP_D\phi)^m}{m!}, \tag{2}$$

where k is the minimum number of assets (sensors) independently detecting the target required for a collaborative detection of the target, while N is the total number of assets (sensors) in the surveillance region $\mathscr{S}$. The parameter P_D is the detection probability of an individual sensor, defined as constant within a given detection radius R_D. Note that the parameter k is used to define the level of collaboration in this framework. The variable ϕ represents the likelihood of a sensor being within distance R_D of a particular target track path to have an opportunity to detect the target (i.e., being within range of the target at some point during the track history). Explicitly, it is given by

$$\phi(\mathbf{y}_T, v, \theta) = \int_{\Omega_T(\mathbf{y}_T, v, \theta)} f(\mathbf{x}) d\mathbf{x}, \tag{3}$$

where $f(\mathbf{x})$ is the distribution of sensors in the space, and the region Ω_T is the two dimensional region (defined by a specific target track) comprised of the subset of $\mathscr{S}$ that is within detection radius R_D of the track.

The relationship between target path and the probability of successful search criteria (for $k = 2$) is illustrated in Figure 1. Figure 1(a) shows a notional path through a rectangular search region in the presence of deployed passive sensors with detection circles as shown. A subset of this path is highlighted and magnified in Figure 1(b) to show a constant velocity segment of this path (from the given Markov parameters) and the subset of the sensors which detect this segment (and subsequently the given path). Note that one can view the detection process from a sensor frame of reference, that is, a detection occurs when two or more sensor circles contain the target segment, or through a target frame of reference, where the center of the sensor circles must be within the pill-shaped region (shaded area in Figure 1(b)) to detect the target. It is through this target frame of reference that we efficiently calculate P_{ST} given a distribution on sensor position. In particular, the expressions in (2) and (3) represent the random search [18] of a moving target "seeking" the fixed sensors when the problem is viewed from a target frame of reference. The resultant probability of successful search, P_{SS}, for this time interval is given by marginalizing the probability $P_{ST}(N_D \ge k)$ over the uncertainty description of the target track as

$$P_{SS}(N_D \ge k)$$
$$= \int_0^{2\pi} \int_{v_{min}}^{v_{max}} \int_{\mathscr{S}} P_{ST}(N_D \ge k) f_T(\mathbf{y}_T) \tag{4}$$
$$\times f_v(v) f_\theta(\theta) d\mathbf{y}_T dv d\theta,$$

where the functions $f_T(\mathbf{y}_T)$, $f_v(v)$, and $f_\theta(\theta)$ are probability density functions (PDF's) for target motion parameters of position, speed, and course, respectively. In addition, by increasing (or decreasing) k, we subsequently increase (decrease) the required level of collaboration among the distributed sensors.

In practice, a target track is successfully found by a collaborative sensor system based on sensors sharing detection information. Thus, it is not only dependent on the requisite

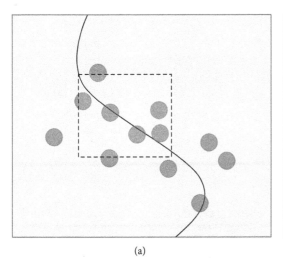
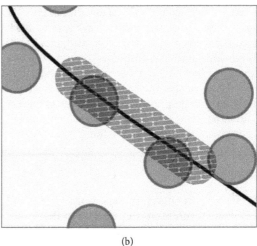

(a)   (b)

FIGURE 1: Notional example showing the connection between sensor placement and track coverage. (a) shows the target track path and the location of sensors with their coverage region. (b) is a blowup of the square box drawn in (a), showing a nominal "target pill" region representing a finite-time segment of the target track path.

number of sensors performing successful detections, but it also requires those sensors to communicate their results to other neighboring sensors. In the absence of full communication connectivity amongst the sensors, a graph model of the network node locations is used to assess the overall connectivity of the network in a probabilistic sense. Let $P_{\text{CON}}(f(\mathbf{x}), N, r_c)$ represent the probability of connectivity of a sensor network of N nodes of communication range r_c that are spatially distributed according to the distribution $f(\mathbf{x})$. The probability of connectivity for the network is the probability that there exists some multihop path between any two nodes of the network, thus it is the probability that any network node can communicate with the rest of the network. The computation of $P_{\text{CON}}(f(\mathbf{x}), N, r_c)$ for a fixed number N of nodes can be performed by known methods [19, 20]. Now the operational success of a search operation is the conditional probability of successful search conditioned on network connectivity. Mathematically, this is given by the joint probability expression $P_{\text{SS}} \cdot P_{\text{CON}}$ where P_{SS} is as given in (4). We note that both terms in this joint probability have a dependence on the sensor placement distribution $f(\mathbf{x})$. However, we assume that the sensors in our applications are densely spaced with respect to communications, such that every sensor can communicate reliably with all other nodes within the network. Such an assumption is common in passive detection systems, where the passive detection radius is often much smaller than the reliable communication distance. Thus, for the remainder of this paper, we consider only the case of completely connected networks (i.e., $P_{\text{CON}} = 1$) and, therefore, the objective corresponding to an operational success of search is given by P_{SS} alone. The extension of our optimization technique to problems with limited connectivity is a subject of future work.

In order to numerically calculate the objective (4) over a variety of distributions from flat (uniform within search region $\mathcal{S}$) to highly nonuniform, we represent the sensor density function as a mixture of N_G circular Gaussian functions, as

$$f(\mathbf{x}; \mathbf{w}) = \frac{1}{2\pi\sigma^2} \sum_{j=1}^{N_G} w_j \exp\left(-\frac{1}{2\sigma^2}(\mathbf{x} - \mathbf{x}_j)^T (\mathbf{x} - \mathbf{x}_j)\right), \quad (5)$$

with modal weights w_j, constant modal variance σ^2, and fixed (spaced equidistant in $\mathcal{S}$) positions $\mathbf{x}_j$, which has been shown to be a useful model for density approximation in many applications [21]. The number (and subsequent spacing) of the Gaussian modes required, as well as the value of the variance parameter σ, are chosen using a heuristic rule. The heuristic [22] is based on the flexibility of the overall density representation; that is, the relationship between the width of a Gaussian mode and the modal spacing; should be such that a wide variety of function forms of $f(\mathbf{x})$ can be represented. After experimentation on many test problems, we determined an appropriate relationship to be

$$N_G = \left(\left\lceil \frac{L}{3R_D} \right\rceil\right)^2, \quad (6)$$

where L is the length of the search region $\mathcal{S}$ along one dimension (assuming that $\mathcal{S}$ is square). The variance parameter is given as $\sigma = 2R_D$ for $R_D \ll L$. As R_D increases relative to L, this parameter should be made smaller relative to R_D; however, for the scale in this paper the given heuristic is applicable.

We note that P_{SS} provides a measure on the ability of multiple collaborative sensors to detect the target in a manner consistent with the spatiotemporal relationship of target motion and sensor position [17]. This is commonly referred to as track-before-detect and is an effective technique for reducing false alarms in distributed detection applications through collaboration defined by the aforementioned spatiotemporal relationship. It is also a method of multisensor filtering of contacts that is commonly used within many data fusion methods. Thus P_{SS} is, in general, a measure of track coverage in a surveillance region. However, as the length of the time interval tends to zero, P_{SS} becomes the more familiar metric of area coverage, that is, coverage independent of target motion. In that context, the expression in (2) is simply the composite area coverage provided by a set of independent sensors provided that their locations are randomly sampled from a common spatial distribution function $f(\mathbf{x})$.

3. Numerical Model

To optimize the placement of assets, the integrals in (3) and (4) must be evaluated with respect to changes in the sensor density function $f(\mathbf{x})$. In both cases these integrals do not have closed form solutions, and thus, must be evaluated numerically. Note first that the evaluation of the integral in (3) is significantly simplified by the representation of sensor density function defined in (5). Namely, through the fixed position and circular variance, the integral can be separated by mode (as a sum of the integrals of each mode) and in dimension (the two-dimensional integral can be separated by independence into the product of two one-dimensional integrals) independent of the modal weights. The latter property allows much of the computation to be done once, prior to entering the optimization, simplifying subsequent objective evaluations. This improvement in efficiency makes the optimization practical on standard desktop computers with no special coding requirements. Further simplification can be made by noting that for constant R_D (sensor performance independent of position in $\mathcal{S}$) the region of integration Ω_T given a target trajectory is a pill-shaped region with area $2R_D v\tau + \pi R_D^2$. This region can be well approximated by a rectangle of equal area for $v\tau \gg R_D$ which allows the integral in (3) to be evaluated using standard error functions commonly used for evaluation of integrals involving Gaussian functions [22]. The implementation utilized in this paper allows for spatial variability of R_D by including an additional step in which the equivalent rectangle is replaced by a series of rectangles (a partitioning) which approximate the track-dependent region (within which sensors have an opportunity to detect the target) by interpolation of an underlying R_D function. The number of segments that each track is partitioned (i.e., the number of rectangles) is determined a priori and depends on the extent of the spatial variability of R_D in the search region $\mathcal{S}$.

The mathematical detail required to evaluate (3) consists of the following. Consider an arbitrary target track of fixed length as defined above. Define an arbitrary point along this track $\mathbf{y}_{t_i}$ and a set $A_{t_i} = \{\mathbf{x} : \|\mathbf{y}_{t_i} - \mathbf{x}\| \le R_D(\mathbf{x})\}$, which is the set of all points in $\mathcal{S}$ from which an arbitrary sensor can detect a target at the specified point along the target track (with probability P_D). Then the general form of the "pill" shaped region of integration can be written as $\Omega_T = \bigcup_{i=1}^{\infty} A_{t_i}$. Next, define an approximation to this region as $\Omega^m = \bigcup_{j=1}^{m} A_{t_j}$ where t_j, $j = 1,\ldots,m$ refer to m equally spaced points spanning the length of the arbitrary track and construct

disjoint sets B_{t_j} from sets A_{t_j} by the recursion $B_{t_j} = A_{t_j} - U^{j-1}$ given $U^k = \bigcup_{j=1}^{k} A_{t_j}$ and $U^0 = \emptyset$ (the empty set). Then the integral in (3) can be approximated as

$$
\begin{aligned}
\int_{\Omega_T} f(\mathbf{x})\, d\mathbf{x} &= \int_{\mathcal{S}} I_{\Omega_T}(\mathbf{x}) f(\mathbf{x})\, d\mathbf{x} \\
&\approx \int_{\mathcal{S}} I_{\Omega^m}(\mathbf{x}) f(\mathbf{x})\, d\mathbf{x} \qquad (7) \\
&= \sum_{j=1}^{m} \int_{\mathcal{S}} I_{B_{t_j}}(\mathbf{x}) f(\mathbf{x})\, d\mathbf{x},
\end{aligned}
$$

where $I_A(\mathbf{x})$ is the set indicator function of the set A.

Assuming that the integral in (3) is well approximated by the above and that the function P_{ST} (as in (2)) changes slowly over the target track parameters in $\mathcal{S}$, the numerical evaluation of the integral in (4) can be done simply, provided that the PDFs of the target track parameters are continuously differentiable and slowly changing over their support. Since this is true for the examples in this paper, then in this work the integral is evaluated by gridding the track parameters (and associated weights) evenly over the track parameter space. This allows the triple integral in (4) to be well approximated by a triple sum weighted by the product of the corresponding values of the PDFs over the target parameter grid. The numerical evaluation of the sum as shown above provides a robust computation of the required integral of $f(\mathbf{x})$ over the region Ω_T.

4. Formulation of Optimization

The problem of optimum deployment of assets for collaborative multisensor surveillance, restricted to the mathematical model in (4), is one of maximizing search effectiveness in a fixed region. From an optimal planning perspective, the problem is one of maximizing the likelihood of achieving the surveillance mission, where the mission can take on various forms. We represent this as a minimization problem of the form

$$
\min_{f} P_{MF}, \qquad (8)
$$

where P_{MF} is the probability of mission failure and $f = f(\mathbf{x})$ is a function representing the sensor distribution over the region $\mathcal{S}$. In practice, this mission failure may take a variety of forms, but we are primarily concerned with the joint probability of not detecting a target within our surveillance region, combined with the risk associated with that target's presence. In particular, for the small time interval of interest which determines the path interval of interest, we have

$$
\begin{aligned}
P_{MF} \\
= \int_0^{2\pi} \int_{v_{\min}}^{v_{\max}} \int_{\mathcal{S}} (1 - P_{ST})\, \psi(\mathbf{y}_T)\, f_T(\mathbf{y}_T) \\
\times f_v(v) f_\theta(\theta)\, d\mathbf{y}_T\, dv\, d\theta \\
= \int_{\mathcal{S}} f_T(\mathbf{y}_T)\, \psi(\mathbf{y}_T)\, d\mathbf{y}_T
\end{aligned}
$$

$$- \int_0^{2\pi} \int_{v_{\min}}^{v_{\max}} \int_{\mathscr{S}} P_{\text{ST}} \left(\mathbf{y}_T \right) \cdot \left[f_T \left(\mathbf{y}_T \right) \psi \left(\mathbf{y}_T \right) \right]$$

$$\times f_v \left(v \right) f_\theta \left(\theta \right) d\mathbf{y}_T \, dv \, d\theta, \tag{9}$$

where $\psi(\mathbf{y}_T)$ is a consequence (risk) function. The consequence function is dependent on the location of target track $\mathbf{y}_T$ and is defined to measure the relative risk posed by various tracks over that of others (such as those in proximity to an HVU, if that is the intention of the surveillance region). The first integral in (9) does not depend on the choice of the sensor location density $f(\mathbf{x})$, so it does not impact the optimization leading to an effective minimization objective of

$$J = - \int_0^{2\pi} \int_{v_{\min}}^{v_{\max}} \int_{\mathscr{S}} P_{\text{ST}} \left(\mathbf{y}_T \right)$$

$$\cdot \left[f_T \left(\mathbf{y}_T \right) \psi \left(\mathbf{y}_T \right) \right] f_v \left(v \right) f_\theta \left(\theta \right) d\mathbf{y}_T \, dv \, d\theta. \tag{10}$$

The optimization problem of (8) is now given in the form

$$\min_f J(f) \tag{11}$$

for the objective functional J given in (10).

If all target locations and tracks are equally important, then the consequence function $\psi(\mathbf{y}_T)$ is necessarily equal to unity, leading to $J = -P_{\text{SS}}$ (see (4)). In such cases, the optimization problem of (11) is equivalent to

$$\max_f P_{\text{SS}}. \tag{12}$$

We seek the $f(\mathbf{x})$ which maximizes the probability of successful search, leading to a density function from which sensors will then be placed [22]. When our goal is more specific, that is for protection of an HVU, the consequence function $\psi(\mathbf{y}_T)$ is used to represent the relative risk of various target tracks, and the solution of the same optimization problem ((10) and (11)) yields the solution of minimizing the expected risk to the HVU. Thus, the optimization problem of (10) and (11) is generically utilized as the asset layout optimization problem, with the understanding that a variety of specific problems are addressed by varying the form of the consequence function.

To compute the objective functional J as shown in (10), the target motion distribution parameters must be known, as well as the effective sensor performance P_D and R_D, which are generally functions of location in the region. In this work, we adopt a notional model for the spatial dependence of sensor performance in a rectangular region of interest, depicted in Figure 2. As in the previously defined model, sensor performance is measured by a spatially dependent radius of detection $R_D(\mathbf{x})$ which corresponds to a fixed probability of detection P_D (note that in Figure 2 we show $R_D(\mathbf{x})$ normalized to the size of the region L, where the R_D corresponds to a value of $P_D = 0.9$). In practice, sensor performance predictions such as these can be formulated using historical information on the environment and are

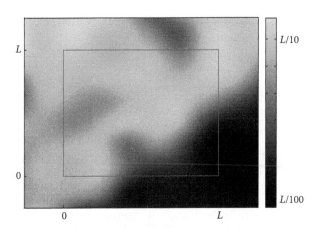

FIGURE 2: Sensor detection range map for the example problems. The region drawn in the center represents the surveillance region for sensor placement.

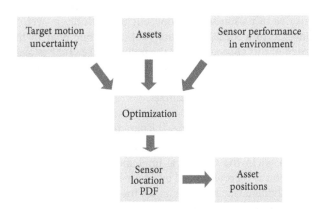

FIGURE 3: Sensor optimization algorithm flow diagram.

common in passive acoustic sensor applications, both in air [23] and undersea [24] domains. The sensor performance and number of sensors provide the necessary inputs for computation of P_{ST} (as in (2)) for any specified target track. When combined with the target motion distribution parameters and consequence function, they provide a complete description of the objective J for any distribution $f(\mathbf{x})$ of sensor locations. Figure 3 shows a functional description of the overall approach, where it becomes clear that the "inputs" to the optimization, that is *a priori* knowledge of target, environment, and asset availability, are utilized to find the optimal distribution of assets. The specific placement of the individual sensor assets from the distribution is done using a sampling procedure from the resulting distribution, leading to a placement map for the surveillance region.

5. Numerical Procedure for Optimization

Recall from (5) that the modal positions representing the sensor distribution are fixed and thus the optimal distribution with respect to the surveillance objective (9) is parameterized only through the modal weights. Thus the numerical objective for optimization becomes

$$\min_{\mathbf{w}} J(\mathbf{w})$$

$$\text{subject to} \sum_{j}^{N_G} w_j = 1, \quad 0 \leq w_j \leq 1, \forall j. \tag{13}$$

We implement a genetic algorithm to perform the optimization defined in (13). The genetic algorithm cannot be run to any guarantee of convergence [25] but is rather run to a prescribed number of generations (iterations). If a theoretically optimal result is desired, the result of the genetic algorithm may be used as the starting point for a nonlinear program (NLP). These stages are complementary in that the genetic algorithm is insensitive to its start and will make significant progress toward a global solution but is devoid of satisfactory stopping criteria (i.e., no guaranteed final convergence). The NLP on the other hand can be quite sensitive to its starting solution but theoretically proven to converge to a local maximum [26]. Thus one goal in the design of this approach is for the potential use of the genetic algorithm to initialize an NLP in the neighborhood of a globally optimal solution, and thus we can attain convergence to a global maximum, if desired.

Genetic algorithms operate on a discrete set of parameters in the form of a binary string. The parameters in this problem are the weights $\{w_j\}_{j=1}^{N_G}$ representing the sensor distribution $f(\mathbf{x})$ in $\mathcal{S}$. In the numerical implementation, each weight parameter w_j is represented by a four-bit binary string, with N_G individual Gaussian modes for the representation in (5). Thus, the string length is $4N_G$.

A genetic algorithm starts with some random values of the parameters of interest represented in the form of a binary string as described above. A set of these strings is produced which is referred to as a *population*. This type of algorithm is an iterative search where iterations are referred to as *generations*. At each generation (iteration), the binary strings which make up the population undergo a series of operations. Thus, starting with a randomly generated population, each string is evaluated by the objective function J returning a value corresponding to each string. Typically, the value of the objective is mapped into a more convenient form (to improve scaling) referred to as fitness [27]. However, in this implementation fitness is set to the evaluated objective J, as this quantity is well scaled.

A standard form of genetic algorithm [27] was implemented with each generation consisting of three genetic operations defined in the evolutionary vernacular as *selection*, *mating*, and *mutation*. These operations utilize the fitness associated with each binary string in the population to pseudorandomly select the best (with respect to the objective J) parameter combinations, randomly combine the selected strings, and apply some random perturbations to the resulting strings, respectively. Specifically, the selection approach utilized, referred to as "roulette," selects binary strings by first scaling the fitness of the population members to sum to unity. Next, the cumulative sum of the fitness is calculated,

creating an interval $(0, 1)$, with subintervals proportional to the fitness of each binary string. A random uniform number is then generated and the subinterval in which the number falls determines the string that is selected. Thus, a string (population member) with high fitness, relative to other strings, will be selected with high probability while one with low fitness will be selected with low probability. In this implementation, the string with the highest fitness (at each generation) is kept as a *survivor*; that is, the best string gets passed on to the next generation unchanged. Therefore, $N_{pop} - 1$ strings are selected to pass to the next generation (where N_{pop} is the fixed number of strings in a population), and these strings make up what is referred to as the *mating pool*. In the next phase, strings in the mating pool are randomly (without regard to fitness) paired up and then randomly combined to create new parameter strings. This operation is called *crossover*. Crossover consists of randomly breaking two strings (at the same point) and then combining the leading part of one with the trailing part of the other. Finally, each of these newly formed strings is passed to the *mutation* operation which flips bits (i.e., change 0 to 1, or vice versa) within each string randomly at some specified (*a priori*) probability. This is essentially a random perturbation of the parameters meant to avoid premature convergence to local minima. Once these operations are complete, the new strings are grouped with the survivor string and these strings become the new population passed on to the next generation (iteration). This process is repeated for some predefined set of generations. From numerical experimentation on a variety of problems, a population size of 100 run over 200 generations was suitable for producing meaningful results for the numerical examples in this paper.

On completion of the genetic algorithm, the optimal sensor density is obtained and the sensors are then placed using a numerical sampling procedure. The procedure consists of a sequential (conditional) sampling where an asset location is selected (among a grid of possible locations) which maximizes the relative entropy between the prior form of the PDF $f(\mathbf{x})$ (discretized and normalized to sum to unity, in order to convert to a probability mass function) and the posterior probability mass function (PMF) calculated by selecting the asset. The relative entropy between two PMFs is written as [28]

$$D(p_1||p_0) = \sum_{\mathbf{s} \in \mathcal{S}} p_1(\mathbf{s}) \log\left(\frac{p_1(\mathbf{s})}{p_0(\mathbf{s})}\right) \tag{14}$$

and represents a measure of divergence of one PMF relative to the other. The conditional sampling procedure used to place sensors from $f(\mathbf{x})$ treats individual sensor placement as a Bayes recursion where a unique posterior is generated by a positional-dependent likelihood update, defined as corresponding to a possible sensor location. The procedure starts with the definition of two grids (uniformly spaced points in $\mathcal{S}$), written as $\mathbf{z}_i$, $i = 1, \ldots, m$ and $\mathbf{v}_j$, $j = 1, \ldots, n$ where $\mathbf{z}_i$ represents discretely sampled points of $f(\mathbf{x})$, and $\mathbf{v}_j$ represents all possible sensor locations for placement. Next, the prior is calculated from the final form (after optimization) of $f(\mathbf{x})$ as

$$p_0(\mathbf{z}_i) = \frac{I_{\mathbf{z}_i}(\mathbf{x}) f(\mathbf{x})}{\sum_{i=1}^{m} I_{\mathbf{z}_i}(\mathbf{x}) f(\mathbf{x})}, \qquad (15)$$

where

$$I_{\mathbf{z}_i}(\mathbf{x}) = \begin{cases} 1, & \mathbf{x} = \mathbf{z}_i \\ 0, & \mathbf{x} \neq \mathbf{z}_i \end{cases} \qquad (16)$$

is the indicator function. The posterior probability resulting from selecting (placing) a sensor at position $\mathbf{v}_j$ is defined as

$$\pi^i(\mathbf{z}) = \begin{cases} \dfrac{p_0(\mathbf{z})}{\psi_j}, & \mathbf{z} \in \overline{B}_j \\[2mm] \dfrac{\alpha \cdot p_0(\mathbf{z})}{\psi_j}, & \mathbf{z} \in B_j, \end{cases} \qquad (17)$$

where $\mathcal{S} = B_j \cup \overline{B}_j$, $B_j \cap \overline{B}_j = \emptyset$ (i.e., a disjoint partitioning of $\mathcal{S}$ with respect to sensor position $\mathbf{v}_j$) and $B_j = \{\mathbf{z} : \|\mathbf{z} - \mathbf{v}_j\|_2 \leq R_D(\mathbf{v}_j)\}$ is a ball of spatially dependent radius R_D (with respect to constant P_D) centered at point $\mathbf{v}_j$. The sensor coefficient $\alpha = 1 - P_D$ plays the role of decreasing mass within the radius of the placed sensor, while the sensor-dependent normalizing constant is written as

$$\psi_j = \sum_{\mathbf{z} \in \overline{B}_j} p_0(\mathbf{z}) + \sum_{\mathbf{z} \in B_j} \alpha \cdot p_0(\mathbf{z}). \qquad (18)$$

This normalizing constant is required so that each posterior probability is a proper PMF (i.e., sums to unity over its support). The posterior with respect to all possible sensor grid points is calculated as in (15), and a sensor is placed at a specified position, by choosing the posterior which maximizes the relative entropy with respect to the prior. This is formalized as

$$\pi^* = \arg\max_j D\left(\pi^j \middle\| p_0\right), \qquad (19)$$

where this process is repeated in a sequential fashion to place all N sensors. Upon the placement of each sensor, the posterior with respect to the chosen location acts as the prior for placing the next sensor.

6. Numerical Examples

The problem of sensor placement as defined above depends on many factors. These factors can be primarily sensor dependencies from environmental variability [29] or can be dominated by other factors such as target behavior [30]. To illustrate these dependencies, we present several numerical examples. Throughout the examples, we consider the number of available sensor assets N to be fixed. The planning problem is to place these sensors optimally in a square planar region $\mathcal{S}$ of size $L \times L$. For these examples, the optimality criteria are to maximize the probability of surveillance mission success, corresponding to minimization of the probability of mission failure P_{MF}.

As an introductory example, and to demonstrate the utility of the optimization approach, we define a nominal environment (constant detection range given by $R_D = L/15$) with target parameters for which intuitive solutions exist. We seek to optimally place $N = 28$ sensors, such that we obtain the maximum P_{SS} (corresponding to minimizing P_{MF}) with a requirement of at least two sensor reports during a time interval τ. The target is assumed to be traveling in a known fixed heading (assumed north) at constant speed v over the fixed time interval τ (where $v\tau = L/2$) with a start position randomly distributed within the search region. For this problem, the expected optimal placement is a "barrier" formation perpendicular to the target course [22]. In particular, due to random starting positions, we should observe a two-line barrier perpendicular to the target course. Figure 4(a) illustrates the optimization results from this problem, where we see that the barrier structure results, as expected. A second nominal example considers a similar problem but with target heading defined as random. In this case, the optimization result, shown in Figure 4(b), produces a sensor layout in a "box-like" structure, which may not be intuitively obvious but has been shown to be optimal [22]. These nominal examples show the dependence that the target behavior has on the optimal sensor layouts.

In a typical approach to deployment of sensors under limited knowledge of the environment, it is reasonable to consider some nominal sensor detection performance. However, given current environmental modeling capabilities, we assume that sensor detection performance can be provided to some acceptable level of fidelity. Figure 2 shows a $1.5L \times 1.5L$ region containing the region of interest, defined by the inner box. The underlying color map depicts sensor coverage as a function of position within the region. The sensor performance is limited by environmental factors that are beyond our control, and the optimization seeks to maximize mission performance (minimizing P_{MF}) in surveillance of the given region with a limited number of sensors. In particular, for the region in Figure 2, the lower right part of the region exhibits a sharp dropoff in individual sensor coverage.

An additional input to the optimization is the characterization of target behavior. The numerical examples that follow were produced assuming that target position and heading are uniformly random within the search region $\mathcal{S}$. That is, all reference track positions (previously defined as $\mathbf{y}_T$) are equally likely. Furthermore, assume that the target of interest travels at a fixed speed v over time intervals of length τ. This defines a track length of $v\tau$, which is given as $v\tau = L/8$ for these numerical examples. The track length is scalable over varying combinations of speed and time (as it is simply the product of the two) and represents *a priori* knowledge of the target of interest, which will result in increased surveillance performance over that of situations where there is very little known (and thus can be assumed) of the anticipated target behavior.

In Figure 5, we illustrate three example consequence (risk) functions $\psi(\mathbf{y}_T)$ of interest. The first function shown in Figure 5(a) is the nominal unity function that is equivalent to the problem of optimizing cumulative probability of detection (see (12) and the surrounding discussion). The second

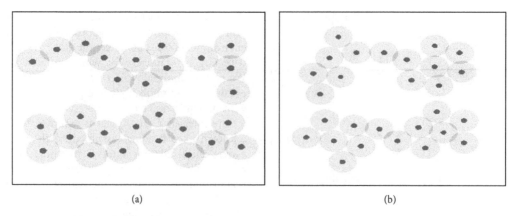

FIGURE 4: Optimal sensor placement for surveillance of fixed speed target in nominal environment. (a) is for a target with a known course; (b) is for a target with an unknown course.

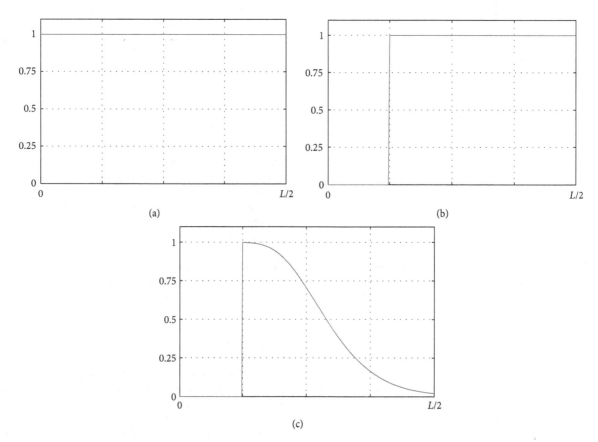

FIGURE 5: Consequence (risk) function $\psi(\mathbf{y}_T)$ versus range for each of the three example cases.

consequence function shown in Figure 5(b) represents a protection problem for an HVU, whereby any targets within a certain distance to the HVU are too close to provide a surveillance response, and, thus, provide zero surveillance risk, with all others providing nominal risk. This may seem counterintuitive, to have zero risk closest to the HVU, but the point here is to maximize surveillance performance, and this case illustrates the situation in which the surveillance mission is no longer operational when targets are too close to the HVU. Alternatively, if one were to weight the consequence

very high near the HVU, an obviously optimal solution is to only try to detect those targets and ignore all targets that are not directly in proximity to the HVU, which is not desired if the risk is already passed. The third consequence function, shown in Figure 5(c), is perhaps the most operationally relevant, in that it incorporates the features of the second case along with degradation in risk for targets further from the HVU. In this case, the risk degradation follows a log-normal function, as described by [31]. Such a consequence is representative of scenarios in which there is a greater

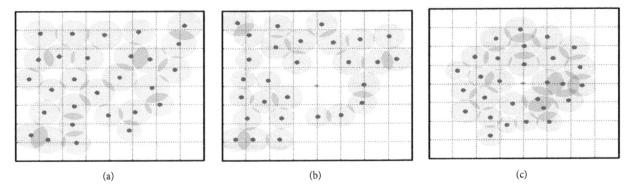

(a)	(b)	(c)

FIGURE 6: Optimal sensor distributions for each of the three consequence functions of Figure 5 for scenarios with no cooperation between sensors. Circle size represents the detection range of the sensor (which is a function of position).

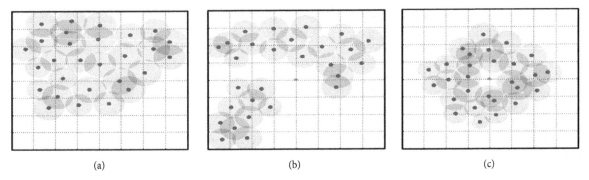

(a)	(b)	(c)

FIGURE 7: Optimal sensor distributions for each of the three consequence functions of Figure 5 for scenarios with $k = 2$ cooperation between sensors. Circle size represents the detection range of the sensor (which is a function of position).

importance to detect targets closer to the HVU, up to a point at which they are so close that response becomes impractical. Specifically, the log-normal consequence function takes the form

$$\psi\left(\mathbf{y}_T\right)$$

$$= \begin{cases} 0, & \|\mathbf{y}_T - \mathbf{x}_0\| < r_0 \\ \dfrac{1}{2}\left[1 - \mathrm{erf}\left[\dfrac{\ln\left(\|\mathbf{y}_T - \mathbf{x}_0\|/\alpha\right)}{\sqrt{2}\beta}\right]\right], & \|\mathbf{y}_T - \mathbf{x}_0\| \geq r_0 \end{cases}$$

$$(20)$$

for an HVU at location $\mathbf{x} = \mathbf{x}_0$ with a minimal response distance r_0. The parameters α, β in (20) are shape parameters that control the slope and taper of the log-normal consequence function. These three example consequence functions illustrate various applications of the consequence function $\psi(\mathbf{y}_T)$ to show how seemingly different scenarios are solved using the same field optimization approach.

Figure 6 illustrates the results of the optimization process applied to the three consequence functions of Figure 5 for a scenario with $N = 28$ sensors performing noncollaborative surveillance. By noncollaborative surveillance, we consider the sensors to behave completely autonomously ($k = 1$ in (2)), and extended coverage is obtained only through the effective spacing of the individual sensors with respect to the target prior information, that is, since there is no collaboration between sensors, the surveillance relies only upon individual

sensors to detect a target if present. In Figure 6, along with the sensor positions, we include opaque circles corresponding to the coverage capability radius R_D of each sensor. The circle size varies according to the local sensing capabilities attributable to the local environmental conditions, as shown in Figure 2. The effect for the first consequence function (for unity risk), as shown in Figure 6(a), is to place the sensors somewhat evenly to best cover the requirement of single sensor coverage in the field. Fewer sensors are located where there is lower detection capability (lower right corner) since the additive coverage is small. For the second consequence function, note that there are no sensors placed near the HVU (see Figure 6(b)), as expected. When compared to the first consequence function, note that the sensors are still spread evenly but now pushed slightly closer to the edges, in order to still cover as much of the area as possible. The third consequence function provides a different type of optimal configuration, as shown in Figure 6(c). In this case, the sensors tend to encircle the HVU in an annulus, as the annular region is the region of highest consequence if detections are missed. This effect appears more significant than the effect of avoiding the low coverage in the lower right corner, and more sensors are added to the lower right section of the annular region to make up for the lower individual sensor coverage. Note that each of these results were created from the same optimization procedure, with the only distinction between the three cases being the specific form of the consequence function $\psi(\mathbf{y}_T)$.

TABLE 1: Comparison of optimal and nominal values of the objective J for the distributions shown in Figures 6 and 7.

	Objective value for consequence function a		Objective value for consequence function b		Objective value for consequence function c	
	Uniform placement	Optimal placement	Uniform placement	Optimal placement	Uniform placement	Optimal placement
Noncollaborative Sensors	0.46	0.60	0.45	0.55	0.52	0.80
Collaborative Sensors	0.14	0.28	0.14	0.28	0.18	0.60

In practical situations with many sensors, there is performance enhancement opportunity through the use of collaboration [32, 33]. Historically, such problems are solved using optimal processing strategies given a fixed location of sensors [34, 35]. However, the optimization framework developed herein permits the optimization of sensor placements for a given level of collaboration. For instance, the parameter k in (2) may be adjusted to represent the number of sensors that must concurrently detect a target over the time interval of interest τ. Any detections that are spatially or temporally isolated will not count towards the probability P_{ST} used as the performance objective, as they are likely false positives. Recall that the requirement of multiple detections need not occur simultaneously, only over the time interval of interest. Thus, the performance objective cannot be translated into a simple geometrical overlap requirement, that is, a goal in which maximal overlap is sought. In fact, since this objective depends on target track parameters which have spatiotemporal features, there are many scenarios for which non-intuitive patterns of sensors will be optimal. In particular, as complexity (from such factors as environmental sensitivity or higher levels of collaboration) is added, results formed through intuition become less likely to approach optimal, reinforcing the need for an optimization framework which can factor in these complexities.

To illustrate the impact of multiple sensor collaboration on the optimal patterns, the examples of Figure 6 are repeated with a requirement of $k = 2$ detections to occur over the time interval of interest. In this case the goal is to optimally deploy the same sensors in the same variable environment, but we now require two separate sensor detections ($k = 2$) over the previously defined time interval τ. The resulting optimal patterns for the three consequence functions are shown in Figure 7. Comparison with Figure 6 shows that the increased detection requirement coupled with the relatively short target track length results in a more clustered approach to the deployment. For the third consequence function the deployment pattern has only subtle differences compared to Figure 6. This is attributed to the effect of having more than a suitable number of sensors for covering the annular region of primary interest.

In Table 1 we show the numerical values of the performance objectives for each of the scenarios presented in Figures 6 and 7. These objective values are also compared to the equivalent objective values obtained with uniform placement patterns of the assets for each situation. Observe that in each case the optimization approach resulted in better performance in the objective J than for the uniform

distribution, as expected. In these examples the $N = 28$ sensors represent a sparse coverage with respect to the search region $\mathscr{S}$, particularly for general surveillance (consequence function a) and for cases requiring multiple detections. This sparsity explains some of the general trends seen in the results. For instance, for both consequence functions a and b there is little or no difference between the results for collaborating and independent sensors. This is because the reduction in the search space due to the presence of the HVU is not significant with respect to the level of sensor coverage sparsity. However, the coverage numbers increase significantly for consequence function c, where the form of the consequence function $\psi(\mathbf{y}_T)$ increases the spatial dependence of the objective with respect to the position of the HVU. Overall the increased coverage due to optimization is much more significant for collaborative sensors than for independent sensors. This is due to the added sensitivity of sensor placement when using collaboration based on spatiotemporal target dependence.

An important byproduct of these numerical results is that for a number of diverse surveillance missions, a common optimization procedure can be utilized for positioning sensors to either meet specific performance criteria, or to get the best performance possible. This can be applied in two ways, the obvious one being as a predeployment tool for positioning sensors for a specific mission, the other being a guide to repositioning sensors to react to a change in mission. In either case these examples show that through proper modeling of the problem, optimal positioning of sensor assets can be achieved, without resorting to costly simulations. In fact, the results attained for these examples were produced with a per case computation time of approximately 20 minutes on a Pentium IV 3 GHz processor with code implemented in MATLAB.

7. Conclusion

We have developed an optimization approach to place distributed sets of sensors to collaboratively perform surveillance against moving targets over extended areas. In particular, a genetic algorithm solution was provided to find the spatial sensor density functions that maximize effectiveness against moving targets. These density function representations provide a computationally efficient method for determining sensor locations for planning and were applied to situations with environmentally induced sensor spatial variability and varying forms of target risk. By illustrating the effective performance of our method on problems of general area surveillance and risk-based surveillance in protection of an asset, we have shown how the general technique applies to seemingly dissimilar problems. The numerical solutions that were obtained were shown to compare favorably against nominal layouts of sensors in the scenarios that were examined. Future work includes the extension of this method to problems with limited network connectivity between the sensor nodes.

Acknowledgments

This work has been supported by the Office of Naval Research code 321MS and by the In-house Laboratory Independent Research program of the Naval Undersea Warfare Center.

References

[1] D. H. Wagner, W. C. Mylander, and T. J. Sanders, *Naval Operations Analysis*, Naval Institute Press, Annapolis, Md, USA, 1999.

[2] S. Olariu and J. V. Nickerson, "Protecting with sensor networks: perimeters and axes," in *Proceedings of the Military Communications Conference (MILCOM '05)*, vol. 3, pp. 1780–1786, October 2005.

[3] I. F. Akyildiz, W. Su, Y. Sankarasubramaniam, and E. Cayirci, "A survey on sensor networks," *IEEE Communications Magazine*, vol. 40, no. 8, pp. 102–114, 2002.

[4] D. Estrin, D. Culler, K. Pister, and G. Sukhatme, "Connecting the physical world with pervasive networks," *IEEE Pervasive Computing*, vol. 1, no. 1, pp. 59–69, 2002.

[5] H. Qi, S. S. Iyengar, and K. Chakrabarty, "Distributed sensor networks—a review of recent research," *Journal of the Franklin Institute*, vol. 338, no. 6, pp. 655–668, 2001.

[6] T. Clouqueur, V. Phipatanasuphorn, P. Ramanathan, and K. K. Saluja, "Sensor deployment strategy for detection of targets traversing a region," *Mobile Networks and Applications*, vol. 8, no. 4, pp. 453–461, 2003.

[7] S.S. Dhillon and K. Chakrabarty, "Sensor placement for effective coverage and surveillance in distributed sensor networks," in *Proceedings of the Wireless Communications and Networking Conference*, vol. 3, pp. 1609–1614, March 2003.

[8] P. K. Biswas and S. Phoha, "Self-organizing sensor networks for integrated target surveillance," *IEEE Transactions on Computers*, vol. 55, no. 8, pp. 1033–1047, 2006.

[9] M. F. Duarte and Y. H. Hu, "Vehicle classification in distributed sensor networks," *Journal of Parallel and Distributed Computing*, vol. 64, no. 7, pp. 826–838, 2004.

[10] Y. Zou and K. Chakrabarty, "Sensor deployment and target localization in distributed sensor networks," *ACM Transactions on Embedded Computer Systems*, vol. 3, no. 1, pp. 61–91, 2004.

[11] E. H. Aboelela and A. H. Khan, "Wireless sensors and neural networks for intruders detection and classification," in *Proceedings of the International Conference on Information Networking (ICOIN '12)*, pp. 138–143, 2012.

[12] A. Arora, P. Dutta, S. Bapat et al., "A line in the sand: a wireless sensor network for target detection, classification, and tracking," *Computer Networks*, vol. 46, no. 5, pp. 605–634, 2004.

[13] S. Martínez and F. Bullo, "Optimal sensor placement and motion coordination for target tracking," *Automatica*, vol. 42, no. 4, pp. 661–668, 2006.

[14] K. Hadi and C. M. Krishna, "Management of target-tracking sensor networks," *International Journal of Sensor Networks*, vol. 8, no. 2, pp. 109–121, 2010.

[15] Y. Bar-Shalom, X. R. Li, and T. Kirubarajan, *Estimation with Applications to Tracking and Navigation: Theory, Algorithms, and Software*, Wiley-Interscience, 2001.

[16] B. Ristic, S. Arulampalam, and N. Gordon, *Beyond the Kalman Filter: Particle Filters for Tracking Applications*, Artech House, 2004.

[17] T. A. Wettergren, "Performance of search via track-before-detect for distributed sensor networks," *IEEE Transactions on Aerospace and Electronic Systems*, vol. 44, no. 1, pp. 314–325, 2008.

[18] B. O. Koopman, *Search and Screening: General Principles with Historical Applications*, Pergamon Press, 1980.

[19] M. Desai and D. Manjunath, "On the connectivity in finite ad hoc networks," *IEEE Communications Letters*, vol. 6, no. 10, pp. 437–439, 2002.

[20] A. Ghasemi and S. Nader-Esfahani, "Exact probability of connectivity in one-dimensional ad hoc wireless networks," *IEEE Communications Letters*, vol. 10, no. 4, pp. 251–253, 2006.

[21] G. McLachlan and D. Peel, *Finite Mixture Models*, John Wiley & Sons, 2000.

[22] T. A. Wettergren and R. Costa, "Optimal placement of distributed sensors against moving targets," *ACM Transactions on Sensor Networks*, vol. 5, no. 3, article 26, pp. 1–25, 2009.

[23] R. J. Kozick, B. M. Sadler, and D. K. Wilson, "Signal processing and propagation for aeroacoustic sensor networks," in *Frontiers in Distributed Sensor Networks*, S. S. Iyengar and R.R. Brooks, Eds., CRC Press LLC, 2004.

[24] C. Ferla and M. B. Porter, "Receiver depth selection for passive sonar systems," *IEEE Journal of Oceanic Engineering*, vol. 16, no. 3, pp. 267–278, 1991.

[25] G. Rudolph, "Convergence analysis of canonical genetic algorithms," *IEEE Transactions on Neural Networks*, vol. 5, no. 1, pp. 96–101, 1994.

[26] R. Fletcher, *Practical Methods of Optimization*, John Wiley & Sons, 2nd edition, 1987.

[27] D. E. Goldberg, *Genetic Algorithms in Search, Optimization, and Machine Learning*, Addison Wesley Longman, 1989.

[28] T. M. Cover and J. A. Thomas, *Elements of Information Theory*, Wiley-Interscience, 1991.

[29] R. Stolkin, L. Vickers, and J. V. Nickerson, "Using environmental models to optimize sensor placement," *IEEE Sensors Journal*, vol. 7, no. 3, pp. 319–320, 2007.

[30] S. A. Musman, P. E. Lehner, and C. Elsaesser, "Sensor planning for elusive targets," *Mathematical and Computer Modelling*, vol. 25, no. 3, pp. 103–115, 1997.

[31] J. S. Przemieniecki, *Mathematical Methods in Defense Analyses*, American Institute of Aeronautics and Astronautics, Reston, Va, USA, 3rd edition, 2000.

[32] J. F. Chamberland and V. V. Veeravalli, "Decentralized detection in sensor networks," *IEEE Transactions on Signal Processing*, vol. 51, no. 2, pp. 407–416, 2003.

[33] S. Ferrari, "Track coverage in sensor networks," in *Proceedings of the American Control Conference*, pp. 2053–2059, Minneapolis, Minn, USA, June 2006.

[34] R. Niu, P. K. Varshney, and Q. Cheng, "Distributed detection in a large wireless sensor network," *Information Fusion*, vol. 7, no. 4, pp. 380–394, 2006.

[35] D.E. Penny, "Multi-sensor management for passive target tracking in an anti-submarine warfare scenario," in *IEE Colloquium on Target Tracking: Algorithms and Applications*, vol. 3, pp. 1–5, 1999.

4

MDS-Based Wormhole Detection Using Local Topology in Wireless Sensor Networks

Xiaopei Lu, Dezun Dong, and Xiangke Liao

College of Computer Science, National University of Defense Technology, Hunan 410073, China

Correspondence should be addressed to Xiaopei Lu, luxp02@gmail.com

Academic Editor: Shuai Li

Wormhole attack is a severe threat to wireless sensor networks (WSNs), which has received considerable attentions in the literature. However, most of the previous approaches either require special hardware devices or depend on rigorous assumptions on the network settings, which greatly limit their applicability. In this work, we attempt to relax the limitations in prior work, and propose a novel approach to detect wormhole attacks by only local topology information in WSNs. The basic idea is as follows. Each node locally collects its neighborhood information and reconstructs the neighborhood subgraph by multidimensional scaling (MDS). Potential wormhole nodes are detected by validating the legality of the reconstruction. Then, a refinement process is introduced to filter the suspect nodes and to remove false positives. Our approach solely relies on the local connectivity information and is extremely simple and lightweight, which makes it applicable in practical systems. Extensive simulations are conducted, and the results demonstrate the effectiveness and superior performance of our approach.

1. Introduction

Wormhole attack is a severe threat to wireless networks, which has attracted considerable attentions since it was introduced in previous works [1]. Recently, wormhole attack has become a more critical problem, especially in large-scale WSNs [2]. In a wormhole attack, the adversary places two radio transceivers, which are connected through high-speed channel. Each transceiver, captures signals in the network and delivers them to the other end. These signals are replayed, respectively, at the two ends. Then, two distant sensor nodes that are, respectively, around these two transceivers will consider each other as a close neighbor. By building these tunnels, wormhole attacker can fundamentally change the network connectivity, create a set of shortcut paths, attract a large amount of network traffic, and launch many kinds of attacks, such as selectively dropping or modifying packets and breaking the order of packets. Moreover, by attracting network traffic and collecting and analyzing network data, the attacker can perform many other more aggressive and severe attacks, such as denial of service attacks, network

hijacking, and man-in-the-middle attacks. Since wormhole attacks are independent of the MAC layer protocol and immune to the cryptographic techniques, most of traditional security mechanisms are vulnerable to them.

To address wormhole attack in WSNs, a number of countermeasures have been proposed in the literature. Those solutions are respectively based on catching different symptoms of wormhole attack. However, most of them have various limitations, for example, requiring additional hardware devices, depending on special assumptions on the network settings. For instance, a number of methods are based on additional hardware devices, such as GPS [3], special radio frequency (RF) hardware [4], and directional antennas [5], which all significantly increase the hardware cost of the systems. Another kind of solutions depends on special assumptions on the network, such as global tight clock synchronization [6], special guarding nodes [7, 8], and attack-free initial networks [9, 10], which all greatly limit their applicability. In order to relax these limitations, a number of topology-based solutions are proposed [11–16]. These methods can detect wormholes by capturing various symptoms on the network topology, by only exploring the network topology information. However, most of them still have various limitations, for example, centralized algorithms, requiring unit disk graph (UDG) model or relatively high node density, high false positive rate, and so forth. To sum up, wormhole attack has not been well addressed presently, especially in large-scale practical systems.

In this work, we propose a purely new topology-based wormhole detection approach in WSNs. We basically focus on exploring the abnormal structures introduced by wormhole attacks to the network topology. Each node v locally collects its k-hop neighborhood information and obtains the neighborhood subgraph. Then, we construct an estimation distance matrix that consists of the shortest distances (i.e., hop counts) of all node pairs in this subgraph. Next, the estimation distance matrix is used to reconstruct the subgraph and embed it on a plane by *multidimensional scaling (MDS)*, during which each node will be assigned a virtual position (i.e., node coordinates). The basic idea of our wormhole detection approach is based on an important observation as follows. If node v is a normal node, the layout of the MDS would well accord with the estimation distances, which means the distortion factor of the reconstruction would be relatively small. Otherwise, if node v is a wormhole node, its neighborhood subgraph cannot be smoothly embedded on a plane or at least would produce a great distortion factor. Based on this observation, we can detect potential wormhole nodes by validating whether the distortion factor of each node exceeds a threshold. Finally, we propose a simple but novel necessary condition for wormhole links and utilize it to filter the suspect nodes in a *refinement process*. Then, all wormhole nodes and wormhole links can be explicitly identified, with almost no false positives. Figure 1 briefly illustrates the detection results by our approach and the state-of-the-art methods. Black points in the gray regions denote real wormhole nodes, and circles denote detected wormhole nodes by wormhole detection algorithms. The given network graphs in Figures 1(a)–1(d), respectively, present the detection results by MDS-VOW method [12], LCT method [16], and our approach. We can see that MDS-VOW method can hardly work on this kind of wormhole attack, LCT method can detect all wormhole nodes, but with many false positives, and our approach can effectively detect all wormhole nodes with no false positives.

The main contributions of this work are as follows. Our approach does not require any additional hardware devices, but only needs each node to locally collect its k-hop neighborhood information. The algorithm is very simple and the overhead is extremely low, which makes it very applicable in practical WSNs. Moreover, not only can our approach identify all wormhole nodes and wormhole links, but also it produces very few false positives (almost no false positives according to extensive simulations).

The rest of this paper is organized as follows. We discuss related works in Section 2 and introduce the problem formulation in Section 3. Section 4 presents our detection approach in details. We evaluate this design through extensive simulations in Section 5 and conclude this work in Section 6.

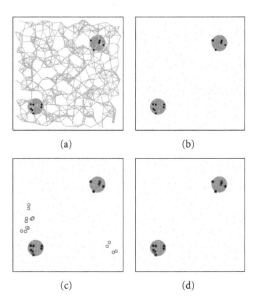

FIGURE 1: An illustration of wormhole detection results by different approaches. Gray areas denote the impact range of wormhole antennas. Black points in the gray areas denote real wormhole nodes that are directly affected by wormhole antennas. Circles denote detected wormhole nodes by respective detection approaches. (a) The original sensor network. 400 nodes are deployed over a square region. The average node degree is 7.5. Edges connecting wormhole nodes at different ends are omitted. (b) Detection results of MDS-VOW. Most of wormhole nodes are not detected. (c) Detection results of LCT. A number of false positives are produced. (d) Detection result of our approach.

2. Related Work

2.1. Wormhole Detection. A number of countermeasures have been proposed in the literatures. Existing methods are all based on capturing various symptoms induced by wormholes. In this section, we review and analyze the prior work.

The first line of existing solutions is based on the distance or timing analysis of data transmissions. Some methods attempt to detect wormhole attacks by validating the legality of packet traverse distance or time. By appending the location or time information of the sending nodes in each packet, they verify whether the hop-by-hop transmission is physically possible and accordingly detect the wormholes. However, such methods require the preknowledge of node locations by special hardware devices such as GPS [3, 6] or depend on the assumption of accurate globally synchronized clocks to capture the packet propagation time [4, 6]. These methods significantly increase the hardware cost of sensor nodes, and it is unclear whether these techniques would be effective in resource constraint WSNs.

Another line of existing solutions uses special communication devices. Some methods provide physical layer mechanism by using special radio frequency hardware to perform authentications in packet modulation and demodulation [6]. Hu and Evans [5] propose to adopt directional antennas to find and prevent infeasible communication links. The requirement of special hardware devices limits the applicability of these methods.

The third line of existing solutions is based on the discovery and maintenance of node neighborhood. For instance, LiteWorp [7] assumes that the network is attack-free before a time point, and each node collects its 2-hop neighbors. Then, LiteWorp selects a number of guard nodes to detect wormhole channels by overhearing the infeasible transmissions among those nonneighboring nodes. Mobi-Worp [8] is further proposed to complement LiteWorp by introducing some location-aware mobile nodes. Obviously, the assumption of attack-free environment significantly limits the applicability of these methods.

The forth line of existing solutions detects wormhole attacks by observing the symptom of traffic flow mismatch based on statistical analysis on the network traffic. For instance, Buttyan et al. [9] propose to detect wormhole attacks by capturing the abnormal increase of neighbor number and the decrease of the shortest path lengths that are induced by wormhole channels. This method is centralized because the base station needs to detect wormhole attacks by hypothesis testing based on the prestatistics of normal networks. Another statistical approach [10] is based on the observation that the wormhole links are selected for routing with abnormally high frequency. They identify wormhole links by comparing them with normal network statistics. However, these methods all require the prestatistics of normal network (i.e., attack-free environments).

The last line of existing solutions, which our approach would belong to, is based on the network topology. Wormhole attacks drastically change the network connectivity by introducing fake links among nodes near wormhole antennas, which will result in various abnormal symptoms to the network topology. Lazos et al. [11] present a graph-based framework to tackle wormhole attacks. They assume that a number of guard nodes that have extraordinary communication range exist in the network. The direct communication links between guard nodes and regular nodes would form special geometric structures, and the presence of wormholes would break these structures. Wang and Bhargava propose MDS-VOW [12] to reconstruct the whole network using MDS technique and detect wormhole links by capturing the abnormal features of the "network layout" introduced by wormholes. However, this method is centralized, and it can only work for special cases with only one infected node at both ends of the wormhole attack. In [13], the authors propose a wormhole detection approach with only local connectivity information. In networks with UDG model, their approach can accurately detect wormholes by looking for "forbidden substructures" that should not be present in a normal connectivity graph. However, it is inaccurate under non-UDG graph. Dong et al. [14] propose a distributed connectivity-based wormhole detection method. Each node collects its k-hop neighborhood and checks whether the boundary of its k-hop neighborhood subgraph has one or two circles. Its basic idea is based on the observation that the neighborhood that encloses a wormhole link will have two cycles and single cycle otherwise. However, Wormcircle requires relatively high node density to ensure that boundary detection algorithm works well. In another work [15], they propose to leverage global topological properties to detect

wormhole attacks. They consider a legitimate multihop wireless network deployed on the surface of a geometric terrain as a 2-manifold surface of genus 0. Wormholes would introduce singularities or higher genus into the network topology. Ban et al. [16] propose local connectivity test (LCT) to identify wormhole attacks. Their basic idea is that removing the wormhole would disconnect its neighborhood from two components. Their algorithm works well in relatively dense and regular networks but results in many false positives in sparse or random networks.

To sum up, the wormhole attack problem has not been perfectly addressed presently. Existing solutions have various limitations, which make them lack applicability in practical WSNs. In this work, we attempt to propose a new wormhole detection approach to relax the limitations in prior work.

2.2. MDS and Its Applications. Multidimensional scaling was originally a method for visualizing dissimilarity data, which was developed from the behavioral and social sciences for studying the structure of objects. MDS takes a dissimilarity matrix among objects as input and produces a layout of the objects in a low-dimensional space as output. Its basic goal is to create a configuration of objects in a low-dimensional space (e.g., one, two, or three dimensions), and the distances between object pairs are close to the original dissimilarities.

Recently, MDS was applied in WSNs for solving the localization problem. As a fundamental problem in wireless networks, localization problem has been widely studied [17–22]. Shang et al. [17] propose a MDS-based localization algorithm that only relies on mere connectivity information and well tolerates measurement error. Ji and Zha [18] propose a distributed MDS-based sensor localization mechanism that presents a multivariate optimization-based iterative algorithm to calculate the positions of the sensors. In this work, we apply MDS to reconstruct the neighborhood subgraph of each node in WSNs. The input is the distance matrix of all node pairs, and the output is a set of virtual positions of all nodes. The virtual positions are used to calculate a virtual distance matrix of all node pairs. Then, the dissimilarity of these two distance matrices is utilized to evaluate the legality of the reconstruction.

3. Problem Formulation

3.1. Network Model. In our model, a WSN consists of a set of sensor nodes deployed over a plane region. Each node has a unique identity (ID). Nodes are only capable of communicating with other nodes in their proximity. We use G to denote the communication graph, where vertices and edges depict the nodes and communication links, respectively. We do not require the sensor nodes to be equipped with any special hardware, or achieve accurate globally synchronized clocks. Moreover, we do not place any restrictions on the network settings or topology, for example, static or dynamic nodes, node density, communication model, the uniformity of deployment, attack-free initial environment, and so forth. We set an assumption to the network as follows.

Each vertex v in the network G is capable of collecting its k-hop neighbor information. We use $N_G^k(v)$ to denote the neighbors of vertex v that are away from v within k hops in G. Let X be a vertex set in G, and let $G(X)$ be the vertex-induced subgraph by X, which consists of vertexes in X and edges among them. The k-hop neighborhood subgraph of vertex v is denoted by $\Gamma_G^k(v) = G(N_G^k(v) \cup v)$. This assumption is common in the literatures and is realistic in practical WSNs. It is worth noting that k would be a relatively small value, for example, $k = 2$ is sufficient for our algorithm, which makes our approach extremely lightweight.

3.2. Threat Model. In this work, wormhole attacks are defined based on the minimum capabilities required by the attacker to perform these attacks. In particular, the attacker does not need to compromise any node or have any knowledge of the network protocol used. Wormhole endpoints deployed by the adversary do not have valid network identities and do not become part of the network. We assume that in the network exist mechanisms that authenticate legitimate nodes and establish secure links between authenticated nodes. Although wormhole attacks impact neighboring discovery mechanisms in the physical or link layer greatly, transmitted data over encrypted network protocols remain transparent and unobservable to the wormhole attacker. These assumptions are common in prior work [3–6, 12, 13].

Then, we set an assumption on the threat model as follows. Each wormhole link e in network G is long enough to well separate nodes at the two ends of it. We denote nodes at the two ends of e by $V_1(e)$ and $V_2(e)$ and denote the shortest distance between $V_1(e)$ and $V_2(e)$ by $d_G(V_1(e), V_2(e))$. Then, we assume that $d_G(V_1(e), V_2(e)) > 2k$, where $2k$ presents the length of the wormhole attack, that is, the shortest distance between nodes at the two ends of the wormhole without wormhole links. The length of the wormhole determines the threat level of the wormhole attack. Longer wormholes are more dangerous because they have larger impact range and longer impact distance. For a short wormhole attack, its impact on the network connectivity would be negligible since only a small fraction of nodes are affected.

4. Local MDS-Based Wormhole Detection

In this section, we present the analysis and design details of our MDS-based wormhole detection approach.

4.1. Overview of Our Approach. Wormhole attacks introduce essential changes to the network topology. In order to detect wormhole attacks by only topology information, we have to capture the typical topological characteristics of wormhole links. The main idea of our detection approach is based on an observation as follows.

Each node v in the network G collects its k-hop neighborhood information, in particular, $k = 2$. The shortest distances (i.e., hop count) between all node pairs in the neighborhood subgraph $\Gamma_G^k(v)$ are used to construct an estimation distance matrix. Then, the distance matrix is used to reconstruct the subgraph by applying MDS on the subgraph and embedding it on a plane. There would be two conditions. First, if v is a normal node, the reconstructed subgraph would be relatively approximating to the original network. Thus, the embedded distance between each node pair would be relatively close to their estimation distance. Otherwise, if v is a wormhole node, its 2-hop neighborhood subgraph would contain all the wormhole nodes. Topologically, each wormhole node would connect with all nodes at the other end. Therefore, if we still constrainedly embed the subgraph on a plane, the distance constraints cannot be well maintained during the reconstruction. Based on this observation, we let all nodes in the network perform local MDS-based reconstruction and detect potential wormhole nodes according to the legality of their reconstructions. Additionally, we introduce a simple and effective necessary condition of wormholes to filter the suspect nodes detected by the previous process. Through this refinement process, we can remove most of false positives and identify all wormhole links.

As discussed previously, our detection approach mainly includes two components: (1) performing local MDS-based reconstruction and (2) performing refinement process. The first component obtains a number of suspect wormhole nodes. The second component filters the suspect nodes and presents the final detection results. We, respectively, describe these two components in detail as follows.

4.2. Local MDS-Based Reconstruction. For ease of representation, we divide this component into three subprocesses, as described hereinafter.

4.2.1. Distance Estimation. For an arbitrary node v in network G, it first collects its k-hop neighborhood information and obtains its k-hop neighborhood subgraph $\Gamma_G^k(v)$. Next, a classical shortest-path algorithm, for example, Dijkstra's shortest path algorithm, is applied to calculate the shortest distances between all node pairs in $\Gamma_G^k(v)$. Then, the shortest distance matrix $M[\Gamma_G^k(v)]$ is constructed, which is an $n \times n$ matrix (n denotes the number of nodes). Each element in $M[\Gamma_G^k(v)]$ is utilized as the estimation distance between each node pair.

4.2.2. Network Reconstruction. Using the shortest distance matrix $M[\Gamma_G^k(v)]$ as input parameter, we apply MDS to reconstruct the k-hop neighborhood subgraph of v. We denote the reconstructed network by $\overline{\Gamma}_G^k(v)$, in which each node would be assigned a virtual position (i.e., node coordinations). Then, the Euclidian distance between each node pair is calculated in $\overline{\Gamma}_G^k(v)$, and a virtual distance matrix $M[\overline{\Gamma}_G^k(v)]$ is produced.

4.2.3. Wormhole Judgement. Then, we describe how to decide whether a node is a wormhole node candidate by its reconstructed neighborhood subgraph. First, the distortion factor of the MDS reconstruction is calculated for each node v. The distortion factor is defined as follows.

Definition 1 (distortion factor). The distortion factor $\lambda(v)$ is defined as the root mean square error (RMSE) between the shortest distance matrix $M[\Gamma_G^k(v)]$ and the reconstructed virtual distance matrix $M[\overline{\Gamma}_G^k(v)]$, that is, $\lambda(v) = \sqrt{(1/(n \times n)) \sum_{i=1,j=1}^n (M[\overline{\Gamma}_G^k(v)](i,j) - M[\Gamma_G^k(v)](i,j))^2}$.

As discussed previously, each node produces large distortion factor if it is a wormhole node and little distortion factor otherwise. Based on this observation, we set a predefined threshold and label nodes that produce distortion factors above this threshold as suspect wormhole nodes. In our experiment, we set the threshold to be the median value of the distortion factors of all nodes in G, that is, $\lambda_{\text{threshold}} = (\lambda_{\max} + \lambda_{\min})/2$ and $\lambda_{\max} = \max\{\lambda(v) : v \in V(G)\}$, $\lambda_{\min} = \min\{\lambda(v) : v \in V(G)\}$, respectively.

Then, we present an efficient way to generate the threshold and distribute it to all nodes. Each node floods a message that contains its distortion factor and records the maximum and minimum values of all distortion factors in all flooding messages it receives. Each node only relays messages that contain a new maximum or minimum value. Thus, only two messages that, respectively, contain the globally maximum and minimum values would be flooded to the whole network. After the flooding is finished, each node calculates the threshold from the maximum and minimum values it records and compares it with its own distortion factor. If its distortion factor exceeds the threshold, it is labeled as a suspect wormhole node and normal node otherwise.

After the implement of this component, a number of suspect wormhole nodes are produced.

4.3. Performing Refinement Process. There is still an issue to be addressed. Some normal nodes may be wrongly labeled as suspect wormhole nodes, and false positives will be introduced. Too many false positives would result in normal links being removed and consequentially degrade the network capacity. In order to address this issue, we introduce this refinement process to filter the suspect nodes and remove false positives. By fully investigating the topology changes introduced by wormholes, we are able to capture some typical topological characteristics of wormhole links. Let X and Y denote two sets that, respectively, contain wormhole nodes at the two ends of a wormhole in network G; let $X \times Y$ denote the edge set between an arbitrary node pair $x \in X$ and $y \in Y$. Then, we present Theorem 2.

Theorem 2. *Given a network graph G and two wormhole node sets X and Y, the following two conditions hold.*

(1) *The subgraph G' that contains node set $X \cup Y$ and edge set $X \times Y$ is a complete bipartite subgraph of G.*

(2) *In the subgraph G'', which is constructed by removing all edges in $X \times Y$ from G, the k-hop neighbor sets of an arbitrary vertex pair $x \in X$ and $y \in Y$ have no common elements, that is, $N_{G''}^k(x) \cap N_{G''}^k(y) = \varnothing$.*

Proof. We first prove condition 1. Because X and Y, respectively, contain and only contain nodes at the two ends of a

wormhole, each node v at one end is given the illusion that all nodes at the other end are its direct neighbors. Thus, there will be an edge between v and each node at the other end. According to the construction of G', it will obviously be a complete bipartite subgraph of G.

We then prove condition 2. If there are two nodes $x \in X$ and $y \in Y$ and $N_{G''}^k(x) \cap N_{G''}^k(y) \neq \varnothing$, the shortest distance between x and y must be less than $2k$, that is, $d(x,y) < 2k$. Consequentially, the shortest distance between node sets X and Y would be less than $2k$, that is, $d_{G''}(X,Y) < 2k$, which will contradict with our assumption in the threat model.

Theorem 2 is a necessary condition of wormholes and is utilized to filter suspect wormhole nodes. First, all connected components are found in these suspect nodes. We denote the set of such connected components by $\mathcal{C}$. Isolated nodes can be certainly excluded. Next, all maximal complete bipartite subgraphs (MCBSs) are found in these connected components. In order to improve the detection rate, we expand each connected component by adding all 1-hop neighbors of the nodes in the component into this component. By doing this, all wormhole nodes can be included in the component if at least one wormhole node at both ends of the wormhole is suspect node. The algorithm in [23] that finds the maximal complete bipartite subgraphs in any graph is applied on each $C \in \mathcal{C}$. Let $\mathcal{B}$ be the set of maximal complete bipartite subgraphs generated by this algorithm, and let $B = (X, Y)$ be an element in $\mathcal{B}$, where X and Y are the two partitions of the bipartite graph. Then, condition 2 in Theorem 2 is applied on each $B \in \mathcal{B}$. If $N_{G''}^k(X) \cap N_{G''}^k(Y) = \varnothing$, all nodes in B will be labeled as final wormhole nodes. Otherwise, they are excluded. Till now, the final detection results are produced.

Moreover, our ultimate goal of detecting wormhole attacks is to neutralize them without breaking regular network functions. In particular, we want to eliminate the high volume of traffic passing through the wormhole links that create the wormhole effect with keeping the sensing and computational capabilities of the nodes. After detecting all wormhole nodes, this can be easily done by removing edges $X \times Y$ in each bipartite subgraph $B \in \mathcal{B}$.

4.4. Algorithm and Discussion. We present Algorithm 1 that describes our wormhole detection approach. Then, several parameters that may influence the performance of our algorithm are discussed as follows.

First, we discuss the influence of k. In our simulations, k is set to be small constant $k = 2$. The reasons are twofold. First, small k introduces low communication overhead of each node for collecting its k-hop neighborhood information. Second, if v is a wormhole node, its 2-hop neighbors would cover all wormhole nodes. Therefore, setting $k = 2$ is sufficient for capturing the abnormal embedding chrematistics induced by this wormhole. Actually, setting k to be a larger value is even adverse to the detection, because larger k induces larger subgraph, which will reduce the proportion of wormhole nodes in the subgraph and accordingly degrade the distinguishability of wormhole nodes.

Then, we discuss the influence of $\lambda_{\text{threshold}}$. The selection of the threshold dramatically impacts the detection accuracy

Input:
    A network graph $G(V, E)$.
Output:
    A set of complete bipartite graphs $\mathcal{B}$.
(1) **for** each $v \in V$ **do**
(2)   Collect k-hop neighborhood subgraph $\Gamma_G^k(v)$.
(3)   Calculate the shortest distance matrix $M[\Gamma_G^k(v)]$.
(4)   Reconstruct the subgraph by MDS.
(5)   Calculate the virtual distance matrix $M[\overline{\Gamma}_G^k(v)]$.
(6)   Calculate the distortion factor $\lambda(v)$.
(7)   Flood $\lambda(v)$ to the network.
(8)   Calculate the threshold $\lambda_{\text{threshold}}$.
(9)   **if** $\lambda_v > \lambda_{\text{threshold}}$ **then**
(10)   Add v to the suspect node set S.
(11)   **end if**
(12) **end for**
(13) Find all connected components $\mathcal{C}$ from S.
(14) **for** each $C \in \mathcal{C}$ **do**
(15)   Find each MCBS B from C.
(16)   Add B to the MCBS set $\mathcal{B}$.
(17) **end for**
(18) **for** each $B = \{X, Y\}$ in $\mathcal{B}$ **do**
(19)   **if** $N_{G''}^k(X) \cap N_{G''}^k(Y) = \varnothing$ **then**
(20)   Remove edges $X \times Y$.
(21)   **else**
(22)   Remove B from $\mathcal{B}$.
(23)   **end if**
(24) **end for**

ALGORITHM 1: Our wormhole detection algorithm.

of our approach. In particular, lower threshold guarantees to catch all wormhole nodes, but causes more false positives, which will increase the workload of refinement process. Otherwise, a higher threshold induces fewer false positives but may produce false negatives. Comparatively, we are more concerned with detecting all wormhole nodes. Therefore, our approach will be on the aggressive side and select a relatively lower threshold. In our simulations, the threshold is set to be the median value of all distortion factors. Moreover, it is also a concerning issue, which makes the generation and distribution of the threshold easier.

5. Evaluation

In this section, we conduct extensive simulations to evaluate the effectiveness and performance of our design and compare it with the state-of-the-art methods.

5.1. Simulation Setup

5.1.1. Node Deployment. Two node deployment models are used: perturbed grid and random deployment. Perturbed grid model is adopted [24] to approximate manual deployments of nodes, in which all nodes are placed on an $m \times n$ grid and perturbed around their initial positions with a perturbed ratio p. Let each cell in the grid be a square with edge length d. Then, the node with coordinate (x, y) will be

randomly placed in the region $[x - pd, x + pd] \times [y - pd, y + pd]$. In random deployment model, each node is assigned a coordinate randomly drawn from the network field.

5.1.2. Communication Model. Although our approach does not require specific communication models, both UDG and quasi-UDG models are adopted to build the networks. In the UDG model, there is a link between nodes u and v if and only if their distance is no larger than R, where R is the communication radius. In quasi-UDG model, nodes u and v have a link if their distance is no larger than ρR and have a link with probability q if their distance is within $[\rho R, R]$, where $0 < \rho < 1$.

5.1.3. Wormhole Position. The wormhole position is a crucial factor for wormhole detection, because it could impact the significance of wormhole symptoms. Especially when multiple wormholes exist in the network, their relative position will dramatically influence the wormhole detection. In the simulations, our approach is evaluated for detecting wormholes placed at different positions of the network. Moreover, multiple wormholes with different relative positions are also evaluated.

5.2. Simulation Results. In this subsection, we present the results of the simulations under various network settings and compare them with the state-of-the-art MDS-VOW [12] and LCT [16] methods.

The basic network contains 1600 nodes deployed over a square region. In all simulations, $p = 2$ for perturbed grid model, and $\rho = 0.75$ for quasi-UDG model. The average node degree varies from 4 to 13. A set of wormhole nodes are placed at the diagonal of the network. The average number of wormhole nodes is 15. We require all algorithms to detect wormholes that are not shorter than 8 hops, that is, the shortest distance between nodes at the two ends of the wormhole is not less than 8. All simulations take 100 runs with random network generation and present the average results.

First, four sets of simulations are conducted to evaluate the number of false positives of our approach. Each set of simulations adopts different node deployments and communication models. The results are, respectively, presented in Figures 2(a)–2(d). From the results, we can obtain several observations as follows.

5.2.1. Influence of Node Density. The results in Figure 2 indicate that the number of false positives decreases for all approaches as the node degree increases. And our approach always greatly outperforms LCT method. However, when the degree is very low, there are still some false positives. The reason is analyzed as follows. In extremely sparse networks, there would be some special cases called bridge links, as shown in Figure 3. Although it is a normal link in the network, it topologically accords with the property of wormhole links. Some of these links may be wrongly labeled as wormhole candidates in MDS-based reconstruction and cannot be filtered by the refinement process.

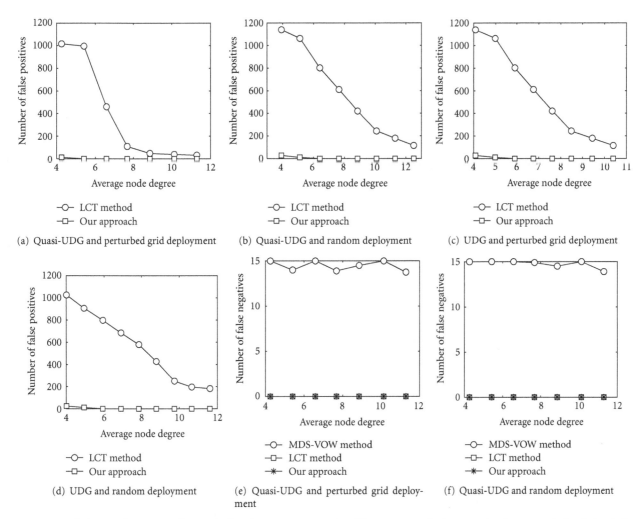

FIGURE 2: Simulation results. 1600 nodes are deployed over a square region. The average node degree varies from 4 to 13. In all simulations, $p = 2$ for perturbed grid model, and $\rho = 0.75$ for quasi-UDG model. A wormhole is launched at the diagonal of the network. The average number of wormhole nodes is 15. (a)–(d) evaluate the number of false positives under various network settings. (e)-(f) evaluate number of false negatives.

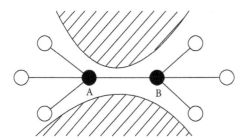

FIGURE 3: An example of bridge link. Link between nodes A and B may be aggressively labeled as wormhole link. The hatched areas denote holes of network deployment.

5.2.2. Influence of Node Deployment. It is shown in Figure 2 that our approach always produces few false positives for both perturbed grid distribution and random distribution. LCT produces fewer false positives for perturbed grid

model than random deployment model. The reason is that perturbed grid model produces more regular networks.

5.2.3. Influence of Communication Model. Figure 2 demonstrates that our approach is not clearly influenced by the communication model. And it also demonstrates that our approach always induces much fewer false positives under both UDG and quasi-UDG models.

Then, we evaluate the number of false negatives of our approach, as shown in Figures 2(e) and 2(f). The results show that our approach can always detect all wormhole attacks. More results are constant under UDG model and are omitted here. The MDS-VOW method cannot even detect any wormholes because it does not work for the general wormhole model.

More simulations are conducted by placing wormholes at different positions in the network. The results are constant and are omitted due to the space limit. To sum up, our approach still works well in sparse and irregular networks

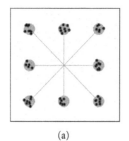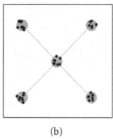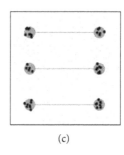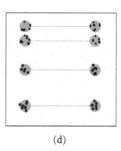

(a)	(b)	(c)	(d)

FIGURE 4: Detection results for multiple wormholes. 900 nodes are deployed over a square region. Perturbed grid deployment with $p = 1.5$ and quasi-UDG with $\rho = 0.75$ are adopted to generate the networks. The average node degree is 7.5. Multiple wormholes are placed at different positions in the network.

and is not clearly influenced by the communication model. Moreover, our approach produces few false positives. It is worth noting that LCT method can obtain better results by increasing the shortest length of wormholes required to be detected. However, that will greatly restrict its applicability and increase the communication and computation cost.

5.3. Multiple Wormholes. In this subsection, our approach is evaluated for detecting multiple wormholes.

When the distance between two different wormholes is long enough, they will not affect each other. Thus, our approach can well detect all wormhole nodes, as shown in Figures 4(a)–4(c). Otherwise, if multiple wormholes are close, they may interfere with each other, which makes the detection more difficult. Particularly, if the distances of both ends of the wormholes are relatively short, as shown in Figure 4(d), our approach fails to detect the wormholes. The reason is as follows. When both ends of two wormholes are very close to each other, wormhole nodes at different ends are connected by short paths through wormhole links in the adjacent wormhole. Therefore, these nodes would be filtered during the refinement process. Actually, to the best of our knowledge, this situation cannot be solved by any purely topology-based detection methods.

6. Conclusions

As a severe threat to WSNs, wormhole attack has received considerable attentions during the past decade. However, most of existing countermeasures lack applicability for requiring special hardware devices or depending on rigorous assumptions on the network. In this work, we fundamentally analyze the essential wormhole symptoms by topological methodology and propose a local MDS-based wormhole detection approach. Our approach does not depend on any hardware requirements and is extremely simple and lightweight, which make it quite feasible in practical WSNs. Extensive simulations are conducted, and the results show that our approach can effectively identify all wormhole nodes for a large class of network instances.

Acknowledgments

The first author is supported by the National Natural Science Foundation of China (NSFC) under Grants no. 60903224 and no. 61202484. D. Dong is supported by NSFC under Grants no. 61272482 and no. 61170261.

References

[1] K. Sanzgiri, B. Dahill, B. Levine, and F. Belding-Royer, "A secure routing protocol for Ad Hoc networks," in *Proceedings of the IEEE International Conference on Network Protocols (IEEE ICNP '02)*, 2002.

[2] X. Mao, X. Miao, Y. He, X.-Y. Li, and Y. Liu, "CitySee: urban CO_2 monitoring with sensors," in *Proceedings of the 32nd IEEE International Conference on Computer Communications (IEEE INFOCOM '12)*, 2012.

[3] W. Wang, B. Bhargava, Y. Lu, and X. Wu, "Defending against wormhole attacks in mobile ad hoc networks," *Wireless Communications and Mobile Computing*, vol. 6, no. 4, pp. 483–503, 2006.

[4] S. Capkun, L. Buttyan, and J. P. Hubaux, "Sector: secure tracking of node encounters in multi-hop wireless networks," in *Proceedings of the ACM Workshop on Security in Ad Hoc and Sensor Networks (ACM SASN '03)*, 2003.

[5] L. Hu and D. Evans, "Using directional antennas to prevent wormhole attacks," in *Proceedings of the Network and Distributed System Security Symposium Conference (NDSS '04)*, 2004.

[6] Y. C. Hu, A. Perrig, and D. B. Johnson, "Packet leashes: a defense against wormhole attacks in wireless networks," in *Proceedings of the 22nd Annual Joint Conference on the IEEE Computer and Communications Societies (IEEE INFOCOM '03)*, pp. 1976–1986, April 2003.

[7] I. Khalil, S. Bagchi, and N. B. Shroff, "LITE WORP: a lightweight countermeasure for the wormhole attack in multihop wireless networks (DSN '05)," in *Proceedings of the International Conference on Dependable Systems and Networks*, pp. 612–621, July 2005.

[8] I. Khalil, S. Bagchi, and N. B. Shroff, "MOBIWORP: mitigation of the wormhole attack in mobile multihop wireless networks," in *Proceedings of the Securecomm and Workshops (SECURECOMM '06)*, September 2006.

[9] L. Buttyan, L. Dora, and I. Vajda, "Statistical wormhole detection in sensor networks," in *Proceedings of the Security and Privacy in Ad-hoc and Sensor Networks (IEEE ESAS '05)*, vol. 3813, pp. 128–141, 2005.

[10] N. Song, L. Qian, and X. Li, "Wormhole attacks detection in wireless ad hoc networks: a statistical analysis approach," in *Proceedings of the 19th IEEE International Parallel and Distributed Processing Symposium (IPDPS '05)*, April 2005.

[11] L. Lazos, R. Poovendran, C. Meadows, P. Syverson, and L. W. Chang, "Preventing wormhole attacks on wireless ad hoc networks: a graph theoretic approach," in *Proceedings of the IEEE Wireless Communications and Networking Conference, Broadband Wirelss for the Masses—Ready for Take-off (WCNC '05)*, pp. 1193–1199, March 2005.

[12] W. Wang and B. Bhargava, "Visualization of wormholes in sensor networks," in *Proceedings of the ACM Workshop on Wireless Security (WiSe '04)*, pp. 51–60, October 2004.

[13] R. Maheshwari, J. Gao, and S. R. Das, "Detecting wormhole attacks in wireless networks using connectivity information," in *Proceedings of the 26th IEEE International Conference on Computer Communications (IEEE INFOCOM '07)*, pp. 107–115, May 2007.

[14] D. Dong, M. Li, Y. Liu, and X. Liao, "WormCircle: connectivity-based wormhole detection in wireless ad hoc and sensor networks," in *Proceedings of the 15th International Conference on Parallel and Distributed Systems (ICPADS '09)*, pp. 72–79, December 2009.

[15] D. Dong, M. Li, Y. Liu, X. Y. Li, and X. Liao, "Topological detection on wormholes in wireless ad hoc and sensor networks," in *Proceedings of the 17th IEEE International Conference on Network Protocols (ICNP '09)*, pp. 314–323, October 2009.

[16] X. Ban, R. Sarkar, and J. Gao, "Local connectivity tests to identify wormholes in wireless networks," Proceedings of the 12th ACM International Symposium on Mobile Ad Hoc Networking and Computing (ACM MobiHoc '11), 2011.

[17] Y. Shang, W. Ruml, Y. Zhang, and M. P. J. Fromherz, "Localization from mere connectivity," in *Proceedings of the PROCEEDINGS OF The Fourth ACM International Symposium on Mobile Ad Hoc Networking and Computing (MOBIHOC '03)*, pp. 201–212, June 2003.

[18] X. Ji and H. Zha, "Sensor positioning in wireless ad-hoc sensor networks using multidimensional scaling," in *Proceedings of the IEEE Computer and Communications Societies (IEEE INFOCOM '04)*, pp. 2652–2661, March 2004.

[19] S. Li and F. Qin, "A dynamic neuralnetwork approach for solving nonlinear inequalities defined on a graph and Its application to distributed, routing-free, range-free localization of WSNs," *Neurocomputing*. In press.

[20] S. Li, Y. Lou, and B. Liu, "Bluetooth aided mobile phone localization: a nonlinear neural circuit approach," *Transactions on Embedded Computing Systems*. In press.

[21] S. Li, B. Liu, B. Chen, and Y. Luo, "Neural network based mobile phone localization using bluetooth connectivity," *Neural Computing and Applications*. In press.

[22] S. Li, Z. Wang, and Y. Li, "Using laplacian eigenmap as heuristic information to solve nonlinear constraints defined on a graph and its application in distributed range-free localization of wireless sensor networks," *Neural Processing Letters*. In press.

[23] D. Eppstein, "Arboricity and bipartite subgraph listing algorithms," *Information Processing Letters*, vol. 51, no. 4, pp. 207–211, 1994.

[24] Y. Zhang, W. Liu, W. Lou, and Y. Fang, "Location-based compromise-tolerant security mechanisms for wireless sensor networks," *IEEE Journal on Selected Areas in Communications*, vol. 24, no. 2, pp. 247–260, 2006.

5

Study on Routing Protocols for Delay Tolerant Mobile Networks

Haigang Gong and Lingfei Yu

School of Computer Science and Engineering, University of Electronic Science and Technology of China, Chengdu 611731, China

Correspondence should be addressed to Haigang Gong; hggong@uestc.edu.cn

Academic Editor: Nianbo Liu

Delay tolerant mobile networks feature with intermittent connectivity, huge transmission delay, nodal mobility, and so forth. There is usually no end-to-end path in the networks and it poses great challenges for routing in DTMNs. In this paper, the architecture of DTMNs is introduced at first, including the characteristics of DTMNs, routing challenges, and metric and mobility models. And then, the state-of-the-art routing protocols for DTMNs are discussed and analyzed. Routing strategies are classified into three categories: nonknowledge-based approach, knowledge-based approach, and social-based approach. Finally, some research issues about DTMNs are presented.

1. Introduction

With the rapid development of low-power wireless communication technology and integrated circuit technology, there emerge a large number of low-cost, portable wireless devices. These devices are organized into a wireless ad hoc network and communicate with each other by multihop transmissions, which have great potential for many applications. For example, wireless sensor networks (WSNs) [1], composed of densely deployed low-power, low-cost sensor nodes, could be applied in scenarios such as military surveillance [2], disaster relief [3], health monitoring [4], environment monitoring [5], and smart home [6]. Another example is vehicular ad hoc networks (VANETs), in which vehicles equip with short range RF modules and exchange data when they meet, widely used in traffic safety [7], traffic efficiency [8], and information service [9].

Data gathering and routing is one of the fundamental functions of the low-power wireless ad hoc network and there have been lots of research works on routing issues [10–14]. However, authors assume that the network is full connected in these works, that is to say, there exists an end-to-end path between the source node and destination node, which is unreasonable in the real environment. In fact, if nodes are deployed randomly in the region, the density of nodes in some subregions would be higher than other subregions, leading to the phenomena of network partition,

as shown in Figure 1. Once the network is partitioned, it is not fully connected any more. Secondly, the environment often has great impacts on the low-power communication. For instance, if there are electromagnetic fields or some obstacles, nodes will not communicate with each other even if they are within the transmission range, disconnecting the network. Thirdly, nodes are often powered by batteries, which is hard to rechargeable. When the energy of the battery exhausts, nodes cannot transmit data any more, degrading the network connectivity. Moreover, if nodes move with animals such as ZebraNet [15] and SWIM [16], data transmission only occurs when nodes meet each other. The mobility of nodes introduces opportunistic connectivity and there is not a stable end-to-end path in the network, leading to partially connected network.

Above all, the network is often not fully connected in the real environments and the network connectivity is intermittent and opportunistic, which is the characteristic of delay tolerant networks (DTNs) [17]. DTNs feature with sparse and intermittent connectivity, long and variable delay, high latency, high error rates, highly asymmetric data rate, and no stable end-to-end path. Obviously, traditional routing protocols are not well suitable for DTNs. For example, on-demand routing protocols such as AODV [18] and DSR [19] for MANET try to find an end-to-end path and table-driven routing protocols such as DSDV [20] and WRP [21] need to build route table. They are both hard to be adaptive to

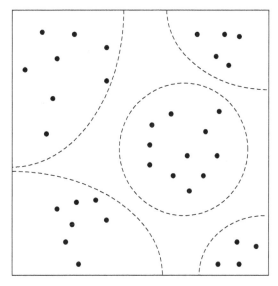

FIGURE 1: The phenomena of network partition.

the intermittent connectivity and dynamic network topology. New protocols must be designed for delay tolerant networks.

With the improvement of the portability of the wireless nodes, the mobility of nodes has been greatly improved. The enhanced mobility deteriorates the network connectivity further and challenges network routing. Harras et al. discuss the characteristics of delay tolerant mobile networks (DTMNs) and present routing issues of DTMNs in [22]. However, DTMNs are application specific and there are different types of DTMNs such as delay tolerant mobile sensor networks (DTMSNs) [23] composed of tiny sensor nodes, mobile social networks (MSNs) [24] when nodes attached to the human, and vehicular delay tolerant networks (VDTNs) [25]. Undoubtedly, there is not a universal routing protocol running in different types of DTMNs and routing protocols should be application specific, too.

The key issue of routing for DTMNs is to find an opportunistic connectivity between the nodes and transmit data to the nodes when they meet with each other if possible. Some methods have been proposed to achieve opportunistic communication in such challenged networks, trying to achieve the higher delivery ratio with the shorter delivery delay. Each of them has its own pros and cons and is just suitable in certain domains. Flooding is the simplest approach to transmit data to the destination but it wastes network resources extremely. In order to reduce the network overheads, some of them employ the history of contacts made by the nodes to route the data. Some other schemes try to forward messages to the neighbor node with the higher probability to communicate with the destination node. There are also some approaches that predict the behavior of the nodes and assist to route messages by the prediction knowledges. In addition, some other mechanisms are proposed, including infrastructure assisted method, that is, placement of stationary waypoint stores, using some mobile nodes to bridge the disconnection in the network, message

replication, network coding, and leveraging prior knowledge of mobility patterns. Authors classify the routing protocols for delay tolerant networks into two categories: flooding-based approach and forwarding-based approach [26–28]. In [29], authors categorize the routing protocols into flooding-based method, history-based method, and special device-based method. In our opinions, the routing protocols should be divided into two categories: nonknowledge-based protocols and knowledge-based protocols. The former is to transmit messages to the next hop without any information indicating whether the next hop is an appropriate relay node. The latter relays messages with the assistance of the collected information about the network state and chooses a suitable next hop based on the knowledge. Moreover, social behavior analysis has been introduced to resolve the routing issues when the nodes are attached to the human and could achieve better performance by using social relationship or human mobility in real life environment, in which the routing schemes are called social-based protocols. In fact, the social-based protocols often utilize the knowledge of the social structure of the network and should be classified into the knowledge-based protocols. However, we discuss them separately from the former two categories in order to present routing schemes by using the social interaction of the nodes more clearly. In this paper, we study the existing routing protocols for DTMNs and give an analysis of them with respect to the important challenging issues and performance metrics.

The rest of the paper is organized as follows. Section 2 presents the architecture of DTMNs, including the characteristics of the DTMNs, routing challenges for the DTMNs, evaluation metrics of routing protocols for the DTMNs, and mobility model of the nodes. In Section 3, the states-of-the-arts of previous routing protocol for DTMNs are introduced and the existing problems are discussed. Section 4 presents some open issues about the DTMNs and Section 5 concludes the paper.

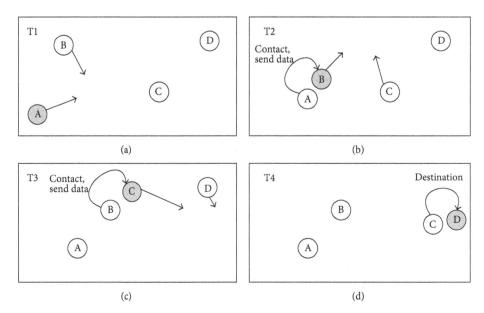

FIGURE 2: Data transmission in DTMNs.

2. Network Architecture

The concept of delay tolerant networking was initially proposed as an approach for the interplanetary Internet (IPN) [30]. Deep space communication suffers from very long latencies, low bandwidth, and intermittent scheduled connectivity. Fall proposes an overall architecture of DTN in [17], and it operates as an overlay above the transport layer to provide services such as in-network data storage and retransmission, and data forwarding. DTN technology has been introduced into wireless ad hoc network in the past few years. According to the mobility of the nodes, the network can be classified into two categories. (1) Network with some controllable nodes. In the network, most of the nodes are static and only a few movable nodes. The managed mobile nodes bridge the sparse disconnected network, store data from static nodes, and carry data to the destination. This method substantially saves the energy of the nodes as they only transmit over a short range. (2) Network with mobile nodes. In the second category, most of the nodes are movable and they have to transmit data occasionally when they contact with each other, introducing more challenges for routing messages. In this section, we firstly describe the characteristics of DTMNs, then analyze the routing challenges in DTMNs and metrics to evaluate the performance of the routing protocols, and finally discuss some mobility models, which have great influence on the network performance.

2.1. Characteristics of DTMNs. DTMN distinguishes itself from conventional networks by the following characteristics. (1) Intermittent connectivity. The connectivity of DTMNs is very poor. In most cases, it is impossible to have an end-to-end path. A node connects to other nodes only occasionally and the link is the scarcest resource in the network. (2) Delay tolerable. The end-to-end transmission

latency is dominated by the queuing delay. Messages have to be stored in the message queue until the node meets a neighbor node. Obviously, opportunistic connection will lead to long latency so that applications have to tolerate the large transmission delay. (3) Sparse density. Node density is normally much lower in DTMNs compared with the traditional densely deployed networks, which further deteriorates network connectivity. (4) Node mobility. Since the nodes are attached to randomly moving objects, the network topology changes frequently. Besides, the buffer size of sensor nodes is usually limited. Since data messages may be stored in the buffer queue for quite a long time before being sent out, queue management is a challenge.

Clearly, a node only transmits its messages to the next hop when it meets other nodes and chooses an appropriate neighbor. As shown in Figure 2, node A wants to send message to node D at T1 but there is no connection between them. Node A has to store the messages and carries them while moving. Then node A contacts node B at T2 and node A will send the messages to node B because node B moves to node D. And then, node B meets node C at T3 and relays the messages to node C. Node C carries the messages and meets node D at T4, then the messages are sent to the destination node.

2.2. Routing Challenges. One of the main design goals of DTMNs is to exchange data between the nodes and employ the opportunistic links among the nodes for transmission. Clearly, the design of routing protocols in DTMNs is influenced by many challenging factors. In the following, we summarize some of the routing challenges that affect routing and forwarding in DTMNs.

2.2.1. Intermittent Connectivity. As mentioned before, intermittent connectivity is the inherent property of DTMNs. DTMN is a partially connected network because of node mobility, sparse deployment, and poor communication quality. The network connectivity varies with time. Consequently, it is hard to find an end-to-end connection between the source node and the destination node so that routing techniques in conventional network are not well suitable for DTMNs. Intermittent connectivity means that the links between the nodes are opportunistic. How to get an opportunistic link and transmit a message is a challenging issue in DTMNs.

2.2.2. High Latency. High latency is also a fundamental property of DTMNs. In general, the transmission delay from a source node to a destination node is composed of four components: waiting time, queuing time, transmission delay, and propagation delay [31]. The waiting time is the interval that a message carried by node until it meets another node, depending on the contact time and the message arrival time. The queuing time is the time it waits for the higher priority messages to be sent out. This depends on the data rate and the traffics in the network. The transmission delay is the time it takes for all the bits of the message to be transmitted, which is determined by data rate and the length of message. The propagation delay is the time a bit takes to propagate across the connection, which depends on the distance between two nodes. Obviously, messages have to be buffered in the queue of the nodes due to intermittent connectivity, incurring more waiting time and queuing time. Moreover, the low data rate of DTMNs introduces more transmission delay. The design of routing protocols for DTMNs should reduce the delivery latency as shorter as possible.

2.2.3. Limited Resources. The nodes in DTMNs are often equipped with low-power RF module, limited buffer size, irreplaceable battery, and low computation capacity, that is to say, the resources of the nodes are limited. The scarce of resources degrades the performance of the routing protocols.

(1) Buffer Size. When a message is generated, the message is buffered in the message queue of the node. Once the node contacts other nodes, it chooses the next hop and delivers the messages in its queue. However, the node usually waits a long periods of time until it meets another node so that the messages have to be buffered in the queue. If the queue is full, some messages would be dropped off, which decreases the delivery ratio. Routing strategies might need to consider the limited buffer space when making routing decisions. In addition, there must be a scheme to manage buffer.

(2) Energy Efficiency. Nodes in delay tolerant mobile networks are usually powered by the battery, which cannot be replaced easily. Lots of energy will be consumed for sending, receiving, and computing. While researchers have investigated general techniques for saving power in delay tolerant networks [32], none of the routing strategies has incorporated energy-aware optimizations. In fact, most of the previous routing techniques do not consider the energy efficiency. In these works, the RF module of the nodes has to work all the time so as to find the possible links (opportunistic connectivity) to their potential neighbors. Then, the nodes will drain off

their battery quickly and cannot contribute any more for routing, while degrading the performance of DTMNs. Therefore, there is a tradeoff between the energy consumption and network connectivity. How to maintain an acceptable connectivity while keeping the energy consumption slowly is a challenging routing issue for DTMNs.

(3) Process Capability. The nodes in DTMNs may be very small and have small processing capability, in terms of CPU and memory. These nodes will not be capable of running complex routing protocols. To design routing protocols for DTMSN, we must consider the computing capability of the nodes.

2.2.4. Replication Management. Since the connectivity between mobile nodes is poor, it is difficult to form a well-connected network for data transmission. The nodes deliver the message to their neighbors opportunistically when they contact. In order to achieve certain success delivery ratio in such an opportunistic network, data replication is necessary [33]. However, multiple copies of messages will increase transmission overhead, which is a substantial disadvantage for energy limited sensor networks. Replication management mechanism is necessary to control the number of message copies in order to reduce the overhead caused by redundant copies.

2.2.5. Network Topology. Due to nodal mobility or link quality, the network topology of DTMNs may change dynamically and randomly. It is impossible to maintain a stable end-to-end path in the networks, and routing in DTMNs is often on demand. Routing strategies designed for delay tolerant networks must be adaptive to the frequent change of network topology.

2.3. Routing Metrics. To evaluate the performance of the routing protocols for DTMNs, there are two main metrics: data delivery ratio and data delivery delay. Moreover, there are some other metrics to evaluate the performance of the routing strategies for application of specific DTMNs such as energy consumption, the number of replications, and network overhead.

2.3.1. Delivery Ratio. The most important performance metric is the data delivery ratio. Delivery ratio is defined as the fraction of all generated messages that are successfully transmitted to the destination within a specific time interval. In DTMNs, there are two factors to cause data loss. One is that the TTL of message exceeds the tolerable delay of the application. The network is unable to deliver messages within an acceptable amount of time. The second factor is that the queue of the node is full and some messages have to be dropped. If there are no any other copies of the dropped messages, these messages will not arrive at the destination forever. Routing protocols should achieve higher data delivery ratio.

2.3.2. Delivery Delay. Data delivery delay is another metric to evaluate the performance of routing strategies of DTMNs, which is the time interval between when data is generated by the source node and when it is received by the destination. Due to the intermittent connectivity, the delivery delay of DTMNs is much longer than that of the conventional networks. Though applications in DTMNs can tolerate high latency, they can benefit from a short delivery delay. Some applications also have some time window where the data is useful. For example, if a DTN is used to deliver e-mail to a mobile user, the messages must be delivered before the user moves out of the network.

2.3.3. Energy Consumption. As described before, most of the existing routing protocols for DTMNs do not consider the energy efficiency. The RF module of node works all the time to search the possible links to other nodes, which exhausts the battery energy quickly. Once the battery is exhausted, the node is dead and cannot deliver any more data. However, for some data-centric applications, they want to gather data from the network as much as possible. That is to say, energy consumption of the node must be considered to design routing protocols in order to achieve longer network lifetime. The longer the network lifetime is, the more data the network collects. Routing techniques should make a tradeoff between the energy consumption and data delivery ratio.

2.3.4. Number of Replications. In order to get higher data delivery ratio, some routing protocols employ replication strategies and they transit more messages than others. The intuition is that having more copies of the message increases the probability that one of them will find its way to the destination and decreases the average time for one to be delivered. Unfortunately, the redundant replications waste a number of network resources such as buffer, bandwidth, and energy. The more the number of replications is, the more the wasted resources are. Routing protocols should achieve higher data delivery ratio with less replications.

2.3.5. Network Overhead. Usually, there are some control messages to assist in forwarding messages efficiently. These messages are network overheads. A good routing protocol should create little network overhead and it makes tradeoff between the data delivery ratio/delay and the delivery overhead.

2.4. Mobility Model. The mobility model is designed to describe the movement pattern of mobile users, and how their location, velocity, and acceleration change over time. Since mobility patterns may play a significant role in determining the performance of the routing protocols, it is desirable for mobility models to emulate the movement pattern of targeted real life applications in a reasonable way [34]. We classify the mobility models into four categories: random-based mobility model, social mobility model, map-based mobility model, and real dataset-based mobility model.

2.4.1. Random-Based Mobility Model. In random-based mobility models, the nodes move randomly without any restrictions. More specifically, the nodes choose their destination, speed, and direction randomly and independently of other nodes.

The simplest mobility model is the random walk mobility model [35], also called Brownian motion; it is a widely used model to represent purely random movements of the entities of a system in various disciplines from physics to meteorology. However, it cannot be considered as a suitable model to simulate wireless environments, since human movements do not present the continuous changes of direction that characterize this mobility model.

Another example of random mobility model is the random waypoint mobility model [36]. This can be considered as an extension of the random walk mobility model, with the addition of pauses between changes in direction or speed. When the simulation begins, each node randomly chooses a location in the field as the destination. It then moves towards the destination with constant velocity chosen randomly from $[0, V]$. The velocity and direction of the nodes are chosen independently of each other. On arriving at the destination, the node stops for a period of time and then chooses another random destination in the simulation field and moves towards it, as shown in Figure 3. The whole process is repeated again and again until the simulation ends.

The random waypoint model and its variants are designed to emulate the movement of mobile nodes in a simplified way. They are widely used due to their simplicity. However, they may not adequately capture certain mobility characteristics of some realistic scenarios, including temporal dependency, spatial dependency, and geographic restriction.

2.4.2. Social Mobility Model. In some types of DTMNs such as mobile social networks, the nodes are usually attached to the humans and carried by them. Apparently, the mobility of the nodes is determined by human decisions and social behavior. In order to emulate the social behavior, researchers propose social mobility model which is dependent on the structure of the relationships among people carrying the node.

Musolesi and Mascolo propose the community-based mobility model based on social network theory [37]. They think that a network consists of several communities, and the nodes are grouped into one community according to their social relationships among the individuals. The mobility of the nodes is also based on the social relationships. The model also allows for the definition of different types of relationships during a certain period of time (i.e., a day or a week). For instance, it might be important to be able to describe that in the morning and in the afternoon of weekdays, relationships at the workplace are more important than friendships and family ones, whereas the opposite is true during the evenings and weekends.

The idea of using communities to represent group movements in an infrastructure-based WiFi network has also been exploited in [38] and in its time-variant extension is presented in [39]. More specifically, this model preserves two fundamental characteristics, the skewed location visiting preferences and the periodical reappearance of nodes in the same location.

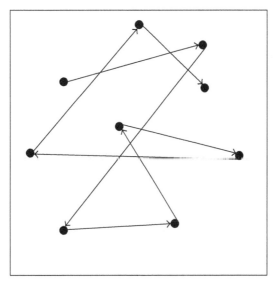

FIGURE 3: Random waypoint mobility model.

An agenda-based mobility model is proposed in [40], in which authors predict the movement of humans based on the trace of the people in the city. Then routing decision is made according to these information.

2.4.3. Map-Based Mobility Model. Map-based mobility model is designed for a specific type of DTMNs, vehicular delay tolerant networks. Different from the random-based mobility model, the movement of the nodes in vehicular delay tolerant networks is not random. The mobility is restricted by the road in the map and the nodes move regularly.

Freeway mobility model is proposed in [41] to emulate the motion behavior of mobile nodes on a freeway. It can be used in exchanging traffic status or tracking a vehicle on a freeway. The freeway mobility pattern is expected to have spatial dependence and high temporal dependence. It also imposes strict geographic restrictions on the node movement by not allowing a node to change its lane.

Manhattan mobility model is also introduced in [41] to emulate the movement pattern of mobile nodes on streets defined by maps in the city. The map is composed of a number of horizontal and vertical streets. Each street has two lanes for each direction. The mobile node is allowed to move along the grid of horizontal and vertical streets on the map. At an intersection of a horizontal and a vertical street, the mobile node can turn left, right, or go straight. The Manhattan mobility model is also expected to have high spatial dependence and high temporal dependence, but differs from the freeway model in giving a node some freedom to change its direction.

The obstacle mobility Model [42] takes a different approach in the objective to obtain a realistic urban network in presence of building constellations. Instead of extracting data from TIGER files, the simulator uses random building corners and Voronoi tessellations in order to define movement paths between buildings. It also includes a radio propagation model based on the constellation of obstacles. According to this model, movements are restricted to paths defined by the Voronoi graph.

2.4.4. Real Dataset-Based Mobility Model. In order to reflect the node behavior in real environment, some institutes try to collect a large number of real data reflecting the mobility of the nodes and their behavior. Based on these data, a real life mobility model could be built. For example, the reality mining project proposed by MIT [43] builds a system for sensing complex social systems with data collected from 100 mobile phones over the duration of 9 months. The collected data can be used to recognize social patterns in daily user activity, infer relationships, identify socially significant locations, and model organizational rhythms.

Haggle project proposed by Cambridge University [44] is an innovative paradigm for autonomic opportunistic communication. Students carry a tiny iMote with Bluetooth to record the contact history. Similarly, Hui and Crowcroft [45] created a human mobility experiment during IEEE Infocom 2006, with the participants labelled according to their academic affiliations. After collecting 4 days of data during the conference period, they replay traces using an emulator and discover that a small label indicating affiliation can indeed effectively reduce the delivery cost, without trading off much against delivery ratio. The intuition that simply identifying community can improve message delivery turns out to be true even during a conference where the people from different subcommunities tend to mix together.

3. Nonknowledge-Based Routing Protocols

In the nonknowledge-based routing approach, it tries to relay messages to the neighboring node without any information about the next hop. For example, the node does not know the likelihood that the next hop meets with the destination node, and the node chooses the next hop randomly or broadcasts.

Flooding is a mechanism which needs relay nodes to store and forward message copies independently through creating multiple duplications of a message in the network. This method could dramatically enhance delivery ratio and reduce average delivery delays at the cost of huge network resource consumption. Numerous optimization approaches have been presented based on flooding striving for reasonable resource consumption.

Direct transmission [46] is a typical nonknowledge-based routing technique. When source node generates messages, it carries the messages moving in the field. Once it contacts with the destination node, the messages are directly sent to the destination. Direct transmission is very simple and there is only one message copy and one transmission. However, the scheme does not employ the opportunistic links and suffers long delivery ratio due to the long waiting time in the buffer, especially when the source node is hard to meet the destination node.

In two-hop relay mechanism [27], the source node will send a message copy to the first n nodes it contacts. Then there is $n + 1$ node carrying the message and moving on. If any node holding the message encounters the destination node, the message will be delivered to the destination. Obviously, this method consumes more network resources, but it achieves better performance than direct transmission since it has better chance to communicate with the destination. For example, assuming that each node has an independent probability P to contact with the destination, then two-hop relay mechanism will deliver the message to the destination node with the probability $1 - (1 - P)^{n+1}$, which is far more than the probability of direct transmission when P is small. Moreover, it can choose the number of copies to control the resources consumption. However, two-hop relay mechanism has the same disadvantage as direct transmission, that is, if all the $n + 1$ nodes cannot encounter the destination node, the message cannot be transmitted.

Tree-based flooding method [27] improves two-hop relay by distributing the task of making copies to other nodes. When a message copy is transferred to a relay node, it will tell the relay node the number of copies it will generate. Because the relay nodes form a tree rooted at the source, the method is called tree-based routing. There are many ways to decide the number of copies the relay node will make. A simple scheme is to allow each node to make unlimited copies, but to restrict the message to travel a maximum of n hops from the source. Tree-based flooding can deliver messages to destinations that are multiple hops away, unlike direct contact or two-hop relay. However, tuning the parameters is a challenging problem.

Vahdat and Becker present epidemic routing in [47]. Epidemic routing works as follows. When a message is sent, it is still in the buffer with a unique ID. Once two nodes contact with each other, they exchange a summary vector including the list of all the messages IDs they have in their buffers. Then they exchange the message they do not have. Though Epidemic Routing uses the knowledge of summary vector, the knowledge does not indicate whether the next hop is the appropriate relay node. So we classify it

into nonknowledge-based category. Epidemic Routing relies upon carriers coming into contact with another connected portion of the network through node mobility. At this point, the message spreads to an additional island of nodes. Through such transitive transmission of data, messages have a high probability of eventually reaching their destination. If the buffer size is large enough, the message will be distributed over the network like epidemic viruses until it arrives at the destination node. Epidemic Routing is relatively simple because it requires no knowledge about the network. Similarly to flooding, the disadvantage of Epidemic Routing is that a great amount of resources are consumed due to the large number of copies and requires large amount of buffer space, bandwidth, and energy.

Authors introduce the idea of immunity to improve the basic Epidemic Routing strategy in [48]. Each node maintains a list of delivered messages, called the immunity list. When two nodes contact with each other, they exchange their immunity lists at first, and then those messages in the immunity lists will not exchange in the future. It is expected to increase the number of delivered messages due to improved buffer and network utilization. Simulation shows statistically significant performance improvement both in delivery ratio and delay for immunity-based epidemic as compared to the basic epidemic protocol.

PREP is another improvement of Epidemic Routing proposed in [49]. The key idea of PREP is to impose a partial priority on the messages for transmission and dropping. The priority calculation is based upon four inputs: the current cost to destination, current cost from source, expiry time and generation time. Each link's average availability is epidemically disseminated to all nodes. As a result of this priority scheme, PREP maintains a gradient of replication density that roughly decreases with increasing distance from the destination. PREP is derived from the recognition that Epidemic routing is unbeatable from the point of view of successful delivery as long as the load does not stress the resources (bandwidth, storage).

Gossip [50] is also nonknowledge-based routing technique. Compared with flooding, Gossip tries to reduce network resources consumption by randomly choosing the relay node rather than delivering message to all nodes it meets. Clearly, the number of message copies is controlled and the resource consumptions decrease. However, randomly selected next hop might not be a suitable relay node and would make negative influence on the performance.

To significantly reduce the overhead of flooding-based schemes, Spyropoulos et al. propose spray and wait (SW) [51], which "sprays" a number of copies into the network at first, and then "waits" till one of these nodes meets the destination. SW routing strategy consists of two phases: spray phase and wait phase. In the spray phase, once a message is generated at source node, the number of message copies is confined by L. L message copies are forwarded by the source node and other relay nodes. If the L nodes with the message copies do not encounter the destination, then enter in to the wait phase. In the wait phase, the L nodes with the message copies performs direct transmission, that is to say, the L nodes carry the message copy till one of them contacts with the destination. SW combines the speed of epidemic routing with the simplicity and thriftiness of direct transmission. At first, it spreads message copies in a manner similar to epidemic routing. When there are enough copies that at least one of them will find the destination quickly with high probability, it stops flooding and performs direct transmission.

Besides flooding-based routing techniques, there are other two types of nonknowledge-based routing strategies: special node-based approach such as SWIM [16] and data MULE [52], and coding based approach [53, 54].

The Shared Wireless Infostation Model (SWIM) architecture proposed by Small and Haas [16] employs the special node called Infostations at various locations. The Infostations are static, and the nodes are attached to moveable whales. Each Infostation is considered as a destination and they are connected. The mobile nodes forward data to the Infostations when they contact with any of the Infostations. So in effect, SWIM is similar to the epidemic scheme, except that in the SWIM, each Infostation is a destination.

Shah et al. [52] present a system called Data MULE. The special node in the system is called MULEs. The MULEs are mobile nodes and move around the sensor area randomly. The MULES try to collect data from the static sensor nodes and carry data back to the base station. Furthermore, there are some other routing schemes using special node to assist in forwarding message [55–61].

There are two types of coding-based strategies: network coding [53] and erasure coding [62]. The former embeds the decoding algorithms into the coded message blocks and the latter adds redundancy into the message blocks. In network coding-based strategies [53, 54], fragmentation and network coding taken are used to reduce resource consumption. In these strategies, each message is partitioned into K fragment packets when it is originated. Those fragments are flooded in the network, and relay nodes firstly combine the fragments and encode them into a new packet then forwarding. At last, when the destination obtains coded packets which collect all the K fragments, it attempts to decode the K source packets and the message is delivered. This method reduces the buffer and transmission consumption at the cost of long time waiting for the destination to receive a sufficient number of coded packets.

Chen et al. [62] apply erasure coding, but combine it with some replication techniques. Liao et al. [63] also propose a method where the message is erasure coded and then routed using estimation-based routing. The same authors further improve this approach in [64] by utilizing the knowledge of the mobility pattern of the network to route the erasure coded blocks.

4. Knowledge-Based Routing Protocols

Nonknowledge-based routing strategies relay message blindly and consume huge network resources. To forward messages efficiently, knowledge about the network could be used to optimize routing strategies and improve the performance. Knowledge about the network include link metric, history contact, mobility pattern, and network topology. According to the knowledge, a node can select the next hop which has the highest likelihood to communicate with the destination node.

4.1. Link Metric-Based Approach. Similarly to traditional networks, DTMNs can be considered as a graph and each link is assigned a weight. Then the shortest path algorithm such as Dijsktra's algorithm is run to get a best route. Link weights are based on some performance metric: the highest bandwidth, lowest latency, and the highest delivery ratio. In DTMNs, the most important metric is the delivery ratio, since the network must be able to reliably deliver data. A secondary metric is the delivery latency. Thus, the challenge is to determine a system for assigning link metrics that maximize the delivery ratio and minimize the delivery latency. Some metrics may also attempt to minimize resource consumption, such as buffer space or power.

Jain et al. utilize link metrics for routing in delay tolerant networks in [65]. Their object is to minimize the end-to-end delivery latency. The intuition is that this minimizes the amount of time that a message consumes to buffer space, and thus it should also maximize the delivery ratio since there is more space available for other messages. Their work uses a metric, that is, the time it will take for a message to be sent over each link. Since this value may depend on the time a message arrives at a node, the authors present a time-varying version of Dijkstra's shortest path algorithm.

Feng et al. propose minimum expected delay-based routing (MEDR) [66] protocols for delay tolerant mobile sensor networks. In MEDR, each sensor maintains two important parameters: minimum expected delay (MED) and its expiration time. According to MED, messages will be delivered to the sensor that has at least a connected path with their hosting nodes and has the shortest expected delay to communicate directly with the sink node. Because of the changing network topology, the path is fragile and volatile, so MEDR uses the expiration time of MED to indicate the time of the path and avoid wrong transmissions.

Jones et al. present a metric called the minimum estimated expected delay (MEED), where the weights are based purely on the history contact record [67]. MEED estimates the transmission delay to the next hop and assumes that the future delay will be similar to the past. The delay metrics are distributed over the network by an epidemic protocol. The node computes the shortest path based on all received link states of the network. MEED maintains a single message copy and selects the next hop with the shortest delay to the destination. Compared to direct transmission, MEED reduces the delivery delay efficiently. But MEED introduces more network overheads when distributing the link states over the network, especially when the network topology changes frequently.

Tan et al. [68] present a shortest expected path routing (SEPR) for DTN scenario. The forwarding probability of the link is calculated from the history of encounters. Based on this, the shortest expected path is calculated. The meet and visit routing (MV routing) proposed by Burns et al. [69] improves SEPR by using only the frequency of node contacts. It uses the frequency of the past contacts of nodes and also the visit to certain regions.

Moreover, Wang and Song propose a distributed real-time data traffic statistics assisted routing protocol (DRTAR) [70] for vehicular ad hoc network. In DRTAR, each vehicle estimates the state of the partitioned network of each road by the real-time statistics of records of neighbors. Based on the estimated delay of all roads, each vehicle can compute the appropriate routing path for message forwarding.

4.2. Prediction-Based Approach. To improve routing performance in opportunistic scenarios, prediction-based approaches have been designed for DTMNs. These approaches calculate and predict the state of network (i.e., message delivery probability, nodes' contact schedule, etc.) based on history information.

ZebraNet [71] is one of the earliest schemes to make routing decisions by the history of encounters. The object of the project is to monitor zebra movement in their habitat and wireless nodes are attached to the zebras. Each mobile node has a hierarchy level, which is calculated from the frequency of its contact with the base station. The hierarchy level of each node varies with time, depending on its frequency of contact with the base station. When a node encounters other nodes, it transmits the messages to another node with higher hierarchy level. In this way, the history of the node's encounter with the base station becomes the metric for data forwarding.

PRoPHET is probabilistic routing protocol proposed by Lindgren et al. [72]. PRoPHET uses the history of encounters to compute the delivery predictability of the nodes. The delivery predictability indicates the likelihood to meet the destination node. Each node maintains the delivery predictability of every other node for all known destinations. When nodes meet each other, they exchange the information of delivery predictability. Moreover, it also incorporates transitivity information to decide the next hop. PRoPHET has a higher delivery ratio than epidemic, with much lower communication overhead.

Spray and focus (SF) proposed in [73] improves spray and wait by substituting wait phase for focus phrase. The works of SF in the spray phase are the same as that of SW. In the focus phase, message carriers would select appropriate relay node based on predicted utility and then forward it. Spray and focus are demonstrated to achieve both good latency and low bandwidth overhead, thereby significantly reducing resource consumption in flooding routing.

PER proposed by Yuan et al. [74] predicts messages' delivery on the ground of probability distribution of future contact schedules and chooses a suitable next hop in order to improve the end-to-end delivery probability. In PER, a model based on a time-homogeneous semi-Markov process is designed to predict the probability distribution of the time of contact and the probability that the two nodes encounters in the future. When making decision, there are three metric functions for nodes in PER, which means nodes could select one of them to choose relay nodes.

Wang and Wu [75] present a replication-based efficient data delivery called RED, which consists of two components for data delivery and message management. Firstly, data delivery uses a history-based method like ZebraNet to calculate the delivery probabilities of sensor nodes. Secondly,

the message management algorithm decides the optimal erasure coding parameters based on sensor's current delivery probability to improve the data delivery ratio. However, the optimization of erasure coding parameters used in [75] is usually inaccurate, especially when the source is very far away from the sinks. They also propose a FAD protocol in [76] to increase the data delivery ratio in DTMSNs. Besides using the same delivery probability calculation method as RED, FAD further discusses how to constrain the number of data replications in the sensor network by using a fault tolerance value associated with each data message. However, that protocol still has a quite high transmission overhead.

Xu et al. present a novel data gathering method named relative distance-aware data delivery scheme (RDAD) in [77]. RDAD introduces a simple non-GPS method with small overhead to gain the relative distance from a node to sink and then to calculate the node delivery probability which gives a guidance to message transmission. RDAD also employs the message survival time and message maximal replication to decide message's transmission and dropping for minimizing transmission overhead. Simulation results have shown that RDAD does not only achieve a relatively long network lifetime but also gets the higher message delivery ratio with lower transmission overhead and data delivery delay than FAD approach.

Similarly, a distance-aware replica adaptive data gathering protocol (DRADG) is proposed in [78]. DRADG economizes network resource consumption through making use of a self-adapting algorithm to cut down the number of redundant replicas of messages and achieves a good network performance by leveraging the delivery probabilities of the mobile sensors as main routing metrics.

So far, the routing techniques we discussed do not consider the energy efficiency of the network. However, for some data-centric applications, they want to gather data from the network as much as possible. That is to say, energy consumption of the node must be considered to design routing protocols in order to achieve longer network lifetime. The longer the network lifetime is, the more data the network collects. Routing techniques should make a tradeoff between the energy consumption and data delivery ratio.

Wang et al. develop a cross-layer data delivery protocol for DFT-MSN in [79]. They think that there is a tradeoff between link utilization and energy efficiency. The goal is to make efficient use of the transmission opportunities whenever they are available, while keeping the energy consumption at the lowest possible level. But the sleeping period of sensor nodes is determined by their working cycles and their buffered message. If a node moves around the sink and its sleeping period is too long according to [79], it will not deliver any data to the sink.

To make tradeoff between opportunistic connectivity and energy consumption, a data delivery protocol with periodic sleep (DPS) tailored for DTMSN is proposed in [80]. Based on their delivery probability and their distance to the sink, sensor nodes choose their sleep schedule to save the energy. The higher the delivery probability and the shorter the distance to the sink, the less the time they sleep in order to improve the connectivity around the sink. Simulation results show that DPS achieves acceptable delivery ratio and delay with a very long network lifetime. In the long lifetime, the network can gather more data from sensor nodes than other approaches.

4.3. Context-Aware Approach. Some other protocols use the context information to aid in data forwarding. Musolesi et al. propose a context-aware adaptive routing (CAR) in [81], in which some context information such as the energy, moving speed, location, and communication probability are used to calculate utility. The node chooses the next hop that has the highest utility to transfer the messages. Based on CAR, Mascolo et al. present SCAR (sensor context-aware routing) [82], a routing approach which uses the context of the sensor node (history neighbors, battery level, etc.) to foresee which of the neighbors are the best relay nodes for data forwarding. In addition, SCAR controls the number of message copies like spray and wait.

Leguay et al. propose MobySpace [83], which utilizes the mobility pattern of nodes as context information. A MobySpace consists of Mobypoints. Each Mobypoint summarizes some characteristics of a node's mobility pattern. Nodes with similar mobility patterns are close in MobySpace. They are the optimum carriers of messages. The same concept on multicopy routing schemes is presented in [84].

Opportunistic routing with window-aware replication (ORWAR) is a resource-efficient protocol for opportunistic routing in delay-tolerant networks presented by Sandulescu and Nadjm-Tehrani [85]. ORWAR exploits the context of mobile nodes (speed, direction of movement, and radio range) to estimate the size of a contact window. This knowledge is exploited to make better forwarding decisions and to minimize the probability of partially transmitted messages. As well as optimizing the use of bandwidth during overloads, it helps to reduce energy consumption since partially transmitted messages are useless and waste transmission power. Another feature of the algorithm is the use of a differentiation mechanism based on message utility. This allows allocating more resources for high utility messages. More precisely, messages are replicated in the order of the highest utility first and removed from the buffers in the reverse order.

Grossglauser and Vetterli [86] propose another algorithm that was based on context information. Here the context information was the time lag between the last encounter with the destination. The main purpose of the work is to show that node mobility can be exploited to disseminate destination location information without incurring any communication overhead. To achieve this, each node maintains a local database of the time and location of its last encounter with every other node in the network. The database is consulted by packets to obtain estimates of their destination's current location. As a packet travels towards its destination, it is able to successively refine an estimate of the destination's precise location, because node mobility has "diffused" estimates of that location.

4.4. Position-Based Approach. Position-based routing (also called geographic routing) is a routing principle that relies on geographic position information, which is based on the idea that the source sends a message to the geographic location of the destination instead of using the network address. Position-based routing requires that each node can determine its own location and that the source is aware of the location of the destination. With this information, a message can be routed to the destination without knowledge of the network topology or a prior route discovery.

Greedy perimeter stateless routing (GPSR) presented by Karp and Kung [87] is a typical routing protocol for wireless ad hoc networks that uses the positions of routers and a packet's destination to make packet forwarding decisions. GPSR makes greedy forwarding decisions using only information about a router's immediate neighbors in the network topology. When a packet reaches a region where greedy forwarding is impossible, the algorithm recovers by routing around the perimeter of the region.

Geographic source routing (GSR) [88] combines position-based routing with topological knowledge, as a promising routing strategy for vehicular ad hoc networks in city environments. Greedy perimeter coordinator routing (GPCR) [89] is a position-based routing protocol. The main idea of GPCR is to take advantage of the fact that streets and junctions form a natural planar graph, without using any global or external information such as a static street map. GPCR consists of two parts: a restricted greedy forwarding procedure and a repair strategy which is based on the topology of real-world streets and junctions and hence does not require a graph planarization algorithm.

5. Social-Based Routing Protocols

In the recent years, social structures have been used to help forwarding in intermittently connected networks. Social behavior analysis has been introduced to resolve the routing issues when the nodes are attached to the human and could achieve better performance by using social relationship or human behavior in real-life environment.

5.1. Social Relationship-Based Approach. In society, there are inherent social relationships between people such as relatives, friends, colleagues, and schoolmates. The relationships usually remain stable in a long period of time. Based on the social relationships, message could be forwarded efficiently.

Hui and Crowcroft have proposed a routing algorithm called LABEL which takes advantage of communities for routing messages [45]. LABEL partitions nodes into communities based on only affiliation information. Then ach node in the network has a label telling others about its affiliation. A node only chooses to forward messages to destinations, or to the next-hop nodes belonging to the same group (same label) as the destinations. LABEL significantly improves forwarding efficiency over oblivious forwarding using their dataset, but it lacks a mechanism to move messages away from the source when the destinations are socially far away.

BUBBLE combines knowledge of the community structure with knowledge of node centrality to make forwarding decisions [90]. Centrality in BUBBLE is equivalent to popularity in real life, which is defined as how frequently a node interacts with other nodes. People have different popularities in the real life so that the nodes have different centralities in the network. Moreover, people belong to small communities like in LABEL. When two nodes encounter, the node forwards the message up to the node with higher centrality (more popular node) in the community until it reaches the same level of centrality as the destination node. Then, the message can be forwarded to the destination community at the same ranking (centrality) level. BUBBLE reduces the resource consumption compared to epidemic and PRoPHET. However, this reduction may not be large since the ranking process creates significant communication overhead. In addition, this protocol still uses multicopy forwarding which means that it is not efficient in terms of resource consumption.

SimBet presented in [91] makes routing decisions by centrality (betweenness) and similarity of nodes. Centrality means popularity as in BUBBLE. More specifically, the centrality value captures how often a node connects nodes that are themselves not directly connected [7]. Similarity is calculated based on the number of common neighbors of each node. SimBet routing exchanges the preestimated centrality and locally determined similarity of each node in order to make a forwarding decision. The forwarding decision is taken based on the similarity utility function (SimUtil) and betweenness utility unction (BetUtil). When the nodes contact with each other, the node selects the relay node with higher SimBet utility for a given destination.

SimBetAge [92] improves SimBet by introducing a new parameter, freshness. Routing decision is made based on freshness, betweenness, and similarity. Betweenness and similarity are the same as in SimBet and they are proportional to the freshness in SimBetAge. SimBetAge employs a weighted time-dependent graph, in which the weight of an edge is called the edge freshness, where $w(e, t) = 0, e = (A, B)$ means that nodes A and B have not been connected from the initial time t_0 to time t and $w(e, t) = 1$ represents a permanent connection between A and B. The similarity of two nodes in SimBetAge is proportional to the freshness of a common neighbor between the two nodes. In order to have a more accurate calculation of betweenness compared to SimBet, SimBetAge takes all possible paths in a network into account, whereas SimBet only uses the shortest path between nodes.

LocalCom proposed by Li and Wu [93] is a community-based epidemic forwarding scheme in disruption tolerant network. LocalCom detects the community structure using limited local information and improves the forwarding efficiency based on the community structure. It defines similarity metrics according to nodes' encounter history to depict the neighboring relationship between each pair of nodes. A distributed algorithm, which only utilizes local information, is then applied to detect communities and the formed communities have strong intracommunity connections.

In social greedy [94], forwarding decision is made by the closeness and social distance. Closeness is calculated by the common attributes (address, affiliation, school, major, city, country, etc.) of the two nodes. The more common the attributes, the closer the two nodes. Social greedy forwards a message to the next node if it is socially closer to the destination. Social greedy outperforms the LABEL protocol.

However, the delivery ratio of Epidemic and BUBBLE is better than social greedy.

PeopleRank approach [95] uses a tunable weighted social information to rank the nodes. PeopleRank is inspired by the PageRank [96] algorithm employed by Google to rank web pages. By crawling the entire web, the algorithm measures the relative importance of a page within a graph (web). Similar to the PageRank idea, PeopleRank gives higher weight to nodes if they are socially connected to other important nodes of the network. With the emergence of Online Social Network platforms and applications such as Facebook, Orkut, or MySpace, information about the social interaction of users has become readily available. Moreover, while opportunistic contact information is changing constantly, the links and nodes in a social network remain rather stable. The idea of PeopleRank is to use this more stable social information to augment available partial contact information in order to provide efficient data routing in opportunistic networks.

5.2. Human Behavior-Based Approach. Another social-based routing strategy employs the regularity of human behavior to aid in routing decision.

Liu and Wu present a cyclic MobiSpace [97], which is a MobiSapce where the mobility of the node exhibits a regular cyclic pattern as there exists a common motion cycle for all nodes. In a cyclic MobiSpace, if two nodes were often in contact at a particular time in previous cycles, then the probability that they will be in contact around the same time in the next cycle is high. Cyclic MobiSpace is common in the real world: (1) most objects' motions exhibit regularity as they are repetitive, time sensitive, and location related; (2) a common motion cycle usually exists because most objects' motions are based on human-defined or natural cycles of time such as hour, day, and week nodes. Based on this phenomenon, routing in cyclic MobiSpace (RCM) scheme is proposed. Routing decision is made by the expected minimum delay (EMD), which is the expected time that an optimal forwarding scheme takes to deliver a message at a specific time from a source to a destination, in a network with cyclic and uncertain connectivity. When nodes contact, messages would be relayed to the next hop with minimum EMD.

Liu et al. consider that there are preference locations that people visit frequently and they propose preference location-based routing strategy (PLBR) [98]. Firstly, PLBR provides the approach of acquiring one's preference locations and then calculates the closeness metric which is used to measure the degree of proximity of any two nodes proposed. On the basis of that, the data forwarding algorithm is presented. The closeness is defined to indicate the similarity of the preference locations that the two nodes visit. The higher the closeness of the two nodes, the more the common preference locations. If the closeness of the two nodes is high, the probability of the two nodes to contact is high. The messages would be forwarded to the next hop with the highest closeness. However, the calculation of the closeness requires the preference locations of the destination node, introducing large network overheads.

An expected shortest path routing (ESPR) [99] scheme improves PLBR by utilizing the stable property of human that they have preference locations in their mobility traces, and the direct distance between node pairs can be calculated according to the similarity of their location visiting preferences. Then an expected shortest path length (ESPL) can be achieved by Dijkstra algorithm. Messages are forwarded to nodes which are closer to the destination than the previous nodes in the message delivery history. In addition, ESPR also employs the priority of message in the queue management.

CSI [100] is a behavior-oriented service as a new paradigm of communication in mobile human networks, which is motivated by the tight user-network coupling in future mobile societies. In such a scenario, messages are sent to the inferred behavioral profiles, instead of explicit IDs. At first, user behavioral profiles are constructed based on traces collected from two large wireless networks, and their spatiotemporal stability is analyzed. The implicit relationship discovered between mobile users could be utilized to provide a service for message delivery and discovery in various network environments. CSI shows that user behavioral profiles are surprisingly stable. Leveraging such stability in user behaviors, the CSI service achieves delivery rate very close to the delay-optimal strategy with minimal overhead.

Hot area-based routing protocol (HARP) scheme presented in [101] is based on the observation that there are some hot areas with higher nodal density and the node in the hot area has higher delivery probability to the destination. In HARP, the delivery probability is determined by the transmission ranking and the popular degree. Transmission ranking indicates the likelihood that sensor nodes communicate with the sink nodes. And popular degree reflects the popularity of sensor nodes. In the real world, some nodes may be more popular and interact with sink nodes more often than others in the network. The more hot areas a sensor node visits, the higher its popular degree is.

6. Open Issues

6.1. Energy Efficiency. Energy efficiency is an important issue for wireless ad hoc networks and there are lots of researches on energy efficiency in traditional wireless ad hoc networks such as WSNs. However, the existing routing strategies for delay tolerant networks seldom consider the energy consumptions of the nodes, shortening the network life time. In the previous works for DTMNs, the RF module of nodes has to work all the time so as to find the possible links (opportunistic connectivity) to their potential neighbors. Then, the nodes will drain off their battery quickly and cannot contribute any more for data gathering. Therefore, routing protocol should make a tradeoff between the energy consumption and data delivery ratio. In DTMNs with intermittent connectivity, it is helpful to find the link to keep the radio working all the time at the cost of rapidly exhausted battery. On the contrary, periodically working of the RF module saves energy but leads to lower connectivity. How to maintain an acceptable connectivity while keeping the energy consumption slowly is a challenging issue for DTMNs.

6.2. Security Routing. Existing routing protocols for DTMNs focus on improving the delivery ratio and reducing the

delivery delay, but do not consider security issue. To our knowledge, there is little study on the security of data delivery in DTMNs. In DTMNs with intermittently connectivity, it is argued that the issue of security and privacy is not so important. In fact, DTMNs face all the security threats that a traditional network faces. Just like PC, the nodes in DTMNs are often controlled by people. There might be some malicious attackers using the nodes to transmit bad data in the network. So, security routing is a promising issue for DTMNs.

6.3. Selfish Routing. In the previous routing techniques, there is a common assumption that all nodes in the network are unselfish and coordinated. Each node is willing to receive and relay the messages sent by other nodes. In fact, there would be some selfish nodes, which want to preserve their own resources while using the services of others and consuming the resources of others, especially in social network. In the real world, most people are socially selfish, that is, they are willing to forward packets for nodes with whom they have social ties but not others, and such willingness varies with the strength of the social tie. Social selfishness will affect node behaviors. As a forwarding service provider, a node will not forward packets received from those with whom it has no social ties, and it gives preference to packets received from nodes with stronger ties when the resource is limited. Thus, a DTMNs routing algorithm should take the social selfishness into consideration.

6.4. Social Routing. Utilizing the social behavior and relationship of humans is still a very promising research area. In fact, the handheld devices are more and more popular today so that most of people carry some handheld devices. Knowledge of the social structure of people can enable these devices to be the bridge between the disconnectedness and to forward message more efficiently.

6.5. Cross-Layer Design. Generally speaking, cross-layer design refers to protocol design done by actively exploiting the dependence between protocol layers to obtain performance gains. This is unlike layering, where the protocols at the different layers are designed independently. Knowledge has to be shared between layers to obtain the highest possible adaptivity. So, how to use the information of other layers to assist in routing decision and optimizing forwarding is an interesting topic.

7. Conclusion

In this paper, we introduce delay tolerant mobile networks and discuss the characteristics of the DTMNs. The intermittent connectivity of DTMNs influences the routing performance significantly. Then routing challenges and routing metrics are analyzed. Moreover, mobility models are also discussed because they affect the forwarding efficiency directly. Then we study the existing routing protocols for delay tolerant mobile networks in depth. The routing strategies for DTMNs are categorized into nonknowledge based, knowledge based, and social based. In fact, it is not possible to classify each of the schemes into exactly one of the many classes. More and more routing techniques are hybrid in nature and may be categorized into more than one category. Finally, we give some research issues about routing for DTMNs, including energy efficiency, security routing, selfish routing, social routing, and cross-layer design.

Acknowledgments

This work is supported by National Science Foundation under Grant no. 60903158, 61003229, 61103226, 61170256, 61173172 and the Fundamental Research Funds for the Central Universities under Grant no. ZYGX2010J074 and ZYGX2011J073.

References

[1] I. F. Akyildiz, W. Su, Y. Sankarasubramaniam, and E. Cayirci, "Wireless sensor networks: a survey," *Computer Networks*, vol. 38, no. 4, pp. 393–422, 2002.

[2] G. Simon, M. Maroti, A. Ledeczi et al., "Sensor network-based countersniper system," in *Proceedings of the 2nd International Conference on Embedded Networked Sensor Systems (SenSys '04)*, pp. 1–12, Baltimore, Md, USA, November 2004.

[3] J. M. Kahn, R. H. Katz, and K. S. J. Pister, "Next century challenges: mobile networking for smart dust," in *Proceedings of the 5th Annual ACM/IEEE International Conference on Mobile Computing and Networking (MobiCom '99)*, pp. 271–278, 1999.

[4] T. Gao, D. Greenspan, M. Welsh, R. R. Juang, and A. Alm, "Vital signs monitoring and patient tracking over a wireless network," in *Proceedings of the 27th Annual International Conference of the Engineering in Medicine and Biology Society (IEEE-EMBS '05)*, pp. 102–105, September 2005.

[5] M. A. Batalin, M. Rahimi, Y. Yu et al., "Call and response: experiments in sampling the environment," in *Proceedings of the 2nd International Conference on Embedded Networked Sensor Systems (SenSys '04)*, pp. 25–38, November 2004.

[6] N. Noury and T. Herve, "Monitoring behavior in home using a smart fall sensor," in *Proceedings of 1st Annual International Conference on Microtechnologies in Medicine and Biology*, pp. 607–610, 2000.

[7] Q. Xu, T. Mak, J. Ko, and R. Sengupta, "Vehicle-to-vehicle safety messaging in DSRC," in *Proceedings of the 1st ACM International Workshop on Vehicular Ad Hoc Networks (VANET '04)*, pp. 19–28, October 2004.

[8] J. Eriksson, H. Balakrishnan, and S. Madden, "Cabernet: vehicular content delivery using WiFi," in *Proceedings of the 14th Annual International Conference on Mobile Computing and Networking (MobiCom '08)*, pp. 199–210, September 2008.

[9] R. Panayappan, J. M. Trivedi, A. Studer, and A. Perrig, "VANET-based approach for parking space availability," in *Proceedings of the 4th ACM International Workshop on Vehicular Ad Hoc Networks (VANET '07)*, pp. 75–76, September 2007.

[10] J. Kulik, W. Heinzelman, and H. Balakrishnan, "Negotiation-based protocols for disseminating information in wireless sensor networks," *Wireless Networks*, vol. 8, no. 2-3, pp. 169–185, 2002.

[11] K. Sohrabi, J. Gao, V. Ailawadhi, and G. J. Pottie, "Protocols for self-organization of a wireless sensor network," *IEEE Personal Communications*, vol. 7, no. 5, pp. 16–27, 2000.

[12] W. R. Heinzelman, A. Chandrakasan, and H. Balakrishnan, "Energy-efficient communication protocol for wireless microsensor networks," in *Proceedings of the 33rd Annual Hawaii International Conference on System Siences (HICSS '00)*, pp. 3005–3014, IEEE Computer Society, Maui, Hawaii, USA, January 2000.

[13] C. Intanagonwiwat, R. Govindan, D. Estrin, J. Heidemann, and F. Silva, "Directed diffusion for wireless sensor networking," *IEEE/ACM Transactions on Networking*, vol. 11, no. 1, pp. 2–16, 2003.

[14] A. Manjeshwar and D. P. Agrawal, "TEEN: a routing protocol for enhanced efficiency in wireless sensor networks," in *Proceedings of the 15th International Workshop on Parallel and Distributed Computing Issues in Wireless Networks and Mobile Computing*, pp. 2009–2015, IEEE Computer Society, San Francisco, Calif, USA, April 2000.

[15] P. Juang, H. Oki, Y. Wang, M. Martonosi, L. S. Peh, and D. Rubenstein, "Energy-efficient computing for wildlife tracking: design tradeoffs and early experiences with ZebraNet," in *Proceedings of the 10th International Conference on Architectural Support for Programming Languages and Operating Systems*, pp. 96–107, October 2002.

[16] T. Small and Z. J. Haas, "The shared wireless infostation model: a new ad hoc networking paradigm," in *Proceedings of the 4th ACM International Symposium on Mobile Ad Hoc Networking and Computing (MobiHoc '03)*, pp. 233–244, June 2003.

[17] K. Fall, "A delay-tolerant network architecture for challenged internets," in *Proceedings of the Conference on Applications, Technologies, Architectures, and Protocols for Computer Communications (SIGCOMM '03)*, pp. 27–34, August 2003.

[18] C. E. Perkins and E. M. Royer, "Ad-hoc on-demand distance vector routing," in *Proceedings of the 2nd IEEE Workshop on Mobile Computing Systems and Applications (WMCSA '99)*, pp. 90–100, February 1999.

[19] D. Johnson and D. Maltz, "Dynamic source routing in ad-doc wireless networks," *Mobile Computing*, vol. 36, pp. 153–181, 1996.

[20] C. E. Perkins and P. Bhagwat, "Highly dynamic destination sequenced distance-vector routing (DSDV) for mobile computers," *Computer Communication Review*, vol. 24, no. 4, pp. 234–244, 1994.

[21] S. Murthy and J. J. Garcia-Luna-Aceves, "An efficient routing protocol for wireless networks," *Mobile Networks and Applications*, vol. 1, no. 2, pp. 183–197, 1996.

[22] K. A. Harras, K. C. Almeroth, and E. M. Belding-Royer, "Delay tolerant mobile networks (DTMNs): controlled flooding in sparse mobile 9 networks," in *Proceeding of 4th IFIP International Conference on Networking Technologies, Services, and Protocols*, pp. 1180–1192, 2005.

[23] Y. Wang, F. Lin, and H. Wu, "Poster: efficient data transmission in delay fault tolerant mobile sensor networks," in *Proceeding of IEEE International Conference on Network Protocols*, pp. 1021–1034, 2005.

[24] P. Hui, A. Chaintreau, J. Scott, R. Gass, J. Crowcroft, and C. Diot, "Pocket switched networks and human mobility in conference environments," in *Proceedings of the ACM SIGCOMM Workshop on Delay-Tolerant Networking (WDTN '05)*, pp. 244–251, ACM, Philadelphia, Pa, USA, August 2005.

[25] P. Pereira, A. Casaca, J. Rodrigues, V. Soares, J. Triay, and C. Cervello-Pastor, "From delay-tolerant networks to vehicular delay-tolerant networks," *IEEE Communications Surveys & Tutorials*, vol. 14, no. 4, pp. 1166–1182, 2011.

[26] J. Shen, S. Moh, and I. Chung, "Routing protocols in delay tolerant networks: a comparative survey," in *Proceedings of the 23rd International Technical Conference on Circuits/Systems, Computers and Communications*, p. 1577, 2008.

[27] E. P. Jones and P. A. Ward, "Routing strategies for delay tolerant networks," *Computer Communication Review*. In press.

[28] M. Liu, Y. Yang, and Z. Qin, "A survey of routing protocols and simulations in delay-tolerant networks," in *Proceedings of the 6th International Conference on Wireless Algorithms, Systems, and Applications (WASA '11)*, vol. 6843 of *Lecture Notes in Computer Science*, pp. 243–253, 2011.

[29] R. J. D'Souza and J. Jose, "Routing approaches in delay tolerant networks: a survey," *International Journal of Computer Applications*, vol. 1, no. 17, pp. 8–14, 2010.

[30] S. Burleigh, A. Hooke, L. Torgerson et al., "Delay-tolerant networking: an approach to interplanetary internet," *IEEE Communications Magazine*, vol. 41, no. 6, pp. 128–136, 2003.

[31] S. Jain, K. Fall, and R. Patra, "Routing in a delay tolerant network," in *Proceedings of the Conference on Applications, Technologies, Architectures, and Protocols for Computer Communications (SIGCOMM '04)*, vol. 34, pp. 145–158, ACM Press, October 2004.

[32] H. Jun, M. H. Ammar, and E. W. Zegura, "Power management in delay tolerant networks: a framework and knowledge-based mechanisms," in *Proceedings of the 2nd Annual IEEE Communications Society Conference on Sensor and Ad Hoc Communications and Networks (SECON '05)*, pp. 418–429, September 2005.

[33] H. Wu, Y. Wang, H. Dang, and F. Lin, "Analytic, simulation, and empirical evaluation of delay/fault-tolerant mobile sensor networks," *IEEE Transactions on Wireless Communications*, vol. 6, no. 9, pp. 3287–3296, 2007.

[34] F. Bai and A. Helmy, "A survey of mobility modeling and analysis in wireless adhoc networks," in *Wireless Ad Hoc and Sensor Networks*, Springer, 2006.

[35] C. Bettstetter, "Mobility modeling in wireless networks: categorization, smooth movement, and border effects," *ACM SIGMOBILE Mobile Computing and Communications Review*, vol. 5, no. 3, pp. 55–66, 2001.

[36] C. Bettstetter, H. Hartenstein, and X. Pérez-Costa, "Stochastic properties of the random waypoint mobility model," *Wireless Networks*, vol. 10, no. 5, pp. 555–567, 2004.

[37] M. Musolesi and C. Mascolo, "A community based mobility model for ad hoc network research," in *Proceedings of the 2nd International Workshop on Multi-Hop Ad Hoc Networks: From Theory to Reality (REALMAN '06)*, pp. 31–38, ACM Press, May 2006.

[38] T. Spyropoulos, K. Psounis, and C. S. Raghavendra, "Performance analysis of mobility-assisted routing," in *Proceedings of the 7th ACM International Symposium on Mobile Ad Hoc Networking and Computing (MobiHoc '06)*, pp. 49–60, ACM, New York, NY, USA, 2006.

[39] W. Hsu, T. Spyropoulos, K. Psounis, and A. Helmy, "Modeling time-variant user mobility in wireless mobile networks," in *Proceedings of the 26th IEEE International Conference on Computer Communications (INFOCOM '07)*, pp. 758–766, May 2007.

[40] Q. Zheng, X. Hong, and J. Liu, "An Agenda Based Mobility Model," in *Proceeding of 39th ANnual Symposium on Simulation (ANSS 2006)*, pp. 188–195, 2006.

[41] F. Bai, N. Sadagopan, and A. Helmy, "Important: a frame work to systematically analyze the impact of mobility on performance o frouting protocols fo rad hoc networks," in *Proceeding of the 22th IEEE Annual Joint Conference on Computer Communications and Networking (INFOCOM '03)*, pp. 825–835, 2003.

[42] The Obstacle Mobility Model moment, http://moment.cs.ucsb.edu/mobility/.

[43] N. Eagle and A. Pentland, "Reality mining: sensing complex social systems," *Personal and Ubiquitous Computing*, vol. 10, no. 4, pp. 255–268, 2006.

[44] C. Diot, M. Martin, and N. Erik, Haggle project[EB/OL], 2004, http://www.haggleproject.org.

[45] P. Hui and J. Crowcroft, "How small labels create big improvements," in *Proceedings of the 5th Annual IEEE International Conference on Pervasive Computing and Communications Workshops (PerComW '07)*, pp. 65–70, March 2007.

[46] M. Grossglauser and D. N. C. Tse, "Mobility increases the capacity of ad hoc wireless networks," *IEEE/ACM Transactions on Networking*, vol. 10, no. 4, pp. 477–486, 2002.

[47] A. Vahdat and D. Becker, "Epidemic routing for partially connected ad hoc networks," Tech. Rep., Duke University, Durham, NC, USA, 2000.

[48] P. Mundur, M. Seligman, and N. L. Jin, "Immunity-based epidemic routing in intermittent networks," in *Proceedings of the 5th Annual IEEE Communications Society Conference on Sensor, Mesh and Ad Hoc Communications and Networks (SECON '08)*, pp. 609–611, June 2008.

[49] R. Ramanathan, R. Hansen, P. Basu, R. Rosales-Hain, and R. Krishnan, "Prioritized epidemic routing for opportunistic networks," in *Proceedings of the 1st International MobiSys Workshop on Mobile Opportunistic Networking (MobiOpp '07)*, pp. 62–66, June 2007.

[50] X. Zhang, G. Neglia, and J. Kurose, "Performance modeling of epidemic routing," in *Proceeding of the International Federation for Information Processing Networking*, pp. 535–546, 2006.

[51] T. Spyropoulos, K. Psounis, and C. S. Raghavendra, "Spray and wait: an efficient routing scheme for intermittently connected mobile networks," in *Proceedings of the ACM SIGCOMM Workshop on Delay-Tolerant Networking (WDTN '05)*, pp. 252–259, August 2005.

[52] R. C. Shah, S. Roy, S. Jain, and W. Brunette, "Data MULEs: modeling a three-tier architecture for sparse sensor networks," in *Proceedings of the 1st International Workshop on Sensor Network Protocols and Applications*, pp. 30–41, IEEE Computer Society Press, Anchorage, Alaska, USA, 2003.

[53] Y. Jiang, Y. Li, L. Zhou, D. Jin, L. Su, and L. Zeng, "Optimal opportunistic forwarding with energy constraint for DTN," in *Proceedings of the IEEE Conference on Computer Communications Workshops (INFOCOM '10)*, pp. 1–2, March 2010.

[54] Y. F. Lin, B. C. Li, and B. Liang, "Stochastic analysis of network coding in epidemic routing," *IEEE Journal on Selected Areas in Communications*, vol. 26, no. 5, pp. 794–808, 2008.

[55] F. Farahmand, I. Cerutti, A. N. Patel, Q. Zhang, and J. P. Jue, "Relay node placement in vehicular delay-tolerant networks," in *Proceedings of the IEEE Global Telecommunications Conference (GLOBECOM '08)*, vol. 27, no. 1, pp. 2514–2518, November 2008.

[56] W. Zhao, Y. Chen, M. Ammar, M. D. Corner, B. N. Levine, and E. Zegura, "Capacity enhancement using throwboxes in DTNs," in *Proceedings of IEEE International Conference on Mobile Ad Hoc and Sensor Sysetems (MASS '06)*, pp. 31–40, October 2006.

[57] M. M. B. Tariq, M. Ammar, and E. Zegura, "Message ferry route design for sparse ad hoc networks with mobile nodes," in

Proceedings of the 7th ACM International Symposium on Mobile Ad Hoc Networking and Computing (MOBIHOC '06), pp. 37–48, May 2006.

[58] A. A. Somasundara, A. Ramamoorthy, and M. B. Srivastava, "Mobile element scheduling for efficient data collection in wireless sensor networks with dynamic deadlines," in *Proceedings of the 25th IEEE International Real-Time Systems Symposium (RTSS '04)*, pp. 296–305, December 2004.

[59] Y. Gu, D. Bozdağ, and E. Ekici, "Mobile element based differentiated message delivery in wireless sensor networks," in *Proceedings of the International Symposium on a World of Wireless, Mobile and Multimedia Networks (WOWMOM '06)*, pp. 83–92, 2006.

[60] Y. Gu, D. Bozdağ, E. Ekici, F. Özgüner, and C.-G. Lee, "Partitioning based mobile element scheduling in wireless sensor networks," in *Proceedings of the 2nd Annual IEEE Communications Society Conference on Sensor and Ad Hoc Communications and Networks (SECON '05)*, pp. 386–395, September 2005.

[61] M. Shin, S. Hong, and I. Rhee, "DTN routing strategies using optimal search patterns," in *Proceedings of the 3rd ACM Workshop on Challenged Networks (CHANTS '08)*, pp. 27–32, September 2008.

[62] L. J. Chen, C. H. Yu, T. Sun, Y. C. Chen, and H. H. Chu, "A hybrid routing approach for opportunistic networks," in *Proceedings of the ACM SIGCOMM workshop on Challenged Networks (CHANTS '06)*, pp. 213–220, September 2006.

[63] Y. Liao, K. Tan, Z. Zhang, and L. Gao, "Combining erasure-coding and relay node evaluation in delay tolerant network routing," Microsoft Technical Report MR-TR, 2006.

[64] Y. Liao, K. Tan, Z. Zhang, and L. Gao, "Estimation based erasure-coding routing in delay tolerant networks," in *Proceedings of the International Wireless Communications and Mobile Computing Conference (IWCMC '06)*, pp. 557–562, July 2006.

[65] S. Jain, K. Fall, and R. Patra, "Routing in a delay tolerant network," in *Proceedings of the Conference on Applications, Technologies, Architectures, and Protocols for Computer Communications (SIGCOMM '04)*, vol. 34, pp. 145–158, ACM Press, October 2004.

[66] Y. Feng, M. Liu, X. Wang, and H. Gong, "Minimum expected delay-based routing protocol (MEDR) for delay tolerant mobile sensor networks," *Sensors*, vol. 10, no. 9, pp. 8348–8362, 2010.

[67] E. P. C. Jones, L. Li, and P. A. S. Ward, "Practical routing in delay-tolerant networks," in *Proceedings of the ACM SIGCOMM Workshop on Delay-Tolerant Networking (WDTN '05)*, pp. 237–243, August 2005.

[68] K. Tan, Q. Zhang, and W. Zhu, "Shortest path routing in partially connected ad hoc networks," in *Proceedings of IEEE Global Telecommunications Conference (GLOBECOM '03)*, pp. 1038–1042, December 2003.

[69] B. Burns, O. Brock, and B. N. Levine, "MV routing and capacity building in disruption tolerant networks," in *Proceedings of the 24th Annual Joint Conference of the IEEE Computer and Communications Societies (INFOCOM '05)*, vol. 1, pp. 398–408, March 2005.

[70] X. Wang and C. Song, "Distributed real-time data traffic statistics assisted routing protocol for vehicular networks," in *Proceedings of the 16th IEEE International Conference on Parallel and Distributed Systems (ICPADS '10)*, pp. 863–867, December 2010.

[71] P. Juang, H. Oki, Y. Wang, M. Martonosi, L. S. Peh, and D. Rubenstein, "Energy-efficient computing for wildlife tracking: design tradeoffs and early experiences with ZebraNet," in *Proceedings of the 10th International Conference on Architectural Support for Programming Languages and Operating Systems*, vol. 37, pp. 96–107, October 2002.

[72] A. Lindgren, A. Doria, and O. Schelén, "Probabilistic routing in intermittently connected networks," *ACM SIGMOBILE Mobile Computing and Communications Review*, vol. 7, no. 3, pp. 19–20, 2003.

[73] T. Spyropoulos, K. Psounis, and C. S. Raghavendra, "Spray and focus: efficient mobility-assisted routing for heterogeneous and correlated mobility," in *Proceedings of the 5th Annual IEEE International Conference on Pervasive Computing and Communications Workshops (PerComW '07)*, pp. 79–85, March 2007.

[74] Q. Yuan, I. Cardei, and J. Wu, "Predict and relay: an efficient routing in disruption-tolerant networks," in *Proceedings of the 10th ACM International Symposium on Mobile Ad Hoc Networking and Computing (MobiHoc '09)*, pp. 95–104, May 2009.

[75] Y. Wang and H. Y. Wu, "Replication-based efficient data delivery scheme (RED) for delay/fault-tolerant mobile sensor network (DFT-MSN)," in *Proceedings of the 4th Annual IEEE International Conference on Pervasive Computing and Communications Workshops (PerComW '06)*, pp. 485–489, March 2006.

[76] Y. Wang and H. Y. Wu, "Delay/fault-tolerant mobile sensor network (DFT-MSN): a new paradigm for pervasive information gathering," *IEEE Transactions on Mobile Computing*, vol. 6, no. 9, pp. 1021–1034, 2007.

[77] F. L. Xu, M. Liu, H. G. Gong, G. H. Chen, J. P. Li, and J. Q. Zhu, "Relative distance-aware data delivery scheme for delay tolerant mobile sensor networks," *Journal of Software*, vol. 21, no. 3, pp. 490–504, 2010.

[78] Y. Feng, H. Gong, M. Fan, M. Liu, and X. Wang, "A distance-aware replica adaptive data gathering protocol for delay tolerant mobile sensor networks," *Sensors*, vol. 11, no. 4, pp. 4104–4117, 2011.

[79] Y. Wang, H. Y. Wu, F. Lin, and N. F. Tzeng, "Cross-layer protocol design and optimization for delay/fault-tolerant mobile sensor networks (DFT-MSN's)," *IEEE Journal on Selected Areas in Communications*, vol. 26, no. 5, pp. 809–819, 2008.

[80] H. Gong, L. Yu, and F. Xu, "A data delivery protocol with periodic sleep for delay tolerant mobile sensor networks," *Journal of Convergence Information Technology*, vol. 7, no. 16, pp. 36–43, 2012.

[81] M. Musolesi, S. Hailes, and C. Mascolo, "Adaptive routing for intermittently connected mobile ad hoc networks," in *Proceeding of the 6th IEEE International Symposium on World of Wireless Mobile and Multimedia Networks (WoWMoM '05)*, pp. 183–189, June 2005.

[82] C. Mascolo, M. Musolesi, and B. Pásztor, "Opportunistic mobile sensor data collection with SCAR," in *Proceeding of the 4th International Conference on Embedded Networked Sensor Systems*, pp. 343–344, 2006.

[83] J. Leguay, T. Friedman, and V. Conan, "Evaluating MobySpace Based Routing Strategies in Delay Tolerant Networks," Université Pierre et Marie CURIE, Laboratoire LiP6-CNRS, Thales Communications.

[84] J. Leguay, T. Friedman, and V. Conan, "Evaluating mobility pattern space routing for DTNs," in *Proceedings of the 25th IEEE International Conference on Computer Communications (INFOCOM '06)*, April 2006.

[85] G. Sandulescu and S. Nadjm-Tehrani, "Opportunistic DTN routing with window-aware adaptive replication," in *Proceedings of the 4th Asian Internet Engineering Conference (AINTEC '08)*, pp. 103–112, November 2008.

[86] M. Grossglauser and M. Vetterli, "Locating nodes with EASE: last encounter routing in ad hoc networks through mobility diffusion," in *Proceedings of the 22nd Annual Joint Conference of the IEEE Computer and Communications Societies (INFOCOM '03)*, vol. 3, pp. 1954–1964, April 2003.

[87] B. Karp and H. T. Kung, "GPSR: greedy perimeter stateless routing for wireless networks," in *Proceedings of the 6th Annual International Conference on Mobile Computing and Networking (MobiCom '00)*, pp. 243–254, August 2000.

[88] C. Lochert and H. Hartenstein, "A routing strategy for vehicular ad hoc networks in city environments," in *Proceeding of IEEE Intelligent Vehicles Symposium*, pp. 156–161, June 2003.

[89] C. Lochert and M. Mauve, "Geographic routing in city scenarios," *ACM SIGMOBILE Mobile Computing and Communications Review*, vol. 9, no. 1, pp. 69–72, 2005.

[90] P. Hui, J. Crowcroft, and E. Yoneki, "BUBBLE rap: social-based forwarding in delay tolerant networks," in *Proceedings of the 9th ACM International Symposium on Mobile Ad Hoc Networking and Computing (MobiHoc '08)*, pp. 241–250, May 2008.

[91] E. M. Daly and M. Haahr, "Social network analysis for routing in disconnected delay-tolerant MANETs," in *Proceedings of the 8th ACM International Symposium on Mobile Ad Hoc Networking and Computing (MobiHoc '07)*, pp. 32–40, September 2007.

[92] J. Ágila Bitsch Link, N. Viol, A. Goliath, and K. Wehrle, "SimBetAge: utilizing temporal changes in social networks for pocket switched networks," in *Proceedings of the 1st ACM Workshop on User-Provided Networking: Challenges and Opportunities*, pp. 13–18, December 2009.

[93] F. Li and J. Wu, "LocalCom: a community-based epidemic forwarding scheme in disruption-tolerant networks," in *Proceedings of the 6th Annual IEEE Communications Society Conference on Sensor, Mesh and Ad Hoc Communications and Networks (SECON '09)*, pp. 1–6, 2009.

[94] K. Jahanbakhsh, G. C. Shoja, and V. King, "Social-greedy: a socially-based greedy routing algorithm for delay tolerant networks," in *Proceedings of the 2nd International Workshop on Mobile Opportunistic Networking (MobiOpp '10)*, pp. 159–162, February 2010.

[95] A. Mtibaa, M. May, C. Diot, and M. Ammar, "PeopleRank: social opportunistic forwarding," in *Proceedings of the 29th IEEE International Conference on Computer Communications (INFOCOM '10)*, pp. 1–5, March 2010.

[96] S. Brin and L. Page, "The anatomy of a large-scale hypertextual web search engine," *Computer Networks and ISDN Systems*, vol. 30, no. 1-7, pp. 107–117, 1998.

[97] C. Liu and J. Wu, "Routing in a cyclic mobispace," in *Proceedings of the 9th ACM International Symposium on Mobile Ad Hoc Networking and Computing (MobiHoc '08)*, pp. 351–360, May 2008.

[98] J. Liu, H. Gong, and J. Zeng, "Preference location-based routing in delay tolerant networks," *International Journal of Digital Content Technology and Its Applications*, vol. 5, no. 12, pp. 468–474, 2011.

[99] J. Liu, M. Liu, and H. Gong, "Expected shortest path routing for social-oriented intermittently connected mobile network," *Journal of Convergence Information Technology*, vol. 7, no. 1, pp. 94–101, 2012.

[100] W. J. Hsu, D. Dutta, and A. Helmy, "CSI: a paradigm for behavior-oriented delivery services in mobile human networks," *Ad Hoc Networks*, vol. 6, no. 4, pp. 13–24, 2011.

[101] H. Gong, X. Wang, L. Yu, L. Wu, and C. Song, "Hot area based routing protocol for delay tolerant mobile sensor network," *Journal of Convergence Information Technology*, vol. 4, no. 15, pp. 450–457, 2012.

6

A Novel Hybrid Self-Organizing Clustering Routing Algorithm

Peng Zhu[1] and Fei Jia[2]

[1] *Department of Information Management, School of Economics and Management, Nanjing University of Science and Technology, 200 Xiao Ling Wei Street, Nanjing 210094, China*
[2] *Division of Education Affairs, Nanjing Forest Police College, Nanjing 210046, China*

Correspondence should be addressed to Peng Zhu, pzhu@ieee.org

Academic Editor: Mugen Peng

This paper discusses the distributed routing algorithm of wireless self-organized network and puts forward a new type of hybrid self-organizing clustering routing protocol by combining energy sense and maximum connectedness. This routing protocol adopts a mechanism which is mainly based on cluster routing with the theory of "on demand-based plane routing discovery mechanism" becoming secondary. The routing discovery and routing maintenance algorithm are also described in this paper. As the emulation experiment result shows, there is no significant difference between the routing protocol and the demand-based routing protocol; however, when there are quite a number of nodes in the network, the performance can be greatly enhanced compared with the demand-based routing protocol. The routing protocol discussed in this paper has better extendability, lower routing overhead, and better data transmission rate; thus it can extend network lifetime and enhance the network performance.

1. Introduction

In most cases, the on-demand routing protocol works effectively; however, as the network scale expands and the node number increases, the number of the routing control messages increases dramatically; as a result, the network congestion is caused and the network performance index decreases [1]. At present, the clustering algorithm is recognized as an effective self-organized method which can improve network extendability, realize smaller route and control overhead, reduce number of nodes that share same channels, and also reduce the collision rate [2]. In addition, the cluster algorithm can help implementation of the functions such as routing selection and resource management. As a commonly used clustering algorithm, the maximum link degree clustering algorithm (MAXD) [3], its node firstly derives number of the neighboring nodes via the interaction control message and then broadcasts its connectedness to the neighboring nodes. Among this node and all other neighboring ones, the node with maximum connectedness to the neighbor one should be selected as the cluster head. If the maximum connectedness between the nodes and their neighborhoods are the same, the node with smallest ID should be selected as the cluster

head. The one-hop neighboring node of the cluster head becomes the member node in the cluster. The above-said procedure can be repeated until all nodes join one certain cluster. This cluster algorithm has the advantage of fewer number of clusters, that is to say, there are no many average hops between the source node and the destination one. By using the algorithm, the packet delivery delay can be reduced, but the overlapping between the created clusters is still high, and the network lifetime can be affected because the network loading balance is not taken into consideration. In such a background, we put forward a new self-organized clustering routing protocol based on link degree and energy aware. In this paper, the proposed clustering routing protocol is denoted as NSCR.

The basic principle of the NSCR is described as follows. On one hand, by referring to the theory of "on demand-based plane routing discovery mechanism" at the initial stage, the routing protocol later evolves as a mechanism which is mainly based on cluster routing; thus the theory of "on demand-based plane routing discovery mechanism" becomes secondary. On the other hand, when choosing the cluster head node, the system considers node connectedness and remaining energy. At the same time, each cluster head node chooses one candidate cluster head node (means the node which will become the cluster head once the node in the cluster head is not the head node) in its one-hop neighbor domain; when energy of the cluster head node is smaller than a certain value, the candidate node works as the new cluster head node instead, so that the network load balance can be achieved and network lifetime can be extended.

The rest of the paper is organized as follows. In Section 2, we present related works. Section 3 describes the proposed algorithm. Experimental results are reported in Section 4 and conclusions are drawn in Section 5.

2. Related Work

Grouping sensor nodes into clusters has been widely pursued by the research community in order to achieve the network scalability objective. The objective of clustering is mainly to generate stable clusters in environments with sensor nodes. In addition to supporting network scalability, clustering has numerous advantages [4].

"Self-organizing" is defined as the process where a structure or pattern appears in a system without intervention by external directing influences. It organizes through direct interaction in a peer-to-peer method [5]. Several self-organizing clustering protocols were studied as follows. Tournus et al. [6] propose a routing to self-organization, in which thin films obtained by deposition of size-selected CoPt clusters on graphite surface. The preformed clusters can easily diffuse on the surface and gather to form "islands" or "bunches" of clusters. By changing the cluster size, very different morphologies can be obtained, going from large-ramified islands to bunches of noncontacting clusters having the size of the initially deposited particles. Ahmed et al. [7] propose that energy efficiency and enhanced backbone capacity are obtained by exploiting the geometric orientation of cooperative nodes in wireless sensor network. The cooperative communication in wireless sensor networks gives people leverage to get the inherent advantages of its random node's locations and the direction of the data flow. Depending on the channel conditions and the transmission distance, the number of cooperative nodes is selected, that participate in an energy-efficient transmission/reception. Hasan and Jue [8] associate survivability and energy efficiency with the clustering of WSNs and show that such a proactive scheme can actually increase the lifetime. They present an easy-to-implement method named DED (distributed, energy-efficient, and dual-homed clustering) which provides robustness for WSNs without relying on the redundancy of dedicated sensors, that is, without depending on node density. DED uses the already gathered information during the clustering process to determine backup routes from sources to observers, thus incurring low message overhead. It does not make any assumptions about network dimension, node capacity, or location awareness and terminates in a constant number of iterations. Ahmed et al. [9] presents an energy-efficient selection of cooperative nodes with respect to their geographical location and the number of nodes participating in cooperative communications in wireless sensor networks. The cooperative communication in

wireless sensor networks gives people leverage to get the inherent advantages of its random node's locations and the direction of the data flow. Depending on the channel conditions and the transmission distance, the number of cooperative nodes is selected, that participate in an energy-efficient transmission/reception. Simulation results show that increasing the cooperative receive diversity decreases the energy consumption per bit in cooperative communications. It has also been shown that the network backbone capacity can be increased by controlled displacement of antennas at base station at the expense of energy per bit. Sun and Gu [10] propose and evaluate an energy-efficient clustering scheme based on LEACH (low energy adoptive clustering hierarchy), that is, LEACH-Energy Distance (LEACH-ED). In LEACH-ED, cluster heads are elected by a probability based on the ratio between residual energy of node and the total current energy of all of the sensor nodes in the network. LEACH-ED is another self-organized protocol that is based on LEACH. AbdelSalam and Olariu [11] propose to construct what they call a network skeleton that is constructed immediately after network deployment and provides a topology that makes the network more tractable. The skeleton provides sensors with coarse localization information that enables them to associate their sensory data with the geographic location in which the data was measured. Moreover, it promotes a geographic routing scheme that simplifies data communication across the network through skeleton sensors. Younis et al. [12] propose REED (Robust Energy-Efficient-Distributed clustering) for clustering sensors deployed in hostile environments in an interleaved manner with low complexity. REED is a self-organized clustering method which constructs independent sets of CH overlays on the top of the physical network to achieve fault tolerance. Each sensor must reach at least one CH from each overlay. Sangjoon [13] introduces a clustering strategy and self-organizing scheme for cluster-based wireless sensor networks, while maintaining the merits of a clustering approach. This scheme is a clustering method to configure cluster by diffusing an interest from a sink node. When a sink node diffuses an interest, every node decides which node is elected as a cluster head or intermediary node by sending and receiving messages.

In summary, the routing protocol in the above-mentioned studies often consider connectivity or energy awareness singly, and their research results always have some defects. In this regard, combined with flat-based routing mechanism and clustering arithmetic, this paper presents an on-demand self-maintenance clustering routing protocol based on connectivity and energy awareness which cited a mechanism with clustering routing key point and with flat-based on-demand routing supplementary point. This protocol keeps the advantages of flat-based on-demand routing, improves the scalability, and enhances the network performance.

3. Algorithm Description

Extensive research has been conducted in the area of clustering routing algorithm in dynamic network, including MANETs and mobile sensor networks; a great deal of algorithms and protocols have been proposed. Most of the

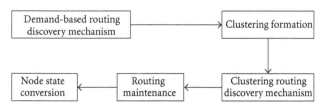

FIGURE 1: Algorithm Description.

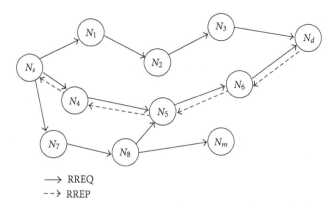

$\longrightarrow$ RREQ

$--\rightarrow$ RREP

FIGURE 2: Demand-based routing discovery mechanism.

research focused on reducing routing overhead and increasing latency of the network. There are, without doubt, some open issues that are still worth to investigate. In our work, we assume the following content as our clustering routing protocol.

The ad hoc network, which consists of multiple free moving nodes, can be extracted as an undirected graph of $G = (V, E)$. Among the parameters, V means network node set and E means bidirectional link set between nodes. For any symmetrical link $(i, j) \in E$ and $(j, i) \in E$. For any node $i, j \in V$ which has the unique ID, the node can provide remaining energy information at any time. If the distance between node i and node j is smaller than the transmission radius R, then the transmission between the two nodes can be achieved successful; the two nodes are called one-hop neighbor to each other.

The self-organized clustering routing protocol (NSCR) proposed by this paper starts performing route query when there is data which needs to be transmitted; in such a case, the nodes form a cluster. In addition, the system considers node connectedness and remaining energy of cluster head election, and at the same time it sets the candidate cluster head. The proposed algorithm consists of five parts as shown in Figure 1.

3.1. Demand-Based Routing Discovery Mechanism. When the source node (s) wants to communicate with the destination node (d), it initiates the routing discovery procedure. At the beginning, all nodes are in pending state, meaning that it is not in the cluster.

The source node (s) firstly checks its own routing table, to see whether there is routing information to the destination node (d). If no, it creates RREQ [14] and then broadcasts the RREQ to all neighboring nodes. RREQ = (Type, Source_addr, Dest_Addr, Dest_squence, RList, ToL). Among the parameters, Type means packet type, Source_addr means source address of the packet, Dest_Addr means destination address of the packet, and Dest_squence means packet serial number. Please note that (Source_addr, Dest_squence) can uniquely identify the RREQ, RList records the route information, and ToL means RREQ's value of lifetime.

After the intermediate node (m) receives one RREQ, it performs the following procedure.

Step 1. Substract 1 from ToL. If ToL value is 0, the intermediate node (m) shall discard the RREQ because the value means that RREQ's value of life is 0.

Step 2. Check whether the RREQ has been received according to RREQ's (Source_addr, Dest_squence). If yes, the intermediate node (m) discards the RREQ; otherwise, it checks whether the Rlist of RREQ carries the node address; if yes, it discards the RREQ.

Step 3. If the intermediate node (m) which carries the route information to the destination node returns the RREP [15] to the source node (s) after it receives the RREQ; otherwise, the intermediate node (m) continues broadcasting the RREQ. At the same time, the node (m) records the neighbor address carried in the RREQ and creates the reverse path.

Step 4. When there are a number of roads between the intermediate node (m) and the destination node (d) can be selected, the algorithm selects the optimal next hop node (k) from the alternative nodes to transmit information according to the probability P_{mk}^d. The trust value between the alternative next hop node (k) and the intermediate node (m) should be greater than a threshold value

$$P_{mk}^d = \frac{\left(D_{mk}^d\right)^\alpha}{\sum_{j \in N_s^d} \left(D_{mj}^d\right)^\alpha}. \qquad (1)$$

Among the parameters, D_{mk}^d means the distance of the path (m, k) on which the current node (m) reaches the destination node (d) through node (k). The distance of same paths to reach different destination nodes is mutative. N_s^d means the nodes set in which the neighbor nodes of node (m) can reach the destination node (d) and α means the parameter of wayfinding control information, $\alpha \gg 1$.

Step 5. After the destination node (d) receives the RREQ from the source node (s), it triggers the routing response procedure, which sends the RREP to the source node (s) in the created reverse path.

Figure 2 shows the demand-based routing discovery mechanism.

(i) Node Weight Calculation Method. In the reverse path where the destination node (d) sends the RREP to the source node (s), the passed node v and its neighboring node weight in the RREP can be obtained via calculation.

Definition 1. Weight (W_v) of node (v) is associated with its connectedness and the current remaining energy. The connectedness can be obtained from node (v), and the weight can be derived by combining the current remaining energy. Weight W_v of node (v) is defined as follows:

$$W_v = \alpha \frac{C_v}{C_{\max}} + (1 - \alpha) \frac{E_{re}}{E_{\max}}, \quad 0 \le \alpha \le 1. \quad (2)$$

Among the parameters, C_v means connectedness, $C_{\max}$ means maximum connectedness in one-hop neighbor domain, E_{re} means current remaining energy, and $E_{\max}$ means maximum initial energy. In case that the node energy is sufficient, when considering reducing the transmission delay, a big value of α should be taken; when considering achieving the energy balance, a small value of α should be taken, so that the network lifetime can be extended.

(ii) Generating Clustering Head Node. Node v broadcasts its weight to its neighboring nodes, and at the same time it updates neighboring node information list based on broadcast information of the neighboring nodes. After this procedure is finished, node v obtains weight and ID of its one-hop neighboring nodes. Then, node (v) compares the weights of this node with all other one-hop neighboring nodes and selects the node with maximum weights as the cluster head. If the maximum weight of the nodes is same, the node with smallest ID shall be selected as the cluster head. In the meanwhile, the node (as new cluster head) sends cluster head broadcast message to all its one-hop neighboring nodes; upon receiving the broadcast message from the cluster head, the neighboring nodes become member of the cluster and add the cluster head address into the head list.

(iii) Generating Distributed Gateway and Gateway Nodes. The member node i broadcasts the distributed gateway request message to its neighboring nodes. If the neighboring node j which receives the message finds that its cluster head node is different from that of the sending node i, then the neighboring node j shall returns a distributed gateway response message to node i; in such a case, node i becomes a distributed gateway in the cluster; later it adds its neighboring node j into its neighboring gateway list, and at the same time, the node i sends the distributed gateway message to its neighboring head node so as to allow the cluster head node to add the node i into its own distributed gateway list.

After this phase ends, the cluster is completely formed. The node is thus comprised of cluster head, gateway, distributed gateway, ordinary member, and pending node. All cluster head nodes are not directly neighbored to each other, which means that they are out of one-hop transmission range. The distance between cluster head node and cluster member node is always one hop.

3.2. Clustering Routing Discovery Mechanism. If the node becomes a cluster member, then the system shall set a cluster routing tag in the RREQ it sends and then query the routing according to the cluster routing discovery mechanism. In addition, the node which forwards RREQ determines

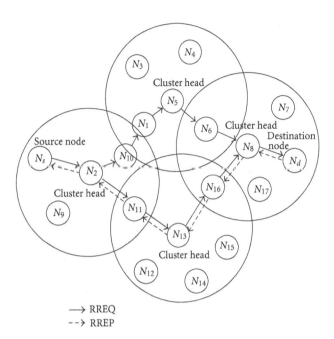

→ RREQ
--> RREP

FIGURE 3: Clustering routing discovery mechanism.

whether to query the routing by adopting cluster routing discovery mechanism or demand-based plane routing discovery mechanism according to the fact whether the cluster routing tag is set in the received RREQ. If the node fails to find the route in the specified time, the plane routing discovery mechanism based on demand shall be used for routing discovery [16]. Figure 3 shows the clustering routing discovery mechanism.

State of any node v can be converted under certain conditions.

(i) Clustering Head Node. When the cluster head node finds its cluster member is 0, it converts its own state to pending; when remaining energy of the cluster head node is below one certain value, the candidate head node becomes the head and the previous head node becomes an ordinary member.

(ii) Clustering Ordinary Member Node. When the cluster ordinary member node finds the cluster head in its neighboring node is not the same as its own cluster head, then its state shall be converted to distributed gateway. When the cluster ordinary member node receives the broadcast message from the heads in different clusters, its state can be converted to gateway. If the cluster ordinary member node is selected as the candidate node, when remaining energy of the cluster head node is below one certain value, its state becomes cluster head.

(iii) Gateway Node. If the gateway node finds that its cluster head is not reachable, then it deletes this node from its cluster head list. If the cluster head list contains only one head node, and the head in one-hop neighbor domain is not the same as its own cluster head, then its state shall be converted to distributed gateway; otherwise, its state shall be converted to cluster ordinary member.

(iv) Distributed Gateway Node. If the distributed gateway node finds that the node in its neighbor domain does not include the node from other clusters, then its state shall be converted to cluster ordinary member. When it finds the new cluster head node, its state shall be converted to gateway.

3.3. Routing Maintenance. After the routing discovery is finished, the network link loses effectiveness and reestablishes itself because it is affected by mode movement, energy reduction, and so forth. At the same time, the network topology structure also changes; so some nodes shall join new clustering from the old one, thus causing clustering structure change. In such a situation, the routing protocol requires the node to obtain state of the neighboring node via the broadcast message sent in a periodic manner and informs the nodes affected by disconnected links to perform the maintenance mechanism such as updating routing table by sending routing error group; besides, the related cluster maintenance mechanism should be adopted to maintain stability of the cluster structure.

(i) Local Routing Repair. If the node detects that its link to one neighboring node disconnects, then all routes using this link shall also fail. In this case, the direct route repair method can be adopted for route maintenance at link disconnection node. When the intermediate node m detects the link disconnection, it firstly puts the data from source node s into cache and then sends the route request to start new routing discovery by taking this node as the source node. If the destination node d receives the request, it replies with the routing response; upon the route is repaired successfully, the link disconnection node sends the data packets to the destination one in the new routing.

(ii) Self-Maintenance of Clustering Head Node. The clustering ordinary member node v in the cluster head node's one-hop neighboring domain can be used to obtain the weight $W_{candidate}(v)$ that is related to candidate cluster head node. $W_{candidate}(v)$ is associated with three parameters: similarity between node v and its clustering head node, connectedness of node v, and remaining energy. In general, the higher the similarity of node v is, the higher the connectedness is and the greater the remaining energy is; hence, the $W_{candidate}(v)$ becomes bigger, and the chance of being selected as the candidate cluster head node is greater.

Definition 2. Weight $W_{candidate}(v)$ of node v's candidate cluster head node is defined as follows:

$$W_{candidate}(v) = \alpha S + \beta \frac{C_v}{C_{max}} + \gamma \frac{E_{re}(v)}{E_{max}}. \quad (3)$$

Among the parameters, S means similarity between node v and its clustering head node h, C_v means connectedness of node v, C_{max} means node v and maximum connectedness of one-hop neighboring domain, E_{re} means current remaining energy of node v, and E_{max} means maximum initial energy of the node, $0 \le \alpha, \beta, \gamma \le 1$ and $\alpha + \beta + \gamma = 1$.

Definition 3. Similarity between node v and its cluster head node h is defined as S:

$$S = \frac{|N_v| \cap |N_h|}{|N_v| \cup |N_h|}. \quad (4)$$

Among the parameters, N_v means one-hop neighbor domain of node v, $|N_v|$ means number of nodes in one-hop neighbor domain of node v, N_h means one-hop neighbor domain of the cluster head, and $|N_h|$ means number of nodes in one-hop neighbor domain of cluster head.

The clustering head node sends the candidate head request message to the node whose $W_{candidate}(v)$ is maximum in the clustering in unicast mode after comparison; the node which receives the message returns the candidate head request message to the cluster head node, which indicates that the node works as the candidate cluster head. When remaining energy of the cluster head node is below one certain value, the candidate head node becomes the new head node, replacing the previous one. The previous head node becomes an ordinary member node in the cluster.

(iii) Joining and Quitting the Clustering. When status of node v is standby, if it receives the clustering head node broadcast message, it shall send cluster join request message to the clustering head node. After node v receives the response message from the clustering head node, it saves the head node address, which indicates node v has joined the clustering. To reduce the overhead, the on demand-based method [17] is adopted to allow new nodes to join the clustering. When the clustering member nodes are not in head node's one-hop neighboring domain, they modify their statuses to pending state, which indicates that they have quit the clustering.

4. Experiment and Result Analysis

4.1. Experiment Design. By routing protocol simulation based on the Linux environment, the simulation experiment adopts NS-2 [18] as the emulation tool. NS-2 is a discrete event-driven network simulation tool; it is open source and free software and can be extended according to the needs of users. NS-2 can perform a variety of network protocols, offer a variety of data sources, achieve a variety of router queue management algorithms, bring about multicast and MAC algorithm, and provide communication model, random topology, and node mobility model generation tool. The scenario documents used in the simulation experiments are generated by the stochastic modeling tools. When the emulation begins, each node waits for a stopping duration at the initial location and then moves to a randomly selected direction with a random speed between 0 and the maximum moving speed. If the node reaches the randomly selected destination, it waits for the same period of stopping duration and then repeats the procedure described earlier until the emulation ends. All moving procedures should be recorded in the scenario documents. In the experiment, the average value is used as reference.

4.2. Parameter Settings. In the emulation scenario, we set a flat rectangular virtual environment with size as 1500 m × 1000 m and set the emulation duration as 2000 s. During the emulation, half of the nodes move randomly in the waypoint mode and the other half stay still. The maximum moving speed of all the nodes is 40 m/s, and the node stopping duration is 50 s. Besides, CBR data source is used, the data transmission rate is 10 packets per second [19], and MAC protocol is using 802.11DCF.

In this paper, two simulation scenarios are set.

(i) Simulation Scenario 1. The number of nodes is set to 100, 150, 200, 250, 300, 350, 400, 450, and 500, respectively.

(ii) Simulation Scenario 2. The number of nodes is set to 5, 10, 20, 40, 80, 120, 160, 250, and 300, respectively.

In order to analyze the performance of routing protocols, the following performance indicators of the routing protocols are assessed. First, lifetime: it refers to the time interval from the beginning of the simulation to the time when the first node in the network runs out of energy. Lifetime can be used to measure the viability of the ad hoc network. Second, routing overhead: it is used to establish and maintain the number of control packets generated by routing. Routing overhead can be used to measure routing protocol's scalability and ability to adapt to network congestion. Third, packet delivery fraction: it means the ratio of the total number of packets the destination node receives with the total number of packets the source node sends. Packet delivery fraction can be used to measure the efficiency of the routing protocol. Fourth, number of clusters: it directly reflects the structure and characteristics of the cluster network.

4.3. Result Analysis. In the emulation experiment, according to the parameters and performance indicators proposed in Section 4.2, we select representative plane on-demand distance vector (AODV) routing protocol [20] and maximum connectivity clustering algorithm (MAXD) as references, do simulation experiments to the proposed clustering routing protocol NSCR via AODV and MAXD, and select some representative simulation results be analyzed and discussed.

(i) Life Time of the Ad hoc Network. In simulation scenario 1, lifetime of the ad hoc network in NSCR clustering algorithm is greatly extended compared with the MAXD. The reason is that the NSCR clustering algorithm considers the node energy in the cluster head election process and thus adopts the candidate cluster head mechanism; by doing so, the network loading is balanced and lifetime of the ad hoc network is extended. Figure 4 shows the comparison of the lifetime of the network between NSCR and MAXD.

(ii) Routing Overhead. Figure 5 shows the routing overhead for both NSCR and AODV in simulation scenario 2. As the figure shows, when the number of the nodes in the network is only a few, routing overhead of NSCR and AODV is almost the same; however, as the number of network nodes increases, especially when the number of nodes exceeds 100,

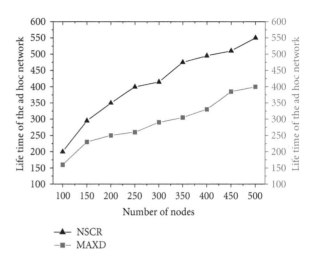

FIGURE 4: Life time of the Ad hoc network.

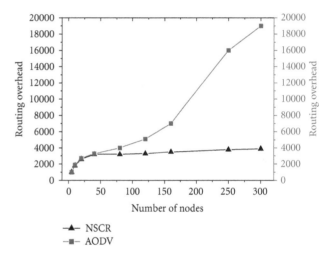

FIGURE 5: Routing overhead.

AODV's routing overhead increases at a relatively big pace; when the number reaches 200, AODV's routing overhead increases significantly but at the same time NSCR's routing overhead goes up in a slow pace. This phenomenon is mainly due to the NSCR routing protocol considers cluster routing mechanism, which to a certain extent improves the network scalability and reduces the network congestion. This experiment result shows that NSCR routing protocol can control network routing overhead effectively.

(iii) Packet Delivery Fraction. In simulation scenario 2, packet delivery fraction of both NSCR and AODV decreases when the number of the nodes in the ad hoc network increases, but the packet delivery fraction of NSCR is obviously higher than that of AODV when there are quite a number of nodes in the ad hoc network. The cause of this phenomenon is for the following reasons: on one hand, the NSCR reduces the routing control information and network congestion by using the cluster routing discovery mechanism; on the other hand, NSCR uses the partial

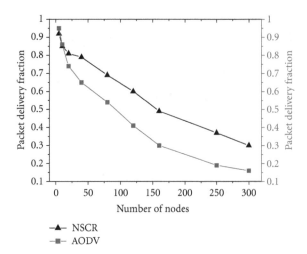

FIGURE 6: Packet delivery fraction.

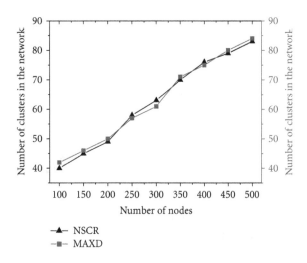

FIGURE 7: Number of clusters.

routing repair to implement routing maintenance, which can reduce packet loss caused by link disconnection. Figure 6 shows the comparison of packet delivery fraction of NSCR and AODV.

(iv) Number of Clusters. In simulation scenario 1, the number of clusters produced by NSCR and MAXD is similar, which indicates that the NSCR clustering algorithm maintains the advantages of clustering algorithm of MAXD. Figure 7 shows the comparison of the number of clusters of NSCR and MAXD.

5. Conclusion

This paper puts forward a demand-based self-maintenance clustering routing protocol based on energy sense and maximum connectedness cluster algorithm. By analyzing basic principle of the clustering routing protocol, describing protocol work mechanism, and conducting the emulation experiments, the paper concludes that there is no much difference

between performance of the proposed clustering routing protocol and demand-based plane routing protocol when the network is in a small scale. However, when there are quite a number of network nodes, their performance can be significantly improved compared with the demand-based plane routing discovery protocol. The HSCR routing protocol has better extendability, lower routing overhead, and better data transmission rate; at the same time, compared with the maximum connectedness cluster algorithm, the HSCR has the advantage of maximum connectedness cluster algorithm; thus it can extend network lifetime and meet routing requirement of the ad hoc network.

Acknowledgment

This research was supported by Ministry of Education of the People's Republic of China, Humanities and Social Sciences Project (no. 12YJC870036).

References

[1] S. Jingfang, W. Muqing, Z. Yan, and Z. Qinjuan, "Robust on-demand routing mechanism for wireless multi-hop networks," *IET Communications*, vol. 5, no. 5, pp. 620–628, 2011.

[2] M. Peng, Y. Liu, D. Y. Wei, W. B. Wang, and H. H. Chen, "Hierarchical cooperative relay based heterogeneous networks," *IEEE Wireless Communications*, vol. 18, no. 3, pp. 48–56, 2011.

[3] A. Bari, S. Wazed, A. Jaekel, and S. Bandyopadhyay, "A genetic algorithm based approach for energy efficient routing in two-tiered sensor networks," *Ad Hoc Networks*, vol. 7, no. 4, pp. 665–676, 2009.

[4] K. Lee and H. Lee, "A self-organized and smart-adaptive clustering and routing approach for wireless sensor networks," *International Journal of Distributed Sensor Networks*, vol. 2012, Article ID 156268, 13 pages, 2012.

[5] F. Dressler, *Self-Organization in Sensor and Actor Networks*, John Wiley & Sons, New York, NY, USA, 2007.

[6] F. Tournus, L. Bardotti, and V. Dupuis, "Size-dependent morphology of CoPt cluster films on graphite: a route to self-organization," *Journal of Applied Physics*, vol. 109, no. 11, Article ID 114309, 4 pages, 2011.

[7] I. Ahmed, M. G. Peng, and W. B. Wang, "Exploiting geometric advantages of cooperative communications for energy efficient wireless sensor networks," *International Journal of Communications, Networks and System Sciences*, vol. 1, no. 1, pp. 55–61, 2008.

[8] M. M. Hasan and J. P. Jue, "Survivable self-organization for prolonged lifetime in wireless sensor networks," *International Journal of Distributed Sensor Networks*, vol. 2011, Article ID 257156, 11 pages, 2011.

[9] I. Ahmed, M. G. Peng, and W. B. Wang, "Energy efficient cooperative nodes selection in wireless sensor networks," in *Proceedings of the International Conference on Parallel Processing Workshops (ICPPW'07)*, pp. 273–277, Xian, China, September 2007.

[10] Y. J. Sun and X. P. Gu, "Clustering routing based maximizing lifetime for wireless sensor networks," *International Journal of Distributed Sensor Networks*, vol. 5, no. 1, article 88, 2009.

[11] H. S. AbdelSalam and S. Olariu, "A lightweight skeleton construction algorithm for self-organizing sensor networks," in *Proceedings of the IEEE International Conference on Communications (ICC'09)*, pp. 426–430, Dresden, Germany, June 2009.

[12] O. Younis, S. Fahmy, and P. Santi, "An architecture for robust sensor network communications," *International Journal of Distributed Sensor Networks*, vol. 1, no. 3-4, pp. 305–327, 2005.

[13] J. Sangjoon, "Self-organizing clusters for routing algorithm by diffusing an interest in wireless sensor networks," in *Proceedings of the 5th ACIS International Conference on Software Engineering Research, Management, and Applications (SERA'07)*, pp. 702–707, Busan, South Korea, August 2007.

[14] C. L. Chang and T. L. Lin, "Delay-based RREQ routing scheme for wireless mesh network," *Journal of Internet Technology*, vol. 10, no. 2, pp. 103–109, 2009.

[15] R. D. Bai, M. Singhal, and Y. Luo, "Enhancing performance by salvaging route reply messages in on-demand routing protocols for MANETs," *Ad Hoc & Sensor Wireless Networks*, vol. 5, no. 3-4, pp. 161–188, 2008.

[16] X. X. Wu, G. Ding, and W. W. Zhu, "Load-based route discovery through searching range adaptation for MANET throughput improvement," *IEEE Transactions on Vehicular Technology*, vol. 58, no. 4, pp. 2055–2066, 2009.

[17] B. Awerbuch, R. Curtmola, D. Holmer, C. Nita-Rotaru, and H. Rubens, "ODSBR: An on-demand secure Byzantine resilient routing protocol for wireless ad hoc networks," *ACM Transactions on Information and System Security*, vol. 10, no. 4, article 18, 2008.

[18] J. L. Font, P. Iñigo, M. Domínguez, J. L. Sevillano, and C. Amaya, "Analysis of source code metrics from ns-2 and ns-3 network simulators," *Simulation Modelling Practice and Theory*, vol. 19, no. 5, pp. 1330–1346, 2011.

[19] C. E. A. Campbell, K. K. J. Loo, O. Gemikonakli, S. Khan, and D. Singh, "Multi-channel distributed coordinated function over single radio in wireless sensor networks," *Sensors*, vol. 11, no. 1, pp. 964–991, 2011.

[20] G. Li and H. M. Sun, "Discovering AODV-based multipath routes in wireless ad hoc networks," *Security and Communication Networks*, vol. 5, no. 4, pp. 374–383, 2012.

7

Detection and Mitigation of Node Replication Attacks in Wireless Sensor Networks: A Survey

Wazir Zada Khan,[1] **Mohammed Y. Aalsalem,**[2]
Mohammed Naufal Bin Mohammed Saad,[1] **and Yang Xiang**[3]

[1] *Electrical and Electronic Engineering Department, Universiti Teknologi PETRONAS,
Bandar Seri Iskandar, 31750 Tronoh, Perak, Malaysia*
[2] *School of Computer Science & Information System, Jazan University, Jazan 15112, Saudi Arabia*
[3] *School of Information Technology, Deakin University, 221 Burwood Highway, Burwood, Melbourne, VIC 3125, Australia*

Correspondence should be addressed to Wazir Zada Khan; wazirzadakhan@yahoo.com

Academic Editor: Muhammad Khurram Khan

Wireless sensor networks are a collection of a number of tiny, low-cost, and resource-constrained sensor nodes which are commonly not tamper proof. As a result, wireless sensor networks (WSNs) are prone to a wide variety of physical attacks. In this paper, we deem a typical threat known as node replication attack or clone node attack, where an adversary creates its own low-cost sensor nodes called clone nodes and misinforms the network to acknowledge them as legitimate nodes. To instigate this attack, an adversary only needs to physically capture one node, and after collecting all secret credentials (ID, cryptographic keys, etc.), an adversary replicates the sensor node and deploys one or more clones of the compromised node into the network at strategic positions, damaging the whole network by carrying out many internal attacks. Detecting the node replication attack has become an imperative research topic in sensor network security, and designing detection schemes against node replication attack involves different threatening issues and challenges. In this survey, we have classified the existing detection schemes and comprehensively explore various proposals in each category. We will also take a glance at some technical details and comparisons so as to demonstrate limitations of the existent detections as well as effective contributions.

1. Introduction

Advancement in technology has made it possible to develop tiny low-cost sensor nodes with off-the-shelf hardware. A wireless sensor network (WSN), which is a distributed and self-organized network, is a collection of such sensor nodes with limited resources that collaborate in order to achieve a common goal. These sensor nodes are comprised of low-cost hardware components with constraints on battery life, memory size, and computation capabilities [1]. Wireless sensor networks are often deployed in harsh and hostile environments which are inaccessible and even hazardous areas to perform various monitoring tasks. For example, they can be used to monitor factory instrumentation, pollution levels, freeway traffic, and the structural integrity of buildings [2]. Some of the other applications of WSNs include patient monitoring, climate sensing, control in office buildings, and home environmental sensing systems for temperature light, moisture, and motion.

WSNs are viable solutions for a wide variety of real-world challenges; however, a set of new security challenges arise in sensor networks due to the fact that current sensor nodes lack hardware support for tamper-resistance (because it is uneconomical to enclose each node in a tamper resistant hardware) and are often deployed in unattended environments where they are vulnerable to capture and compromise by an adversary. Taking an example of a battlefield, WSNs must tackle the threats and attacks from attackers because these areas are sometimes physically accessible to camouflaged enemies [3] who would like to acquire the private locations of soldiers from or inject wrong commands into the sensor network [4]. Similarly, an unattended WSN can be deployed in hostile environments which imply the existence of an adversary. For example, WSN can be used to monitor firearm discharge, illicit crop cultivation, drug/weapons smuggling, human trafficking, nuclear emissions in a rogue region and other illegal activities [5]. Thus, it is very important to ensure the security of sensor networks in such scenarios.

The unattended nature of wireless sensor networks can be exploited by adversaries which are able to launch an array of different physical attacks including node replication attack, signal or radio jamming, denial of service (DoS) attack, node outage, eavesdropping, and Sybil attack. and other attacks like sinkhole, wormhole, and selective forwarding attack. Threats to sensor networks can be either layer dependent or layer independent. Attacks in the former category can be application dependant and are specific to different OSI layers targeting specific network functionalities such as routing, node localization, time synchronization, and data aggregation, while the attacks in the latter category are application independent affecting a wide variety of applications from object tracking and fire alarming to battlefield surveillance, and these attacks are not launched on any OSI layer. The attacks of the latter category are also application independent [2]. This attack taxonomy is also shown in Figure 1. In order to protect wireless sensor networks from layer dependent attacks, many schemes have been proposed. To alleviate the effects of routing disruption attacks, secure routing schemes have been proposed [6, 7]. Authentication schemes [8–10] are used to mitigate false data injection attacks. Data aggregation can be secured by using secure data aggregation protocols proposed in [11–14]. To defend localization and time synchronization protocols from different attacks, and threats many protocols have been proposed in [15–21]. Nevertheless, most of these schemes are attack resilient, rather than they can detect and remove the source of attack. Thus, there is a need to detect and revoke the sources of attacks as soon as possible to substantially reduce the costs and damages incurred by employing attack resilient approaches.

In this comprehensive survey, we consider a very severe and important physical attack on WSN which is called node replication attack or clone attack. It is also known as identity attack. In this attack, an adversary first physically captures only one or few of legitimate nodes, then clones or replicates them fabricating those replicas having the same identity (ID) with the captured node, and finally deploys a capricious number of clones throughout the network. This whole process of node replication attack and the various stages are shown in Figure 2. This vexing problem arises from the actuality that sensor nodes are unshielded. It is stated in [22] that an experienced attacker can completely compromise a typical sensor node by using only a few readily available tools, and it can then obtain copies of that node memory and data within 1 min of discovering it. The clones or replicas may even be selectively reprogrammed to subvert the network by launching further insider attacks like falsifying sensor data or suppressing legitimate data, extracting data from the network and disconnect the network by triggering correct execution of node revocation protocols that rely on threshold voting schemes and staging denial of service (DoS) attacks. Clone nodes may create a black hole, initiate a wormhole attack

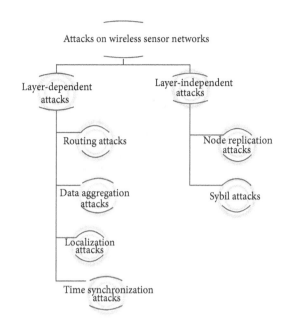

FIGURE 1: Classification of attacks on wireless sensor networks.

with a collaborating adversary, or may also leak data in an environment in which sensed data must be kept private [23]. If these replicated nodes or clones remain undetected or unattended for a long time, they can further commence the changes in protocol behavior and intrusion into the systems security [24]. It is easy for an adversary to launch such attacks due to the fact that the clones, created by an adversary, have legitimate information (codes, key materials, and credentials), and they may be considered as legitimate nodes and totally honest by its neighbors which are participating in the network operation in the same way as the noncompromised nodes.

The above mentioned traditional security schemes for WSNs are inept to detect and prevent node replication attack. Thus, in the last few years, a number of detection and prevention techniques/schemes have been proposed in the literature. According to [2], the detection schemes are classified on a high level as network-based or radio-based detection. Only one instance of radio-based detection is found in [25]. The former category is further categorized into two types as for mobile WSNs and for stationary WSNs. Both techniques for mobile and stationary WSNs are further divided into two broad categories, namely, centralized and distributed. This can be summarized with Figure 3 which shows a detailed classification of all replica detection schemes. This categorization provides a first step to better understand the node replication detection schemes.

A WSN can be either stationary or mobile. In static wireless sensor networks (SWSNs), the sensor nodes are stationary or static; that is, the sensor nodes are deployed randomly, and after deployment their positions do not change. On the other hand, in mobile wireless sensor networks (MWSNs), the sensor nodes can move on their own, and after deployment, they can interact with the physical environment by controlling their own movement. Advances in robotics have made it possible to develop such mobile sensors which

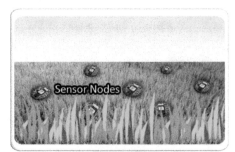

Step 1: Sensor Nodes Deployed in Field

Step 4: Replicate or make clones of captured nodes

Step 2: Capture one sensor node physically

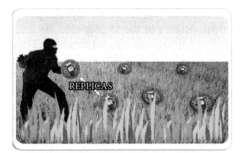

Step 5: Deploy these clones at strategic positions

Step 3: Collects all secret credentials

Figure 2: Steps of node replication attack.

are autonomous and have the ability to sense, compute, and communicate like static sensors. The prime difference between static and mobile WSNs is that mobile nodes are able to reposition and organize themselves in the network, and after initial deployment, the nodes spread out to gather information [26, 27]. Mobile nodes can communicate with one another when they are within the range of each other, and only then they can exchange their information gathered by them. Another important difference is that in static WSNs fixed routing or flooding is used for data distribution, while in mobile WSNs dynamic routing is used. As static and mobile WSNs differ in their characteristics hence replication detection schemes for stationary and mobile WSNs will be substantially different. In a static or stationary WSN, a sensor node has a unique deployment position, and thus if one logical node ID is found to be associated with two or more physical locations, node replication is detected. But this is inapplicable to mobile WSNs where sensor nodes keep roaming in the deployment field. So, replication detection in such mobile WSN involves different scenarios and techniques.

For mobile WSNs, both centralized and distributed techniques have been proposed in the literature. In the case of stationary WSNs, centralized techniques are further categorized into five types, namely, straightforward base station-based technique, key usage-based technique, SET operations techniques, cluster head-based techniques and neighborhood social signature-based techniques. The distributed techniques for stationary WSNs are further divided into four types naming Node to Network Broadcasting, claimer-reporter-witness-based techniques, neighbor-based and generation- or group-based techniques. On the other hand, mobile centralized detection techniques are further divided into two types including key usage-based and node speed-based techniques. The mobile distributed detection techniques are divided into three main types, namely, node meeting-based, mobility-assisted-based, and information-exchange-based techniques. This inclusive categorization can be summarized with Figure 3 which provides a first step in better understanding node replication detection schemes.

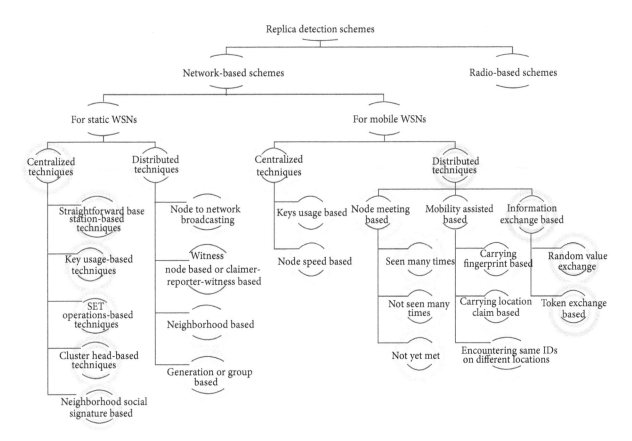

FIGURE 3: Taxonomy of replica detection schemes.

1.1. Motivation. With the rapid use of vast technologies in WSNs, the threats and attacks to WSN are escalating and are also being diversified and deliberate. A typical threat called node replication attack is a very severe and niggling problem in which an adversary replicates a sensor node after physically capturing it and then uses these replicas to disrupt the network operations by redeploying them at strategic positions of the network. Thus the research related to node replication attack in WSNs has been followed with much interest in recent years. The research of authentication and security techniques is already quite mature but such solutions fail to detect node replication attack and thus no longer provide WSN with adequate security from this attack. Furthermore, the detection of node replication attack in mobile WSN is far different and more challenging than in static WSNs.

The development of replica/clone detection techniques suitable for static WSNs and mobile WSNs is therefore regarded as an essential research area which will make WSN (either static or mobile) to be more secure and reliable. Most recently, Zhu et al. [2] did a survey on the countermeasures of node replication attack which has pointed out some valuable technical weaknesses and advantages of some of the techniques, but latest progress of replica detection schemes is absent, and it also lacks the detailed analysis of all existing techniques for mobile WSNs.

This motivates us to present our paper as a complete guideline of replica/clone detection schemes both for static

and mobile WSNs. Moreover, in this paper we have identified the advantages and shortcomings of all the techniques/schemes. Finally, some variations of node replication attack are also identified and discussed. This paper is helpful in understanding all the replica detection schemes developed so far, and it can assist the researchers and developers in the development of new, robust, and effective detection schemes.

1.2. General Adversary Model. Conventionally, some assumptions are made about an adversary in order to scrutinize security of a sensor network. First of all, an adversary is a smart and powerful attacker who can launch a clone attack [4], and it has the ability to secretly capture a limited number of legitimate sensor nodes [28]. Secondly, an adversary can create replicas by using cryptographic information which is obtained from the compromised node. An adversary has also full control over the compromised and replicated nodes and can communicate with them at any time. Thirdly, the main goal of an adversary is to protect its replicas from being detected by the detection protocol used in the network because if any replicas are detected, besides starting a revoke process to revoke replicas, the network may start a sweeping process to sweep out [29] the compromised node and may also draw human intervention. Thus, it is mostly assumed that nodes controlled by an adversary still follow the replica detection protocol as an adversary always wants to be overlooked. Fourthly, an adversary is so powerful that it is able to subvert the nodes that will possibly act as witnesses. To cope with such an adversary, it could be possible to assume that nodes are tamper-proof. But as tamper proof hardware is expensive and energy demanding, a large part of the literature has assumed that nodes in the network are not tamper resistant.

In case of mobile WSNs, the method of attack is the same but difference is that an adversary is mobile. The scenario of mobile WSN is that the sensors are unable to transmit sensed data at their will because the sink is not always present. Thus, the data accumulated in their memories become targets of many adversaries. In [30], a mobile adversary model is proposed in which mobile adversary visits and travels around the network trying to compromise a subset of sensors within the time interval when sinks are not present in the network. The time taken by a mobile adversary to compromise a set of sensors is much shorter than the time between two successive data collections of a sink.

1.3. Node Replication Attack and Its Effects on the Security Goals of WSNs. High level security issues are basically identical to the security requirements of both static and mobile WSNs. Thus, when dealing with security of WSNs, one is faced with achieving some of the following common security goals including availability, authenticity, confidentiality, and data integrity. When node replication attack is launched by an adversary, all of these security goals are affected severely because of two reasons. First, if any proper, specific, and efficient detection scheme is not used to identify and revoke these replicas because the existing general purpose security protocols would allow the replica nodes to encrypt, decrypt, and authenticate all of their communications as if they were original captured nodes. Second, when the detection probability of the detection technique used is very low to detect these clones or replicas. Node replication attack is significantly harmful to the networks because these replicas or clones have legitimate keys, and they are recognized as legitimate members of the network, since they carry all cryptographic materials extracted from the captured nodes so that an adversary can use them to mount a variety of insider attacks [2]; for example, it can monitor all the information passing through the nodes or monitor significant fraction of the network traffic that passes through the nodes, falsify sensor data, launch denial of service (DoS) attack, extract data from the network, inject false data to corrupt the sensor's monitoring operation, subvert data aggregation, and jam legitimate signals and can also cause continual disruption to network operations by undermining common network protocols.

Availability ensures the survivability of network services despite attacks [31]. In case of node replication attack, an adversary is able to compromise the availability of WSN by launching a denial of service (DoS) attack, which can severely hinder the network's ability to continue its processing. By jamming legitimate signals, the availability of the network assets to authorized parties is also affected.

Authenticity is a security goal that enables a node to ensure the identity of the sensor node it is communicating with. In case of node replication attack, an adversary creates clone nodes which are seemingly legitimate ones (identical to the original captured node) as they have all the secret credentials of the captured node; thus, it is difficult for any node to differentiate between a clone node and the original or legitimate node. Also the existing authentication techniques cannot detect clone nodes as they all hold legitimate keys. This is how the authenticity of the network is affected.

Confidentiality is the assurance that sensitive data is being accessed and viewed only by those who are authorized to see it. But when node replication attack is launched, confidentiality of data is not assured as clone nodes are the duplicated nodes of the compromised ones, and thus they behave like original compromised nodes. These clone nodes can have all the data that contains trade secrets for commercial business, secret classified government information, or private medical or financial records, and thus by misusing such sensitive data, it can damage the network or organization, person, and governmental body.

Data integrity ensures that the contents of data or correspondences are preserved and remain unharmed during the transmission from sender to receiver. Integrity represents that there is a guarantee that a message sent is the message received meaning that it was not altered either intentionally or unintentionally during transmission. But in case of node replication attack, an adversary can falsify sensor data or can inject false data to corrupt the sensitive data and thus subverting the data aggregation using the replicated or clone nodes.

1.4. Evaluation Metrics for Replication Detection Techniques. For the performance analysis and evaluation of replica detection protocols, four vital evaluation metrics are mostly used by all the detection schemes. These are communication overhead, storage or memory overhead, detection probability and detection time [26].

Communication overhead is defined as the average number of messages sent by a sensor node while propagating the location claims. *Storage overhead* defines the average number of the location claims stored in a sensor node. *Detection probability* is an important evaluation metric which shows how accurately a protocol can identify and detect the clones or replicas. The *detection time* is simply the delay between actual replica node deployment and detection.

To make the current survey more comprehensive and detailed, here in Section 2 we have discussed all the existing schemes for the replica detection in stationary WSNs which are accordingly compared in Section 3. Section 4 describes all the replication detection schemes in mobile WSNs proposed so far in the literature which are then compared in Section 5. In Section 6, we have highlighted some important issues and challenges associated with the node replication attack in both static and mobile WSNs. Finally, Section 7 concludes the paper.

2. Detection Techniques for Stationary WSNs

Many techniques have been proposed for the detection of node replication attack in static WSNs which are categorized mainly into two types as centralized and distributed techniques.

2.1. Centralized Techniques. In centralized techniques base station is considered to be a powerful central which is responsible for information convergence and decision making. During the detection process every node in the network sends its location claim (ID, Location Info) to base station (sink node) through its neighboring nodes. Upon receiving the entire location claims, the base station checks the node IDs along their location, and if it finds two different locations with the same ID, it raises a clone node alarm.

2.1.1. On the Detection of Clones in Sensor Networks Using Random Key Predistribution. This technique falls into the category of key usage based techniques. Brooks et al. [32] have proposed a cloned key detection protocol in the context of random key predistribution [33]. The basic idea is that the keys employed according to the random key predistribution scheme should follow a certain pattern, and those keys whose usage exceeds a threshold can be judged to be cloned. In the protocol, counting Bloom filters is used to collect key usage statistics. Each node makes a counting Bloom filter of the keys it uses to communicate with neighboring nodes. It appends a random number (nonce) to the Bloom filter and encrypts the result using base station public key; this encrypted data structure is forwarded to base station. Base station decrypts the Bloom filters it receives, discards duplicates, and counts the number of time each key used in the network. Keys used above a threshold value are considered cloned. Base station makes a bloom filter from the cloned keys, encrypts the list using its secret key and broadcasts this filter to the sensor network using a gossip protocol. Each node decrypts base stations bloom filter removes cloned keys from its keying, and terminates connections using cloned keys.

2.1.2. SET: Detecting Node Clones in Sensor Networks. This technique falls into the category of base station-based techniques. Choi et al. [23] have proposed a clone detection approach in sensor networks called SET. In SET, the network is randomly divided into exclusive subsets. Each of the subsets has a subset leader, and members are one hop away from their subset leader. Multiple roots are randomly decided to construct multiple subtrees, and each subset is a node of the subtree. Each subset leader collects member information and forwards it to the root of the subtree. The intersection operation is performed on each root of the subtree to detect replicated nodes. If the intersection of all subsets of a subtree is empty, there are no clone nodes in this subtree. In the final stage, each root forwards its report to the base station (BS). The BS detects the clone nodes by computing the intersection of any two received subtrees. SET detects clone nodes by sending node information to the BS from subset leader to the root node of a randomly constructed subtree and then to the BS.

2.1.3. Real-Time Detection of Clone Attacks in Wireless Sensor Networks. This technique falls into the category of neighborhood social signature-based techniques. Xing et al. [34] have proposed real-time detection of clone attacks in WSN. In their approach, each sensor computes a fingerprint by incorporating the neighborhood information through a superimposed s-disjunct code [35]. Each node stores the fingerprint of all neighbors. Whenever a node sends a message, the fingerprint should be included in the message, and thus neighbors can verify the fingerprint. The messages sent by clone nodes deployed in other locations will be detected and dropped since the fingerprint does not belong to the same "community." The motivation behind their scheme for detection of clone attacks is exploring the social characteristics of each sensor. Once they are deployed, these sensors reside within a fixed neighborhood. The sensor and its neighborhood form a small "community," or a "social network." A cloned sensor can have the same legitimate credentials (ID, keys, etc.) as the original node, but cannot have the same community neighborhood. Thus, each sensor can be distinguishably characterized by its social community network. In a small community, a newcomer can be easily recognized if speaking with a different accent. Similarly, a clone node can be easily identified by its neighbors if carrying a "social signature" belonging to a different community.

2.1.4. Hierarchical Node Replication Attacks Detection in Wireless Sensor Networks. This technique falls into the category of cluster head-based techniques. Znaidi et al. [36] have proposed a cluster head selection-based hierarchical distributed algorithm for detecting node replication attacks using a Bloom filter mechanism including the network reactions. More precisely, the algorithm relies on a cluster head selection performed using the local negotiated clustering algorithm (LNCA) protocol [37]. Each cluster head exchanges the member node Ids through a Bloom filter with the other cluster heads to detect eventual node replications. The algorithm works in three steps. In the first step all the material required for Bloom filter computations and for cryptographic operations that will be performed in the network predistributed in each sensor node. The second step performs the cluster head election. In the third step, Bloom filter construction is performed by each cluster head, and the Bloom filter verification is performed by the other cluster heads.

2.1.5. CSI: Compressed Sensing-Based Clone Identification in Sensor Networks. This technique falls into the category of base station-based techniques. Yu et al. [38] have proposed a centralized technique called compressed sensing-based clone identification (CSI) for static wireless sensor networks. The basic idea behind CSI is that each node broadcasts a fixed sensed data (α) to its one hop neighbors. Sensor nodes forward and aggregate the received numbers from descendant nodes along the aggregation tree via compressed sensing-based data gathering techniques. Base station (BS), as the root of the aggregation tree, receives the aggregated result and recovers the sensed data of the network. According to the reconstructed result, the node with the sensory reading greater than α is the clone since a nonclone node can only report the number once.

2.2. Distributed Techniques. In distributed techniques, no central authority exists, and special detection mechanism called claimer-reporter-witness is provided in which the detection is performed by locally distributed node sending the location claim not to the base station (sink) but to a randomly selected node called witness node. Distributed techniques are classified into four types and these are described below.

2.2.1. Node-to-Network Broadcasting (N2NB) and Deterministic Multicast (DM).

This technique falls into the category of node-to-network broadcasting. The N2NB and DM protocols are two unappealing examples proposed by Parno et al. [28]. Both of protocols received relatively less attention. In N2NB, each node floods the entire network with authenticated broadcast to claim its own location (instead of its neighbors). Each node stores the location information for its neighbors, incurring a storage cost of $O(d)$. Each node upon receiving a conflicting claim invokes a revocation procedure against the offending nodes, and eventually any replica will be cut off by all its neighbors (thus isolated from the WSN). The N2NB protocol achieves 100% detection rate as long as the broadcast reaches every node if the network size is assumed to be n and certain duplicate suppression algorithm is employed so that each node only broadcasts a given message once.

The DM protocol is a good example to illustrate the claimer-reporter-witness framework. The claimer is a node which locally broadcasts its location claim to its neighbors, each neighbor serving as a reporter, and employs a function to map the claimer ID to a witness. Then the neighbor forwards the claim to the witness, which will receive two different location claims for the same node ID if the adversary has replicated a node. One problem can occur that the adversary can also employ the function to know about the witness for a given claimer ID, and may locate and compromise the witness node before the adversary inserts the replicas into the WSN so as to evade the detection.

2.2.2. Distributed Detection of Node Replication Attacks in Sensor Networks.

Both RM and LSM fall into the category of witness node-based techniques. Parno et al. [28] have introduced two more distributed algorithms for the detection of clone nodes in wireless sensor networks which are quite mature schemes as compared to DM. The first protocol is called randomized multicast (RM) which distributes location claims to a randomly selected set of witness nodes. The birthday paradox [39] predicts that a collision will occur with high probability if the adversary attempts to replicate a node. Their second protocol, line-selected multicast (LSM), exploits the routing topology of the network to select witnesses for a node location and utilizes geometric probability to detect replicated nodes.

In RM, each node broadcasts a location claim to its one-hop neighbors. Then, each neighbor selects randomly witness nodes within its communication range and forwards the location claim with a probability to the nodes closest to chosen locations by using geographic routing. At least one witness node is likely to receive conflicting location claims according to birthday paradox when replicated nodes exist in the network. In LSM, the main objective is to reduce the communication costs and increase the probability of detection. Besides storing location claims in randomly selected witness nodes, the intermediate nodes for forwarding location claims

can also be witness nodes. This seems like randomly drawing a line across the network, and the intersection of two lines becomes the evidence node of receiving conflicting location claims.

2.2.3. A New Protocol for Securing Wireless Sensor Networks against Node Replication Attacks.

This technique falls into the category of generation- or group-based techniques. Bekara and Laurent-Maknavicius [40, 41] have proposed a new protocol for securing WSN against node replication attack by limiting the order of deployment using symmetric polynomial for pair-wise key establishment and defined group-based deployment model. Their scheme requires sensors to be deployed progressively in successive generations (or group). Each node belongs to a unique generation. In their scheme, only newly deployed nodes are able to establish pairwise keys with their neighbors, and all nodes in the network know the number of the highest deployed generation. Therefore, the clone nodes will fail to establish pair-wise keys with their neighbors since the clone nodes belong to an old deployed generation.

2.2.4. A Randomized, Efficient, and Distributed Protocol for the Detection of Node Replication Attacks in Wireless Sensor Networks.

This technique falls into the category of witness node-based techniques. Conti et al. have proposed a randomized, efficient, and distributed protocol called RED [42, 43] for the detection of node replication attack. It is executed at fixed intervals of time and consists in two steps. In first step, a random value, *rand*, is shared between all the nodes through base station. The second step is called detection phase. In the detection phase, each node broadcasts its claim (ID and location) to its neighboring nodes. Each neighbor node that hears a claim sends (with probability p) this claim to a set of g pseudorandomly selected network locations. The pseudo random function takes as an input ID, random number, and g. Every node in the path (from claiming node to the witness destination) forwards the message to its neighbor nearest to the destination. Hence, the replicated nodes will be detected in each detection phase. When next time the RED executes, the witness nodes will be different since the random value which is broadcasted by the BS is changed.

2.2.5. Efficient Distributed Detection of Node Replication Attacks in Sensor Networks.

These techniques falls into the category of witness node-based techniques. Zhu et al. [44, 45] have proposed two distributed protocols for detecting node replication attacks called single deterministic cell (SDC) and parallel multiple probabilistic cells (P-MPC). In both protocols, the whole sensor network is divided into cells to form a geographic grid. In SDC, each node ID is uniquely mapped to one of the cells in the grid. When executing detection procedure, each node broadcasts a location claim to its neighbors. Then, each neighbor forwards the location claim with a probability to a unique cell by executing a geographic hash function [46] with the input of node ID. Once any node in the destination cell receives the location claim, it floods the location claim to the entire cell. Each node in the destination cell stores the location claim with a probability. Therefore, the clone nodes will be detected with a certain probability since the location claims of clone nodes will be forwarded to the same cell. Like SDC, in the P-MPC scheme, a geographic hash function [46] is employed to map node identity to the destination cells. However, instead of mapping to single deterministic cell, in P-MPC the location claim is mapped and forwarded to multiple deterministic cells with various probabilities. The rest of the procedure is similar to SDC.

2.2.6. (Space-Time)-Related Pairwise Key Predistribution Scheme for Wireless Sensor Networks.
This technique falls into the category of base station-based techniques. Fei et al. [47] have proposed a polynomial based space-time-related pairwise key predistribution scheme (PSPP-PKPS, for short PSPP) for wireless sensor networks, which relates the keying material of a node with its deployment time and location. In PSPP, the keying material of a node can only work at its initial deployment location. If a node leaves its deployment location, its keying material will become invalid. By using this idea, their scheme provides resistance against the clone attack.

2.2.7. A Neighbor-Based Detection Scheme for Wireless Sensor Networks against Node Replication Attacks.
This technique falls into the category of neighborhood-based techniques. Ko et al. [48] have proposed a real time neighbor-based detection scheme (NBDS) for node replication attack in wireless sensor networks. The main idea of their scheme is that when a person moves to another community, he will meet new neighbors and tell his new neighbors where he comes from through chatting. But new neighbors will not check if he lies or not. However, if some of his new neighbors ask his previous neighbors whether this newcomer really comes from the community that he claims, the identity of the newcomer can be implicitly verified. If previous neighbors say that this person still lives in the original neighborhood, the newcomer can be detected as a replica. This observation motivates their research on node replication attacks, and replicas are detected in the same way.

2.2.8. Distributed Detection of Node Capture Attacks in Wireless Sensor Networks.
This technique falls into the category of base station-based techniques. Ho [49] has proposed a node capture detection scheme for wireless sensor networks. Their scheme detects the captured sensor nodes by using the sequential analysis. They use the fact that the physically captured nodes are not present in the network during the period from the captured time to the redeployment time. Accordingly, captured nodes would not participate in any network operations during that period. By leveraging this intuition, the captured nodes can be detected by using the sequential probability ratio test (SPRT) [50]. The protocol first measures the absence time period of a sensor node and then compares it to a predefined threshold. If it is more than threshold value, the sensor node is considered as a captured node. The efficient node capture detection capability depends on a properly configured threshold value.

2.2.9. Memory Efficient Protocols for Detecting Node Replication Attacks in Wireless Sensor Networks.
These techniques fall into the category of witness node-based techniques. Zhang et al. [3] have proposed four memory efficient multicast protocols for replication detection, namely, memory efficient multicast with Bloom filters (B-MEM), memory efficient multicast with Bloom filters and Cell Forwarding (BC-MEM), memory efficient multicast with cross forwarding (C-MEM), and memory efficient multicast with cross and cell forwarding (CC-MEM). The first protocol B-MEM use Bloom filters to compress the information stored at the sensors and the location claim $C\alpha$ of a node α is multicast via its neighbors to a number of randomly selected locations in the network. Each neighbor β has a probability p to participate in the multicast. If it does, it becomes a witness node and sends $C\alpha$ to a random location in the network. The node closest to that location will be another witness node w to store $C\alpha$. The watcher nodes on the routing path P from β to w only store the membership of $ID\alpha$ and $l\alpha$ in the Bloom filters. Such membership information can help them detect any conflicting location claim $C'\alpha$ received later, and guide $C'\alpha$ along P to either β or w, which will then broadcast both $C\alpha$ and $C'\alpha$ to the entire network in order to revoke node α and its replicas.

The second protocol BC-MEM is designed on top of B-MEM. It adopts a cell forwarding technique that not only solves the crossover problem but also reduces the memory overhead. The deployment area is divided into virtual cells. In each cell an anchor point is assigned for every node in the network. The anchor point for a node α is determined by α ID. The node closest to the anchor point is called the anchor node for α. In B-MEM, when a location claim is forwarded on a line segment, all intermediate nodes on the line serve as watchers, while the first node and the last node serve as witnesses. In contrast, in BC-MEM a claim is not forwarded on the line segment. It is forwarded to the anchor point in the next cell where the line segment intersects. The claim is forwarded from one anchor node to another until reaching the last cell. The anchor nodes in the intermediate cells are watchers, and the anchor nodes in the first and last cells are witnesses.

The third protocol C-MEM is designed on top of B-MEM. It incorporates a new cross forwarding technique to solve the crowded center problem. B-MEM stores the information about a location claim along randomly selected line segments, which are likely to pass the center area of the deployment. On the other hand, C-MEM first selects a random point (called the cross point) in the network and forwards the location claim to that point. From there, it forwards the claim along the horizontal and vertical lines that pass the cross point. While the node closest to the cross point is a witness node, the nodes along the horizontal and vertical lines are watchers. Since the cross points for all location claims are distributed uniformly at random in the network, it is no longer true that the lines pass the center area more frequently. C-MEM does not use cell forwarding.

The fourth protocol CC-MEM combines cross forwarding and cell forwarding to solve both the crowded center problem and the crossover problem, such that it can detect node replication attack with high probability and low overhead.

2.2.10. Active Detection of Node Replication Attacks. This technique falls into the category of base station-based techniques. Melchor et al. [51] have proposed a distributed protocol for the detection of replication attack for wireless sensor networks, in which each node verifies at random a few other nodes in the network. The proposed protocol does not build a distributed database of location claims that will contain local conflicting claims when replicas exist. The idea is that each node will actively test if 1 k other random nodes are replicated or not; they call them the scrutinized nodes. In order to test whether a scrutinized node α is replicated or not, 2 k nodes are randomly chosen in the network and asked to forward to α a request for a signed location claim. If two replicas exist, each will probably receive a request, and if both answer, two conflicting claims will be obtained by the queerer.

2.2.11. Randomly Directed Exploration. An Efficient Node Clone Detection Protocol in Wireless Sensor Networks (RDE). This technique falls into the category of witness node-based techniques. Zhijun et al. [52] have presented a novel clone node detection protocol called randomly directed exploration. This protocol does not call for any unrealistic assumptions. Each node only needs to know its neighbor nodes. During the detection procedure, nodes issue claiming messages containing neighbor list with a maximum hop limit to randomly selected neighbors. The previous transmission of a claiming message forms a direction, and then the intermediate node tries to follow the direction to forward the message. During forwarding messages, the intermediate nodes explore the claiming messages for node clone detection. In such a simple way, the proposed protocol can efficiently detect clone nodes in the dense sensor networks. In addition, the protocol consumes almost minimum memory during detection, and communication payload is satisfactory. It can scale to large configurations. They have implemented the protocol in the OMNet++ simulation framework.

2.2.12. Random-Walk-Based Approach to Detect Clone Attacks in Wireless Sensor Networks. These two techniques fall into the category of witness node-based techniques. Zeng et al. [4] have proposed two protocols RAndom WaLk (RAWL) and Table-assisted RAndom WaLk (TRAWL) for the detection of clone attack in wireless sensor networks. The RAndom WaLk (RAWL) starts several random walks randomly in the network for each node a, and then selects the passed nodes as the witness nodes of node a. RAWL works in four steps in each execution. In the first step, each node broadcasts a signed location claim. In the second step, each of the node neighbors probabilistically forwards the claim to some randomly selected nodes. In the thirds step, each randomly selected node sends a message containing the claim to start a random walk in the network, and the passed nodes are selected as witness nodes and will store the claim. In the fourth step, if any witness receives different location claims for same node ID, it can use these claims to revoke the replicated node.

The second protocol, Table-assisted RAndom WaLk (TRAWL), is based on RAWL and adds a trace table at each node to reduce memory cost. Usually, the memory cost is due to the storage of location claims, but in TRAWL each node only stores $O(1)$ location claims (although the size of the trace table is still $O(\sqrt{n}\log n)$, the size of a table entry is much smaller than the size of a location claim). When a randomly chosen node starts a random walk, all the passed nodes will still become witness nodes. However, now they do not definitely store the location claim, instead, they store the location claim independently with probability $c_2\sqrt{n}\log n$, where c_2 is a constant. Also, each witness node will create a new entry in its trace table for recording the pass of a location claim.

2.2.13. CINORA: Cell-Based Identification of Node Replication Attack in Wireless Sensor Networks. Gautam Thakur [24] has proposed two distributed methods for detecting node replication attack based on intersecting sets called CINORA-Inset and restricted cell two-phase authentication model called CINORA-Hybrid. Initially, the sensor network is divided into geographical cells similar to the existing cellular network. However, their approach does not deterministically map a nodes identity to a cell. In CINORA-Inset, location claims from the nodes are distributed among a subset of cells to detect any replication. These cells are generated from a nonnull intersecting subset algorithm. The inherent property of this algorithm is for any two subsets C_i and C_j of total $1 \le i$, $j \le N$ cells, and $C_i \cap C_j \ne \emptyset$. Thus, during the authentication phase at least one cell receives conflicting location claims if adversary has ever attempted to replicate a legitimate node. In CINORA-Hybrid a base station-based two-phase authentication scheme is used in which a sensor node has a valid residence entry permit for a cell. If permitted and nodes current residing cell is different or two (or more) similar permits are detected with different location claims, then that identity node is removed from the network.

2.2.14. A Note-Based Randomized and Distributed Protocol for Detecting Node Replication Attacks in Wireless Sensor Networks. This technique falls into the category of witness node-based techniques. Meng et al. [53] have proposed a note-based randomized and distributed protocol called NRDP, for detecting node replication attacks, which introduces no significant overhead on the resource-constrained sensors. This protocol does not need the geographic locations of nodes as well. Three types of nodes are assumed in the network, namely, a *claimer node, a reporter node*, and *a witness node*. A node which broadcasts a claim message is a *claimer node*. Neighbor node which forwards a claim message is a *reporter node*. And the destination node of a claim message is a *witness node*. This protocol works in two phases: neighbor discovery period and replication detection period. In the beginning of NRDP, it is a neighbor discovery period in which each node in the network broadcasts a message within its one-hop neighbors. After neighbor discovery period, each node in the network gets a neighbor list. The replication detection period starts when the neighbor discovery period ends. Replication detect period consist of two steps. The first step is called request-note step and the second step is called send claim step. In *request-note step*, node α randomly chooses a node γ from its neighbor list as its reporter node, and then sends a request-note message to the reporter node. Upon receiving α request-note message, node γ replies with a signature note message which contains a note. The parameter time is fresh time of the note. Nodes in the network use it to identify the validity of a note received in different iterations. Note is an evidence to prove that the reporter node of a claimer node is existing and valid. In the *send-claim step*, every node generates a claim message, which includes a signed subneighbor list and a note from the corresponding reporter node. The parameter list in the claim message is an ID list, which consists of q α's neighbor node IDs. And the reporter node γ must be in the list. Each node α then broadcasts the claim message in one-hop neighbors. When the reporter node receives corresponding claim message, it first verifies the signature and the time fresh of the note contained in the claim message. Further, the reporter node verifies that the list in the claim message contains its ID. If all the verifications succeed, using a pseudorandom function, the reporter node calculates g witness nodes for the claimer node. This function takes in input, the ID of the claimer node, which is the first argument of the claim message, the current rand value, and the number g of witness nodes that has to be generated. The witness nodes of a certain node change in different iterations. A trusted entity broadcasts a seed *rand* to the network before each detection iteration starts. This prevents the adversary from anticipating the witness nodes in a given protocol iteration. The reporter node analyzes the claim message, then generates a forwarded claim message, and forwards the forwarded claim message to all the g witness nodes. The forwarded claim message just contains the subneighbor list signed by claimer node, without note. When a node receives a claim message, it first checks whether it is the corresponding reporter node. If it is the reporter node of the claimer node, it checks the signature, the fresh of the note, and the list in the claim message. If it is not the reporter node, with probability pc it does the checking jobs as the reporter node does. It is necessary for nonreporter node neighbors to do the checking jobs with probability pc. This can prevent a claimer node from specifying a nonexisting neighbor node as its reporter node. Each node in the network has to specify an actual neighbor node as its reporter node, or it will be detected as a replicated node by its neighbor nodes.

Each witness node that receives a forwarded claim message verifies the signature and time fresh firstly. Then, it compares the claim to each previously stored claim. If it is the first time received claim contains IDα, then it simply stores the claim. If a claim from IDα has been received, the witness checks whether the claimed neighbor list is the same as the stored claim. If a conflict is found, the witness detects a node replication attack. Then, the witness triggers a revocation procedure for IDα. Actually, because there is always only one reporter node for a claimer node, if the claimer node is a valid node, its corresponding witness nodes would never receive more than one forwarded claim message from the claimer node. Therefore, once a witness node receives two

claims containing the same ID in one detection iteration, it detects a replication attack. The two signature claims become evidence to trigger the revocation of the replicated node. The witness node forwards both claims to the base station. The base station will broadcast a signature message within the network to revoke the replicated node.

2.2.15. Distributed Detection of Replication with Deployment Knowledge in Wireless Sensor Networks.
This technique falls into the category of group-based techniques. Ho et al. [54] have proposed three group deployment knowledge-based schemes for the detection of node replication attack in wireless sensor networks. Their schemes are based on the assumption that nodes are deployed in groups. By taking advantage of group deployment knowledge, the proposed schemes perform replica detection in a distributed, efficient, and secure manner. The sensors can be preloaded with relevant knowledge about their own group's membership and all group locations. Then, the sensors in the same group should be deployed at the same time in the location given to that group. The three proposed schemes are basic, location claim, and multigroup approaches. The first scheme is the basic scheme in which each node only accepts the messages from the member's of their own group (trusted nodes) not from other groups (untrusted nodes). It stops intercommunication between groups. An advantage of this basic scheme is low communication and computational or memory overhead. But the problem that is even honest nodes suffer from communication due to the fact that the deployment points are far away from their group. The network becomes poorly connected and not suitable for high resilient applications. To solve this problem, second scheme is proposed which also forwards messages from untrusted nodes as long as they provide provable evidence that they are not replicas but based on only predetermined locations for replica detection. The second scheme achieves high replication detection capability with less communication, computational, and storage overheads as compared to the first scheme, but there is a risk of DoS by flooding fake claims.

The third scheme protects against this kind of aggressive adversary. Every sensor node sends its neighbor's location claims to multiple groups rather than a single group. This scheme has higher communication overhead. It can provide a trade-off between the overhead and resilience to attack. This scheme provides very strong resilience to node compromise, since attacker needs to compromise multiple groups of nodes to prevent replicas being undetected.

2.2.16. Distributed Detection of Node Replication Attack Resilient to Many Compromised Nodes in Wireless Sensor Networks.
This technique falls into the category of group-based techniques. Sei and Honiden [55] have proposed a distributed protocol for the detection of node replication attack that is resilient to many compromised nodes. Their method does not need any reliable/trusted entities. To prevent an attacker from learning the location of a witness node of a compromised node, the protocol uses a one-time seed for each replicated node detection process; that is, each node has the role of

starting a detection process, and it is preloaded with the assigned turn number and seed for the turn.

When node has a turn starting detection process, it sends the seed and its ID with a signature. Other nodes verify the signature and execute the detection process if the verification succeeds. They divide nodes into groups to increase resiliency to fault nodes and compromised nodes. The role of the starting detection process is not assigned to each node but to each group. If at least one node of a group survives, the group can start the detection process during its turn. An attacker must compromise the first node of a group which has the next turn starting detection process if he wants to learn the location of the witness node in the next detection process.

2.2.17. A Resilient and Efficient Replication Attack Detection Scheme for Wireless Sensor Networks. This technique falls into the category witness node-based techniques. Kim et al. [56] have presented a distributed, deterministic approach to detect node replication attack. Their scheme works in three steps: initialization, witness node discovery phase, and node revocation phase. In initialization phase, before deployment, a base station (BS) associates a particular location coordinate (hereafter referred to as the verification point, vp) with each node id using geographic hash function F. A vp is the target location coordinate in the network where each sensor node will be verified, and it can be predetermined by a network operator to a certain extent with experience. In witness node discovery phase, the replicas with the same id but different deployment locations are detected through location claim message. In the last phase of node revocation base station BS floods the revocation node lists after checking out the revocation request message received from the witness nodes. Once a BS receives this revocation request message, it checks whether the revocation request message is correctly encrypted by witness node using a pair-wise key shared with witness node. If the key is correct, a BS floods a list of replica nodes including reporter node through the network. If the key fails, which means that an attacker sent the forged replica revocation message, the BS regards that reporter node has been compromised.

3. Comparison of Node Replica Detection Schemes for Static WSNs

In this paper, we have addressed an important attack on WSN referred to as node replication attack or clone node attack. So far, many techniques have been proposed to detect node replication attack in static WSNs which are broadly categorized into centralized and distributed techniques. We have compared all the techniques according to their year of publication, identifying their shortcomings.

3.1. Centralized Techniques. Centralized techniques are considered to be the first solutions for detecting replicated nodes which are simple but suffer from several common drawbacks. Some of the limitations of centralized techniques are found to be fairly serious like the base station which introduces a single point of failure, and any compromise of the base station will render the solution useless; also, even if there are no attacks the nodes surrounding the base station will suffer an undue communication burden which may shorten the lifetime of a network, and this approach also incurs an observable processing delay. Consequently, centralized detections have barely an advantage over distributed detections making a distributed solution a necessity. The asymptotic performance of centralized techniques (including their memory and communication cost) is shown in Table 1. Localized voting protocols are also considered as the first naïve solutions for the detection of clone nodes which are unable to deal with distributed node replication attacks, in which replicas are placed at least two hops away from each other. In order to detect replicas which are spreading anywhere in the network a fully distributed solution is needed that also incurs small memory and energy overhead.

In 2004, one of the first solutions for detecting replicated nodes was proposed by Dutertre et al., outlined in [57] which was based on a centralized base station for node replica detection. This scheme was the most straightforward one and a naive solution that provided a low defense against node replication attacks, suffering from several drawbacks as mentioned before.

In 2007, Brooks et al. [32] proposed a clone detection protocol which was based on random pairwise key pre-distribution schemes and used to tackle with detection of cloned cryptographic keys rather than clones sensor nodes. This solution seemed effective but only when the size of the keys predistributed to each node is small and more clones exist in the network, thus implying poor detection accuracy. Moreover, it is assumed in the protocol that the connections between all nodes are possibly equal, while practically in WSNs, any sensor node can only communicate with a limited number of neighbors within a finite wireless communication radius. Another drawback of this solution is that it has neglected to ensure that the participating clones report their keys honestly to the base station.

Choi et al. [23] proposed another centralized detection technique named SET in 2007 which was an attempt to reduce the detection overhead by computing set operations. But the message authentication codes used for additional security resulted in even higher detection cost in terms of computation and communication. Moreover, SET protocol is highly complex due to its complicated components, and unexpectedly an adversary can misuse the detection protocol to revoke honest nodes.

Another centralized approach was proposed in 2008 by Xing et al. [34] which used social fingerprint for the detection of clones, but it was purely based on fixed WSNs, and thus neither node addition nor disappearance can be handled. Furthermore, besides all the common limitations of centralized solutions, it cannot handle a sophisticated replica which can cleverly compute by itself a fingerprint consistent with its neighborhood in order to flee the detection at the sensor side. A more intelligent replica can dodge and avoid the detection at the base station simply by not communicating with the base station.

The most recent solution for the detection of node replication attack or clones is a centralized technique given

TABLE 1: Asymptotic performance of centralized schemes.

Type of scheme	Technique/scheme	Communication cost	Memory cost
Key usage based	Brooks et al. scheme [32]	$O(n \log n)$	—
Base station based	SET [23]	$O(n)$	$O(d)$
	CSI [38]	$O(n \log n)$	—
Neighborhood social signature based	Xing et al. scheme [34]	$C \cdot (1 + \text{ratio})$	$O(d) + \min(M, \omega \cdot \log_2 M)$
Cluster head-based techniques	Znaidi et al. scheme [36]	$O(t^2)$	$O(t)$

n: no. of nodes in the network, ω: the column weight in the superimposed s-disjunct code, C: message generated by sensor node, d: degree of neighboring nodes, M: the number of rows in the superimposed s-disjunct code, ratio $= \log_2 M / L_{\text{packet}} \times 100\%$, and L_{packet}: the bit-length of a regular message.

by Yu et al. [38] in 2012. They have used a novel concept of compressed sensing for the identification of clones in the sensor network. This technique has the lowest communication overhead, but it suffers from all the common drawbacks of centralized techniques as BS is responsible for the aggregation of the result (decision) about the identification of clones in the network.

Considering the limitations of centralized detection schemes, the researchers move to a distributed solution for detecting clones, and the first naïve solution that was proposed was called node-to-network broadcasting (N2NB). Although the scheme was simple it also suffered from high memory and communication cost for large sensor networks.

3.2. Distributed Techniques. We have investigated a dozen distributed detection protocols by asymptotically comparing their communication and memory costs, and they are shown in Table 2. As all the proposed solutions use different motivations and assumptions and thus have their respective strengths and weaknesses, we cannot make any general or definite remarks that which solution is the best one.

Distributed techniques for the detection of clone node attack are categorized into three main classes, namely, witness node-based, neighbor-based, and generation-based or group-based techniques. All the three categories have their own pros and cons. For neighbor-based technique [48], the neighboring nodes should be static and any addition or removal of nodes is not possible throughout the detection process because in doing so the detection process is affected severely. For the generation- or group-based techniques [40, 41, 54, 55] all the nodes are deployed in groups, and no new node can be added in a particular group. Also, nodes should have location or network information before node deployment. These techniques only prevent the node replication attack but are unable to detect the clone nodes.

The witness node-based techniques use a framework called claimer-reporter-witness framework in which a node referred to as claimer locally broadcasts it, location claim to its neighbors. Each neighbor serves as a reporter and employs a function to map the claimer ID, to a witness. The neighbor forwards the claim to the witness and if it receives two different location claims for the same nodded id then it means that the adversary has replicated a node. The adversary can also employ a function to know about the witness for the given claimer ID and may also locate and compromise the witness node before she inserts the replicas into the wireless sensor networks in order to evade the detection.

A relatively more mature distributed detection scheme was proposed in 2007 by Parno et al. [28] known as deterministic multicast (DM) which was the first to use a framework called claimer-reporter-witness framework. Although its design goal was to reduce communication cost, it was treated as an unfavorable protocol because of its several drawbacks. Firstly, it does not provide much security as an adversary only needs to compromise all the g witnesses for a given claimer id deploying as many replicas as she desires without activating an alarm. Secondly, it does not work for large g as both the network communication and the node storage are proportional to g, and with very small g, an adversary can produce unlimited replicas. Considering DM as unappealing due to its deterministic property, Parno et al. [28] have proposed and developed two more techniques as improvements of DM protocol, namely, randomized multicast (RM) and line selected multicast (LSM). The security was improved but at the price of increased communication/memory costs. In both of these protocols the problem lies in the selection of witness nodes (i.e., Probabilities) and also it is not always true that location claims of clone nodes are received to the same witness node. Moreover, both RM and LSM are unable to detect masked replication attack. To decrease the communication cost of RM protocol, LSM was developed as a less expensive version of RM, but it suffers from uneven distribution of witnesses nodes. As majority of witness nodes are selected from the center of the network, thus the energy of these nodes is depleted soon, and also they become the point of interest for the adversary.

Zhu et al. [44, 45] proposed two techniques called single deterministic cell (SDC) and parallel multiple probabilistic cells (P-MPC) in 2007 as the variations of DM. Practically, both of these techniques depend upon the careful selection of a cell size (s) because if the cell size is too large, they incur high communication cost like N2NB, and if s is too small, it will be very easy for an adversary to trounce them by compromising all nodes in the g deterministic tiny cells. An important problem with SDC is that in order to reduce the broadcast overhead, it requires to execute the flooding only when the first copy of a node location claim arrives at the cell, and the following copies are ignored. In doing this, the node in the cell that first receives the location claim is unable to distinguish between claims of original node and replica node.

Another attempt to detect clones was made by Conti et al. [42, 43] in 2007 who have proposed a randomized, efficient, and distributed protocol named RED by combining

TABLE 2: Asymptotic performance of distributed schemes.

Type of scheme	Technique/scheme	Communication cost	Memory cost
Node-to-network broadcasting	N2NB [28]	$O(n^2)$	$O(1)$
Witness node	DM [28]	$O(g \log \sqrt{n}/d)$	$O(g)$
	RM [28]	$O(n^2)$	$O(\sqrt{n})$
	LSM [28]	$O(n\sqrt{n})$	$O(\sqrt{n})$
	RED [42, 43]	$O(g \cdot p \cdot dn\sqrt{n})$	$O(g \cdot p \cdot d)$
	SDC [44, 45]	$O(r \cdot \sqrt{n}) + O(s)$	$O(\omega)$
	P-MPC [44, 45]	$O(r \cdot \sqrt{n}) + O(s)$	$O(\omega)$
	B-MEM [3]	$O(k \cdot n \cdot \sqrt{n})$	$O(tk + t'k\sqrt{n})$
	BC-MEM [3]	—	$O(tk + t'k\sqrt{n'})$
	C-MEM [3]	—	$O(t + t'\sqrt{n})$
	CC-MEM [3]	—	$O(t + t'\sqrt{n'})$
	Melchor et al. [51]	$O(\sqrt{n})$	$O(d)$
	RDE [52]	$O(d \cdot n \cdot \sqrt{n})$	$O(d)$
	RAWL [4]	$O(\sqrt{n}\log n)$	$O(\sqrt{n}\log n)$
	TRAWL [4]	$O(\sqrt{n}\log n)$	$O(1)^2$
	Kim et al. [56]	$O(\sqrt{n})$	$O(\sqrt{n})$
Generation or group based	Bekara and Laurent-Maknavicius [40, 41]	$O(\sqrt{n})$	$O(1)$
	Basic scheme [54]	$O(m)$	$O(m)$
	Location claim base scheme [54]	$O(m + d)$	$O(d + 2m)$
	Multigroup base scheme [54]	$3 * O(m + d)$	$O(d + 2 * m (1 + D_{\max}))$
	Sei and Honiden [55]	$O(r)$	$O(r \cdot \sqrt{n})$
—	Ho [49]	$O(n\sqrt{n})$	$O(n)$
Neighborhood based	NBDS [48]	$O(r \cdot \sqrt{n})$	$O(r)$

n: no. of nodes in the network, d: degree of neighboring nodes, g: no. of witness nodes, r: communication radius, s: the number of sensors in a cell, p: probability that neighboring node will forward the location claim, ω: the column weight in the superimposed s-disjunct code, and ξ: distinct IDs from set of nodes as monitor.

the benefits of both DM and RM. This protocol is considered to be the most promising detection protocol which has solved the crowded center problem as the selection of witness nodes is random and fully distributed. Also, RED [4] is such an "area oblivious" protocol that associates sensor nodes with almost even responsibility, and the selection of witness nodes is pseudorandom which leads to a uniform witness distribution. Besides these advantages, the only drawback of RED is the deterministic selection of witness nodes and that the infrastructure for distributing RED's random seed may not always be available. RED is also unable to detect masked replication attack.

Bekara et al. [40, 41] in 2007 proposed a solution for preventing WSN from node replication attack which exploits the fact that excluding new nodes from joining the network can prevent replication attacks. The main drawback of this scheme is that the sensor nodes are bound to their groups and geographic locations.

In 2009, Zhang et al. [3] have proposed four memory efficient multicast protocols for the detection of replicated nodes, namely, Bloom filter MEM, Bloom filters and cell forwarding MEM, cross forwarding MEM, and last is cross forwarding and cell forwarding MEM. B-MEM is an extension of LSM, but it incurs additional memory consumption per node, and it may also lower the detection rate of LSM due to false verifications (false positives of Bloom filters).

BC-MEM requires highly accurate localization due to its cell division and anchor node selection which may not be affordable for current generation of WSNs. Also, an adversary can elude BC-MEM by compromising certain deterministic anchor nodes. In case of both C-MEM and CC-MEM, cross forwarding achieves high detection probability for convex deployment field (particularly for rectangle-shaped deployment field), but for other irregular topologies considered by LSM (like thin cross and large H), these two schemes may work poorly by dropping the detection rate significantly.

A simplified version of N2NB was proposed by Zhang et al. [3] in 2009 known as randomly directed exploration (RDE). Its network communication overhead is reduced, but storage cost remains the same with N2NB. The detection rate is also decreased and may not be very significant even for a convex deployment field concluding that RDE appears to be feasible only for an ideal network model.

Another work in this area is done by Zeng et al. [4] in 2010 who have proposed two detection protocols, namely, RAndom WaLk (RAWL) and Table-assisted RAndom WaLk (TRAWL) for the detection of node replication attack. Both of these protocols are an extension of LSM and thus suffer from the same drawbacks. Although they have much higher detection probability than LSM, both RAWL and TRAWL require more than twice the communication overhead of LSM.

For an inclusive survey, we have also analyzed some other distributed techniques which are neither very popular nor have promising results in detecting node replication attack. These techniques include Ho et al. [54] proposed in 2009, Kim et al. [56] proposed in 2009, and Meng et al. [53] proposed in 2010.

4. Detection Techniques for Mobile WSNs

Mobility has become an important area of research for WSN community. In mobile WSNs, mobility plays a key role in the execution of the application as the introduction of mobile entities can resolve some problems and offer many advantages over the static WSNs. The node replica detection techniques developed for static WSNs, do not work when the nodes are expected to move as in mobile WSNs, and thus they have turned out to be ineffective for mobile WSNs. As a result some techniques (still not mature enough) have also been developed for mobile WSNs to detect the replica or clone nodes. These techniques are classified into two main classes as centralized and distributed and are described below.

4.1. Centralized Techniques

4.1.1. Fast Detection of Replica Node Attack in Mobile Sensor

Networks Using Sequential Analysis. Ho et al. [58, 59] have proposed a mobile replica detection scheme based on the sequential probability ratio test (SPRT) [50]. Their protocol is based on the fact that an uncompromised mobile node should never move at speeds in excess of the system-configured maximum speed. As a result, an uncompromised (original) mobile sensor node measured speed will appear to be at most the system-configured maximum speed as long as speed measurement system with low error rate is employed. On the other hand, replica nodes will appear to move much faster than original nodes, and thus their measured speeds will likely be over the system-configured maximum speed because they need to be at two (or more) different places at once. Accordingly, if it is observed that a mobile node measured speed is over the system-configured maximum speed, it is then highly likely that at least two nodes with the same identity are present in the network. By leveraging this intuition, the SPRT is performed on every mobile node using a null hypothesis that the mobile node has not been replicated and an alternate hypothesis that it has been replicated. In using the SPRT, the occurrence of a speed that either lessens or exceeds the system-configured maximum speed will lead to acceptance of the null and alternate hypotheses, respectively. Once the alternate hypothesis is accepted, the replica nodes will be revoked from the network.

4.1.2. A New Protocol for the Detection of Node Replication

Attacks in Mobile Wireless Sensor Networks. Deng and Xiong [60] have proposed a new protocol to detect the replicas in mobile WSNs. They have used the idea of polynomial-based pair-wise key pre-distribution and Bloom Filters which insure that the replicas can never lie about their real identifiers and collect the number of pair-wise keys established by each sensor node. Replicas are detected by looking at whether the number of pair-wise keys established by them exceeds the threshold. The protocol works in three steps, node initialization, pair-wise establishment, and detection. In node initialization, before nodes are deployed, the key server randomly generates a bivariate symmetric polynomial over a finite field. After deployment between nodes, pairwise keys are established. Each node periodically constructs a report, which includes its ID and counting Bloom filter (or compressed counting Bloom filter), and sends it to the base station. At base station, counting bloom filters collect the number of pairwise keys established by each node. Nodes whose number of pair-wise keys exceeds the threshold value are considered to be the clones.

4.2. Distributed Techniques

4.2.1. Mobile Sensor Networks Resilient against Node

Replication Attacks. Chia et al. [61] proposed a novel protocol, called extremely efficient detection (XED), against node replication attack in mobile sensor networks. The idea behind XED is motivated from the observation that for the networks without replicas, if a sensor node s_i meets the other sensor node s_j at earlier time and s_i sends a random number r to s_j at that time, then when s_i and s_j meet again, s_i can ascertain whether this is the node s_j met before by requesting the random number r. Based on this observation, a "remember and challenge strategy" is proposed. Once two sensor nodes, s_i and s_j, are within the communication ranges of each other, they first, respectively, generate random numbers $rs_i \rightarrow s_j$ and $rs_j \rightarrow s_i$ of b bits, and then they exchange their generated random numbers. They also use a table to record the node ID, the generated random number, and the received random number in their respective memory. In case the pair of two nodes met before, the above procedure is also performed such that the random number stored in the memory is replaced by the newly received random number. Consider the example shown in Figure 4, in which the sensor node s_i meets another sensor node s_j. If s_i never meets s_j before, they exchange random numbers. Otherwise, the sensor node s_i requests the sensor node s_j for the random number $rs_i \rightarrow s_j$ exchanged at easier time. For the sensor node s_i, if the sensor node s_j cannot replies or reply a number which does not match the number in s_i memory, s_i announces the detection of a replica. When the replicas meet the genuine nodes, the replicas can always pretend that they meet for the first time. However, if the genuine nodes have a record showing that they ever met at earlier time, the replicas are also detected.

4.2.2. Efficient and Distributed Detection of Node Replication

Attacks in Mobile Sensor Networks. Chia et al. [62] proposed an efficient and distributed detection (EDD) scheme and its variant, storage-efficient EDD (SEDD) scheme to detect the node replication attack. The idea behind EDD and SEDD is motivated from the following observations. For a network without replicas, the number of times, $\mu 1$, in which the node u encounters a specific node v, should be limited in a given time

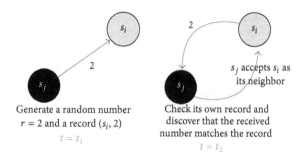

Generate a random number
$r = 2$ and a record $(s_i, 2)$
$t = t_1$

s_j accepts s_i as
its neighbor

Check its own record and
discover that the received
number matches the record
$t = t_2$

FIGURE 4: The operations between two genuine nodes in XED at time t_1 and t_2 (gray and black nodes are genuine) [61].

interval of length T with high probability. For a network with two replicas v, the number of times, $\mu2$, in which u encounters the replicas with the same ID v, should be larger than a threshold within the time interval of length T. According to these observations, if each node can discriminate between these two cases, each node has the ability to identify the replicas. The EDD scheme is composed of two steps: offline step and online step. The offline step is performed by the network planner before the sensor deployment. The goal is to calculate the parameters, including the length T of the time interval and the threshold ψ used for discrimination between the genuine nodes and the replicas. On the other hand, the online step will be performed by each node per move. Each node checks whether the encountered nodes are replicas by comparing ψ with the number of encounters at the end of a time interval. It can be observed from EDD that each node should maintain a list L, leading to $O(n)$ storage overhead. A storage-efficient EDD (SEDD) scheme is proposed based on the tradeoff between storage overhead and time interval length. The basic idea behind SEDD is that instead of monitoring all nodes, each node only monitors a subset of nodes, called monitor set, in a specific time interval. When the cardinality of the monitor set is selected as ξ, the simplest way for each node to select the nodes to be monitored at the beginning of a time interval is to randomly pick ξ distinct IDs from $\{1, \ldots, n\}$. Since the storage overhead is equal to the number of nodes being monitored, the storage overhead is reduced to the cardinality of the monitor set, $O(\xi)$, in the SEDD scheme.

4.2.3. Patrol Detection for Replica Attacks on Wireless Sensor

Networks. Wang and Shi [63] have employed mobile nodes as patrollers to detect replicas distributed in different zones in a network, in which a basic patrol detection protocol and two detection algorithms for stationary and mobile modes are presented. The detection of replicas in stationary sensors is based on the assumptions that if two or more sensors in different locations have the same ID, then all the nodes with the ID will be regarded as compromised nodes or its replicas. Also, for mobile sensors (patroller), if a mobile node moves with a speed higher than the denoted maximum speed, it will be regarded as a replica attack. In the replica detection of static sensor nodes, when a mobile patrol node moves to a new zone, it first discovers its location and then broadcasts

its patrol claim. Each node will be patrolled by at least two mobile nodes. After receiving the location messages, the stationary node takes the mobile nodes who patrolled him as the anchor nodes and will send the patrol node its location claim. After collecting the answer message, patrol node will check the location of node, and if the distance is larger than the signal range, it ignores the wrong message. Otherwise, it will check the ID of the answer message by using the security assumption "A legitimate ID only has one location." Then, it saves the answer from the original node (benign node) in a whitelist, saves the replica node ID in a blacklist, and revokes the replica ID by refusing to distribute secret material and broadcasting its two answer messages to other mobiles nodes. Then, patrol node will move to another location to send his patrol claim in another interval. After a round, it collects all the saved information of the white- and blacklists to the user when collecting the sensing data. If the replicas are deployed in a zone where a patrol node collects their answer message in a patrol interval, then the patroller can revoke them immediately after he receives the second answer and the distance between the two locations exceeds. Else if the replicas' answers are collected by different patrol nodes, then they will be found by the base station or by exchange messages of patrollers after a round. If the adversary compromises and replicates the patrol node, firstly, an original mobile patroller will wait for the answer message after he reaches a new position and sends his claim in time T, so there is a static period interval after the patrol broadcasts his claim. Accordingly, if the patroller node moves and changes its position in time $(T, T + \text{interval})$, then it is highly likely that at least two nodes with the same identity are present in the network. Further, the mobile patroller should never move faster than the system-configured maximum speed $V_{\max}$.

4.2.4. Single-Hop Detection of Node Clone Attacks in Mobile

Wireless Sensor Networks. Lou et al. [64] have proposed a node clone attack detection protocol, namely, the single hop detection (SHP) for mobile wireless sensor networks. The SHD protocol exploits the fact that at any time, a physical node (or equivalently, its node ID and private key) cannot appear at different neighborhood community; otherwise, there must be replicas in the network. The neighborhood community of a node is characterized by its one-hop neighbor node list, which is readily available in a typical WSN since sensor nodes need to know their neighbors in order to communicate with each other. The SHD protocol consists of two phases, the fingerprint claim and the fingerprint verification phases. In the fingerprint claim phase each node is required to sign its neighbor node list. The signed neighbor node list is a fingerprint of its current neighborhood community, hereafter referred to as fingerprint claim. The fingerprint claim is broadcasted in one-hop neighborhood. Upon reception of a fingerprint claim from a neighboring claim node, the receiver node will decide whether to become a witness node of the claim node. When it decides to become a witness node, the node will then verify the fingerprint claim and finally store the fingerprint claims of the witnessed nodes locally if the claim passed the verification process. In the fingerprint verification phase, when two nodes meet with each other, they exchange their witnessed node lists, and this can be done by piggybacking the witnessed node list in the two nodes and then checking for a possible fingerprint claim conflict with received claims. In a fingerprint claim conflict, there are two fingerprint claims with the same ID and private key claiming two different neighborhood communities, which implies two detected replicas.

4.2.5. Detecting Node Replication Attacks in Mobile Sensor

Networks: Theory and Approaches. Zhu et al. [65] have proposed two replica detection algorithms for mobile sensor networks. First algorithm is a token-based authentication scheme proposed for the detection of replication attack in which the replicas do not cooperate (nonconspiring case). For the case in which the replicas cooperate by communicating with each other in an efficient manner, a detection method is proposed which is based on statistics and the random encounters between physical nodes. In the first algorithm, the base station periodically broadcasts to the entire sensing region a timestamp protected by a broadcast authentication protocol. The broadcast announces the beginning of a detection round. Upon hearing the timestamp, a genuine mobile node randomly selects a secret seed $s_i \in \{0, 1\}^l$, where l is a common security parameter, and empties its local storage of the previously received tokens. The detection consists of a token exchange phase and a mutual authentication phase When a mobile node first meets with another mobile node in the detection round, they will exchange a token with each other and will record the tokens in their memories. When these mobile nodes meet again in the same detection round, each will ask the other for the previously exchanged token. Upon receiving the correct reply, each believes that the other is authenticated. Otherwise, in case of replica, when genuine node asks a replica node (to whom it met before) about the token they have exchanged in their first meeting, the replica node will reply in no or with a wrong token which will mark him as replica.

The second algorithm is a statistics-based detection scheme for detecting replicas that cooperate with each others. This idea is partially inspired by [66] whose detection principle is that if a node is not "seen again" by others, it is likely that the node has been captured. Similarly, herein, the principle is that if in a certain detection round a node is "seen again" too many times by others, it is likely that the node is a replica. Every genuine node contains a step counter "T" and also its "acquaintance list" consisting of n Boolean variables. Each time a mobile node meets another mobile node, it increases the counter T by 1. If this is its first meeting with any mobile node, it treats it as an acquaintance and sets the corresponding bit in the list to 1. Once the acquaintance list contains all 1's, the statistics stops. In the nondetection stage each node reports its numbers of meetings with others when dropping by the base station. The base station is employed for centralized analysis. Finally, the node with more encounters is detected as replica, and base station finally broadcasts the entire network for replicated IDs.

4.2.6. Emergent Properties: Detection of the Node Capture

Attack in Mobile Wireless Sensor Networks. Conti et al. [66] have proposed two algorithms for the detection of node capture attack in mobile wireless sensor networks. Their first algorithm is simple distributed detection (SDD) in which the attack is detected using only information local to the nodes. The second algorithm is called cooperative distributed detection (CDD) which exploits node collaboration to improve the detection performance. Both of the proposed algorithms are based on the simple observations that if node a will not remeet node b within a certain period of time, then it is possible that node b has been captured. Hence, node a can autonomously know the probability that a "not yet remet" node has been actually captured by the adversary. The SDD follows the above simple observation that each node a is given the task of tracking a specific set T_a of other nodes. For each node $b \in T_a$ that a gets into the communication range of, a set the corresponding meeting time to the value of its internal clock and start the corresponding timeout, that will expire after λ seconds. If the time-out expires (i.e., a and b did not remeet), the network is flooded with an alarm triggered by node a to revoke node b. In CDD, network mobility and node cooperation are leveraged to improve node capture detection. When two nodes a and b exchange information about the nodes (if any) that are tracked by both a and b, that is, the nodes in $T_a T_b$, the node exchanges information only when cooperating nodes are in the same communication radius. This shared information is further used for node capture.

4.2.7. Mobility-Assisted Detection of the Replication in Mobile

Wireless Sensor Networks. Deng et al. [67] have proposed two schemes for the detection of node replication attack in mobile wireless sensor networks. The first is called unary time location storage and exchange (UTLSE), and, second is called multitime location storage and diffusion (MTLSD). In both protocols, after receiving the time-location claims, witnesses carry these claims around the network instead of transmitting them. That means that data are forwarded only when appropriate witnesses encounter each other. Only if two nodes encounter each other, they exchange their time-location claims, that is, if a tracer receives a time location claim from its tracked neighbor node, it does not immediately transmit this time-location claim to the witness if the witness is not currently within its communication range but stores that location claim until encountering the witness. UTLSE detects the replicas by each of the two encountered witnesses which stores only one time-location claim. On the other hand, MTLSD stores more time-location claims for each tracked node and introduces time-location claims diffusion among witnesses. The detection probability of the MTLSD protocol is greater than the probability of protocol UTLSE.

5. Comparison of Node Replica Detection Schemes for Mobile WSNs

Mobile wireless sensor networks (MWSNs) are still in their infancy, and there are many challenges in MWSNs that are still needed to be resolved. These challenges include deployment, localization, self-organization, navigation and control, coverage, energy, maintenance, and data process [26]. In case of localization, node position can be determined once during initialization when sensor nodes are deployed statically [68]. However, when sensor nodes are mobile, they must continuously obtain their positions as they navigate through the whole sensing region. As a result, in mobile WSNs, localization requires additional time and energy and also the availability of a rapid localization service. Due to the dynamic network topology of mobile WSNs, they cannot rely on routing tables or recent route histories as static WSNs do for passing messages through the network because table data become outdated quickly; thus, route discovery data must repeatedly be performed extensively in terms of power, time, and bandwidth.

Ho et al. [58, 59] have proposed a centralized detection scheme for mobile WSNs in which accurate measurement is a prerequisite for acceptable false-negative and -positive rates. In result, it requires dynamic and precise localization system and a tight time synchronization which are both nontrivial tasks. Also, better and accurate sampling entails even much more expensive equipment (GPS) and thus may not be affordable for the current generation of WSNs. Another centralized detection technique is proposed by Deng and Xiong [60] in which there is no way to ensure, the participating clone node will report their keys honestly to the base station. It is possible that an original node number of pairwise keys exceed the threshold value due to its communication. Also as the effectiveness of both the above centralized detection techniques relies on the involvement of the base station, this easily incurs the problems of single-point failure and fast energy depletion of the sensor nodes around the base station.

Yu et al. [61] have proposed distributed detection technique called extremely efficient detection technique (XED) in which the authors have assumed that the replicas cannot communicate and collaborate (or cooperate) with each other which is the weakness of this scheme because in case when the replicas cooperate with each other, they can establish secret channels among each other, and then they can easily deceive the detection technique. Efficient and distributed detection (EDD) is another distributed detection technique for mobile WSNs proposed by Yu et al. [62] which is inapplicable due to high storage overhead for large-scale WSNs.

Zhu et al. [65] have proposed a token-based detection technique which fails when a smart attacker establishes secret channels among replicas as by doing this, replicas can share the tokens and make the protocol exist in name only.

Conti et al. [66] have proposed two solutions, namely, SDD and CDD for the detection of node capture. Their approach is based on a simple observation which completely assumes that there is no membership change in the network; for example, at least no nodes die out (meaning run out of power) which is not the case in reality. Also, it is assumed implicitly that any senor node is able to flood the entire mobile WSN with a broadcast message which is also not possible in reality.

An asymptotic comparison of all the detection schemes for mobile WSNs is shown in Table 3 where their communication and memory costs are compared. As all the proposed solutions use different motivations and assumptions and thus have their respective strengths and weaknesses, we cannot make any general or definite remarks that which solution is the best one.

6. Discussion

Node replication attack or clone attack is one of the most harmful and dangerous threat to an unattended wireless sensor network because in this attack an adversary not only compromises the sensor nodes but can also carry out a large class of internal attacks for instance DoS attack, Sybil attack, and Black hole, and wormhole attack, by surreptitiously inserting arbitrary number of replicas at strategic positions of the network. Furthermore this is more niggling and troublesome because these replicated nodes, under the control of an adversary, having all the keying materials, pretend as authorized users in the network and thus deceiving the network into accepting them as legitimate nodes. It is difficult to identify replicas because of two major reasons. First, since a clone or replica is considered to be completely honest by its neighbors, the legitimate nodes cannot be aware of the fact that they have a clone among them. Voting mechanisms [33, 69] remain unsuccessful to detect clone nodes that are not within the same neighborhood as a voting mechanism is used to detect misbehaving nodes and clones within the neighborhood to agree on the legitimacy of a given node. Thus, there is a need for global countermeasure that can detect clones on the global level. Second, the general purpose security protocols for secure sensor network communication would allow replica nodes to create pair-wise shared keys with other nodes and the base station, and thus in doing so, the replica nodes are able to encrypt, decrypt, and authenticate all of their communications as if they were the original captured nodes.

The process or stages of node replication attack can be described in the form of a flow chart as shown in Figure 5. The flow chart concisely describes the instigation of node replication attack and its detection, from physical node capture, extraction of secret credentials, cloning and redeployment and finally the detection and prevention of node replication attack. At Stage 1, an adversary physically captures a sensor node. After physical capture the sensor node remains absent from the network for a specific period of time. If this absence of a sensor node is detected or a tamper-proof hardware is used, the attack will be prevented. Otherwise, an attacker or an adversary starts extracting all the secret materials of the captured node at Stage 2. At Stage 3, an adversary reprograms the captured node. If an adversary is unable to use a new hardware, it can compromise the node and then exploits the compromised node to disrupt the network operations by its misbehaving activities. At Stage 4, an adversary makes clones or replicas of the captured nodes by using new hardware, and these replicas have the same ID and all other keying materials as that of the captured node. After making clones or replicas, an adversary redeploys them

TABLE 3: Asymptotic performance of schemes against clone node attack in mobile sensor networks.

Nature of scheme	Type of scheme	Technique/scheme	Communication cost	Memory cost
Centralized	Node speed based	Ho et al. scheme [58, 59]	$O(n\sqrt{n})$	$O(n)$
	Key usage based	Deng and Xiong scheme [60]	$O(n\log n)$	—
Distributed	Information exchange based	XED [61]	$O(1)$	$O(4 \cdot d \cdot E[X])$
	Node meeting based	EDD [62]	$O(1)$	$O(n)$
		SEDD [62]	$O(n)$	$O(\xi)$
	Mobility assisted based	Wang and Shi scheme with Base Station [63]	$O(n)$	—
		Wang and Shi scheme with out Base Station [63]	$O(n * \sqrt{k})$	—
		UTLSE [67]	$O(n)$	$O(\sqrt{n})$
		MTLSD [67]	$O(n)$	$O(\sqrt{n})$

n: no. of nodes in the network, ξ: distinct IDs from set of nodes as monitor, d: degree of neighboring nodes, and k: total number of zones.

at strategic positions of the network for further insider attacks at Stage 5. Finally these replicas or clones can be detected by using various detection schemes.

Since clone nodes carry all the cryptographic and keying materials, all the traditional authentication and intrusion detection techniques are ineffective to discover and detect these clones or replicas in the network. Keeping this in mind many techniques have been proposed for the detection of node replication attack and recall that these are broadly categorized into centralized and distributed techniques. Some fairly serious limitations of centralized technique like the base station introduces a single point of failure, and any compromise of the base station will make the solution useless thus making distributed solutions a necessity. One important class of distributed techniques is witness node-based techniques which are considered to the most favorable techniques yet for detecting clone nodes. But according to Zeng et al. [4], replica detection protocols must be non-deterministic and fully distributed in order to circumvent the existing drawbacks of witness-based strategies. The witness node-based strategies ought to fulfill three requirements to have a high probability of detecting clones or replicas. Firstly, the selection of witness-nodes should be nondeterministic as it is more difficult for an adversary to launch clone attacks in nondeterministic protocols successfully because the witnesses of node are not known and are different in each execution of the protocol. Secondly, for any given node, all the nodes should have an equal probability to be the witnesses of that node during the lifetime of the network. Thirdly, the witness-nodes should be selected from all over the network randomly and not from particular area of the network every time meaning that the witness distribution should be uniform throughout the entire network.

There are two types of attacks which are the variations of node replication attack and can be launched by an adversary against witness node-based schemes. These are named as smart attack and masked replication attack. Smart attack is a special witness compromising attack, and in this attack an adversary avariciously chooses which sensor to corrupt in order to maximize its chance for its replicas to go undetected. The adversary finds out the witness nodes which are used to detect replicas and only compromises these witness nodes

to avoid detection. The witness node-based techniques use a framework called claimer-reporter-witness framework in which a node referred to as claimer, locally broadcasts it location claim to its neighbors. Each neighbor serves as a reporter and employs a function to map the claimer ID to a witness. The neighbor forwards the claim to the witness and if it receives two different location claims for the same node ID then it means that the adversary has replicated a node. The adversary can also employ a function to know about the witness for the given claimer ID, and may also locate and compromise the witness node before she inserts the replicas into the wireless sensor network in order to evade the detection. In masked replication attack, the adversary may turn to compromise all the neighbors of a replica so as to prevent a location claim from propagating to any witness thus eliminating the reporters at all. This attack makes it possible for such a replica, whose neighbors have all been compromised, to lie about its physical position. So far, all the witness node-based techniques have assumed a static WSN, and are seemed to be the most promising schemes till yet to detect replicas or clones in static WSN, but alas these witness node-based schemes and location-based replication detection schemes are unable to detect and counter these types of replication attacks.

Nowadays, mobility has become an important area of research for WSN community. In mobile WSNs, mobility plays a key role in the execution of the application [68] as the integration of mobility in WSN can improve the coverage and utility of the sensor network deployment and enables more versatile sensing applications as well. However, besides that the introduction of mobile entities (which freely roam in the network and are autonomous as being able to reposition and organize themselves in the network) can resolve some problems by offering many advantages over the static WSNs the unique properties of mobile WSNs and the dynamic mobile network topology pose many new challenges in the security of mobile WSNs. The idea of detecting clone nodes in static WSNs is extensively based on the elitism of the node location meaning that a sensor node should be allied to a unique deployment position, and if one logical node id is found to be associated with two or more physical locations, the node replication is detected. But noticeably this is not

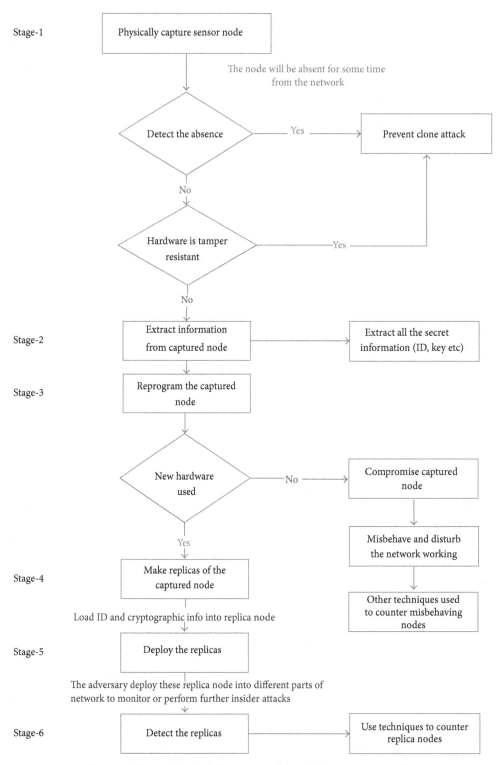

FIGURE 5: Stages of node replication attack in wireless sensor networks.

applicable to the emerging mobile WSNs where the sensor nodes are moving freely all the time in the network. Thus, a little work (which includes significantly different scenarios and techniques) has been done so far to deal with replicas or clones in mobile WSNs.

In mobile WSNs, the adversary is also mobile. In the literature, the assumed scenario of mobile WSN is that the sensors are unable to transmit sensed data at their will because the sink is not always present. Thus, the data accumulated in their memories become targets of many adversaries. In

[30], a mobile adversary model is proposed in which mobile adversary visits and travels around the network trying to compromise a subset of sensors within the time interval when sinks are not present in the network. The time taken by a mobile adversary to compromise a set of sensors is much shorter than the time between two successive data collections of a sink. Thus, it is much difficult to snatch mobile compromised nodes as well as mobile clones.

Another challenge arises in mobile WSNs when a mobile adversary adopts a more sophisticated strategy named "group mobility strategy." In this stratagem, the replicas form a physically close group which always moves together, but only a representative of them communicates with the genuine nodes, whereas the rest of the replicas remain inactive as "silent learners" so that they can learn (from encounters with genuine nodes) about any received token or corresponding meeting instant. Once the replicas have met all the "n" genuine nodes (and thus acquired all the necessary knowledge to pass later authentications), they can scatter in the sensing region, and each behaves actively and independently, until the next detection round starts.

Also, when the mobile replicas communicate and collaborate with each other and share their keys or random numbers, they can make the detection technique fails to thwart them easily. Thus, mobile WSNs offer much more challenges in detecting mobile replicas, and it is highly needed to overcome these challenges by developing some new, different and more efficient detection techniques for detecting mobile replicas or clones.

7. Conclusion

This paper reviewed the state-of-the-art schemes for detection of node replication attack also called clone attack. The existing techniques are broadly categorized into two classes distributed and centralized. Both classes of schemes are proficient in detecting and preventing clone attacks, but both schemes also have some noteworthy drawbacks. However, to sum up, the current study highlights the fact that there are still a lot of challenges and issues in clone detection schemes that need to be resolved to become more applicable to real-life situations and also to become accepted by the resource constrained sensor node.

Acknowledgment

The authors wish to acknowledge the anonymous reviewers for their valuable comments for the improvement of this paper.

References

[1] T. Bonaci, P. Lee, L. Bushnell, and R. Poovendran, "Distributed clone detection in wireless sensor networks: an optimization approach," in *Proceedings of the 2nd IEEE International Workshop on Data Security and Privacy in Wireless Networks (WoWMoM '11)*, Lucca, Italy, June 2011.

[2] W. T. Zhu, J. Zhou, R. H. Deng, and F. Bao, "Detecting node replication attacks in wireless sensor networks: a survey," *Journal of Network and Computer Applications*, vol. 35, no. 3, pp. 1022–1034, 2012.

[3] M. Zhang, V. Khanapure, S. Chen, and X. Xiao, "Memory efficient protocols for detecting node replication attacks in wireless sensor networks," in *Proceedings of the 17th IEEE International Conference on Network Protocols (ICNP '09)*, pp. 284–293, Princeton, NJ, USA, October 2009.

[4] Y. Zeng, J. Cao, S. Zhang, S. Guo, and L. Xie, "Random walk based approach to detect clone attacks in wireless sensor networks," *IEEE Journal on Selected Areas in Communications*, vol. 28, no. 5, pp. 677–691, 2010.

[5] R. Di Pietro, L. V. Mancini, C. Soriente, A. Spognardi, and G. Tsudik, "Data security in unattended wireless sensor networks," *IEEE Transactions on Computers*, vol. 58, no. 11, pp. 1500–1511, 2009.

[6] C. Karlof and D. Wagner, "Secure routing in wireless sensor networks: attacks and countermeasures," in *Proceedings of the 1st IEEE International Workshop on Sensor Network Protocols and Applications*, May 2003.

[7] B. Parno, M. Luk, E. Gaustad, and A. Perrig, "Secure sensor network routing: a cleanslate approach," in *Proceedings of the ACM CoNEXT Conference (CoNEXT '06)*, December 2006.

[8] F. Ye, H. Luo, S. Lu, and L. Zhang, "Statistical en-route filtering of injected false data in sensor networks," in *Proceedings of the IEEE INFOCOM*, 2004.

[9] L. Yu and J. Li, "Grouping based resilient statistical en-route filtering for sensor networks," in *Proceedings of the IEEE INFOCOM*, 2009.

[10] S. Zhu, S. Setia, S. Jajodia, and P. Ning, "An interleaved hop-by-hop authentication scheme for filtering of injected false data in sensor networks," in *Proceedings of the IEEE Symposium on Security and Privacy*, pp. 259–271, May 2004.

[11] H. Chan, A. Perrig, and D. Song, "Secure hierarchical in-network aggregation in sensor networks," in *Proceedings of the 13th ACM Conference on Computer and Communications Security (CCS '06)*, pp. 278–287, November 2006.

[12] J. Deng, R. Han, and S. Mishra, "Security support for in network processing in wireless sensor networks," in *Proceedings of the ACM Workshop on Security in Ad Hoc and Sensor Networks (SASN '03)*, pp. 83–93, 2003.

[13] B. Przydatek, D. Song, and A. Perrig, "SIA: secure information aggregation in sensor networks," in *Proceedings of the 1st International Conference on Embedded Networked Sensor Systems (SenSys '03)*, pp. 255–265, November 2003.

[14] Y. Yang, X. Wang, S. Zhu, and G. Cao, "SDAP: a secure hop-by-hop data aggregation protocol for sensor networks," in *Proceedings of the 7th ACM International Symposium on Mobile Ad Hoc Networking and Computing (MOBIHOC '06)*, pp. 356–367, May 2006.

[15] S. Capkun and J. P. Hubaux, "Secure positioning in wireless networks," *IEEE Journal on Selected Areas in Communications*, vol. 24, no. 2, pp. 221–232, 2006.

[16] S. Ganeriwal, S. Čapkun, C. C. Han, and M. B. Srivastava, "Secure time synchronization service for sensor networks," in *Proceedings of the ACM Workshop on Wireless Security (WiSe '05)*, pp. 97–106, September 2005.

[17] X. Hu, T. Park, and K. G. Shin, "Attack tolerant time synchronization in wireless sensor networks," in *Proceedings of the 27th IEEE Conference on Computer Communications (INFOCOM '08)*, pp. 41–45, Phoenix, Ariz, USA, April 2008.

[18] Z. Li, W. Trappe, Y. Zhang, and B. Nath, "Robust statistical methods for securing wireless localization in sensor networks,"

in *Proceedings of the 4th International Symposium on Information Processing in Sensor Networks (IPSN '05)*, pp. 91–98, April 2005.

[19] D. Liu, P. Ning, and W. Du, "Attack-resistant location estimation in sensor networks," in *Proceedings of the 4th International Symposium on Information Processing in Sensor Networks (IPSN '05)*, pp. 99–106, April 2005.

[20] H. Song, S. Zhu, and G. Cao, "Attack resilient time synchronization for wireless sensor networks," *Ad Hoc Networks*, vol. 5, no. 1, pp. 112–125, 2007.

[21] K. Sun, P. Ning, C. Wang, A. Liu, and Y. Zhou, "TinySeRSync: secure and resilient time synchronization in wireless sensor networks," in *Proceedings of the 13th ACM Conference on Computer and Communications Security (CCS '06)*, pp. 264–277, 2006.

[22] C. Hartung, J. Balasalle, and R. Han, "Node compromise in sensor networks: the need for secure systems," Tech. Rep. CU-CS-988-04, Department of Computer Science, University of Colorado at Boulder, 2004.

[23] H. Choi, S. Zhu, and T. F. L. Porta, "SET: detecting node clones in sensor networks," in *Proceedings of the 3rd International Conference on Security and Privacy in Communication Networks (SecureComm '07)*, pp. 341–350, September 2007.

[24] S. Gautam Thakur, "CINORA: cell based identification of node replication attack in wireless sensor networks," in *Proceedings of the IEEE International Conference on Communications Systems (ICCS '08)*, 2008.

[25] S. Hussain and M. S. Rahman, "Using received signal strength indicator to detect node replacement and replication attacks in wireless sensor networks," in *Data Mining, Intrusion Detection, Information Security and Assurance, and Data Networks Security 2009*, vol. 7344 of *Proceedings of SPIE*, April 2009.

[26] J. Yick, B. Mukherjee, and D. Ghosal, "Wireless sensor network survey," *Computer Networks*, vol. 52, no. 12, pp. 2292–2330, 2008.

[27] I. F. Akyildiz, W. Su, Y. Sankarasubramaniam, and E. Cayirci, "Wireless sensor networks: a survey," *International Journal of Computer and Telecommunications Networking*, vol. 38, no. 4, pp. 393–422, 2002.

[28] B. Parno, A. Perrig, and V. Gligor, "Distributed detection of node replication attacks in sensor networks," in *Proceedings of the IEEE Symposium on Security and Privacy (IEEE S and P '05)*, pp. 49–63, May 2005.

[29] A. Seshadri, A. Perrig, L. van Doorn, and P. Khosla, "SWATT: softWare-based attestation for embedded devices," in *Proceedings of the IEEE Symposium on Security and Privacy (IEEE S and P '04)*, pp. 272–282, May 2004.

[30] R. D. Pietro, L. V. Mancini, C. Soriente, A. Spognardi, and G. Tsudik, "Catch me (If you can): data survival in unattended sensor networks," in *Proceedings of the 6th Annual IEEE International Conference on Pervasive Computing and Communications (PerCom '08)*, pp. 185–194, March 2008.

[31] F. Hu and N. K. Sharma, "Security considerations in ad hoc sensor networks," *Ad Hoc Networks*, vol. 3, no. 1, pp. 69–89, 2005.

[32] R. Brooks, P. Y. Govindaraju, M. Pirretti, N. Vijaykrishnan, and M. T. Kandemir, "On the detection of clones in sensor networks using random key predistribution," *IEEE Transactions on Systems, Man and Cybernetics C*, vol. 37, no. 6, pp. 1246–1258, 2007.

[33] L. Eschenauer and V. D. Gligor, "A key-management scheme for distributed sensor networks," in *Proceedings of the 9th ACM Conference on Computer and Communications Security*, pp. 41–47, Washington, DC, USA, November 2002.

[34] K. Xing, X. Cheng, F. Liu, and D. H. C. Du, "Real-time detection of clone attacks in wireless sensor networks," in *Proceedings of the 28th International Conference on Distributed Computing Systems (ICDCS '08)*, pp. 3–10, Beijing, China, July 2008.

[35] K. Xing, X. Cheng, L. Ma, and Q. Liang, "Superimposed code based channel assignment in multi-radio multi-channel wireless mesh networks," in *Proceedings of the 13th Annual ACM International Conference on Mobile Computing and Networking (MobiCom '07)*, pp. 15–26, September 2007.

[36] W. Znaidi, M. Minier, and S. Ubeda, "Hierarchical node replication attacks detection in wireless sensors networks," in *Proceedings of the 20th IEEE Personal, Indoor and Mobile Radio Communications Symposium (PIMRC '09)*, pp. 82–86, Tokyo, Japan, September 2009.

[37] D. Xia and N. Vlajic, "Near-optimal node clustering in wireless sensor networks for environment monitoring," in *Proceedings of the 21st International Conference on Advanced Networking and Applications (AINA '07)*, pp. 632–641, IEEE Computer Society, Washington, DC, USA, 2007.

[38] C. M. Yu, C. S. Lu, and S. Y. Kuo, "CSI: compressed sensing-based clone identification in sensor networks," in *Proceedings of the IEEE International Conference on Pervasive Computing and Communications Workshops (PERCOM Workshops '12)*, pp. 290–295, Lugano, Switzerland, March 2012.

[39] A. J. Menezes, S. A. Vanstone, and P. C. V. Orschot, *Handbook of Applied Cryptography*, CRC Press, New York, NY, USA, 1996.

[40] C. Bekara and M. Laurent-Maknavicius, "A new protocol for securing wireless sensor networks against nodes replication attacks," in *Proceedings of the 3rd IEEE International Conference on Wireless and Mobile Computing, Networking and Communications (WiMob '07)*, White Plains, NY, USA, October 2007.

[41] C. Bekara and M. Laurent-Maknavicius, "Defending against nodes replication attacks on wireless sensor networks," 2012, http://www-public.it-sudparis.eu/ lauren_m/articles/bekara-SARSSI07.pdf.

[42] M. Conti, R. Di Pietro, L. V. Mancini, and A. Mei, "A randomized, efficient, and distributed protocol for the detection of node replication attacks in wireless sensor networks," in *Proceedings of the 8th ACM International Symposium on Mobile Ad Hoc Networking and Computing (MobiHoc '07)*, pp. 80–89, September 2007.

[43] M. Conti, R. Di Pietro, L. Mancini, and A. Mei, "Distributed detection of clone attacks in wireless sensor networks," *IEEE Transactions on Dependable and Secure Computing*, vol. 8, no. 5, pp. 685–698, 2011.

[44] B. Zhu, V. G. K. Addada, S. Setia, S. Jajodia, and S. Roy, "Efficient distributed detection of node replication attacks in sensor networks," in *Proceedings of the 23rd Annual Computer Security Applications Conference (ACSAC '07)*, pp. 257–266, Miami Beach, Fla, USA, December 2007.

[45] B. Zhu, S. Setia, S. Jajodia, S. Roy, and L. Wang, "Localized multicast: efficient and distributed replica detection in large-scale sensor networks," *IEEE Transactions on Mobile Computing*, vol. 9, no. 7, pp. 913–926, 2010.

[46] S. Ratnasamy, B. Karp, L. Yin et al., "GHT: a geographic hash table for data-centric storage," in *Proceedings of the 1st ACM International Workshop on Wireless Sensor Networks and Applications (WSNA '02)*, pp. 78–87, September 2002.

[47] F. Fei, L. Jing, and Y. Xianglan, "Space-time related pairwise key predistribution scheme for wireless seneor networks," in

Proceedings of the International Conference on Wireless Communications, Networking and Mobile Computing (WiCOM '07), pp. 2692–2696, Shanghai, China, September 2007.

[48] L. C. Ko, H. Y. Chen, and G. R. Lin, "A neighbor-based detection scheme for wireless sensor networks against node replication attacks," in *Proceedings of the International Conference on Ultra Modern Telecommunications and Workshops (ICUMT '09)*, pp. 1–6, St. Petersburg, Russia, October 2009.

[49] J. W. Ho, "Distributed detection of node capture attacks in wireless sensor networks," in *Smart Wireless Sensor Networks*, H. D. Chunch and Y. K. Tan, Eds., pp. 345–360, InTech, Rijeka, Croatia, 2010.

[50] A. Wald, *Sequential Analysis*, Dover, New York, NY, USA, 2004.

[51] C. A. Melchor, B. Ait-Salem, P. Gaborit, and k. Tamine, "Active detection of node replication attacks," *International Journal of Computer Science and Network Security*, vol. 9, no. 2, pp. 13–21, 2009.

[52] Z. Li and G. Gong, "Randomly directed exploration: an efficient node clone detection protocol in wireless sensor networks," in *Proceedings of the 6th IEEE International Conference on Mobile Adhoc and Sensor Systems (MASS '09)*, pp. 1030–1035, Macau, China, October 2009.

[53] X. Meng, K. Lin, and K. Li, "Note based randomized and distributed protocol for detecting node replication attack," in *Algorithms and Architectures for Parallel Processing*, vol. 6081 of *Lecture Notes in Computer Science*, pp. 559–570, 2010.

[54] J. W. Ho, D. Liu, M. Wright, and S. K. Das, "Distributed detection of replica node attacks with group deployment knowledge in wireless sensor networks," *Ad Hoc Networks*, vol. 7, no. 8, pp. 1476–1488, 2009.

[55] Y. Sei and S. Honiden, "Distributed detection of node replication attacks resilient to many compromised nodes in wireless sensor networks," in *Proceedings of the 4th Annual International Conference on Wireless Internet (WICON '08)*, 2008.

[56] C. Kim, S. Shin, C. Park, and H. Yoon, "A resilient and efficient replication attack detection scheme for wireless sensor networks," *IEICE Transactions on Information and Systems*, vol. 92, no. 7, pp. 1479–1483, 2009.

[57] B. Dutertre, S. Cheung, and J. Levy, "Lightweight key management in wireless sensor networks by leveraging initial trust," SDL Technical Report SRI-SDL-04-02, 2004.

[58] J. W. Ho, M. Wright, and S. K. Das, "Fast detection of mobile replica node attacks in wireless sensor networks using sequential hypothesis testing," *IEEE Transactions on Mobile Computing*, vol. 10, no. 6, pp. 767–782, 2011.

[59] J. W. Ho, M. Wright, and S. K. Das, "Fast detection of replica node attacks in mobile sensor networks using sequential analysis," in *Proceedings of the IEEE INFOCOM*, pp. 1773–1781, Rio de Janeiro, Brazil, April 2009.

[60] X. M. Deng and Y. Xiong, "A new protocol for the detection of node replication attacks in mobile wireless sensor networks," *Journal of Computer Science and Technology*, vol. 26, no. 4, pp. 732–743, 2011.

[61] C. M. Yu, C. S. Lu, and S. Y. Kuo, "Mobile sensor network resilient against node replication attacks," in *Proceedings of the 5th Annual IEEE Communications Society Conference on Sensor, Mesh and Ad Hoc Communications and Networks (SECON '08)*, pp. 597–599, June 2008.

[62] C. M. Yu, C. S. Lu, and S. Y. Kuo, "Efficient and Distributed Detection of Node Replication Attacks in Mobile Sensor Networks," in *Proceedings of the 70th IEEE Vehicular Technology Conference (VTC Fall '09)*, pp. 20–23, Anchorage, Alaska, USA, September 2009.

[63] L. M. Wang and Y. Shi, "Patrol detection for replica attacks on wireless sensor networks," *Sensors*, vol. 11, no. 3, pp. 2496–2504, 2011.

[64] Y. Lou, Y. Zhang, and S. Liu, "Single hop detection of node clone attacks in mobile wireless sensor networks," in *Proceedings of the International Workshop on Information and Electronics Engineering (IWIEE)*, 2012.

[65] W. T. Zhu, J. Zhou, R. Deng, and F. Bao, "Detecting node replication attacks in mobile sensor networks: theory and approaches," *Security and Communication Networks*, vol. 5, no. 5, pp. 496–507, 2012.

[66] M. Conti, R. Di Pietro, L. V. MAncini, and A. Mei, "Emergent properties: detection of the node-capture attack in mobile wireless sensor networks," in *Proceedings of the 1st ACM Conference on Wireless Network Security (WiSec '08)*, pp. 214–219, Alexandria, Va, USA, 2008.

[67] X. Deng, Y. Xiong, and D. Chen, "Mobility-assisted detection of the replication attacks in mobile wireless sensor networks," in *Proceedings of the 6th Annual IEEE International Conference on Wireless and Mobile Computing, Networking and Communications (WiMob '2010)*, pp. 225–232, October 2010.

[68] I. Amundson and X. D. Koutsoukos, "A survey on localization for mobile wireless sensor networks," in *Proceedings of the 2nd International Conference on Mobile Entity Localization and Tracking in GPS-Less Environments (MELT '09)*, vol. 5801 of *Lecture Notes in Computer Science*, pp. 235–254, 2009.

[69] H. Chan, A. Perrig, and D. Song, "Random key predistribution schemes for sensor networks," in *Proceedings of the IEEE Symposium on Security And Privacy (IEEE S and P '03)*, pp. 197–213, May 2003.

8

Successful Deployment of a Wireless Sensor Network for Precision Agriculture in Malawi

Million Mafuta,[1,2] **Marco Zennaro,**[3] **Antoine Bagula,**[4] **Graham Ault,**[1]
Harry Gombachika,[2] **and Timothy Chadza**[2]

[1] *Electronic and Electrical Engineering Department, University of Strathclyde, Royal College Building,*
204 George Street, Glasgow G1 1XW, UK
[2] *Electrical Engineering Department, University of Malawi-The Polytechnic, Chichiri, Blantyre, Malawi*
[3] *T/ICT4D Laboratory, The Abdus Salam International Centre for Theoretical Physics, Strada Costiera, 11-34151 Trieste, Italy*
[4] *ISAT Laboratory, University of Cape Town, 18 University Avenue, Rhodes Gift, Cape Town 7707, South Africa*

Correspondence should be addressed to Million Mafuta; mmafuta@poly.ac.mw

Academic Editor: Danny Hughes

This paper demonstrates how an irrigation management system (IMS) can practically be implemented by deploying a wireless sensor network (WSN). Specifically, the paper describes an IMS which was set up in Manja township, city of Blantyre. Deployment of IMS in rural areas of developing countries like Malawi is a challenge as grid power is scarce. For the system to be self-sustained in terms of power, the study used solar photovoltaic and rechargeable batteries to power all electrical devices. The system incorporated a remote monitoring mechanism through a General Packet Radio Service modem to report soil temperature, soil moisture, WSN link performance, and photovoltaic power levels. Irrigation valves were activated to water the field. Preliminary results in this study have revealed a number of engineering weaknesses of deploying such a system. Nevertheless, the paper has highlighted areas of improvement to develop a robust, fully automated, solar-powered, and low-cost IMS to suit the socioeconomic conditions of small scale farmers in developing countries.

1. Introduction

In precision agriculture (PA), various parameters including soil type and temperature vary dramatically from one region to the other; consequently, any irrigation system must be flexible to adapt to such variations. Off-the-shelf irrigation controllers are usually expensive and not effective in managing scarce water resources [1, 2]. On the other hand, an irrigation management system (IMS) based on wireless sensor networks (WSNs) can accept any desired irrigation scheduling strategy to meet specific environmental requirements. However, WSNs are still under a developmental stage; as such, they are at times unreliable, fragile, and power hungry and can easily lose communication especially when deployed in a harsh environment like an agricultural field [2]. Unlike laboratory-based simulations and experimental installations, practical deployments have to handle such challenges to be fully beneficial. WSNs have an immense

potential to PA, such that, if well designed, can be a solution to a low-cost IMS suitable for developing countries.

The increase in WSN deployment in industrial, agricultural, and environmental monitoring applications is as a result of being a low power and low data rate hence energy efficient technology. It also offers mobility and flexibility in connectivity which promote network expansion when needed.

Recently, there have been few publications on the application of WSNs to PA. Keshtgary and Deljoo [3] discussed the simulation of WSN for agriculture using OPNET simulation tools in which random and grid topologies were compared. They evaluated the performance of the networks by monitoring delay, throughput, and load. This approach, however, lacks practical aspects where some simulation assumptions are invalid. Zhou and others [4] presented a WSN deployment for an irrigation system using ZigBee protocol. This study did not monitor the performance of communication links between sensor nodes which is vital in practical deployments as it impacts battery performance. Despite having a detailed design for the powering side, they did not monitor battery levels for the sensor nodes.

This paper revisits the problem of the field readiness of WSNs when deployed in PA to assist small scale farmers in the rural areas of developing countries. The main contribution of this paper is the design, implementation, and performance enhancement of a low-cost but efficient IMS that combines sensors and actuators in a wireless sensor/actuator network. This approach could guide the successful deployment of WSN for PA.

The remainder of the paper is organized as follows: Section 2 presents the design of the wireless sensor network for precision agriculture in Malawi (WiPAM); Section 3 presents the performance evaluation of the underlying WSN development; Section 4 discusses challenges and experiences acquired from the WSN practical deployment; finally, conclusion and future work are presented in Section 5.

2. The WiPAM Design

The ultimate purpose of the WiPAM system was to automate irrigation process. Specifically, the study examined the fluctuations in soil moisture in an agricultural field. Such fluctuations were then used by the irrigation controller to initiate irrigation events. In order for the controller to precisely determine when to irrigate, sensor data were automatically gathered at intervals of 30 minutes. However, in order to avoid over irrigation due to late termination of an irrigation event, the sampling interval was reduced from 30 minutes to 2 minutes when the irrigation was in progress.

The general workflow of the system consists of (1) taking soil moisture and temperature samples at predefined time intervals, (2) sending and storing sampled data in a coordinator node, (3) sending the data from the coordinator to a gateway node for forwarding to a remote monitoring station (RMS) through a cellular network, (4) going to sleep, and (5) waking up and repeating the previous steps. Depending on the values stored in the coordinator node, the irrigation valves have to be opened or closed.

In order to realise these functional requirements, the WiPAM was divided into two sections: irrigation station (IS) and RMS which were linked via a cellular network as shown in Figure 1. The RMS was used to capture performance parameters of the IS at a remote site. The parameters included soil moisture level, soil temperature, battery voltage levels of sensor nodes, quality of wireless links, and valve status. The idea was to get timely information without visiting the site physically, consequently, saving time and money.

Section 2.1 discusses the architecture and components of the IS; thereafter, Section 2.2 describes the RMS design.

2.1. Irrigation Station. The workflow of the IS can be mapped into a five-component system architecture depicted by Figure 2 which includes soil moisture sensor, sensor node, coordinator node, gateway node, and irrigation system. Section 2.1.1 discusses the WSN protocol and topology used,

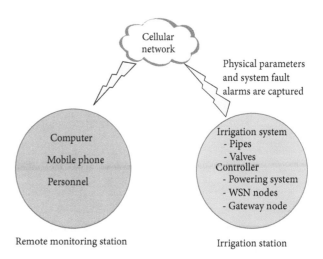

FIGURE 1: The Architecture of the irrigation management system.

after which the single components of the IS are described in Sections 2.1.2 through 2.1.6.

2.1.1. WSN Protocol and Topology. The WSN deployed in this study used ZigBee, an IEEE 802.15.4 networking standard for personal area networks. The physical layer of ZigBee operates in the unlicensed industrial, scientific, and medical radio bands of 868 MHz, 915 MHz, and 2.4 GHz depending on the region. This study adopted the 2.4 GHz band because it is unlicensed in Malawi.

The ZigBee protocol mainly focuses on low-cost and low power consumption. The low power consumption characteristic is really appealing since sensors are usually placed at a remote location where battery power supply is the only option and needs to be sustained. In order to attain a low power consumption characteristic, the ZigBee protocol operates at low data rates (250 kbps at 2.4 GHz). Nonetheless, this imposes its limitation where high data transmission applications are required. Such applications may use other IEEE standards, for instance, Bluetooth (802.15.1) and Wi-Fi (802.11) which offer high data rates of 1 Mbps and 54 Mbps, respectively, but at the expense of battery power. Nevertheless, in PA, sensor data do not require wide bandwidth since it is not necessary to continuously monitor soil moisture and temperature as there could be no significant changes in these parameters in a short period. Hence, ZigBee is well suited for PA in remote areas where high battery performance may be required.

Depending on the situation and environment, ZigBee networks can take three forms of topologies: star; cluster tree, and mesh. A star topology comprises one ZigBee coordinator (ZC) and several other ZigBee end devices (ZEDs). No ZigBee router (ZR) is required in this topology. The ZC communicates with all ZEDs; however, there is no direct messaging between ZEDs (refer to Figure 3). On the other hand, a cluster-tree topology is made up of one ZC and several child nodes which are ZRs and ZEDs [5]. Apart from communicating with its parent node, the ZR may as well have its own child nodes, but there is only one path between any pair of devices in this network. A mesh

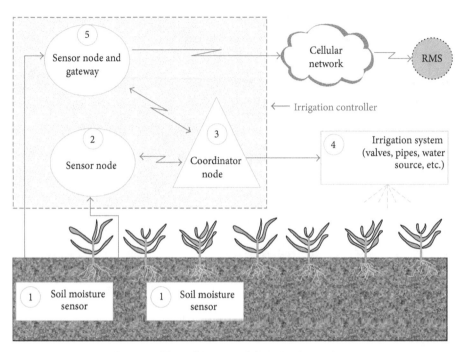

FIGURE 2: The architecture of the irrigation station.

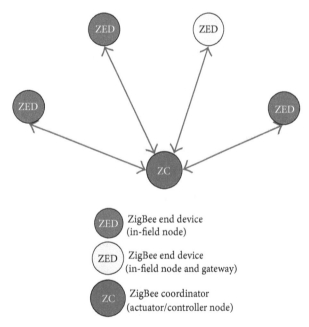

FIGURE 3: Star network topology deployed in this study.

network is accomplished by allowing devices in the cluster-tree to topology communicate with each other using multiple routes. Consequently, the devices are able to send and receive messages reliably even when their preferred path is down or congested. This is the major advantage of a ZigBee mesh network over star and cluster-tree networks. However, a mesh network has no guarantee of bandwidth since no synchronisation is used which requires disabling of beacon mode.

Since the network for this study was small, comprising five devices placed within short distances (7 m), a star topology was chosen (refer to Figure 3). In this topology, three in-field sensor nodes and the gateway node were configured as ZEDs, whereas one node was configured as ZC. The ZC node was used to aggregate data and actuate irrigation valves accordingly. With this topology, there is a considerable potential of battery power saving since all ZEDs spend most of their time asleep, only waking up to make measurements and send the data to the ZC. Otherwise, as the case with cluster tree and mesh, ZRs need to be awake since they provide paths for other devices to the ZC thereby wasting battery power in the process.

2.1.2. The Soil Moisture Sensor. The soil moisture sensor is one of the most important components upon which the efficiency of the irrigation activity heavily relies. The suitability of a soil moisture sensing device depends on the cost, reliability, ease of interfacing to a signal processing device, accuracy, and soil texture. Although it is not possible to single out a sensor that satisfies all of the above selection criteria, the Watermark 200SS (Irrometer Company, Inc., Riverside, CA, USA) was opted for. This sensor scores highly on low-cost, and durability, maintenance-free operation and suitability for soil texture variability since it has a wide measuring range (0 to −239 kPa) [6]. The fact that this sensor monitors water potential makes it superior to other water content-based sensors; knowledge of soil water content is not as important as knowing the level of tension crop roots must exert to extract water.

The measurement of the soil moisture potential (SMP) using Watermark 200SS sensor is done in two stages: (1) reading the frequency of the alternating current signal pushed into the sensor which is then converted to resistance and (2) using a nonlinear calibration equation to convert the Watermark electrical resistance (in kΩ) into SMP (in kPa). Using an Agriculture Board as an interface of the Watermark sensor and a Waspmote microcontroller unit (MCU), it was possible to measure the frequency directly. The following equation developed by the manufacturer of the Agriculture Board [7] was then used to convert the measured frequency to resistance:

$$R = \frac{150390 - 8.19f}{1000\,(0.021f - 1)}\,\mathrm{k}\Omega, \tag{1}$$

where f is the measured frequency expressed in Hz.

There are numerous calibration equations in the literature [8–10] that permit conversion of the Watermark resistance to SMP. However, this study used the equation developed by Shock and others [8] because it is used in many Watermark digital meters and data loggers [11, 12]. Moreover, the manufacturer of the Watermark 200SS sensor uses this equation as a default calibration [10]. The equation is expressed as follows:

$$SMP = -\frac{4.093 + 3.213R}{1 - 0.009733R - 0.01205T}\,\mathrm{kPa}, \tag{2}$$

where R is the sensor resistance (kΩ) and T is the soil temperature (°C) measured within the vicinity of moisture sensor.

Soil temperature was measured with the help of a TP1000 sensor (Omega Engineering Ltd.).

Sensor positioning in the root zone of the plant is crucial, because it determines the amount of water to be applied during each irrigation event. A sensor placed very deep into the soil allows the irrigation system to apply more water up to that depth beyond plant roots; the water below plant roots is lost through deep percolation. On the other hand, a very shallow sensor promotes light irrigation, consequently, failing to apply water into the root zone and therefore stressing the plants. Maize is a deep-rooted crop with approximate maximum rooting depth ranging from 75 cm to 120 cm [13] depending on the characteristics of the soils like the presence of restrictive soil layers. Accordingly, the study placed the soil moisture sensors at a depth of 40 cm. At this sensor depth, about 70% of water uptake by crops takes place [14]; the effective root zone in this case is 60 cm. For ease of installation of the Watermark sensor into the soil, a 1/2 inch, class 315 psi, thin wall polyvinyl chloride (PVC) pipe was used. This gives a good snug fit of the sensor on its collar (refer to Figure 4) and allows the sensor to be pushed easily into an access hole during installation [15].

After successfully attaching sensors to the PVC pipes it was important to precondition them by following wet-dry cycles. The wet-dry process is necessary in order to remove air from sensors [15] which, consequently, improves the response of sensors during the first few irrigation events. Three wet-dry cycles were conducted before installing sensors. Specifically, sensors were soaked in irrigation water for 1 hour then air dried for 24 hours. In addition, sensors were soaked in water for 24 hours just before installation.

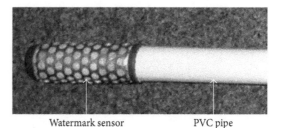

Watermark sensor   PVC pipe

FIGURE 4: Soil moisture sensor (Watermark) attached to a PVC pipe.

2.1.3. The Sensor Node. In this study an open WSN node was used as a sensor node. The advantage of the open source model when applied to WSNs is relevant in terms of cost, personalization, and independence from a single entity as compared to proprietary solutions. In particular, the Waspmote node by Libelium was selected. Waspmotes are built around XBee transceivers which provide flexibility in terms of multiplicity of operating power, protocols, and operating frequencies. According to [16], other Waspmote characteristics include (1) minimum power consumption of the order of 0.7 mA in the hibernate mode; (2) flexible architecture allowing extra sensors to be easily installed in a modular way; (3) the provision of Global Positioning System, General Packet Radio Service (GPRS), and Secure Digital card on board; (4) the provision of a Real Time Clock. Furthermore, Waspmotes are powered with a lithium battery which can be recharged through a special socket dedicated for a solar panel; this option is quite interesting for deployments in developing countries where power supply is either scarce or unstable.

This study deployed four in-field sensor nodes—two in each plot of 8 m × 7 m in size (refer to Figure 5). However, one of these nodes was assigned additional responsibilities of a gateway to relay field data to a remote station for diagnostic purposes by the management personnel.

Since the moisture sensors were coupled to the sensor nodes, it was important to install the nodes at appropriate locations to take into account the variability of spatial distribution of water in the field. Towards that end, sensor nodes were positioned as shown in Figure 5. While it is prudent to place sensor nodes in the mostly dry locations of the field to avoid stressing crops in those locations, caution should also be exercised to avoid over irrigation of the other parts of the field. Consequently, based on topography, it may be necessary to divide a large field into smaller zones which can effectively be irrigated independently. In order to ease the task of establishing appropriate sensor positions and to facilitate even distribution of water in the field, the two plots were leveled independently.

Figure 6 shows the architecture of an in-field sensor node (excluding that of the gateway). This node was equipped with a ZigBee module to be used for communication with a coordinator node described later in Section 2.1.4. The Agriculture Board was used as an interface between the sensors and the Waspmote sensor board.

A software program was developed and uploaded into the sensor nodes to allow them to measure soil moisture, their

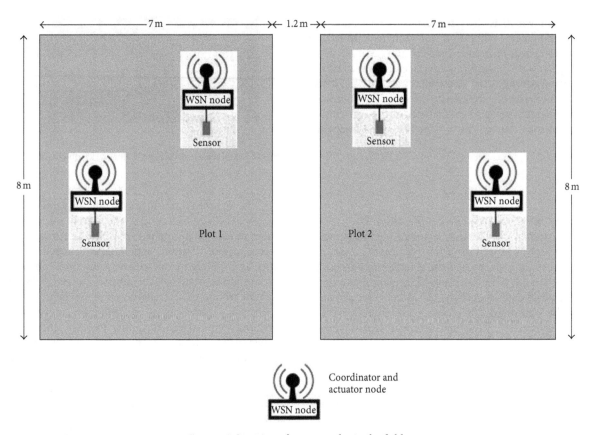

FIGURE 5: Location of sensor nodes in the field.

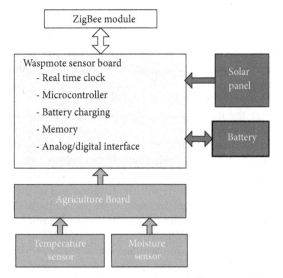

FIGURE 6: The architecture of an in-field sensor node.

battery levels, and soil temperature. The sampling intervals for the measurement of these parameters were 30 minutes when the system was idle and 2 minutes when irrigation was taking place. The rest of the time sensor nodes were in a deep sleep mode to conserve battery power. Once the measurements were completed, the nodes relayed the data

through the XBee transceivers to the coordinator node for processing.

A 30-minute sampling interval was considered a long enough time to preserve battery power for the nodes on one hand, and a short enough time to fully monitor the soil moisture trends. In other words, as it is generally expected, increasing the sampling interval can save a substantial amount of battery power for the sensor nodes at the expense of information. However, in order to avoid over irrigation as a result of late termination of the irrigation event, the study reduced the sampling interval from 30 minutes to 2 minutes when the irrigation was in session. This permitted prompt termination of the irrigation event.

2.1.4. The Coordinator Node. This study used a Waspmote equipped with a ZigBee module as a coordinator node. This component was the heart of the whole system and had several crucial roles to perform. Firstly, as the most capable node in the network, ZC permitted and sanctioned all ZEDs that were in quest of connecting to its network. That is, it was responsible for network formation by assigning addresses to all joining nodes and ensuring security for the network. As such, there was only one ZC for the ZigBee network.

Secondly, the ZC was used to receive and aggregate data from the four in-field sensor nodes discussed earlier in Section 2.1.3. The received sensor data included the Watermark frequency and the soil temperature which were used to derive SMP. The coordinator then decided on whether to irrigate or not depending on the level of the SMP. Four of the input/output (I/O) pins of the Waspmote's sensor board were connected to a latching circuit and were used to initiate or halt the irrigation by sending appropriate pulses to the pins.

Thirdly, the ZC was used to relay data to a gateway node for forwarding to RMS. When receiving data from the sensor nodes the coordinator also captured the Received Signal Strength Indicator (RSSI) of every packet received. This is a measure of the quality of the link between itself and a particular in-field sensor node. The SMP, battery level, soil temperature and RSSI from all four sensor nodes together with its own battery level and system running time were aggregated and prepared suitable for Short Message Service (SMS) transmission system. Thereafter, the SMS data were relayed to the gateway for forwarding to RMS every 15 minutes when irrigation was in progress or every 30 minutes when the irrigation system was in an idle mode. Figure 7 illustrates the architecture of a coordinator and actuator node that carried out the stated functions.

Finally, the ZC node was configured as a controller for the irrigation system. A software program was uploaded to allow the node to effectively schedule irrigation events based on the data received from the four in-field nodes.

2.1.5. The Irrigation System. The irrigation system had four components: latching circuit; solenoid valves; drip pipes; and powering system. It was compelling to use a latching circuit as a means of saving energy for the coordinator node. Unlike sending and holding a pulse for the entire irrigation period which could waste battery power, the latching circuit sanctioned the use of a short pulse from I/O pins of the coordinator's MCU. The latching circuit comprised optocouplers, switching transistors, digital NAND gates (forming reset-set flip-flop), and power transistors. The power transistors were used to switch on/off solenoid valves where irrigation pipes were connected. Switches were incorporated in the latching circuit to allow manual closing and opening of the valves in case of emergency.

It was prudent to use L182D01-ZB10A (SIRAI) solenoid valves because of the low cost, low power consumption (5.5 W when latched), and the possibility of using a 12 V direct current power supply. The two latter features allowed the use of a single 14 W, 12 V solar panel to power both the solenoid valves and the latching circuit. This was more appealing for deployments in rural areas of developing countries where grid power supply is either scarce or unstable.

With the above arrangements, the coordinator node was able to control the irrigation by sending short pulses to its MCU's I/O pins. Specifically, two pins were dedicated for each of the two solenoid valves; in which case when initiating irrigation, the coordinator had to send a HIGH pulse lasting 1 second to the latching circuit through one pin. The latching circuit had to hold this state until the coordinator sent another high pulse to the other pin indicating completion of irrigation and, hence, valves should close.

This study opted for drip irrigation system for the advantages it offers. Unlike the sprinkler system which sprinkles water all over the field, drip irrigation, also known as trickle

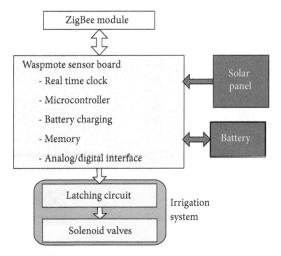

FIGURE 7: The architecture of a coordinator and actuator node.

irrigation, is a type of irrigation system that applies water slowly and directly into the root zone of plants. In this case, scarce water resources are conserved since there is little or no chance for water to evaporate before seeping into the ground. Besides, Humphreys and others [17] found that drip was 33% higher in water productivity than both sprinkler and furrow. However, the biggest challenge of drip irrigation is its high installation cost especially for a large field where a great deal of pipes, drippers, and valves are deployed throughout the field.

Since it is not recommended to apply water directly onto the sensors, this study placed the sensors midway between drippers. This allowed the water to diffuse around the drippers first before reaching the sensors resulting in the correct reporting of the moisture status of the soil.

2.1.6. The Gateway Node. One of the four in-field sensor nodes discussed in Section 2.1.3 assumed the role of a gateway used to send data to the RMS through a cellular network. In addition to a ZigBee module, this particular node was equipped with a GPRS module (refer to Figure 8). Just like any other in-field sensor node in this experiment, it was capturing Watermark frequency, soil temperature, and its battery level. The sensed data were sent to a coordinator for processing. Afterwards, the coordinator sent the processed data back to the gateway every 15 minutes when irrigation was in progress or every 30 minutes when the irrigation system was in an idle mode. The GPRS module residing on top of the gateway node was then used to communicate with the cellular network to forward the SMS data to the RMS for remote system diagnosis.

The sensor data were collected at intervals of 2 minutes or 30 minutes depending on whether the irrigation was in progress or not. However, this study opted for sending the data to the RMS at intervals of 15 minutes when irrigating and 30 minutes otherwise. This arrangement reduced considerably the cost of the remote monitoring system by decreasing the number of SMSs sent. It should be noted that the data transmitted to the RMS were used for diagnostic

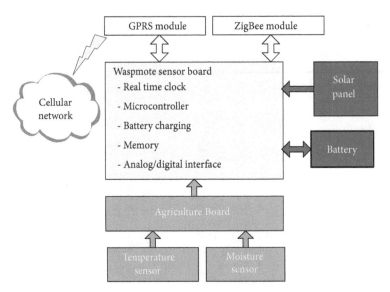

FIGURE 8: The architecture of a gateway node.

purposes only and not for decision making on when to initiate or terminate irrigation. Therefore, the data that were not forwarded to RMS were used by the controller in decision making.

Although it was possible to use the coordinator node to send data directly to a remote server by equipping it with a GPRS module, this study was motivated to use this structure because of the following confounding issues. Firstly, the coordinator was configured to be a nonsleeping device because it was responsible for network setup and maintenance. It was also responsible for actuating solenoid valves in addition to receiving and processing sensor data from all other nodes in the network. As such, it was the busiest node in the network and, consequently, its battery was being depleted extensively. It was therefore necessary to offload SMS sending duties to a gateway node which, otherwise, was less loaded. Obviously, sending the same amount of data through the ZigBee module consumes less power (2 mW) than sending through GPRS to the cellular network (2000 mW) [16].

Secondly, since the coordinator node was the heart of the whole system, its failure was very critical. For instance, when the irrigation process is in session and in the event that the coordinator collapses, the system would fail to terminate the irrigation. In this instance, if the coordinator was responsible for sending the fault alarm to the remote personnel, there was no way the personnel would receive such an alarm. As such, it was imperative that an independent node, in this case the gateway, checks the status of the coordinator, on a regular basis and reports any hitches directly to the personnel.

2.2. Remote Monitoring Station. Figure 9 shows two architectural parts of RMS of which the first is the monitoring personnel who receive valve status and fault alarms directly onto their mobile phone for prompt reaction to the IS. The fault alarms included low battery levels for sensor nodes and wireless communication link failures. The second part is the server which is a computer equipped with a broadband

dongle and was used to store and graphically display both current and historical IS data. The data stored in the server included SMP, soil temperature, battery voltage levels, valve status, and RSSI. There was a possibility of adding a third section to the RMS in the form of Internet connectivity which could allow the IS performance data to be accessed across the globe. However, due to financial limitation this section was not implemented.

Figure 10 presents a conceptual model of the server depicting how data emanating from the broadband dongle were processed and analysed graphically. Firstly, the data from the IS were received directly by the broadband dongle housed in the RMS. It was vital to delegate the data storing capabilities of the dongle to the first database. FrontlineSMS, a free open source software licensed under GNU Lesser General Public License, was used to receive the data because it offers a more user-friendly front-end browser based on Java FrontlineSMS back-end. Additionally, it has group forwarding, auto replying, and message forwarding functionalities.

The raw data stored in the first database were not in the right format and syntax because IS prepared the data to suit the SMS transmission system. Consequently, a Hypertext Preprocessor (PHP) script was used to create a new database where the processed data were stored ready to be graphed and uploaded onto the Internet. The study used PHPlot as a graph library to show the results graphically onto a computer screen.

3. Performance Evaluation

This study assessed the WSN deployment field readiness in agricultural application. Firstly, it investigated the ZigBee radio link performance through measurements of RSSI at different distances of the WSN nodes and different heights of the maize plants. Secondly, the study monitored battery performance for sensor nodes both at night and during the day. Thirdly, it was interesting to assess whether battery performance had a bearing on radio link performance or not.

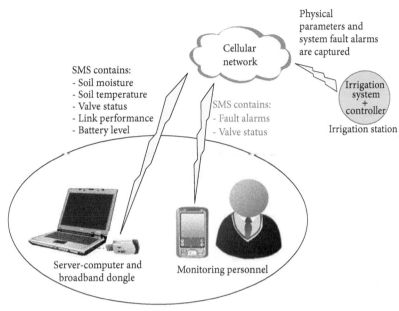

FIGURE 9: The architecture of the Remote Monitoring Station showing two parts and the type of information sent to each part.

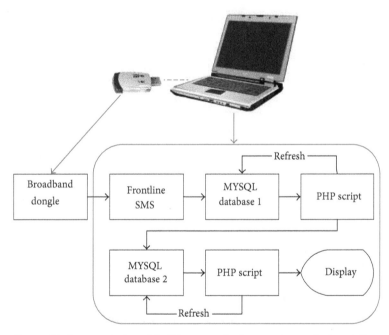

FIGURE 10: A conceptual model of the server for the remote monitoring station.

Finally, the fluctuations of SMP in the agricultural field were monitored.

3.1. Received Signal Strength Indicator. The performance of the WiPAM was assessed in terms of RSSI at different distances and heights of the maize plants. Zennaro and others [18] reported that RSSI is one of the three commonly used WSN link quality estimators which is a signal based indicator, and is computed over the signal present in the channel at a particular time. The other indicators are the link quality

indicator and the packet reception rate. In this experiment the performance of the network was analysed based on RSSI. Accordingly, the study used XBee-ZB modules at 2.4 GHz as radio transceivers whose sensitivity was −96 dBm [16]. This means that the communication link is bound to fail when RSSI goes below −96 dBm.

3.1.1. RSSI over Distance. The four in-field sensor nodes were fixed but the coordinator was moved from one place to another. In the first experiment, the coordinator node was placed in such a way that the relative distances between the respective sensor nodes and the coordinator were 23 m. All the nodes were placed at a height of 60 cm above the ground. In the second experiment, the coordinator was moved closer to the in-field nodes with a distance of 7 m to each node and at the same height as in the first scenario (Figure 5 shows sensor positions for this case).

Figure 11 shows the results of the network performance in terms of RSSI expressed in dBm when the distance between sensor nodes and the coordinator was 23 m. On the other hand, Figure 12 shows the same parameters when the distance was reduced to 7 m. The results show that the communication links were bound to fail when the distance was 23 m since the RSSI was at around −90 dBm which is very close to the receiver sensitivity of −96 dBm. On the other hand, it was essentially improbable for the network to fail when the distance between the nodes and the coordinator was 7 m since the RSSI was at around −58 dBm. These results confirm the FRIIS equation which states that RSSI varies inversely with the square of the distance.

Therefore, it is absolutely imperative in any practical deployment to consider placing sensor nodes in such a way that the distances between the nodes are optimized in accordance with the size of the field.

Furthermore, it is worth to note that multipath fading which was exacerbated by the movement of leaves of the maize plants played a very crucial role on RSSI. This is portrayed by the random fluctuation of the RSSI graphs shown in both Figures 11 and 12.

3.1.2. RSSI over Height of Crops.
As described in the previous section, the sensor nodes were placed at a height of 60 cm above the ground. Monitoring of the link performance commenced when the maize plants were 50 cm tall. At the end of the experiment the crops had grown to about 200 cm thereby covering the in-field sensor nodes completely. Figure 13 shows a scenario in which the sensor is being fully covered by the maize plants.

Figure 14(a) depicts the RSSI for individual nodes as a function of crop height. In order to clearly define the crop height impact on RSSI, the average RSSI for the nodes was plotted against the crop height as shown in Figure 14(b). The graph in this figure shows a slight decrement in the level of RSSI with crop height. However, as depicted by the best-fit line of the average RSSIs, there is no major degradation in the quality of the communication link corresponding to the height of the crops. Nevertheless, it is recommended that more experiments should be conducted to examine this observation especially when the distance between nodes is long. Furthermore, it may be interesting to explore the impact of frequency variation on RSSI.

3.2. Battery Level.
As the system had to be self-sustained in terms of power, solar panels and rechargeable Li-ion batteries were used to power all electronic devices in this system. After evaluating the performance of the system in terms of power usage, it was discovered that the three in-field sensor nodes were more efficient than the coordinator. As generally

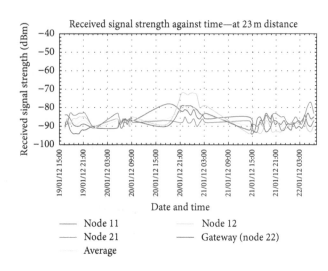

FIGURE 11: Received signal strength against time—at 23 m distance.

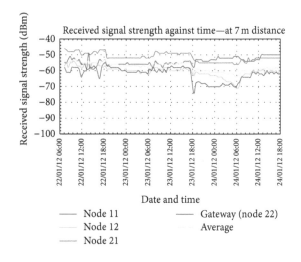

FIGURE 12: Received signal strength against time—at 7 m distance.

FIGURE 13: Sensor node being covered by maize plants.

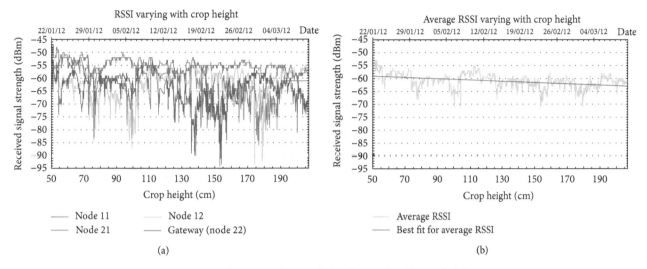

FIGURE 14: Variation of received signal strength with crop height.

expected, this was solely due to the fact that the three in-field sensor nodes were using deep sleeping mode as a way of conserving power. The coordinator node was never put into sleeping mode. In spite of employing sleeping mode, the gateway node had its battery level depleted so quickly because most of its power was being used for sending SMSs to a remote monitoring site. Through these experiments it was found that the 2.5 W solar panels were enough for the three in-field sensor nodes, while the gateway and coordinator had to be powered by 5 W and 7.5 W solar panels, respectively. The batteries of the gateway and the coordinator were changed from 1150 mAh to 2300 mAh and 2450 mAh, respectively, while 1150 mAh batteries sufficed all the other three in-field sensor nodes.

Figure 15 shows the battery levels for all the five sensor nodes used in this experiment. Clearly, the gateway and coordinator batteries were a major concern in this deployment before the changes were effected. The graphs in this figure show that on a number of occasions (e.g., on 3rd, 10th, 12th, and 18th January, 2012) the coordinator battery was depleted completely. At these instances, the system had to be resuscitated by a higher capacity battery which was used for powering the valves. As depicted by the graphs, all the batteries were heavily depleted between 18th January and 21st January when there was no sunshine due to heavy rains. It was after this point in time that the changes in the powering requirements of the gateway and the coordinator were inevitable.

3.3. Battery Level versus RSSI. It was important to investigate the correlation between the battery level and RSSI as performance parameters. Figure 16 shows graphs of the four nodes' battery levels and RSSIs plotted on the same time scale. The results show that there is a correlation between the battery level and the RSSI. Both battery level and RSSI peak at around 3:00 PM and slump dramatically at around 4:00 AM. They

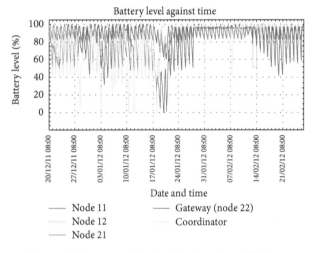

FIGURE 15: Sensor node battery level varying with time.

start to peak again at around 7:00 AM when the sun rises and starts to charge batteries.

Furthermore, it was observed that the random fluctuations of RSSIs were as a result of the interaction of radio waves with the plant cover's dynamic nature affected by air flow in the field. This might have contributed significantly to a weak correlation between RSSIs and battery levels as depicted in Table 1 for node 11, $r(215) = 0.23$, $P < 0.05$; node 12, $r(215) = 0.16$, $P < 0.05$; node 21, $r(215) = 0.2$, $P < 0.05$; node 22, $r(215) = 0.15$, $P < 0.05$.

The results demonstrate the need to balance between power and RSSI requirements to achieve a specified quality of service (QoS). Specifically, the battery discharge level should be minimised where a high level of RSSI is required. Conversely, the RSSI could be compromised in noncritical applications where conservation of battery power is of paramount importance.

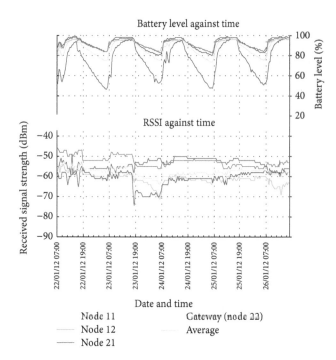

FIGURE 16: Correlation analysis between sensor node battery level and RSSI.

TABLE 1: Correlation analysis between sensor node battery level and RSSI.

Node 11	Node 12	Node 21	Node 22
0.23, 215, 0	0.16, 215, 0	0.24, 215, 0	0.15, 215, 0

3.4. Soil Moisture Potential. Since the main objective of WiPAM was to automate irrigation, it was important for the management personnel to remotely monitor SMP fluctuations in the agricultural field and compare with the set levels. In order to satisfy the plant water needs, irrigation was initiated when the SMP at any of the two sensor locations dropped to −19.2 kPa which represented a 50% management allowable depletion. The irrigation was then terminated when both sensors reported at least −11.3 kPa representing a 10% of depletion from the field capacity (FC) of −9.88 kPa. These threshold levels were established based on the water holding capacity of the soil type at the site. Based on the set SMP threshold levels the personnel precisely predicted the next irrigation event by tracing the displayed graphs of SMP on the computer.

Figure 17 shows how the controller managed the irrigation scheduling by keeping the level of SMP within the stated limits. However, as it can be seen from the graphs, it was really hard for the controller to safeguard the upper limit. Although the controller terminated the irrigation at −11.3 kPa, on most occasions the moisture still rose to just over the FC. This is due to the fact that water diffuses gradually into the soil. As such, by the time the sensor reports a change in water level the system will have already applied a bit more water. This water will continue trickling down for some time. As a solution

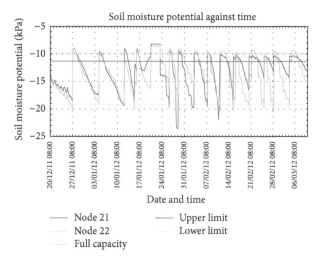

FIGURE 17: Soil moisture potential varying with time.

to this predicament, the study chose a slightly lower cut-off point of SMP than FC so to avoid over irrigation.

In order to contain this problem further, it is recommended that the use of water budget scheduling strategy should be adopted. In this strategy, the irrigation controller computes the amount of water needed for each irrigation event based on the current SMP readings. The controller then irrigates for an estimated duration after which it terminates the irrigation and goes into hibernation for a predetermined period of time. Upon waking up, it measures the SMP and reirrigates if the level is lower than FC; otherwise, it stops the irrigation. This study suggests that in this way over irrigation will be avoided, and hence, water resources will be managed effectively without compromising the crop yield.

The graphs in Figure 17 also show a very interesting phenomenon about how crop water use varies with growth stage. During the early stages there were fewer irrigation events than at later stages when the maize had grown. For instance, there were about three irrigation events between 20 December 2011 and 12 January 2012 (23 days) as compared to five events between 7 and 28 February (21 days).

4. Challenges and Experiences Gained

This study has exposed a number of valuable experiences which can be used to speed up the process of designing new WSN deployments for PA. Firstly, the study revealed a practical challenge concerning the conflict between ZigBee and GPRS modules. When both ZigBee and GPRS modules were powered up, either of them would lose connection which required manual reset. Nonetheless, using an appropriate software configuration in the gateway node, it was possible to turn off one module when the other was active. This was not possible at the coordinator node since its ZigBee module was always required to be on to avoid losing connection with the other network nodes. However, this conflict could be specific to Waspmote and probably dependent on the firmware. It could be solved in a future release of firmware and may not be a general problem.

Secondly, there was a challenge of powering requirements for the sensor nodes which, on several occasions, required site visit to resolve the problem. The batteries for the coordinator and gateway nodes were being heavily depleted. The system, nonetheless, became remarkably resilient to power failure when battery capacities for the gateway and coordinator nodes were increased. The robustness of the system was further enhanced by increasing the sampling time from 5 minutes to 30 minutes when in idle mode and from 1 minute to 2 minutes when irrigating. This implies that where power supply is limited, or in order to reduce the cost of WSN deployment through the use of low capacity batteries and small-sized solar Photovoltaic panels, one needs to consider increasing the sampling time. Therefore, this study concludes that it is advisable for a large network to divide the system into several independent subnetworks so that no single node is used to amass the data from all the other nodes. It was also noted that keeping distances between sensors as short as possible can improve battery performance tremendously as generally expected.

Thirdly, a very crucial requirement of any WSN deployment is close monitoring. Rather than conducting physical site visit, which is time consuming and expensive, it was compelling to monitor the system performance remotely. This was imperative as personnel could timely identify system faults and conduct pre-emptive maintenance by visiting the field only when needed. The study suggests that any successful WSN deployment must involve remote monitoring through a cellular network which is broadly available even in rural areas of developing countries.

Finally, it was also observed that there is a possibility of disturbing the sensors during field work, for example, weeding.

5. Conclusion and Future Work

This paper has demonstrated how an IMS can be implemented based on WSN. It has further evaluated the performance of the design in order to develop a more robust and sustainable system considering the challenges that any practical deployment would face. Specifically, the paper has explored battery performance for sensor nodes, RSSI, and the correlation between the two. The study suggests that sensor battery performance has serious repercussions on the robustness of WSN deployment since it erodes RSSI. The study has also shown that placement of sensor nodes in the agricultural field is critical. The distance between sensor nodes has to be as short as possible in order to improve the resilience of the system remarkably.

Furthermore, it has been revealed that several performance parameters can be monitored cost effectively using a WSN node equipped with a GPRS module and using open source tools that include FrontlineSMS, MYSQL, and PHP. The use of cellular network reduces the cost of the remote monitoring system since an SMS charge is extremely low as compared to satellite communication or Wi-Fi connectivity. Moreover, cellular network coverage is broad even in remote areas of developing countries.

However, a large-scale deployment is proposed in order to assess the ability of the ZC node in handling numerous queries from the in-field sensors. Since WSNs are flexible on the software layer and, hence, can accept any scheduling strategy, it is further proposed that future deployments should focus on improving water application efficiency. In this way, both water and energy used in irrigation water pumping will be conserved. It is envisaged that this will foster installations of low-capacity solar photovoltaic water pumping systems for irrigation to suit the socioeconomic conditions of small scale farmers in developing countries.

While it would be interesting to explore the practical performance of WSN irrigation systems in other areas of Malawi, this paper suggests that such setups would compare well with the current deployment in Blantyre. This is also because Malawi as a small country experiences almost evenly distributed weather conditions.

Conflict of Interests

The authors of this paper declare that the choice of all devices and software applications used in this research was solely on a professional basis. There is no direct financial relation with the trademarks mentioned in this paper that might lead to a conflict of interest.

Acknowledgments

The authors of this paper would like to thank the Community Rural Electrification and Development Project funded by the Scottish Government through the University of Strathclyde for providing the equipment deployed in this study. Furthermore, the authors thank Damien Frame of the University of Strathclyde and Elijah Banda of the Malawi Polytechnic for their tremendous contributions leading to the success of this project. This paper was partly supported by the project "Secured quality of service aware wireless sensor networks: toward effective network and energy management" funded by a Grant from the South African National Research Foundation.

References

[1] S. Fazackerley and R. Lawrence, "Reducing turfgrass water consumption using sensor nodes and an adaptive irrigation controller," in *Proceedings of the IEEE Sensors Applications Symposium (SAS '10)*, pp. 90–94, February 2010.

[2] J. Balendonck, J. Hemming, B. van Tuijl, L. Incrocci, A. Pardossi, and P. Marzialetti, "Sensors and wireless sensor networks for irrigation management under deficit conditions (FLOW-AID)," FLOW-AID, 2008.

[3] M. Keshtgary and A. Deljoo, "An efficient wireless sensor network for precision agriculture," *Canadian Journal on Multimedia and Wireless Networks*, vol. 3, no. 1, pp. 1–5, 2012.

[4] Y. Zhou, X. Yang, L. Wang, and Y. Ying, "A wireless design of low-cost irrigation system using ZigBee technology," in *Proceedings of the International Conference on Networks Security, Wireless Communications and Trusted Computing (NSWCTC '09)*, pp. 572–575, April 2009.

[5] A. Prince-Pike, *Power characterisation of a ZigBee wireless network in a real time monitoring application [M.S. thesis]*, Auckland University of Technology, 2009.

[6] IRROMETER Company, *WATERMARK Soil Moisture Sensor MODEL 200SS*, Riverside, Calif, USA, 2010.

[7] Libelium, "Watermark Sensors Interpretation Reference," Libelium Comunicaciones Distribuidas S.L., pp. 1-6.

[8] C. C. Shock, J. M. Barnum, and M. Seddigh, "Calibration of watermark soil moisture sensors for irrigation management," in *International Irrigation Show*, pp. 139-146, Irrigation Association, San Diego, Calif, USA, 1998.

[9] R. Allen, "Calibration for the watermark 200ss soil water potential sensor to fit the 7-19-96 "calibration no.3" table from irrometer," University of Idaho, Kimberley, Idaho, USA, 2000.

[10] R. B. Thompson, M. Gallardo, T. Agüera, L. C. Valdez, and M. D. Fernández, "Evaluation of the Watermark sensor for use with drip irrigated vegetable crops," *Irrigation Science*, vol. 24, no. 3, pp. 185-202, 2006.

[11] J. Chard, "Watermark soil moisture sensors: characteristics and operating instructions," Utah State University, 2002.

[12] P. R. Johnstone, T. K. Hartz, M. LeStrange, J. J. Nunez, and E. M. Miyao, "Managing fruit soluble solids with late-season deficit irrigation in drip-irrigated processing tomato production," *HortScience*, vol. 40, no. 6, pp. 1857-1861, 2005.

[13] Texas Water Development Board, "Agricultural Water Conservation Practices," 2004.

[14] M. Morris, "Soil moisture monitoring: low-cost tools and methods," National Center for Appropriate Technology (NCAT), pp. 1-12, 2006.

[15] S. Irmak, J. Payero, D. Eisenhauer et al., "Watermark Granular Matrix Sensor to Measure Soil Matrix Potential for Irrigation Management," University of Nebraska-Lincoln Extension, 2006.

[16] Libelium, "Waspmote datasheet, vers. 0.8," Libelium Comunicaciones Distribuidas S.L., pp. 1-6, 2010.

[17] L. Humphreys, B. Fawcett, C. O. Neill, and W. Muirhead, "Maize under sprinkler, drip & furrow irrigation," *IREC Farmers' Newsletter*, no. 170, pp. 35-38, 2005.

[18] M. Zennaro, H. Ntareme, and A. Bagula, "Experimental evaluation of temporal and energy characteristics of an outdoor sensor network," in *Proceedings of the International Conference on Mobile Technology, Applications, and Systems (Mobility '08)*, pp. 99:1-99:5, ACM, New York, NY, USA, September 2008.

9

Efficient Data Dissemination in Urban VANETs: Parked Vehicles Are Natural Infrastructures

Hui Zhao and Jinqi Zhu

School of Computer Science and Engineering, University of Electronic Science and Technology of China, Chengdu, Sichuan 611731, China

Correspondence should be addressed to Hui Zhao, jenniferzhao09@gmail.com

Academic Editor: Ming Liu

Data dissemination is the fundamental operation in vehicular ad hoc networks (VANETs); for example, after an accident or congestion is detected by the corresponding sensors mounted on the vehicles, an alert message should be swiftly disseminated to the vehicles moving towards the affected areas. However, the unique characteristics of VANETs, such as high mobility of vehicle nodes, intermittent connectivity, and rapidly dynamic topology, make data dissemination over them extremely challenging. Motivated by the fact that there are large amounts of roadside parked vehicles in urban areas, this paper proposes a parking-based data dissemination scheme for VANETs. Data to be disseminated are buffered at the roadside parked vehicle, which continuously provides data dissemination services for the vehicles passing by. We analyze the challenging issues in achieving parking-based data dissemination and provide possible solution for each issue. Theoretical results illustrate the effectiveness of our approach, and simulation results based on a real city map and realistic traffic situations show that the proposed data dissemination paradigm achieves a higher delivery ratio with lower network load and reasonable delivery delay.

1. Introduction

Nowadays, to facilitate better road safety and comfort driving, more and more vehicles are equipped with wireless devices and different types of sensors. Consequently, large-scale vehicular networks are expected to be available in the near future. With its popularity, VANETs are envisioned to provide us with numerous useful applications. One typical application is intelligent transportation system; for example, after an accident or congestion is detected by the corresponding sensors mounted on the vehicles, an alert message would be swiftly disseminated to the vehicles moving towards the affected areas via vehicular communication. Taking advantage of this application, incoming vehicles will be informed in advance of these accidents/congestions and the drivers may take another route/appropriate actions. Other applications also include available parking spaces notification and commercial ads dissemination. Undoubtedly, these applications would improve our driving experience greatly.

The basic operation in the aforementioned applications is data dissemination. Unfortunately, VANETs are characterized by rapidly dynamic topology, intermittent connectivity, and high mobility of vehicle nodes, which make data dissemination over it a challenging issue. Most of the existing works take advantage of the inter-vehicle communication to achieve data dissemination [1–4]. The weakness of the inter-vehicle scheme is that data to be disseminated can hardly be kept within a target area in highly mobile environments. Towards solving the problem, two abiding geocast techniques [5] could be adopted. One is periodically broadcasting each data at the deployed server. Another is maintaining each data at selected moving vehicles within the target area. For the first approach, when tens of thousands of messages are routed over a long distance to the target areas, excessive transmissions and severe congestion are inevitable. For the second approach, continuous node selection and message handover are required due to the high mobility of vehicle nodes, which incurs great overheads.

In view of the insufficiency of inter-vehicle data dissemination, some researches put forward the infrastructure-based data dissemination. In [6], Zhao et al. propose to deploy roadside units to assist data dissemination. Data to be disseminated are stored temporarily at roadside units in the target area and broadcasted periodically to the vehicles passing by. This scheme is proved to be effective. However, the deployment of roadside units at the city scale also requires a large amount of investment.

In this paper, we propose a parking-based data dissemination scheme, which harnesses the free resource offered by roadside parking for data dissemination in urban areas. Our proposal is inspired by a real world urban parking report [7], which provides the parking statistics of two surveys in a central area of Montreal city in Canada. It investigated the 61,000 daily parking events in an area of 5,500 square kilometers. According to the report, street parking accounts for 69.2% of total parking, and the average duration of street parking lasts 6.64 hours. It generates many roadside vehicle nodes easy to communicate and enables them to support long-time communication. The basic idea of our parking-based data dissemination scheme is simple: if a vehicle often drives through extensive vehicles parked at roadside, why not let these parked vehicles support data dissemination as roadside infrastructure?

We organize the parked vehicles into different clusters, propose an effective routing scheme to distribute each data message to appropriate roadside parking, and adopt the pub/sub scheme to perform data dissemination. Moreover, we investigate our scheme through theoretic analysis, realistic survey, and simulation. The results prove that our scheme achieves a higher delivery ratio with lower network load and reasonable delivery delay.

The original contributions that we have made in the paper are highlighted as follows.

(i) We exploit the roadside parked vehicles to achieve data dissemination in urban VANETs. Our scheme aims at reducing the overhead brought by inter-vehicle scheme and avoiding the costs brought by constructing roadside infrastructure.

(ii) We tackle the main challenges in realizing parking-based data dissemination, for example, how to manage the roadside parked vehicles and how to route a data message to the targeted parking efficiently.

(iii) We evaluate our parking-based data dissemination scheme through theoretical analysis, realistic survey, and simulation. The numeric results show that our scheme is effective.

The remainder of this paper is structured as follows. Section 2 makes a brief overview of related work. Section 3 presents the system model. In Section 4, we explain our parking-based data dissemination scheme in detail. Section 5 proves the effectiveness of our scheme through theoretical analysis, while Section 6 evaluates our scheme through realistic survey and simulation. Finally, Section 7 summarizes the paper.

2. Related Work

Data dissemination over VANETs is extremely challenging due to the unique characteristics of VANETs. In the last decade, many research effects have been devoted to addressing the data dissemination issues in VANETs. Xu et al. propose an opportunistic dissemination (OD) scheme [8]. In this scheme, the data center periodically broadcasts some data, which will be received and stored by passing vehicles. Whenever two vehicles move into the transmission range of each other, they exchange data. This scheme does not rely on any infrastructure. However, the performance of the OD scheme is poor in areas with high vehicle density due to media access control (MAC) layer collisions. This can easily lead to severe congestion and significantly reduce the data delivery ratio. To mitigate the excessive transmissions and congestion, Korkmaz et al. [9] propose a link-layer broadcast protocol to help disseminate the data. The protocol relies on link-layer acknowledge mechanisms to improve the reliability of the multihop broadcast. However, in the case of network congestion, the link-layer solution is not enough. Furthermore, since many information sources may exist in a given urban area, the amount of broadcasted data from these sources can easily consume the limited bandwidth. In [1], Nekovee M proposes an improved Epidemic scheme, which takes advantage of the clustering characteristics of vehicle flow and broadcasts message at the edge of each cluster. This scheme reduces the communication overhead at some extent. In [2], the notification area is divided into several subareas, and message is disseminated based on each subarea, which effectively limits the broadcast range of each message. In [3], the authors put forward MDDV scheme, which exploits the vehicles called message holder to carry the message to the notification area and broadcast it in this area. In [4], Wu et al. propose a mobile distribution-aware data dissemination scheme MDA for VANETS. In MDA, the subscribers' distribution is predicted, and the forwarding of the notification token is controlled to achieve effective distribution of notification brokers (notification-token holder). Although [1–4] cut down the network overhead to some extent. The data to be disseminated can hardly be kept in the target area owing to the intermittent connectivity of VANETs.

Recently, many approaches have been proposed to realize persistent data availability in VANETs. A basic approach is the server approach in [5], in which the server periodically delivers the message to the destination region using a geocast routing protocol. The deficiency of this approach is that frequent broadcasting at the server would consume a large amount of bandwidth. An alternative approach is the Election approach in [5]. It stores the messages at elected mobile nodes inside the geocast destination region. Due to the high mobility of vehicle nodes, continuous node selection and message handover are required in this case.

To reduce the amount of data poured from the server, Zhao et al. [6] propose the idea of intersection buffering, in which the relay and broadcast station (IBer) is used to buffer data copies at the intersection. The IBer broadcasts each message periodically. As a result, the server does not have to frequently broadcast data to guarantee that each vehicle receives the data. In [10], the authors also propose to use stationary roadside units to improve data dissemination performance. In [11], they further discuss the strategic placement of roadside units. Although the deployment of roadside units could improve the dissemination performance dramatically, the widely deployed roadside units will lead to great investments.

3. System Model

3.1. Assumptions. First, we assume that vehicles are equipped with various types of sensors, GPS, and preloaded electric maps, which are already popular in new cars and will be common in the future. Second, we assume that some vehicle users will share their devices during parking. This could be motivated by effective incentives, as indicated in [12, 13]. Finally, we assume that each data message is attached with the following two attributes: (1) target areas, which are the areas where the data is most likely to be interested, and (2) survival time, which indicates the survival time of the data. This assumption is based on the following observation: the disseminated data are often spatial or/and temporal sensitive; for example, for an accident notification message, it is most likely to be the interest of drivers moving towards the affected area, and this message will be invalid after the traffic accident is properly treated.

3.2. Scenario. As shown in Figure 1, the parked vehicles are widely distributed at the roadside in urban area. At a certain moment, a traffic accident happens in one road segment. Assume that the vehicles are equipped with accident detection sensors and the sensor output is monitored and processed by a microcontroller. After the microcontroller detects this traffic accident based on the input from the sensors, it would broadcast an emergency notification message. To lower the impact of this accident on the traffic condition, the emergency notification message should be forwarded to the vehicles moving towards the affected area, so that the drivers could choose to take another route. Similar applications also include parking statistics dissemination. In [14], it is reported that cruising for parking wastes 47,000 gallons of gasoline and produces 730 tons of CO_2 emissions per year in a small business district of Los Angeles. If drivers are provided with parking data dissemination services, the parking space searching costs would be greatly reduced. With the popularity of VANETs, more and more applications would be emerging in VANETs. While tens of thousands of data messages are flooded into the VANETs, an efficient data dissemination scheme is indispensable. Therefore, it is of great significance to develop highly efficient data dissemination scheme for urban VANETs.

In our parking-based data dissemination scheme, data to be disseminated are buffered at the roadside parked vehicle, which continuously provides services for the vehicles passing by. Overall, our parking-based scheme involves the following four components.

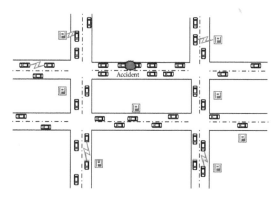

FIGURE 1: A sample scenario.

(1) Data source could be a computer with a wireless interface, a wireless access point, or an infostation [15].

(2) Data forwarders are the vehicles which help to forward a data item from the data source to the targeted parking clusters.

(3) Roadside parking cluster is composed of a group of vehicles which are parked along the same road segment and belong to the same partially connected network.

(4) End users are the vehicle users who have interests in a certain set of data messages while driving.

4. The Proposed Parking-Based Scheme

To facilitate data dissemination, we organize the roadside parked vehicles into clusters. Generally, our proposed parking-based data dissemination scheme is divided into two phases: data forwarding from the data source to appropriate parking clusters within the target area and data dissemination from the parking cluster to vehicles passing by.

4.1. Parking Cluster. A realistic survey [16] provides a quantitative understanding of roadside parking in cities, in which the on-street parking meters in the Ann Arbor city are continuously monitored during six midweek days. It shows that the parking time is 41.40 minutes in average, with a standard deviation of 27.17. The occupancy ratio, defined as occupied space-hour/available space-hour, averages 93.0% throughout one day. Even the occupancy ratio during off-peak time reaches almost 80%. Due to the high stability and utilization of roadside parking, clustering parked vehicles is feasible in urban areas. In our parking-based scheme, we group the vehicles which are parked along the same road segment and are mutually reachable into a cluster and take it as data buffering unit at street level. Considering the fact that vehicle mobility is strictly constrained by traffic rules and street layout, buffering each data at some clusters in the target area is enough. Therefore, we will first introduce how to elect data buffering units from the existing clusters and then give our cluster management scheme.

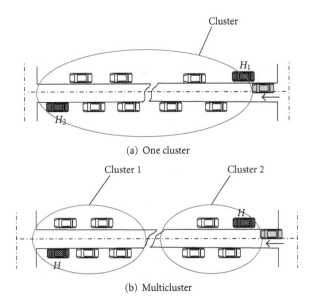

(a) One cluster

(b) Multicluster

Figure 2: Data buffering unit.

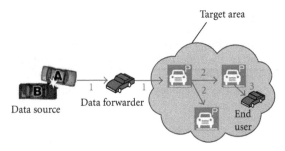

Figure 3: Data forwarding process.

In some road segments, the parked vehicles form one cluster, as shown in Figure 2(a). In other road segments, the parked vehicles are isolated from each other and form different partially distributed groups, as shown in Figure 2(b). To determine whether it should act as data buffering unit, we let each cluster periodically report its distribution to other clusters along the same road (with the help of vehicles traveling across the road). After obtaining the distribution of other clusters along the same road, a cluster decides whether it would work as buffering unit according to following rule: if there is only one cluster along the road, this cluster is undoubtedly elected as data buffering unit; if there are two or more than two clusters along the road, the two clusters located at the two ends of the road are elected as data buffering units. After elected as data buffering unit, a cluster needs to be responsible for the cluster management, including head election and membership management.

In our scheme, we specify the following head selection mechanism. In a scenario in Figure 2(a), the two vehicles located at the two ends of the cluster are elected as cluster head. In a two-way road, the two cluster heads, respectively, provide services for the vehicles coming from the nearest intersection. In a scenario in Figure 2(b), the vehicle which locates at the end of the road segment is elected as cluster head in each cluster; this is also to ensure that a vehicle moving into the road could encounter the cluster head in a short time. After the cluster head is determined, the cluster members periodically report their position to the cluster head. Thus, the cluster head is able to manage all parked vehicles, act as local service access points, and perform the data dissemination operation. Considering the fact that the vehicle works as cluster head might leave at any time, we specify the following rule: while the cluster head is leaving (the engine is started), a new round of head selection is triggered, and the data to be disseminated as well as the

cluster state are transferred from the old cluster head to the new one.

4.2. Data Forwarding from Data Source to Roadside Parking. In our parking-based scheme, the parking clusters help to buffer the data messages in their target area and provide data dissemination service for the vehicles passing by. To realize this one-hop data dissemination, the data source should first distribute each data to the selected parking clusters within the target area. According to the strategy used, this process could be further divided into two phases: routing from data source to one parking cluster (step 1 in Figure 3) and routing from one parking cluster to other parking clusters (step 2 in Figure 3). We will describe them in detail in the following part.

4.2.1. Routing from Data Source to One Parking Cluster. While investigating the routing from the data source to one parking cluster in the target area, we first focus on the most common scenario, in which the location of the data source is out of the target area of the data message. In our scheme, apart from taking advantage of the mobile vehicles, we also exploit the parked vehicles for data forwarding. To be specific, in the straightway mode, the geographically greedy forwarding is used to forward the data message to the intersection ahead. Here, specially, the parked vehicles are deemed as special mobile vehicles (velocity = 0) and involved in the process of geographically greedy forwarding. In the intersection mode, a vehicle finds the next road to forward the packet according to the utility function of each available road, which is determined by the vehicle density (including both the moving vehicles and parked vehicles) in this road and the distance from the next intersection to the target area.

The utility function of a road segment is defined as follows:

$$U = \frac{\rho_m + \rho_p}{d}, \qquad (1)$$

where ρ_m represents the density of mobile vehicles, ρ_p represents the density of parked vehicles, and d is the shortest distance form the next intersection to the target area. If we assume N_m to be the number of parked vehicles in a road segment, N_p to be the number of parked vehicles, L to be the length of this road segment, and r_{pva} to be the ratio of parked vehicles which are willing to provide parking assistance service, we have

$$\rho_m = \frac{N_m}{L}, \tag{2}$$

$$\rho_p = \frac{r_{\text{pva}} N_p}{L}. \tag{3}$$

For N_p, it could be easily obtained, and for N_m, it could be estimated as follows: the cluster head first estimates the driving time within this segment based on the average velocity as $T = L/v$ and then counts the number of vehicles passing by within time period of T.

Using the above data forwarding strategy, a message could be routed to its target area efficiently. After arriving at a road in the target area, the data is propagated along this road. While its carrier encounters the first parking cluster, it forwards the data to this parking cluster. This parking cluster is then responsible for sending the data to the other parking clusters in the same target area. To indicate whether a parking cluster is the first one obtaining the data in the target area, we adopt an additional bit in the head of each message, where 0 represents it has not traversed any parking cluster until now, while 1 represents it has traversed at least one parking cluster.

If the data source is within the target area of a data, the routing process becomes much simpler. Data is sent to a vehicle that moves into its communication range, which works as mobile helper and forward this data along this road, until the carrier encounters a parking cluster.

4.2.2. Routing from One Parking Cluster to Other Parking Clusters.
To effectively route a data to all parking clusters in the target area, we propose a tree-based data forwarding scheme, which forwards each data message from one parking cluster to the other parking clusters in the same target area over a tree structure. We assume that one parking cluster knows the location of other parking clusters within the same target area. This could be realized through a simple mechanism with the help of moving vehicles. For example, each parking cluster periodically broadcasts its location (the location of cluster head) to the parking clusters within two hops (the TTL is set as 2), and adjacent parking clusters exchange the information (similar like <cluster ID, location>) they obtain with each other. This process is similar to Link-State Broadcast [17]. Due to the high occupancy of parking lots, a long broadcast cycle is enough. As some vehicles may move away while others may move in, the location reported from the same cluster at different time might be slightly different. We abstract the parking clusters and the roads in a target area as a weighted connected graph $G(V, E)$, where V is the set of parking clusters and E is the set of roads between two adjacent parking clusters (might be more than one segment). Weight d_{ij} on E is the estimated transmission delay between adjacent parking clusters. Figure 4 shows one such weighted connected graph. We let adjacent parking lot clusters periodically send a delay probe packet to each other and estimate the transmission delay according to the history record. As the transmission delay between two parking lot clusters is affected by their mutual distance, the

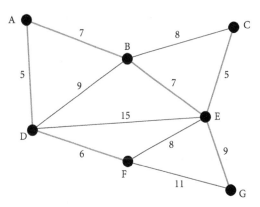

FIGURE 4: One minimum spanning tree.

traffic density, and other factors that change slowly, this approximation is reasonable.

The transmission delay between each pair of parking clusters forms a delay matrix, which is updated periodically. With this delay matrix, each parking vehicle could derive a minimum spanning tree, such that the total estimated transmission delay is minimized while routing over this tree. The minimum spanning tree could be easily acquired at each parking cluster through the classic Kruskal's algorithm or Prim's algorithm, both of which are of polynomial complexity. As these two algorithms are all very simple, we will not elaborate them here. If the minimum spanning tree is not unique, the one covers that the shortest road length is chosen as data forwarding tree. Through this way, we could make sure that each parking cluster in a target area maintains the same MST at the same time point. With this tree obtained in each cluster, each data message records its previous hop and is forwarded along this tree. Here, the data forwarding from one cluster to a next-hop cluster uses the routing approach presented in the previous section.

Although routing a packet along any one spanning tree could make sure that the packet could be received by every parking cluster, routing along the minimum spanning tree could realize the same goal in a shorter time. With this routing scheme, each packet only needs to be replicated while new tree branch appears, which greatly decreases the transmission overhead. Moreover, the consistency among packets buffered at different parking clusters could also be maintained.

4.3. Demand-Driven Data Dissemination.
VANETs are characterized by limited bandwidth. To make full use of this scarce resource, blind data dissemination should be avoided. We observe that the vehicle users usually only have interests in certain types of data items. Thus, we adopt a demand-driven data dissemination scheme. The vehicles users express their interests in certain types of data messages, while the parking cluster delivers the matched ones to them. In this sense, our system is a pub/sub system. The data source acts as publisher, the mobile vehicle acts as subscriber, while the parking cluster acts as a broker, which is used to ensure

that the data from the data source could be delivered to the subscribers.

To achieve the demand-driven data dissemination, the format of a data message is defined as <MsgID, AOI, topic, TTL>, among which the MsgID represents the ID of this data message, AOI represents the target areas, topic indicates the type, and TTL is the survival time of this data message. For the topic, it is represented by a tree as follows in Figure 5.

The data dissemination at the parking cluster includes the following three phases.

(1) Subscribe: an end user customizes a subscription according to his/her requirements, and this subscription is periodically broadcasted in the control channel.

(2) Match: once receiving a subscription, the parking cluster compares it against the stored data messages. This could be realized using the existing matching algorithm [18, 19].

(3) Data dissemination: if there is any data messages which match the subscription, the parking clusters broadcast it in the service channel, which is then received by the subscribers.

Due to the fact that each data item is buffered at multiple parking clusters in the same target area, a vehicle may receive replicas of the same data message while driving in this area. To avoid this problem, we let the subscriber piggyback the IDs of the last n data messages received while broadcasting the subscription. Through this way, we could guarantee that the vehicle users will not be disturbed by replicas of the same data message.

5. Theoretical Analysis

We consider a road segment S with length L. Assume that the number of vehicles moving on this road is K_m, among which the number of vehicles that carry the desired message is K_c. The communication range of each vehicle is R, and there are K_P vehicles parked uniformly along one side of this road. Imagine that a vehicle moves into road S at time 0. We will investigate the probability of getting the desired message through the inter-vehicle-based scheme and the parking-based scheme, respectively, on this road segment.

5.1. Parking-Based Scheme. As the vehicles are uniformly parked along road S, we have the number of vehicles parked within a distance of R of the intersection is

$$N_e = K_p \cdot \frac{R}{L}. \tag{4}$$

Here, the width of the road is neglected. Among the N_e vehicles, the probability of at least one vehicle willing to provide PVA services is

$$p = 1 - \left(1 - \text{pva}_{\text{ratio}}\right)^{N_e}. \tag{5}$$

Substituting N_e with (3), we have the probability for a vehicle getting a data from the parking cluster at the intersection is:

$$p = 1 - \left(1 - \text{pva}_{\text{ratio}}\right)^{K_p R/L}. \tag{6}$$

Now we assume $L = 1000\,\text{m}$, $R = 200\,\text{m}$, $\text{pva}_{\text{ratio}} = 30\%$, and study how the probability p varies with the number of parked vehicles, with the results shown in Figure 6.

We observe that with 40 vehicles parked along a road with a length of 1 km, the probability for the vehicle getting the data at the intersection is higher than 94%. From the parking report [16], we learn that the average number of parked vehicles along a road (in one side) with 1 km is much higher than 40 in urban areas. Thus, while taking advantage of the parking cluster, the probability of getting the desired data at the intersection is greater than 94%.

5.2. Inter-Vehicle Scheme. We assume $N(t)$; $t \geq 0$ denotes the number of encountered mobile vehicles in the time of $(0, t]$. Notice that the $N(t)$, $t \geq 0$ satisfies the conditions of the Poisson process [20]. Therefore, $N(t)$, $t \geq 0$ is a Poisson process. We define W_n as a random variable and have the sequence of $W_0 = 0, \ldots,$ $W_i = t_i, \ldots,$ where t_i stands for the beginning until encountering the number i mobile vehicle. According to the properties of Poisson process, we can derive that $W_n, n = 1, 2, \ldots$ is an Erlang distribution, with the probability density function expressed as

$$f_{W_n}(t) = \begin{cases} \dfrac{\lambda^n}{\Gamma(n)} t^{n-1} e^{-\lambda t}, & \text{if } t \geq 0, \\ 0, & \text{otherwise.} \end{cases} \tag{7}$$

Then, we have the probability of encountering the number n mobile vehicle in the time of $(0, t]$ is

$$F(t) = \int_0^t \frac{\lambda^n}{\Gamma(n)} t^{n-1} e^{-\lambda t} dt = \sum_{k=n}^{\infty} \frac{\lambda t^k}{k!} e^{-\lambda t}. \tag{8}$$

As the possibility for a moving vehicle carrying the desired data item, represented by P, is K_c/K_m, the possibility of obtaining the desired data item from the number n encountered vehicle is

$$p_n = \sum_{k=n}^{\infty} \frac{\lambda t^k}{k!} e^{-\lambda t} (1-P)^{n-1} P. \tag{9}$$

Considering the fact that a moving vehicle might obtain the desired data item from the number $1, 2, \ldots, N(t)$ encountered vehicle, we have

$$p = \sum_{n=1}^{N(t)} \sum_{k=n}^{\infty} \frac{\lambda t^k}{k!} e^{-\lambda t} (1-P)^{n-1} P. \tag{10}$$

This can be further represented by

$$p = \sum_{n=1}^{N(t)} \left(1 - \sum_{k=0}^{n-1} \frac{\lambda t^k}{k!} e^{-\lambda t}\right) (1-P)^{n-1} P. \tag{11}$$

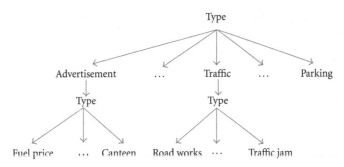

FIGURE 5: Topic representation.

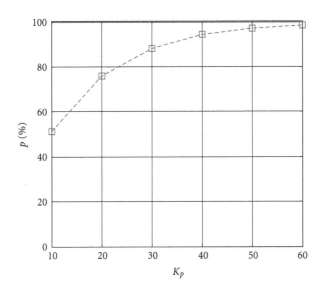

FIGURE 6: Impact of K_p on the probability p.

Now we assume $L = 1000$ m, set $\lambda = 2$, $K_m = 100$, $t = 20$, $N(t) = 60$ (as the average value obtained in our survey), and study the probability p. According to formula (11), if $K_c = 2$, p equals 69%. That is to say, if there are only 2 copies of the same message kept within a road segment, the possibility for a moving vehicle getting the desired message within 20 s is only 69%. Obviously, the parking-based data dissemination scheme outperforms the inter-vehicle-based scheme.

6. Performance Evaluation

In this section, we investigate realistic parking and traffic profile in real urban environments and evaluate the performance of parking-based scheme and other two alternative data dissemination schemes in NS-2.33.

6.1. Survey. We performed a six-week survey on an urban area of Chengdu, a city in China, for collecting realistic parking and traffic profile. Since choosing target area is crucial in performance evaluation, we prefer ordinary urban region with typical parking distribution to downtown areas where the parking is above average. As shown in Figure 7, we extract a real street map with the range of 1600 m × 1400 m,

TABLE 1: Roadside parking in survey.

Street	Policy	Density	Average
R_{04}, R_{15}, R_{26}	No limits	280–320 veh/km	308 veh/km
R_{37}, R_{79}	Strict limits	15–25 veh/km	21 veh/km
R_{01}, R_{12}, R_{23}, R_{45}, R_{56}, R_{67}, R_{48}, R_{68}, R_{89}	Moderate limits	72–180 veh/km	95 veh/km

which contains 10 intersections and 14 bidirectional roads totaled up to 7,860 meters. Each intersection is marked by a number from 0 to 9.

During the survey, we investigated the traffic and roadside parking statistics at 16:00, 18:00, and 22:00 of every Tuesday, Thursday, and Saturday. We counted the vehicles parked along each street within 5 meters and skipped those parked in the middle of obstacles or too far from the roads. To on-street parking lots, only fringed vehicles along road direction were calculated. As shown in Table 1, there are three classes of streets with different parking limits. The first class permits free parking at roadside, as R_{04}, R_{15}, and R_{26}, which results in a very high node density. The second one, as R_{37} and R_{79}, lacks public parking spaces. These

FIGURE 7: Road topology in survey and simulations.

TABLE 2: Performance under default parameters.

Parameter	Default value
Number of vehicle	200
Vehicle velocity	40~80 kph
Size of data message	10 kb
Interval of beacon message	1 second
Data generation rate	0.1/second
Data survival time	30 minutes

TABLE 3: Performance under default parameters.

Scheme	Parking-based	Inter-vehicle	OD
Average delivery ratio (%)	93.2	85.4	80.6
Average delivery delay (s)	3.5	18.2	7.6
Network traffic overhead	1.53×10^4	2.4×10^5	0.7×10^6

streets have a very low vehicle density that comes from some reserved parking spaces and illegal parking. The rest of the streets belong to the third one, which has a moderate vehicle density. Generally, the parked vehicle numbers are stable in different hours of a day. During the survey, we also calculated daily traffic by counting the passing vehicles within fifteen minutes at random positions and found traffic fluctuating from 300 veh/h (vehicle per hour) to 2200 veh/h at different time of one day. If the road width is 20 m, the corresponding moving vehicles within the area range from 60 to 400, with the average speed ranges of 40 km/h to 80 km/h.

6.2. Simulations. Since accurately modeling node movement is very important for simulation, we use the open source software, VanetMobiSim-1.1 [21], to generate realistic urban mobility traces. The generated traffic file can be directly utilized by NS-2.33. To produce sparse traffic and traffic changes, we deploy different vehicle numbers, that is, 50, 100, 150, 200, 250, and 300, to the map. The radio range is set at 250 m, and the MAC protocol is 2 Mbps 802.11. In the simulation, parked vehicle nodes are located on random positions of each street, following the density collected in

Table 1. The average parking time is 41.40 minutes with a standard deviation of 27.17, which is provided in [18]. Since not all parked vehicles are willing to share their wireless devices, a participating ratio of 30% is deployed in default. We assume that the parking clusters are established at the beginning of simulation and are maintained at a cycle of 60 seconds.

To simulate data dissemination, a data source is deployed at the center area of the simulated area, which generates new message with a given time interval. For each message, its target area is specified as a rectangle area which includes four intersections and the roads among them (e.g., the area composed of R_{01}, R_{04}, R_{45}, and R_{15} in Figure 5.), and we assume that 20% of vehicles moving in the target area are interested in it. The default parameters are shown in Table 2.

We mainly discuss three data dissemination mechanisms: our parking-based data dissemination, inter-vehicle-based data dissemination, and OD [8]. For the inter-vehicle based scheme, data messages to be disseminated are routed to the target area using GPSR [22] routing protocol and are maintained within each road segment by the mobile vehicles. While the carrier is leaving a road segment, the maintained data would be transmitted to the furthest vehicle that located within its communication range and drives on the same road segment. Here, similar to our parking-based scheme, we let the message carrier respond to the message subscription within one hop.

The performance of the three mechanisms is measured by the following three metrics.

Data Delivery Ratio. For each message, the delivery ratio is defined as the fraction of subscribers that successfully received this message.

Data Delivery Delay. For each message, the delivery delay is defined as the time spent for a subscriber obtaining this message after entering the target area of this message.

Network Traffic Overhead. The network traffic overhead is defined as the total amount of data generated during the simulation.

The average delivery ratio is the mean value of delivery ratio of all the disseminated messages, and the average delivery delay is the mean value of the delivery delay of all the disseminated messages. For each measurement, 30 simulation runs are used, and each simulation lasts for 60 minutes.

We first test the performance of the above three schemes under the default parameters. The results are shown as Table 3. We notice that compared to the inter-vehicle scheme and OD, parking-based scheme shows better performance. It achieves a higher delivery ratio with less delivery delay at lower overhead. For parking-based scheme, replicas of the same message are maintained at many parking clusters in the target area. Once a vehicle comes to a road with parking cluster, it will get the desired message in short time. Thus, the average delivery ratio is higher and the average delivery delay is lower. In addition, as each message only needs to

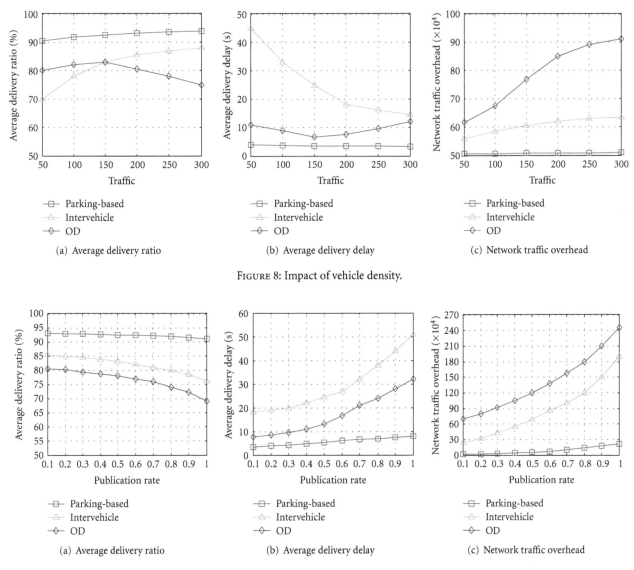

FIGURE 8: Impact of vehicle density.

FIGURE 9: Impact of data publication rate.

be broadcasted within one hop of the parking cluster, the overhead is very low. For the inter-vehicle scheme, data to be disseminated are maintained at the mobile vehicles. Owing to the high mobility of vehicles, frequent handovers among the mobile vehicles are needed to maintain a data message within a road segment. Hence, the network overhead is high. Moreover, there might exist some special cases, in which the vehicle which carries a message leaves a road segment, and it has no chance to perform data handover (there are not any other vehicles within its communication range), and the new coming vehicles have no way to acquire this data. Thus, the delivery ratio is lower and the data delivery delay is higher. For OD, the overhead is much higher than the other two schemes. However, the data delivery ratio is not as high as it should be. In OD, whenever two vehicles move into the transmission range of each other, they will exchange data, which leads to severe congestion and significantly reduces the data delivery ratio.

6.2.1. Impact of Vehicle Density. This group of experiments illustrates the impact of vehicle density on the performance of three data dissemination schemes. Form Figure 8, we observe that the parking-based scheme works well under different road traffic, while the inter-vehicle scheme shows bad performance under sparse traffic. The parking based scheme relies on the roadside parking. As long as there are a certain amount of parked vehicles, the message availability within the target area could be guaranteed. However, the inter-vehicle scheme relies on the moving vehicle, which can hardly ensure the message availability in sparse traffic and thus lead to low delivery ratio. For OD, while the vehicles density increases, the possibility of collisions in media access control (MAC) layer is increased. Thus, the delivery ratio decreases while the delivery delay reduces.

6.2.2. Impact of Data Publication Rate. The data publication rate determines the number of messages to be disseminated

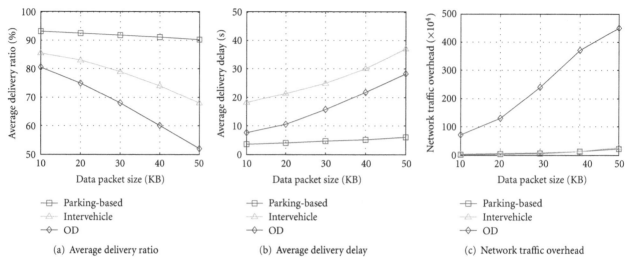

FIGURE 10: Impact of data packet size.

over VANETs. Higher data publication rate means larger network load. Through this group of experiments, we will see how the data publication rate affects the performance of the three data dissemination schemes. As shown in Figure 9, while the data publication rate varies from 1 message/10 s to 1 message/1 s, the delivery ratio of parking based scheme decreases slightly, while the delivery ratio of inter-vehicle scheme drops obviously. This is because parking-based scheme buffers data at roadside parking and performs data dissemination within one hop, which greatly reduces the possibility of transmission collision. The inter-vehicle scheme maintains data at mobile vehicles, which causes frequent handover and excessive transmission while the publication rate is high. With the increase of the publication rate, the overheads of the three schemes are all increased, and that of OD scheme is more obvious. Here, we also observe that the parking based scheme outperforms the other two schemes.

6.2.3. Impact of Data Packet Size. This group of experiments investigates the impact of data packet size on the performance of three data dissemination schemes. As shown in Figures 10(a) and 10(b), the data delivery ratio and delivery delay of parking-based scheme are superior to that of the other two schemes under different data packet size. For the parking-based scheme, data messages are maintained at the roadside parked vehicles, which thus could provide stable data dissemination services for the vehicles passing by. However, for the inter-vehicle scheme, data messages need to be frequently handed over to the vehicles still moving within the road segment. With the increasing data packet size, the handover suffers from more losses; thus, the data delivery ratio is decreased and the data delivery delay is increased. For OD, larger data packet size means much more serious collision. Hence, the performance becomes worse.

7. Conclusion

Data dissemination over VANETs is challenging due to the fact that data messages can hardly be kept in a specified target area. In this paper, we propose the idea of parking-based data dissemination, which leverages the roadside parking to buffer the data to be disseminated and performs data dissemination. We organize the parked vehicles into clusters, offer a routing scheme to distribute each data message to appropriate roadside parking, and introduce the pub/sub scheme into the last stage of data dissemination. Our parking-based data dissemination scheme exhibits a low capital overhead by exploiting the free resources offered by parked vehicles and a low operational overhead via efficient operations. The theoretical analysis demonstrates the superiority of our scheme. At last, the numerical results also show that our scheme achieves a higher data delivery ratio at lower network traffic overhead and reasonable delay.

Acknowledgments

This work is supported by National Science Foundation of China under Grant nos. 61170256, 61103226, 61103227, 61173172, and 61272526 and the Fundamental Research Funds for the Central Universities under Grant nos. ZYGX2011J060, ZYGX2010J074, and ZYGX2011J073.

References

[1] M. Nekovee, "Epidemic algorithms for reliable and efficient information dissemination in vehicular Ad Hoc networks," *IET Intelligent Transport Systems*, vol. 3, no. 2, pp. 104–110, 2009.

[2] M. Caliskan, D. Graupner, and M. Mauve, "Decentralized discovery of free parking places," in *Proceedings of the 3rd ACM International Workshop on Vehicular Ad Hoc Networks (VANET'06)*, pp. 30–39, New York, NY, USA, September 2006.

[3] H. Wu, R. Fujimoto, R. Guensler, and M. Hunter, "MDDV: a mobility-centric data dissemination algorithm for vehicular networks," in *Proceedings of the 1st ACM International Workshop on Vehicular Ad Hoc Networks (VANET'04)*, pp. 47–56, New York, NY, USA, October 2004.

[4] L. Wu, M. Liu, X. Wang, G. Chen, and H. Gong, "Mobile distributionaware data dissemination for vehicular Ad Hoc Networks," *Software Journal*, vol. 22, no. 7, pp. 1580–1596, 2011.

[5] C. Maihöfer, T. Leinmüller, and E. Schoch, "Abiding geocast: time-stable geocast for Ad Hoc networks," in *Proceedings of the 2nd ACM International Workshop on Vehicular Ad Hoc Networks (VANET'05)*, pp. 20–29, ACM, 2005.

[6] J. Zhao, Y. Zhang, and G. Cao, "Data pouring and buffering on the road: a new data dissemination paradigm for vehicular Ad Hoc networks," *IEEE Transactions on Vehicular Technology*, vol. 56, no. 6 I, pp. 3266–3277, 2007.

[7] C. Morency and M. Trépanier, "Characterizing parking spaces using travel survey data," CIRRELT, 2006.

[8] B. Xu, A. Ouksel, and O. Wolfson, "Opportunistic resource exchange in inter-vehicle Ad Hoc networks," in *Proceedings of the IEEE International Conference on Mobile Data Management (MDM)*, pp. 4–12, 2004.

[9] G. Korkmaz, E. Ekici, F. Ozguner, and U. Ozguner, "Urban multi-hop broadcast protocol for inter-vehicle communication systems," in *Proceedings of the 1st ACM International Workshop on Vehicular Ad Hoc Networks (VANET'04)*, pp. 76–85, 2004.

[10] Y. Ding, C. Wang, and L. Xiao, "A static-node assisted adaptive routing protocol in vehicular networks," in *Proceedings of the 4th ACM International Workshop on Vehicular Ad Hoc Networks (VANET'07)*, pp. 59–68, September 2007.

[11] C. Lochert, B. Scheuermann, C. Wewetzer, A. Luebke, and M. Mauve, "Data aggregation and roadside unit placement for a vanet traffic information system," in *Proceedings of the 5th ACM International Workshop on VehiculAr Inter-NETworking (VANET'08)*, pp. 58–65, New York, NY, USA, September 2008.

[12] M. Eltoweissy, S. Olariu, and M. Younis, "Towards autonomous vehicular clouds," in *Ad Hoc Networks*, vol. 49 of *Lecture Notes of the Institute for Computer Sciences, Social Informatics and Telecommunications Engineering*, pp. 1–16, 2010.

[13] S. Olariu, I. Khalil, and M. Abuelela, "Taking VANET to the clouds," *International Journal of Pervasive Computing and Communications*, vol. 7, no. 1, pp. 7–21, 2011.

[14] D. Shoup, "Cruising for parking," *Access*, vol. 30, pp. 16–22, 2007.

[15] R. H. Frenkiel, B. R. Badrinath, J. Borràs, and R. D. Yates, "Infostations challenge: balancing cost and ubiquity in delivering wireless data," *IEEE Personal Communications*, vol. 7, no. 2, pp. 66–71, 2000.

[16] A. Adiv and W. Wang, "On-street parking meter behavior," *Transportation Quarterly*, vol. 41, pp. 281–307, 1987.

[17] J. F. Kurose and K. W. Ross, "A top-down approach featuring the internet".

[18] R. Mcier and V. Cahill, "STEAM: event-based middleware for wireless Ad Hoc networks," in *Proceedings of the 1st International Workshop on Distributed Event-Based Systems (DEBS'02)*, pp. 639–644, 2002.

[19] L. Fiege, F. Gärtner, O. Kasten, and A. Zeidler, "Supporting mobility in content-based publish/subscribe middleware," in *Proceedings of the ACM/IFIP/USENIX International Conference on Middleware (Middleware'03)*, pp. 103–122, 2003.

[20] W. Feller, *An Introduction to Probability Theory and Its Applications*, John Wiley & Sons, New York, NY, USA, 2008.

[21] J. Härri, F. Filali, C. Bonnet, and M. Fiore, "VanetMobiSim: generating realistic mobility patterns for VANETs," in *Proceedings of the 3rd International Workshop on Vehicular Ad Hoc Networks (VANET'06)*, pp. 96–97, ACM, New York, NY, USA, 2006.

[22] B. Karp and H. Kung, "GPSR: greedy perimeter stateless routing for wireless networks," in *Proceedings of the 6th Annual International Conference on Mobile Computing and Networking (MobiCom'00)*, pp. 243–254, ACM, 2000.

10

Connectivity-Aware and Minimum Energy Dissipation Protocol in Wireless Sensor Networks

Dahlila Putri Dahnil, Yaswant Prasad Singh, and Chin Kuan Ho

Faculty of Computing and Informatics, Persiaran Multimedia, 63100 Cyberjaya, Selangor, Malaysia

Correspondence should be addressed to Dahlila Putri Dahnil; dahlilaputri@gmail.com

Academic Editor: Wen-Hwa Liao

This paper formulates an analytical model of energy dissipation in cluster-based wireless sensor networks for network connectivity. The proposed model constructs the analytic expression for the optimal cluster size for minimum energy dissipation. The same model is then applied to control the cluster size which is defined as number of nodes connected to a node (node degree) through transmission power control. The proposed approach constrains the cluster size through node's degree so that all cluster heads maintain a minimum node degree for network connectivity. The simulation results show the total energy dissipation in the network with respect to node's degree, and when cluster heads' degree is above a certain value (threshold), the network remains connected at many more rounds during the network operation.

1. Introduction

One of the main design considerations in cluster-based wireless sensor networks is cluster head election and cluster formation. A cluster size with a large number of member nodes leads to a small number of clusters in the network improving the efficiency of intercluster communication. On the other hand, cluster size with a small number of member nodes leads to increased number of clusters in the network which requires a backbone with a large number of cluster heads and gateways (cluster member linking two different cluster heads) to route the packet for inter-cluster communications [1]. Energy efficiency of clustering protocols can be considered through two different approaches which are the number of clusters formed or the number of members per clusters (cluster size). In context of cluster-based topology, cluster size is related to number of neighbours connected to a cluster head which is defined as node degree and can be referred to as the number of member nodes per cluster. Most of the existing methods control the cluster size with admission or rejection policies during the cluster formation which can be based on the strongest received signal strength [2]. Our proposed method of controlling the number of members per cluster is through transmission power control algorithm [3].

This paper considers the fundamental question of what is the cluster size that gives minimum energy dissipation while maintaining network connectivity. Connectivity can be determined by number of neighbours a node has (node degree) [4]. Node degree is a local property that can be checked by each node to achieve global network property such as connectivity [5]. Connectivity is an important property in wireless sensor networks that enables data to be forwarded or exchanged between nodes in the network. Nodes can cooperate among themselves to route each others' data packets if there exists a path between any two pairs of nodes. Connectivity depends on the number of nodes per unit area and their transmission range. The correct setting of nodes' transmission range is an important consideration for network lifetime [6]. By increasing the transmission power of a node, more nodes can be reached via direct link. Increasing the transmission range can improve connectivity but on the other hand can lead to higher interference, more data collision, and higher energy consumption [7]. Reducing to low transmission power may result in some nodes getting isolated without having any link to other nodes. Connectivity in terms of node degree has been studied by [4, 8, 9]. Node degree is also regarded as one of the important and convenient metrics to measure connectivity of wireless ad hoc networks [10, 11]. It has been shown that the average node degree for an almost fully connected random network of node located randomly using uniform distribution is in the range of 6 to 10 [8]. The results have also been derived to show that to obtain a connected network it is only necessary to keep the average node degree to a certain value [8]. It has been further shown that, for increasing number of nodes in the network, it is essential to have node degree of 5.1774log$N$ to maintain network connectivity, where N is the total nodes in the network [4].

In this paper we work on the fundamental questions of the cluster size that gives minimum energy dissipation while maintaining network connectivity. Cluster size can be the basis for connectivity by implementing minimum constraint to node degree. First we propose to formulate an analytical model of energy dissipation in the network for different cluster sizes. Then we make use of the result from [4] where we take a node degree threshold of Q_{min} = 5.1774log$N$ (rounded to an integer) to constraint cluster size so that cluster size is formed with two aims: (1) to dissipate minimum energy and (2) to maintain connected network. We show the effect of different cluster sizes to energy dissipation using the previously proposed clustering algorithm in [3] to group nodes using suitable power levels to obtain minimum node degree constraint. The energy dissipation model is a part of our effort to extend the algorithm proposed previously in [3] to an energy-efficient clustering algorithm with connectivity.

The remainder of the paper is organized as follows: Section 2 describes the related works on clustering process. Section 3 describes the analytical formulation of energy dissipation for connected sensor networks. The simulation results are presented in Sections 4 and 5 concludes the paper.

2. Related Works

The aim of cluster formation in LEACH is to have k number of clusters per round. The LEACH protocol determines the optimal value of k, which is a system parameter, using the communication energy model based on radio energy dissipation model as in [12]. The research work derived the total energy consumption for transmitting l-bit message at a distance d for a frame and is given by the following:

$$E_{total} = l\left(E_{elec}N + E_{DA}N + k\varepsilon_{mp}d_{toBS}^4 \right.$$
$$\left. + E_{elec}N + \varepsilon_{fs}\frac{1}{2\pi}\frac{M^2}{k}N \right), \tag{1}$$

where E_{elec} = 50 pJ/bit is the energy consumption per bit for the transmitter and receiver circuits to operate, ε_{fs} = 10 pJ/bit/m^2 and ε_{mp} = 0.0013 pJ/bit/m^4 are the amplifier energy, and N is the number of nodes in the network distributed in $M \times M$ region. E_{DA} is the energy consumed for data aggregation, and d_{toBS} is the distance from the cluster head to base station. From (1) the optimum number of clusters k_{opt} is determined by setting the derivative of E_{total} with respect to k to zero which gives the following:

$$k_{opt} = \frac{\sqrt{N}}{\sqrt{2\pi}}\sqrt{\frac{\varepsilon_{fs}}{\varepsilon_{mp}}}\frac{M}{d_{toBS}^2}. \tag{2}$$

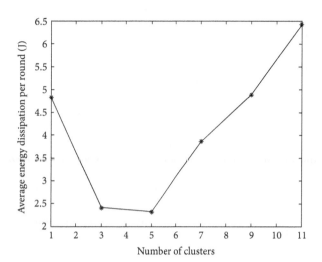

FIGURE 1: Average energy dissipated per round in LEACH as the number of clusters is varied between 1 and 11. This graph shows that LEACH is the most energy efficient when there are between 3 and 5 clusters in the 100-node network, as predicted by the analysis [12].

Experimental results by Heinzelman et al. [12] on 100-node network to verify the analytical results are shown in Figure 1 where the number of clusters is varied between 1 and 11. The average energy dissipated in a round versus cluster numbers is illustrated in Figure 1. Based on Figure 1, the most efficient energy occurs when the number of clusters is from 3 to 5, and the simulation results generated from the experiments agree with the analysis performed in (1). The research work shows that there exists an optimal number of cluster that gives the minimum energy dissipation in the network. This work has shown that achieving optimum number of clusters guarantees the most energy efficient protocol. However, achieving optimum number of clusters does not guarantee connectivity.

The number of neighbors connected to a node or a cluster head (node degree) can be obtained during the clustering process. A fix transmission power or dynamic controlled power levels can associate cluster heads with a number of fully connected nodes. As stated earlier, node degree can be considered as an essential criterion for obtaining connectivity in the network. From this standpoint, we proposed to formulate an analytical model for node degree (Q) to show the energy dissipation as a function of node degree using the same radio energy dissipation model as illustrated in [12].

In wireless sensor networks, adaptive clustering for data routing is well explored as they have been shown to improve network lifetime [13]. Nodes are grouped into clusters with a probability that some nodes become cluster heads and the rest becomes member of clusters. The role of the cluster heads is rotated among the nodes in the network to balance the energy consumption [14]. The aim of clustering in multihop is to have balanced workload among all the nodes in the network by having different cluster sizes [15–17]. However, the effect of different cluster sizes to connectivity is yet to be explored as an important consideration for an efficient intercluster communication. In most recent clustering algorithms the connectivity is usually measured through nodes transmission range and not in terms of node degree [18, 19]. In HEED [18], to ensure multi-hop communications among cluster heads, the selected transmission range among cluster heads varies to ensure connectivity. A sufficiently large network is divided into cells, where each cell is of size $c \times c$. Such network is guaranteed to remain connected if the communication range of node is set to $r_t = (1 + \sqrt{5})c$, where r_t is the node transmission range and c is defined as the square cell size [20]. The connectivity is ensured when the transmission is related to the size of the network deployment area, regardless of how many nodes are there in the network [20]. HEED produces uniformly distributed cluster heads over the entire network [14]. However, good spatial distribution does not always achieve balanced load over the entire network since nodes far from base station tend to exhaust energy more quickly.

The results in EECS [15] propose clustering with reduced transmission range and try to balance the energy of cluster heads by justifying the cluster size. Since the energy consumed by cluster heads is dependent on the distances between cluster heads and the base station, cluster heads located farther from the base station have smaller cluster size compared to cluster heads located closer to the base station. The cluster head election phase has no iteration and is different from HEED. During the election phase candidate nodes broadcast their candidacy using a reduced transmission range where they need to adjust their transmission range to R_{compete}. The aim for R_{compete} transmission range is to obtain optimal cluster heads, k_{opt}, as in [12]. Once the candidates become cluster heads they have to re-adjust their transmission power level so that all nodes in the network can receive their cluster head advertisement message. This step requires each node to be able to readjust their transmission power on every round of the network operation which can be energy costly [21]. During the cluster formation, node computes the cost of every cluster heads in the network and then chooses a cluster head with minimum communication cost which might require nodes to use higher power level. EECS algorithm only proves an optimal transmission range used during cluster heads election which results in optimal number of cluster heads election. However, the optimal transmission range does not always guarantee a connected network. In the following, we consider network connectivity through optimal node degree which also guarantees minimum energy dissipation in the network.

3. Energy Dissipation for Connected Sensor Networks

In the network model assumed in recent literature, nodes can join a cluster after the cluster heads election based on strongest signal strength, node degree, or distance of cluster heads to base station [12, 16–18]. During cluster formation if the cluster heads do not maintain a certain cluster head degree, the connectivity of the network may be lost. The connectivity depends mainly on the number of nodes per unit area and their radio transmission range. Our goals in this paper are that (1) small node degree will result in reduced average distance between cluster members to cluster heads and vice

versa, (2) connectivity can be conserved by maintaining cluster head degree to certain value, (3) controlling the node degree we can create both equal and unequal cluster sizes, and (4) addressing the question of whether or not the network connectivity can be achieved at minimum energy dissipation.

3.1. Energy Dissipation Model with respect to Node Degree. The simplified radio model is used from [12]. Both energies dissipated in cluster heads in a single frame is related to energy spent receiving from members, that is, cluster head degree (Q), aggregating data and sending the aggregated data to base station [12, 22]. We define Q as the number of neighbours connected a node (node degree), so in a cluster there will be $Q + 1$ nodes, (Q noncluster heads node and one cluster head). Assume that N nodes distributed uniformly in a $M \times M$ region. Then if we divide equally, there will be $N/(Q + 1)$ number of clusters.

The area occupied by each cluster is $\pi r^2 = M^2(Q+1)/N$

$$r = \sqrt{\frac{M^2(Q+1)}{\pi N}} \quad r = M\sqrt{\frac{Q+1}{\pi N}}, \tag{3}$$

where r is the transmission range of the cluster head covering a circular area. Energy dissipated in cluster head is associated with energy consumption while receiving data from members (i.e., cluster heads' degree (Q), aggregating members' data, and sending aggregated data to base station) and is given as follows:

$$E_{\text{CH}} = QlE_{\text{elec}} + QlE_{\text{DA}} + lE_{\text{elec}} + l\varepsilon_{\text{mp}}d_{\text{toBS}}^4. \tag{4}$$

Energy dissipated by noncluster head node to transmit to its cluster head is

$$E_{\text{non-CH}} = lE_{\text{elec}} + l\varepsilon_{\text{fs}}d_{\text{toCH}}^2. \tag{5}$$

The energy dissipated in a single cluster is the sum of (4) and (5):

$$E_{\text{cluster}} = E_{\text{CH}} + Q\left(E_{\text{non-CH}}\right),$$

$$E_{\text{cluster}} = QlE_{\text{elec}} + QlE_{\text{DA}}$$
$$+ lE_{\text{elec}} + l\varepsilon_{\text{mp}}d_{\text{toBS}}^4 + Q\left(lE_{\text{elec}} + l\varepsilon_{\text{fs}}d_{\text{toCH}}^2\right),$$

$$E_{\text{cluster}} = Ql\left(2E_{\text{elec}} + E_{\text{DA}} + \varepsilon_{\text{fs}}d_{\text{toCH}}^2\right) + lE_{\text{elec}} + l\varepsilon_{\text{mp}}d_{\text{toBS}}^4. \tag{6}$$

The expected squared distance from nodes to the cluster head (assumed to be at the centre of mass) is

$$E\left[d_{\text{toCH}}^2\right] = \iint \left(x^2 + y^2\right)\rho\left(x, y\right)dx\,dy,$$
$$E\left[d_{\text{toCH}}^2\right] = \iint r^2\rho\left(r, \vartheta\right)r\,dr\,d\theta. \tag{7}$$

Expression (3) gives the radius, r, as follows:

$$r = \sqrt{\frac{M^2(Q+1)}{\pi N}}. \tag{8}$$

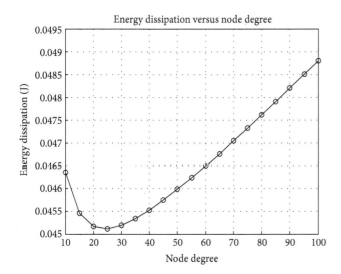

FIGURE 2: Energy dissipation per round with different node degrees for 100-node network.

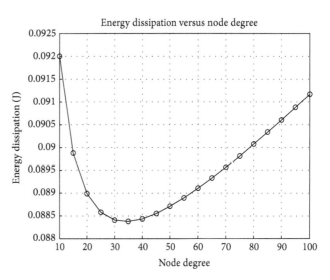

FIGURE 3: Energy dissipation per round with different node degrees for 200-node network.

So, (7) becomes

$$E\left[d_{\text{toCH}}^2\right] = \rho \int_{\vartheta=0}^{2\pi} \int_0^{M\sqrt{(Q+1)/\pi N}} r^3 dr\, d\vartheta,$$

$$E\left[d_{\text{toCH}}^2\right] = \rho \int_{\vartheta=0}^{2\pi} \frac{\left(M\sqrt{(Q+1)/\pi N}\right)^4}{4},$$

$$E\left[d_{\text{toCH}}^2\right] = \rho \int_{\theta=0}^{2\pi} \frac{M^4(Q+1)^2}{4\pi^2 N^2},$$

$$E\left[d_{\text{toCH}}^2\right] = \frac{\rho M^4(Q+1)^2}{2\pi N^2}. \tag{9}$$

If the density of nodes is uniform throughout the cluster area, then

$$\rho = \frac{1}{M^2(Q+1)/N} = \frac{N}{M^2(Q+1)}. \tag{10}$$

The expected distance square is

$$E\left[d_{\text{toCH}}^2\right] = \frac{N}{M^2(Q+1)}\left(\frac{M^4(Q+1)^2}{2\pi N^2}\right),$$

$$E\left[d_{\text{toCH}}^2\right] = \frac{M^2(Q+1)}{2\pi N}. \tag{11}$$

The total energy spent in the network per round is

$$E_{\text{total}} = \frac{N}{Q+1}E_{\text{cluster}} \approx \frac{N}{Q}E_{\text{cluster}},$$

$$E_{\text{total}} = \frac{N}{Q}\left[Ql\left(2E_{\text{elec}} + E_{\text{DA}} + \varepsilon_{\text{fs}}d_{\text{toCH}}^2\right) + lE_{\text{elec}} + lc_{\text{mp}}d_{\text{toBS}}^4\right],$$

$$E_{\text{total}} = Nl\left(2E_{\text{elec}} + E_{\text{DA}} + \frac{\varepsilon_{\text{fs}}M^2(Q+1)}{2\pi N}\right)$$

$$+ \frac{Nl\left(E_{\text{elec}} + \varepsilon_{\text{mp}}d_{\text{toBS}}^4\right)}{Q},$$

$$E_{\text{total}} = 2NlE_{\text{elec}} + NlE_{\text{DA}} + \frac{l\varepsilon_{\text{fs}}M^2(Q+1)}{2\pi}$$

$$+ \frac{Nl\left(E_{\text{elec}} + \varepsilon_{\text{mp}}d_{\text{toBS}}^4\right)}{Q}. \tag{12}$$

Simulation is conducted to see the effect of cluster head degree to the energy dissipation per round on the proposed clustering algorithm as shown in Figure 2. For the experiment, N is set to 100, with deployment area set to 100×100. The base station is located at (50,175), with initial energy $E_0 = 2\,$J, $E_{\text{elec}} = 50\,$nJ/bit, $\varepsilon_{\text{fs}} = 10\,$pJ/bit/m^2 and $\varepsilon_{\text{mp}} = 0.0013\,$pJ/bit/m^4, and $E_{\text{DA}} = 5\,$nJ. It can be seen that as the cluster head degree is small, the energy dissipation per round is high. When the cluster head degree increases from 20 to 30 the energy consumption is at its lowest point. The calculated value from analysis (12) gives the optimal degree range of 20 to 30 which agrees with the simulations. Therefore, the value for optimal node degree, Q_{opt}, can be set between 20 and 30.

We further simulate the energy dissipation for 200 nodes in the network as in Figure 3. It shows that minimum energy dissipation occurs when node degree is between 30 and 40.

We developed here an analytical formulation to show energy efficiency of our previously proposed algorithm (TCAC) [3] which constructs cluster within the minimum cluster size to ensure network connectivity. TCAC clustering algorithm consists of three phases: a Periodical Update, Cluster Head Election, and Cluster Formation as shown in Figure 4.

The pseudocode of the algorithm is as shown in Pseudocode 1.

3.1.1. Description of Cluster Heads Election. The cluster heads election is an important process for any clustering algorithms because it determines how the overall energy is dissipated in the network. A node calculates its probability $P(\text{CCH}_i)$ to

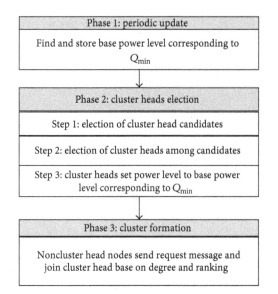

FIGURE 4: Periodical Update, Cluster Head Election, and Cluster Formation phases.

become a cluster head candidate based on its residual energy, E_i, with respect to the average energy of all nodes in the network; E_{avg}. LEACH protocol [12] defines the optimal number of cluster heads, k_{opt}, to achieve minimum energy dissipation per round. We set a clustering parameter where $k_{\text{initial}} > k_{\text{opt}}$ for the election process to get a nonoverlapped cluster heads. The k_{initial} is set to have value $> k_{\text{opt}}$, for example, double of k_{opt}, such that only high-energy nodes will be elected and cover the whole network area. Nodes become cluster head candidates with a probability $P(\text{CCH}_i)$ and are calculated as follows:

$$P\left(\text{CCH}_i\right) = \frac{E_i}{E_{\text{avg}}}, \tag{13}$$

where the E_{avg} is computed as follows:

$$E_{\text{avg}} = \frac{E_{\text{total}}}{k_{\text{initial}}}. \tag{14}$$

Each node generates a random number in the range of $[0, 1]$, and, if the number is less than the calculated probability $P(\text{CCH}_i)$, it elects itself as cluster head candidate. Other nodes that are not elected as candidates (normal nodes) set a timer and wait for cluster heads messages. The average energy of all nodes is obtained when nodes send their current residual energy to their respective cluster heads which aggregate and send this information to other cluster heads in the network. Based on this information, cluster heads will calculate the average energy of all clusters in the network and forward this information to its members for $P(\text{CCH}_i)$ calculation. The probability of becoming cluster heads is computed again on every round and propagated to all cluster heads since intercluster connectivity is ensured on every round. Nodes that have been cluster heads on the previous round will have lower chances of becoming a cluster head on the next round due to depletion of energy during communication with base station.

If the election is based on a static threshold T such as in EECS or based on probability P as in [23], all nodes have the same chance of becoming the cluster heads and forces nodes with low energy to become cluster heads. These cluster head candidates, then, broadcast contending messages, CONTENDMSG, consisting of their residual energy information at base power level. Each candidate compares its energy level with other candidates. If a candidate's energy level is higher than others, the candidate elects itself as cluster head. If its energy is lower than other candidates it has to back-off and become a normal node. In case of ties, candidate nodes with higher degree will be elected as a cluster head. At the end of clustering process, the number of cluster heads elected is smaller than the number of elected cluster head candidates; that is, subset of the candidates become cluster heads. Then, cluster heads execute the transmission power level algorithm to update their degree information. This step ensures that their power level corresponds to Q_{min} that preserves network connectivity. If the acknowledgements received correspond to Q_{min} the cluster heads then transmit CHMSG to announce themselves as cluster heads. The proposed cluster heads election leads to an optimal number of cluster heads being elected, with nonoverlapped and well-distributed cluster heads covering the entire network.

3.1.2. Description of Cluster Formation. Once cluster heads are elected, membership association takes place for noncluster heads nodes. The cluster formation is described as follows: once nodes are elected as cluster heads they send cluster head messages, *CHMSG*. The noncluster head nodes receiving the message will acknowledge a CHMSG message by sending a request message, *REQMSG*, containing its ID to the cluster heads. Noncluster heads nodes that do not receive any cluster head message will send request message across the network after timeout expires. A cluster head can receive multiple requests. Once the cluster head receives the requests it will rank the requests based on received signal strengths and store them in a priority list with the following priority structure (ID, Rank). The node with strongest signal strength is ranked with the highest priority. The cluster head then broadcasts the priority list to all nodes requesting to join its cluster. The priority mechanism indicates two important features: (1) nodes know how close they are to the cluster head relative to all the nodes requesting to join the same cluster, (2) the importance of a node to a cluster head which does not necessarily implies that it is the closest to cluster head, but a node may join a cluster to fulfill the degree threshold of the cluster heads. From the list, noncluster head nodes calculate the degree of each cluster head. Nodes join a cluster to achieve the Q_{min} degree of a cluster. For example, between two clusters a node chooses a cluster that has a degree count less than Q_{min}. In a situation where all the cluster heads have equal degree or more than Q_{min} nodes compare their ranks given by each cluster head and choose to join a cluster with the best rank. Upon joining a cluster, member nodes then readjust their transmission range just enough to communicate to their cluster heads for efficient intracluster communications.

```
Begin (Periodic Update)
   Set transmission power level, P_tx;
   Broadcast UPDATEMSG;
   While Node Degree # Q_min do
      Received Acknowledgement;
      Compute Acknowledgement = Node Degree;
      If Node Degree < Q_min do
         increase P_tx;
      else if Node Degree > Q_min do
         decrease P_tx;
      end
   end
end

Begin (Cluster Head Election)
   Compute probability to become cluster head
   candidate P(CCH_i);
   Generate random number [0,1]
   If random number < P(CCH_i) do
      state ← candidate;
      broadcast CONTENDMSG;
   end
   While state == candidate do
    If received CONTENDMSG from other candidates
       compare energy level;
        If energy level > other candidates do
           state ← cluster head;
           broadcast CHMSG;
         else if energy level < other candidates do
           state ← normal node;
         end
      end
      if state == candidate do
         state ← cluster head;
         broadcast CHMSG;
      end
   end
end

Begin (Cluster Formation)
   CH1 = N + 999;
   While (timer has not expired) do
      if received CHMSG do
       Send REQMSG;
        if received Priority list do
          temporaryCH = min (CH1,CH2);
          if temporaryCH < CH1 do
             CH1 = temporaryCH;
          end
        end
      end
   end
   if CH1 < N + 999 do
    Send JOINMSG to CH1;
    status ← member;
   else if CH1 == N + 999 do
    REQMSG across the network
    Send JOINMSG based on priority list
   end
end
```

PSEUDOCODE 1

TABLE 1: Simulation parameters.

Parameters	Values
Network grid	From (0, 0) to (100, 100)
Sink	(50, 175)
Initial energy	0.5 J
E_{elec}	50 nJ/bit
ε_{fs}	10 pJ/bit/m^2
ε_{mp}	0.0013 pJ/bit/m^4
E_{DA}	5 nJ/bit/signal
Threshold distance (d_0)	87 m
Data size	500 bytes

4. Simulation Results

Simulations are carried out to evaluate the proposed algorithm for its energy efficiency. The nodes are placed according to uniform distribution in an area of dimension 100×100. The base station is located at $x = 50$, $y = 175$. The simulation parameters considered are as described in Table 1. The proposed TCAC is evaluated using the following measures: network lifetime, cluster heads distribution, cluster heads variation, and connectivity.

In the simulation we measure lifetime in terms of number of rounds when the first node dies. We set the optimal number of cluster head $k_{\text{opt}} = 5$ for 100 nodes [12] in the network when we compare LEACH, HEED, and EECS. For HEED, the cluster radius is taken as 25 m and initial $\text{CH}_{\text{prob}} = C_{\text{prob}} = 5\%$ for all nodes. On each experiment, nodes are randomly placed by generating random coordinates using uniform distribution. In our simulation we use various transmission ranges, r, corresponding to different transmission power levels. On each experiment random topology is generated, and each result is the average of 100 experiments. We perform simulation on 100–600 nodes in the network with maximum rounds of 1500 per experiment.

4.1. Network Connectivity Performance Comparison. We conducted experiments comparing HEED, EECS, and TCAC algorithm. We set $n = 100$, base station at (50,200), and the transmission range, r, is set to 47 m. The threshold $Q_{\text{min}} = 11$ for 100 nodes in the network. For EECS, $c = 0.8$, $T = 0.2$, and $R_{\text{compete}} = 25$ m. For LEACH and energy-based LEACH, the cluster heads variation is very big; thus the average rounds when the degree is not maintained above threshold occur at very early rounds. HEED generates single-node clusters and, due to this, the degree falls below threshold at a very early round. Figure 5 shows the simulation results for all the algorithms being compared for network connectivity. It is shown that the TCAC protocol maintains the cluster heads degree above threshold for a longer period of time as compared to LEACH, HEED, or EECS. This result also shows that the TCAC algorithm performs 100 rounds longer in ensuring intercluster connectivity. The advantage of the algorithm is that, when degree is maintained above threshold, the network

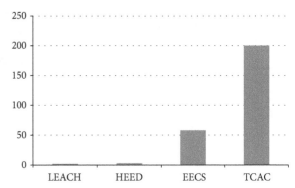

FIGURE 5: The average rounds when cluster heads maintain degree above Q_{min}.

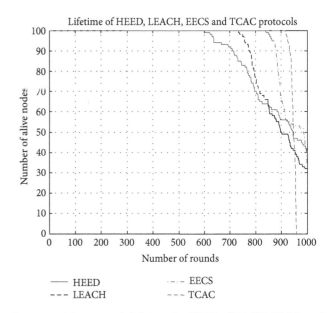

FIGURE 6: The network lifetime for HEED, LEACH, EECS, and TCAC.

remains connected at many more rounds during the network operation.

4.2. Network Lifetime. We have conducted simulation experiments to compare the network lifetime of TCAC algorithm with LEACH, EECS, and HEED where network lifetime is measured as the time elapsed until the first node dies. In this simulation the network lifetime is expressed as number of rounds until the death of first node. It can be observed from the results in Figure 6 that the TCAC algorithm runs for more rounds than the other three algorithms. The energy loss per round in the TCAC algorithm is less than others causing network to run for a longer time. The energy consumption is dependent on how many nodes are connected to cluster heads. The TCAC algorithm ensures there are cluster heads elected at every round covering all nodes, and there will not be any single-node clusters. The simulation results also show a small variation in the number of cluster heads elected per round which is in contrast with other algorithm. The TCAC algorithm also allows dynamically the control of node degree to ensure connectivity.

5. Conclusion

This paper has presented an analytical model of energy dissipation with respect to cluster size. The proposed model considers the number of nodes connected neighbors to a cluster head to form a connected network while extending the network lifetime. When each cluster maintains a degree above certain value, the network remains connected on every round of the operation. We have shown analytically and through simulation that the lowest energy dissipation takes place when the node degree is in the range of 20 to 30 for 100 nodes in the network. The optimal degree ensures network connectivity as well as prolonging lifetime which are important design considerations in wireless sensor networks.

Acknowledgment

This work is financially sponsored by Yayasan Khazanah a foundation established by Khazanah National Berhad.

References

[1] S. Naeimi, H. Ghafghazi, C.-O. Chow, and H. Ishii, "A survey on the taxonomy of cluster-based routing protocols for homogeneous wireless sensor networks," *Sensors*, vol. 12, no. 6, pp. 7350–7409, 2012.

[2] S. Tyagi and N. Kumar, "A systematic review on clustering and routing techniques based upon LEACH protocol for wireless sensor networks," *Journal of Network and Computer Applications*, vol. 36, no. 2, pp. 623–645, 2013.

[3] D. P. Dahnil, Y. P. Singh, and C. K. Ho, "Topology-controlled adaptive clustering for uniformity and increased lifetime in wireless sensor networks," *IET Wireless Sensor Systems*, vol. 2, no. 4, pp. 318–327, 2012.

[4] F. Xue and P. R. Kumar, "The number of neighbors needed for connectivity of wireless networks," *Wireless Networks*, vol. 10, no. 2, pp. 169–181, 2004.

[5] N. M. Freris, H. Kowshik, and P. R. Kumar, "Fundamentals of large sensor networks: connectivity, capacity, clocks, and computation," *Proceedings of the IEEE*, vol. 98, no. 11, pp. 1828–1846, 2010.

[6] C. Bettstetter, "On the minimum node degree and connectivity of a wireless multihop network," in *Proceedings of the 3rd ACM International Symposium on Mobile Ad Hoc Networking & Computing (MOBIHOC '02)*, pp. 80–91, June 2002.

[7] D. P. Dallas and L. W. Hanlen, "Optimal transmission range and node degree for multi-hop routing in wireless sensor networks," in *Proceedings of the 4th ACM International Workshop on Performance Monitoring, Measurement, and Evaluation of Heterogeneous Wireless and Wired Networks (PM2HW2N '09)*, pp. 167–174, October 2009.

[8] J. Ni and S. A. G. Chandler, "Connectivity properties of a random radio network," *IEE Proceedings*, vol. 141, no. 4, pp. 289–296, 1994.

[9] L. Guo, K. Harfoush, and H. Xu, "An analytical model for the node degree in wireless ad hoc networks," *Wireless Personal Communications*, vol. 66, no. 2, pp. 291–306, 2012.

[10] A. V. Babu and M. K. Singh, "Node isolated probability of wireless ad hoc networks in nagakami fading channel," *International Journal of Computer Networks and Communications*, vol. 2, no. 2, pp. 21–36, 2010.

[11] B. R. A. Kumar, L. C. Reddy, and P. S. Hiremath, "Analysis of K-connected MANETs for QoS multicasting using EDMSTs based on connectivity index," *International Journal of Computer Applications*, vol. 3, no. 12, pp. 15–22, 2010.

[12] W. B. Heinzelman, A. P. Chandrakasan, and H. Balakrishnan, "An application-specific protocol architecture for wireless microsensor networks," *IEEE Transactions on Wireless Communications*, vol. 1, no. 4, pp. 660–670, 2002.

[13] K. Sohraby, D. Minoli, and T. Znati, *Wireless Sensor Networks: Technology, Protocols and Applications*, John Wiley & Sons, New York, NY, USA, 2007.

[14] K. A. Darabkh, S. S. Ismail, M. Al-Shurmkan, I. F. Jafar, E. Alkhader, and M. F. Al-Mistarihi, "Performance evaluation of selective and adaptive heads clustering algorithms over wireless sensor networks," *Journal of Network and Computer Applications*, vol. 35, no. 6, pp. 2068–2080, 2012.

[15] M. Ye, C. F. Li, G. H. Chen, and J. Wu, "EECS: an energy efficient clustering scheme in wireless sensor networks 10a.2," in *Proceedings of the 24th IEEE International Performance, Computing, and Communications Conference (IPCCC '05)*, pp. 535–540, April 2005.

[16] G. Chen, C. F. Li, M. Ye, and J. Wu, "An unequal cluster-based routing protocol in wireless sensor networks," *Wireless Networks*, vol. 15, no. 2, pp. 193–207, 2009.

[17] S. Soro and W. B. Heinzelman, "Prolonging the lifetime of wireless sensor networks via unequal clustering," in *Proceedings of the 19th IEEE International Parallel and Distributed Processing Symposium (IPDPS '05)*, April 2005.

[18] O. Younis and S. Fahmy, "HEED: a hybrid, energy-efficient, distributed clustering approach for ad hoc sensor networks," *IEEE Transactions on Mobile Computing*, vol. 3, no. 4, pp. 366–379, 2004.

[19] V. Mhatre and C. Rosenberg, "Design guidelines for wireless sensor networks: communication, clustering and aggregation," *Ad Hoc Networks*, vol. 2, no. 1, pp. 45–63, 2004.

[20] F. Ye, H. Luo, J. Cheng, S. Lu, and L. Zhang, "PEAS: a robust energy conserving protocol for long-lived sensor networks," in *Proceedings of the 23th IEEE International Conference on Distributed Computing Systems*, pp. 28–37, May 2003.

[21] P. Santi, "Topology control in wireless ad hoc and sensor networks," *ACM Computing Surveys*, vol. 37, no. 2, pp. 164–194, 2005.

[22] D. P. Dahnil, Y. P. Singh, and H. Chin-Kuan, "Analysis of adaptive clustering algorithms in Wireless Sensor Networks," in *Proceedings of the 12th IEEE International Conference on Communication Systems (ICCS '10)*, pp. 51–55, November 2010.

[23] S. Bandyopadhyay and E. J. Coyle, "An energy efficient hierarchical clustering algorithm for wireless sensor networks," in *Proceedings of the 22nd Annual Joint Conference on the IEEE Computer and Communications Societies*, pp. 1713–1723, April 2003.

11

Dynamic Key-Updating: Privacy-Preserving Authentication for RFID Systems

Li Lu,[1] Jinsong Han,[2] Lei Hu,[3] and Lionel M. Ni[4]

[1] School of Computer Science and Engineering, University of Electronic Science and Technology of China, Chengdu 611731, China
[2] School of Electronic and Information Engineering, Xi'an Jiaotong University, Xi'an 710049, China
[3] State Key Laboratory of Information Security, Chinese Academy of Sciences, Beijing 100049, China
[4] Department of Computer Science and Engineering, Hong Kong University of Science and Technology, Hong Kong, China

Correspondence should be addressed to Li Lu, lulirui@gmail.com

Academic Editor: Mo Li

The objective of private authentication for Radio Frequency Identification (RFID) systems is to allow valid readers to explicitly authenticate their dominated tags without leaking the private information of tags. In previous designs, the RFID tags issue encrypted authentication messages to the RFID reader, and the reader searches the key space to identify the tags. Without key-updating, those schemes are vulnerable to many active attacks, especially the compromising attack. We propose a strong and lightweight RFID private authentication protocol, SPA. By designing a novel key-updating method, we achieve the forward secrecy in SPA with an efficient key search algorithm. We also show that, compared with existing designs, (SPA) is able to effectively defend against both passive and active attacks, including compromising attacks. Through prototype implementation, we demonstrate that SPA is practical and scalable for current RFID infrastructures.

1. Introduction

The proliferation of RFID applications [1–5] raises an emerging requirement—protecting user privacy [6] in authentications. In most RFID systems, tags automatically emit their unique serial numbers upon reader interrogation without alerting their users. Within the scanning range, a malicious reader thus can perform bogus authentication on detected tags to obtain sensitive information. For example, without privacy protection, any RFID reader is able to identify a consumer's ID via the serial number emitted from the tag. In this case, a buyer can be easily tracked and profiled by unauthorized entities. Nowadays, many companies embed RFID tags with produced items. Those tags indicate the unique information of the items they are attached to. Thus, a customer carrying those items might easily get subject to silent track from unauthorized entities in a much larger span. Some sensitive personal information would thereby be exposed: the illnesses she suffers from indicated by the pharmaceutical products; the malls where she shops; the types of items she prefers, and so on. To prevent such unexpected leakage of private information, a secure RFID system must meet two requirements. First, a valid reader must be able to successfully identify the valid tags; on the other hand, misbehaving readers should be isolated from retrieving private information from these tags.

To address the above issue, researchers employ encryptions in RFID authentication. Each tag shares a unique key with the RFID reader and sends an encrypted authentication message to the reader. Instead of identifying the tag directly, the back-end database subsequently searches all keys that it holds to recover the authentication message and identify the tag. For simplicity, we will denote the reader device and back-end database by the "reader" in what follows. Two challenging issues on the reader side must be addressed in the key storage infrastructure and search algorithm: the search efficiency and the security guarantee. Searching a key should be sufficiently fast to support a large-scale system, while the maintained keys should be dynamically updated to meet security requirements.

Many efforts have been made to achieve efficient private authentication. To the best of our knowledge, the most efficient protocols are tree based [7, 8]. They provide efficient key search schemes with logarithm complexity. In those approaches, each tag holds multiple keys instead of a single key. A virtual hierarchical tree structure is constructed by the reader to organize these keys. Every node in the tree, except the root, stores a unique key. Each tag is associated with a unique leaf node. Keys in the path from the root to the leaf node are then distributed to this tag. If the tree has a depth d and branching factor δ, each tag contains d keys and the entire tree can support up to $N - d^{\delta}$ tags. A tag encrypts the authentication message by using each of its d keys. During authentication, the reader performs a depth-first search in the key tree. In each hierarchy, the reader can narrow the search set within δ keys. Thus, the reader only needs to search $d\delta$ keys for each tag's authentication. Therefore, the key search complexity of identifying a given tag from N tags is logarithmic in N.

The tree-based approaches are efficient, nevertheless, not sufficiently secure due to the lack of a key-updating mechanism. Most tree-based approaches do not update keys of tags dynamically. Since the storage infrastructure of keys in tree-based approaches is static, each tag shares common keys with others. Consequently, compromising one tag will reveal information of other tags. To address this problem, we need to provide a dynamic key-updating mechanism to such approaches. The major challenge of dynamic key-updating in tree-based approaches is consistency. If a single tag updates its keys, some other tags have to update their keys accordingly. Till now, consistent and dynamic key-updating mechanisms have scarcely been seen in the literatures.

In this paper, we propose a strong and lightweight RFID private authentication protocol, (SPA), which enables dynamic key-updating for tree-based authentication approaches. Besides consistency, SPA also achieves forwarding secrecy without degrading key search efficiency. We also show that SPA outperforms existing designs in defending against both passive and active attacks, including the compromising attack.

The rest of this paper is organized as follows. We introduce related work in Section 2. We present the SPA design in Section 3. In Section 4, we analyze the security guarantee of SPA. We evaluate the performance of SPA via a prototype implementation in Section 5. We conclude this paper in Section 6.

2. Related Work

Many approaches have been proposed to achieve private authentication in RFID systems. Weis et al. [9] proposed a hash-function-based authentication scheme, HashLock, to avoid tags being tracked. In this approach, each tag shares a secret key k with the reader. The reader sends a random number r as the authentication request. To respond to the reader, the tag generates a hash value on the inputs of r and k. The reader then computes $h(k, r)$ of all stored keys until it finds a key to recover r, thereby identifying the tag. The search complexity of HashLock is linear to N, where N is the number of tags in the system. Most subsequent approaches in the literature are aimed at reducing the cost of key search. Juels [10] classifies these approaches into three types.

Tree-Based Approaches. Tree based approaches [7, 8, 11] improve the key search efficiency from linear complexity to logarithmic complexity. Molnar and Wagner proposed the first tree-based scheme, which employs a challenge-response scheme [8], which achieves *mutual* authentication between tags and readers. The protocol uses multiple rounds to identify a tag and each round needs three messages. Since it requires $O(\log N)$ rounds to identify a tag, the exchanged messages incur relatively large communication overhead. In [7], the authors provide a more efficient scheme which performs the authentication via one message from the tag to the reader and no further interactions. However, the tree-based approaches are often vulnerable to the *Tag Compromising Attack.* Because tags share keys with others in the tree structure, compromising one tag results in compromising secrets in other tags.

Synchronization Approaches. Synchronization approaches [12] make use of an incremental counter to enhance the authentication security. When successfully completing an authentication, the counter of a tag augments by one. The reader can compare the value of a tag's counter with the record in the database. If they match, the tag is valid and the reader will synchronize the counter record of this tag. However, incomplete authentications lead the tag's counter larger than the one held by the reader. To solve this problem, the reader keeps a window for each tag. Such a window limits the maximum value of the counter held by the tag. If a tag's counter is larger than the record held by the reader but within the window, the reader still regards this tag as valid. Such schemes are vulnerable to the *Desynchronization Attack.* In such an attack, an invalid reader can interrogate a tag many times so that the counter of this tag exceeds the window recorded in the valid reader. In [13], the authors proposed a protocol to mitigate the impact from desynchronization attacks by allowing tags to report the number of incomplete authentications since the last successful authentication with the reader. Dimitriou proposed a scheme in [14], in which a tag increases its counter only after successful mutual authentications. Those protocols, however, degrade the anonymity of tags. An attacker is still able to interrogate a given tag enough times so that the tag will be immediately recognized when replying with unchanged responses.

Time-Space Tradeoff Approaches. Avoine converted the key search problem to an attempt at breaking a symmetric key [15]. In [16], Hellman studied the key-breaking problem and claimed that recovering a symmetric key k from a ciphertext needs to precompute and to store $O(N^{2/3})$ possible keys. Accordingly, the key search complexity is $O(N^{2/3})$ in key-breaking-based approaches. Obviously, those approaches are not efficient compared with tree-based approaches.

3. SPA Protocol

In this section, we first introduce the challenging issues of static tree-based private authentication approaches. We then present the design of SPA.

3.1. Challenges of Tree-Based Approaches. Existing tree-based approaches [7, 8, 11] construct a balanced tree to organize and store the keys for all tags. Each node stores a key and each tag is arranged to a unique leaf node. Thus, there exists a unique path from the root to this leaf node. Correspondingly, those keys on this path are assigned to the tag. For example, tag T_1 obtains keys k_0, $k_{1,1}$, $k_{2,1}$, and $k_{3,1}$, as illustrated in Figure 1. When a reader authenticates a tag, for example, T_1, it conducts the identification protocol shown in Figure 2. $h(k, r)$ denotes the output of a hash function h on two input parameters: a key k and a random number r. The identification procedure is similar to traversing a tree from the root to a leaf. The reader R first sends a nonce r to tag T_1. T_1 encrypts r with all its keys and includes the ciphertexts in a response. Upon the response from T_1, the reader searches proper keys in the key tree to recover r. This is equal to marking a path from the root to the leaf node of T_1 in the tree. At the end of identification, if such a path exists, R regards T_1 as a valid tag. Usually, the encryption is employed by using cryptographic hash functions.

From the above procedure, we see that tags will, more or less, share some nonleaf nodes in the tree. For example, T_1 and T_2 share $k_{2,1}$, while T_1, T_2, T_3, and T_4 share $k_{1,1}$. Of course all tags share the root k_0. Such a static tree architecture is efficient because the complexity of key search is logarithmic. For the example in Figure 1, any identification of a tag only needs $\log_2(8) = 3$ search steps. On the other hand, if the adversary tampers with some tags; however, it obtains several paths from the root to those leaf nodes of the corrupt tags, as well as the keys on those paths. Since keys are not changed in the static tree architecture, the captured keys will still be used by those tags which are not tampered (for simplicity, we denote those tags as *normal* tags). Consequently, the adversary is able to capture the secret of normal tags.

A practical solution is to update keys for a tag after each authentication so that the adversary cannot make use of keys obtained from compromised tags to attack normal ones. However, the static tree architecture makes it highly inflexible to provide consistent key-updating. Suppose we update the keys of T_1 in Figure 1, we have to change k_0, $k_{1,1}$, $k_{2,1}$, and $k_{3,1}$ partially or totally. Note that $k_{1,1}$ is also used by T_2, T_3, and T_4, and $k_{2,1}$ is used by T_2. To keep the updating consistent, the keys of all influenced tags must be updated and re-distributed. A challenging issue is that if the position of a key is close to the root, the key-updating would influence more tags. For example, updating $k_{1,1}$ would influence half of all tags in the system (T_1, T_2, T_3, and T_4). One intuitive idea is to periodically recall all tags and update the keys simultaneously. Unfortunately, such a solution is not practical in large-scale systems with millions or even hundreds of millions of tags. Another solution is collecting those influenced tags only and updating their keys. This is

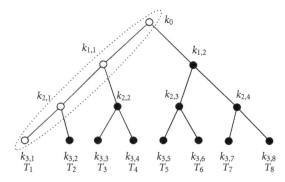

FIGURE 1: A binary key tree with eight tags.

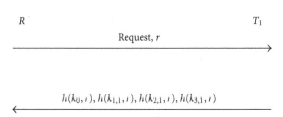

FIGURE 2: A basic RFID authentication procedure.

also difficult because we have to collect a large span of tags even though there is only one tag updating its keys.

This problem motivates us to develop a dynamic key-updating algorithm for private authentication in RFID systems. This is where our proposed SPA enters the picture.

3.2. SPA Overview. SPA comprises four components: *system initialization, tag identification, key-updating,* and *system maintenance.* The first and second components are similar to tree-based approaches such as [7] and perform the basic identification functions. The key-updating is employed after a tag successfully performs its identification with the reader. In this procedure, the tag and the reader update their shared keys. This key-updating procedure will not break the validation of keys used by other tags. SPA achieves this using temporary keys and state bits. A temporary key is used to store the old key for each nonleaf node in the key tree. For each nonleaf node, a number of state bits are used in order to record the key-updating status of nodes in the subtrees. Based on this design, each nonleaf node will automatically perform key-updating when all its children nodes have updated their keys. Thus, SPA guarantees the validation and consistency of private authentication for all tags. SPA also eases the system maintenance in high dynamic systems where tags join or leave frequently by the fourth component.

3.3. System Initialization. For the simplicity of discussion, we use a balanced binary tree to organize and store keys, as shown by an example in Figure 3. Let δ denote the branching factor of the key tree (e.g., $\delta = 2$ when the key tree is a binary tree). We assume that there are N tags T_i, $1 \leq i \leq N$, and a reader R in the RFID system. The reader R assigns the N tags to N leaf nodes in a balanced binary tree S. Each nonleaf

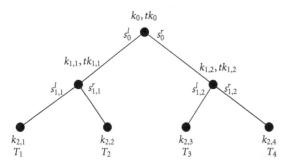

FIGURE 3: A key tree of a system with four tags ($N = 4$).

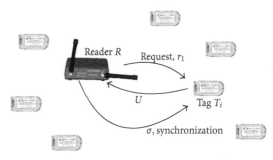

FIGURE 4: Authentication procedure in SPA. After receiving U, Reader R's operations are Step 1, identifying T_i and computes σ; Step 2, sending σ to T_i and key-updating. T_i also updates its keys after checking σ.

node j in S is assigned with two keys, a working key k_j and a temporary key tk_j. The usage of tk_j will be illustrated in Section 3.5. Initially, each key is generated independently randomly by the reader, and $tk_j = k_j$ for all nonleaf nodes.

When a tag T_i is introduced into the system, the reader distributes the ($\lceil \log N \rceil + 1$) keys to T_i. Those keys are corresponding to the path from the root to tag T_i (for a nonleaf node j at the path, if $tk_j \neq k_j$, tag T_i is assigned with k_j). For example, the keys stored in tag T_1 are k_0, $k_{1,1}$ and $k_{2,1}$, as illustrated in Figure 3. Hereafter, we use d to denote the depth of the tree and $(k_0^i, k_1^i, \ldots, k_d^i)$ to denote the secret keys distributed to T_i.

3.4. Tag Identification.
The basic authentication procedure between the reader and tags includes three rounds, as illustrated in Figure 4. In the first round, R starts the protocol by sending a "*Request*" and a random number r_1 (a nonce) to tag T_i, $1 \leq i \leq N$. In the second round, upon receiving the request, T_i generates a random number r_2 (a nonce) and computes the sequence $(h(k_0^i, r_1, r_2), \ldots, h(k_d^i, r_1, r_2))$, where $h(k, r_1, r_2)$ denotes the output of a hash function h on three inputs: a key k and two random numbers r_1 and r_2. T_i replies R with a message $U = (r_2, h(k_0^i, r_1, r_2), \ldots, h(k_d^i, r_1, r_2))$. For simplicity, we denote the elements in U as $u, v_0, \ldots, v_d$. R identifies T_i according to U.

R executes the basic identification procedure to identify T_i, represented as Step 1 in Figure 4. From the root, the reader first encrypts r_1 by using k_0 and compares the result with $h(k_0, r_1, r_2)$ from T_i. If they match, R invokes a recursive algorithm, Algorithm 1, as illustrated in Algorithm 1 to identify T_i. For the key tree in Figure 3, the reader starts from the root and encrypts r_1 by using $k_{1,1}$(or $tk_{1,1}$) and $k_{1,2}$ (or $tk_{1,2}$). Having the results, the reader compares them with received $h(k_1^i, r_1, r_2)$. If $h(k_1^i, r_1, r_2)$ is equal to the result computed from $k_{1,1}$ (or $tk_{1,1}$), the tag belongs to the left subtree; otherwise, it belongs to the right sub-tree.

Level by level, R figures out the path of T_i originated from the root by invoking Algorithm 1. Suppose the path reaches an intermediate node j at level l ($1 \leq l \leq d$) in the tree. At this point, R computes all hash values $h(k_{l+1}, r_1, r_2)$ and $h(tk_{l+1}, r_1, r_2)$ by using the keys of node j's children, then compares them with v_l. Note that v_l is in the authentication message U received from T_i. If there is a match, T_i must belong to the sub-tree of the matched j's

child node. Therefore, R extends the path to that node and continues the identification procedure until reaching a leaf node.

Identifying a tag is similar to traversing from the root to a leaf in the key tree. The path is determined by using Algorithm 1. Instead of using only one key for each node, Algorithm 1 uses both the working key k and the temporary key tk.

3.5. Key-Updating.
After successfully identifying T_i, R invokes the Key-updating algorithm in Step 2, as shown in Figure 4.

When generating new keys, SPA still makes use of the hash function h. Let k_j be the old key of node j. The reader computes a new key k_j' from the old key k_j as $k_j' = h(k_j)$. The key-updating algorithm for the key tree is shown in Algorithm 2. To remain consistent, the nonleaf node j uses temporary key tk_j to store j's old key. In this way, the key-updating of a tag will not interrupt the authentication procedures of other tags belonging to j's sub-tree.

Two important issues must be addressed when updating keys. First, R should update the keys of the identified tag T_i without interrupting the identification of other tags. This is because the keys stored in nonleaf nodes are shared by multiple tags. Those keys should be updated in a consistent manner. Second, each nonleaf node should automatically update its keys when all its children have updated their keys.

To address the two issues, SPA introduces a number of state bits to each nonleaf node. The basic idea behind this mechanism is that each nonleaf node uses these bits to reflect the key-updating status of its children. Once a child has updated its key, the corresponding bit is set to 1. Each node updates its own key when all its state bits become 1.

Without losing generality, we still use balanced binary key tree S to illustrate this mechanism. Each nonleaf node j in S is assigned with two state bits, denoted as s_j^l and s_j^r, s_j^l, $s_j^r \in \{0, 1\}$, where s_j^l (s_j^r) represents the state whether or not the left (right) child of node j has updated its keys. When initializing the key tree S, $s_j^l = s_j^r = 0$ for all nonleaf nodes. At any time, if the key of node j's left (right) child is updated, SPA sets s_j^l (s_j^r) to 1.

```
Fix d ← log N;
SUCCEED ← false;
l ← DepthofNode(n);
    if (v_l = h(k_n, r_1, r_2) ∨ v_l = h(tk_n, r_1, r_2))
        if (l ≠ d)
            if v_l = h(tk_n, r_1, r_2)
                Record n in Synchronization
                Message;
            for i = 1 to δ
                m ← FindChildren(n, i);
                Identification (U, m);
        else if l = d
            SUCCEED ← true;
    if (¬SUCCEED)
        Fail and output 0;
    else Accept and output 1;
```

ALGORITHM 1: Identification (U, node n). Tree-based identification.

```
if n is a nonleaf node
    Store the old key tk_n ← k_n;
Generate a new key k_n ← h(k_n);
m ← FindParent(n);
if n is the left child of m
    Set s_m^l ← 1;
else if n is the right child of m
    Set s_m^r ← 1;
if (s_m^l = 1 ∧ s_m^r = 1)
    Reset s_m^l and s_m^r to 0, and record m in
    Synchronization message;
if m is not the root node
    n ← m;
    Key-updating (n);
```

ALGORITHM 2: Key-updating (node n). Tree-based key-updating.

When R finishes key-updating, it sends a message $\sigma = h(k_d^i, r_1, r_2)$, as shown in Figure 4, and a *synchronization* message to T_i. The former one is used by T_i to authenticate R. The latter one includes the information of the levels on which the nodes have updated their keys in the key tree. After receiving these messages, T_i first verifies whether or not $\sigma = h(k_d^i, r_1, r_2)$. If yes, T_i updates its keys according to the synchronization message. For example, in Figure 3, suppose that R has updated keys $k_{1,1}$ and $k_{2,2}$ at levels 1 and 2 after identifying T_2. The synchronization message is $(1, 2)$. Accordingly, T_2 updates $k_{1,1}$ as $k'_{1,1} = h'(k_{1,1})$ and $k_{2,2}$ as $k'_{2,2} = h(k_{2,2})$, respectively. This algorithm guarantees that the key-updating is consistent and feasible under arbitrary tag access patterns.

The key-updating algorithm is suitable for an arbitrary balanced tree with $\delta > 2$. In such a tree, there are δ state bits maintained in each nonleaf node to indicate the key-updating states of δ children.

3.6. System Maintenance. If a tag T_i is added to the RFID system, R checks whether or not there exists an empty leaf node in the key tree S. If yes, T_i is assigned to an empty leaf node. T_i's keys are then predistributed according to the path from the leaf node to the root of S. If there is no any empty leaf node in the tree S, R creates a new balanced tree S' with the branching factor δ and depth $d - 1$. R then initializes S' by employing the system initialization component described in Section 3.3.

After initialization, R connects the root of S to the root of S'. In this way, S' becomes a sub-tree of S. Hereby, T_i is assigned to an empty leaf node in S' and T_i's keys are pre-distributed according to the path from the leaf node to the root of S. For example, in Figure 5(a), R has 4 tags and each leaf node is occupied in R's key tree. If a new tag T_5 is added to the RFID system, R creates a new sub-tree and assigns a leaf node in this sub-tree to T_5. T_5's keys are k_0, $k_{1,3}$, and $k_{2,5}$.

For any empty leaf node i in the key tree, SPA lets the i's parent node j to set the corresponding state bit s_j to 1. Further, s_j is locked until the node i is assigned to a new tag T_i. This constraint is for protecting the key-updating of other tags from being interrupted. Indeed, since the node i is

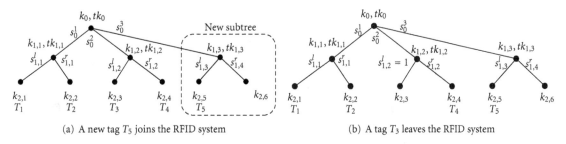

(a) A new tag T_5 joins the RFID system   (b) A tag T_3 leaves the RFID system

FIGURE 5: Tag joining and leaving.

empty, no tag will trigger the change of s_j. Therefore, if s_j is 0, it will never change, such that node j will never update keys. To avoid such an interruption, SPA sets the s_j to 1 to allow other tags update their keys continuously and consistently.

If a tag leaves, R sets the leaf node of the leaving tag to be empty. For example, in Figure 5(b), if the tag T_3 leaves, R empties the leaf node distributed to T_3 and let $s^l_{1,2} = 1$.

3.7. An Example of Key-Updating. For the ease of under-standing, we use an example to explain the key-updating algorithm. Here we show one reader R and four tags a, b, c, d (i.e., four leaf nodes in the key tree). We assume the sequence of tag authentication is (a, b, c, d, a). The original state of the key tree is shown in Figure 6(a). When tag a is identified, R sets the corresponding state bit of a's parent to 1. Meanwhile, R generates a new key of the leaf a as shown in Figure 6(b).

When tag b is identified, the corresponding state bit of b's parent is set to 1, and R updates the keys of the leaf node b and b's parent as shown in Figure 6(c).

When tag c is identified, the situation is similar to that of tag a. Since all state bits of the parent node of a and b are set to 1, R clears the state bits (i.e., reset the state bits to 0) in the key-updating operation as illustrated in Figure 6(d).

When tag d is identified, all state bits of d's parent and the root are set to 1. Thus, R updates the keys of the path from the leaf node of d to the root as shown in Figure 6(e).

Since tag a does not know that the keys of a's parent and the root have been updated, it will still use the old keys for identification. As indicated in the description of Algorithm 2 (Algorithm 2 in Section 3.5), each node stores the old key as the temporary key. After identifying tag a, R informs tag a to update its keys, according to the new keys from the leaf node of a to the root in the tree, as shown in Figure 6(f).

4. Discussion

In this section, we first discuss the security requirements for designing private authentication protocols in RFID systems. To evaluate the security of SPA, we propose an attack model to represent existing attacking scenarios. We then demonstrate the ability of SPA to meet those requirements and to defend against attacks.

4.1. Security Requirements. A private authentication protocol should meet the following security requirements [7].

Privacy. The private information, such as tag's ID, user name, and other private information should not be leaked to any third party during authentication.

Untraceability. A tag should not be correlated to its output authentication messages; otherwise, it may be tracked by attackers.

Cloning Resistance. Attackers should not be able to use bogus tags to impersonate a valid tag. Also, the replay attack should be resisted.

Forward Secrecy. Attackers can compromise a tag to obtain the keys stored in it. In this case, those keys should not reveal the previous outputs of the captured tag.

Compromising Resistance. The privacy of normal tags is threatened if they share some keys with compromised tags. Thus, the number of affected tags should be minimized after a successful compromising attack.

Existing private authentication approaches are able to defend against passive attacks (i.e., eavesdropping), but are vulnerable to active attacks (i.e., cloning and compromising attacks). Therefore, our discussion will focus on how SPA protects tags from active attacks. From the attacker's perspective, two metrics are important for evaluating the capability of SPA in defending against active attacks: (a) *past-exposing probability,* the probability of successfully identifying the past outputs of a compromised tag—this metric reflects the forward secrecy property of an authentication scheme; (b) *correlated-exposing probability,* the probability of successfully tracing a tag when some other tags in the system are compromised.

4.2. Attack Model. Avoine [17] proposes an attack model for RFID system and introduces the concept *untraceability.* The model well-reflects the attack behaviors and impacts on the authentication protocols. Our discussions are mainly based on this model with slight modification as follows.

In our model, the attackers and the RFID system are abstracted into two participants: the *Adversary A* (the attackers) and the *Challenger C* (the RFID system). So, the model is like a game between A and C. A first informs C that A will start to attack. C then chooses two tags to perform SPA protocols. If A can successfully distinguish any

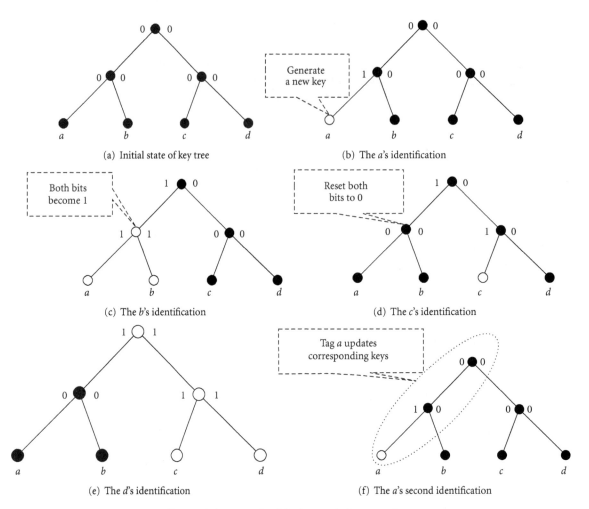

(a) Initial state of key tree

(b) The *a*'s identification

(c) The *b*'s identification

(d) The *c*'s identification

(e) The *d*'s identification

(f) The *a*'s second identification

FIGURE 6: An example of the key-updating procedure.

tag from another one based on their outputs by performing passive or active attacks on the RFID system, we claim that *A* successfully compromises the privacy of the system. For simplicity, Let *P* denote the SPA authentication procedure.

We define four oracles, *Query, Send, Executive,* and *Reveal*, to abstract the attacks on each *T* or *R*. Thus, any attack on a given *R* or *T* can be represented as *A*'s calling on its oracles.

Query (T, m_1, m_3). *A* sends a request m_1 to *T*. Subsequently, *A* receives a response from *T*. *R* then sends the message m_3 to *T*. Note that m_1 and m_3 represent the messages sent from *A* in the first round and third round in a SPA authentication procedure, respectively.

Send (R, m_2). *A* sends a message m_2 to *R* and receives a response. Note that m_2 represents the message sent from *A* in the second round in a SPA authentication procedure.

Execution (T, R). *A* executes an instance of *P* with *T* and *R*, respectively. *A* then modifies the response messages and relays them to both sides accordingly.

Reveal (T). After accessing this oracle of *T*, *A* compromises *T*, which means *A* obtains *T*'s keys. Note that *A* can distinguish any given tag *T* from other tags if it can obtain *T*'s keys.

We claim that an authentication protocol is resistant to attacks *A-O*, if the protocol is resistant to *A* when the adversary has access to the oracles $O \subset \{Query, Send, Executive, Reveal\}$. Based on these oracles, the detailed procedure of a game between *A* and *C* is formalized by following steps.

A tells *C* that the game begins. *C* chooses two tags T_0 and T_1.

For two tags T_0 and T_1 chosen by *C*, *A* accesses the oracles of T_0 and T_1. For T_0 and T_1, let O_{T_0} and O_{T_1} denote the sets of accessed oracles, respectively.

C selects a bit $b \in \{0, 1\}$ uniformly at random, and then provides the oracles of the corresponding tag T_b for *A* to access. For simplicity, we denote T_b as *T*. *A* then accesses *T*'s oracle. Let the set of accessed oracles of *T*, be O_T.

Based on the results from O_{T_0}, O_{T_1} and O_T, *A* outputs a bit b'. If $b' = b$, *A* successfully distinguishes T_0 and T_1; otherwise, *A* loses. Note that *A* can access the oracles in O_{T_0}, O_{T_1}, and O_T in polynomial times. Indeed, if *A* can distinguish T_0 from T_1, it means that A can track all tags in an RFID system.

A passive adversary who can only eavesdrop on the messages delivered by T or R has no access to any oracle. For an active adversary, it can access arbitrary oracles introduced above. For instance, if an adversary applies a cloning attack, it means that it can access the *Query*, *Send*, and *Executive* oracles in this attack model. If an adversary can apply compromising attack, it means that it can access the *Reveal* oracle.

4.3. Security Analysis. In this subsection, we show how SPA achieves the security goals.

Privacy. Due to the pseudorandomness and one-way properties of the cryptographic hash functions, it is safe to claim that the output of the hash function can be seen as a random bit string. Note that the pseudo-randomness of a hash function means no adversary can distinguish the output of the hash function from a real random bit string. Therefore, the messages sent by the reader and tags provide no useful information to an adversary. None of the passive adversaries is able to deduce the original messages based on the output of hash functions, unless it can invert the hash function. It is well known that the probability of inverting a hash function is negligible.

Untraceability. Since the authentication of SPA does not enroll the ID of a tag and all authentication messages are encrypted by a cryptographic hash function, any passive adversary cannot distinguish the tags from others based on their encrypted messages. That is, it cannot track a tag.

Cloning Resistance. In a cloning attack, an adversary monitors a tag, records its messages and resends the message repeatedly [9]. Similar to most previous protocols, in SPA, the reader and the tags generate random numbers r_1 and r_2 to defend against the cloning attack. Since the random numbers r_1 and r_2 are generated uniformly at random, the adversary has to guess them to recover the content of the messages. If the length of r_1 (r_2) is sufficiently long (e.g., 40 bits), the probability of successfully guessing the random numbers is negligible. Thus, SPA is not subject to the cloning attack.

Forward Secrecy. If a tag is captured, the adversary might obtain the tag's current keys. However, the adversary cannot trace back the tag's past communications because the keys are updated by a cryptographic hash function in each authentication procedure. In this way, the adversary still cannot retrieve the past outputs of the tag, unless it is able to invert the cryptographic hash function. Therefore, we can consider that the past-exposing probability of SPA upon the forward secrecy approaches 0. On the contrary, the static key tree protocols [7, 8, 11] cannot update the keys in the system. When an adversary compromised a tag, it can identify the past outputs of the tag from the obtained keys. Thus, the past-exposing probability of the key tree protocols approaches 1.

4.4. Compromising Attack. As we discussed in Section 3.1, a compromised tag may reveal some of the keys of other tags in static tree-based protocols. The adversary is then aware of some paths from the root to the leaf nodes of the compromised tag. Based on those paths, the adversary partially compromises the tree infrastructure. Knowing the "positions" of those nonleaf nodes, the adversary can further identify a sub-tree to which T_i might belong.

Now we use the attack model to discuss the impact of a compromising attack on SPA. The following analysis is based on Avoine's work [18]. The game procedure comprises six phases.

Phase 1. The adversary A has compromised t tags and obtained their complete secret keys.

Phase 2. The system (*challenger*) C chooses two normal tags T_0 and T_1.

Phase 3. A calls oracles O_{T_0} and O_{T_1} (except the *Reveal* oracle), and then receives the results (Note that A cannot compromise T_0 and T_1).

Phase 4. C selects a bit $b \in \{0, 1\}$ uniformly at random, and then provides the oracle O_T (denote T_b as T) to A for accessing (except the *Reveal* oracle).

Phase 5. A calls oracle O_T (except the *Reveal* oracle) and receives the results.

Phase 6. A outputs a bit b', if $b' = b$, A has successfully distinguished T_0 or T_1 from another. Otherwise, A loses.

We assume that A cannot carry out an exhaustive search over the key space. Suppose that A has compromised t tags except T_0 and T_1. Thus, A is aware of several paths from the root to the leaf nodes of those tags, as well as the relevant keys of the nonleaf nodes on those paths. Let M denote the set of those compromised nonleaf nodes in key tree. Let M_i denote the subset of M in which the nodes have the same level i in the key tree. Clearly, $M = \bigcup_{i=1}^{d} M_i$. Correspondingly, let $\overline{M_i}$ denote the set of nodes at level i which have not been compromised by A.

In Phase 5, A impersonates the reader and queries T, T_0, and T_1 with the keys obtained in the RFID system. At this point, there are three possible cases: (1) If neither T_0 nor T_1 has a nonleaf in M, A completely fails. (2) if either T_0 or T_1 (but not both) has a nonleaf node in M, the key subset of T_0 or T_1 including all the keys from the root to this nonleaf node have been compromised. Thus, the adversary can determine which one is T and obtain a correct answer in Phase 6. In this case, A succeeds. (3) If both T_0 and T_1 have an identical nonleaf node in M, A cannot directly distinguish T_0 or T_1 from another. In this case, A can move down to the lower level of the key tree from the current nonleaf node. We denote the keys of T, T_0, and T_1 by $[k_0, \dots, k_d]$, $[k_0^0, \dots, k_d^0]$, and $[k_0^1, \dots, k_d^1]$, respectively, where d is the depth of the key tree. For a given level i, suppose two nodes $n_{i,0}$ and $n_{i,1}$ have an identical parent $n_{i-1,0}$ at the lever $i - 1$, and their keys are

k_i^0 and k_i^1, respectively. Let S_{i-1} denote the sub-tree of key tree S rooted at $n_{i-1,0}$. Thus, $n_{i,0}$ and $n_{i,1}$ are both in S_{i-1}. Let K_i denote the set of keys of the nodes in the interaction of $S_{i-1} \cap M_i$. Let V_i denote the set of the nodes in the interaction of $S_{i-1} \cap \overline{M_i}$. For example, suppose that R maintains a key tree with eight leaf nodes in Figure 7. A has compromised tags T_3, T_5, and T_8. In this case, for the sub-tree S_1, $K_i = \{k_{2,2}, k_{2,3}, k_{2,4}\}$ and $K_i = \{k_{2,1}\}$. Let t_i be the number of keys in K_i, and let δ be the branching factor of the key tree. We also denote a as the number of keys belonging to a nonleaf node (in SPA, any nonleaf node stores two keys k and tk, therefore $a = 2$). We consider the following five cases.

Case 1. If $C_i^1 = ((k_i^0 \in K_i) \wedge (k_i^1 \in V_i))$, then A succeeds.

Case 2. If $C_i^2 = ((k_i^0 \in V_i) \wedge (k_i^1 \in K_i))$, then A succeeds.

Case 3. If $C_i^3 = ((k_i^0 \in K_i) \wedge (k_i^1 \in K_i) \wedge (k_i^0 \neq k_i^1))$, then A succeeds.

Case 4. If $C_i^4 = ((k_i^0 \in V_i) \wedge (k_i^1 \in V_i))$, then A definitively fails.

Case 5. If $C_i^5 = ((k_i^0 \in K_i) \wedge (k_i^1 \in K_i) \wedge (k_i^0 = k_i^1))$, then A fails at level i but it can move to level $i + 1$ to continue its attack.

For $1 \leq i \leq d$, we have

$$\Pr[C_i^1] = \Pr[C_i^2] = \frac{t_i}{a\delta}\left(1 - \frac{t_i}{a\delta}\right),$$

$$\Pr[C_i^3] = \left(\frac{t_i}{a\delta}\right)^2\left(1 - \frac{1}{t_i}\right), \qquad (1)$$

$$\Pr[C_i^5] = \left(\frac{t_i}{a\delta}\right)^2 \cdot \frac{1}{t_i}.$$

Therefore, $\Pr[C_i^1 \vee C_i^2 \vee C_i^3] = (t_i/(a\delta)^2)(2a\delta - t_i - 1)$.

The probability that A succeeds is given by

$$\Pr[\text{Attack Succeeds}]$$

$$= \Pr[C_1^1 \vee C_1^2 \vee C_1^3]$$

$$+ \sum_{i=2}^{d}\left(\Pr[C_i^1 \vee C_i^2 \vee C_i^3] \times \prod_{j=1}^{i-1}\Pr[C_j^5]\right)$$

$$= \frac{t_1}{(a\delta)^2}(2a\delta - t_1 - 1)$$

$$+ \sum_{i=2}^{d}\left(\frac{t_i}{(a\delta)^2}(2a\delta - t_i - 1) \times \prod_{j=1}^{i-1}\frac{t_i}{(a\delta)^2}\right). \qquad (2)$$

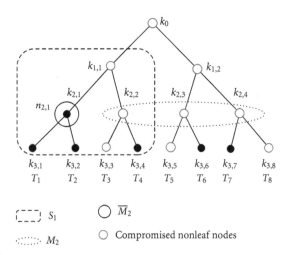

FIGURE 7: An example of the compromising attack.

In (2), t_i, the number of keys known by the adversary at level i, is given by

$$t_1 = \delta\left(1 - \left(1 - \frac{1}{a\delta}\right)^t\right),$$

$$t_i = \delta\left(1 - \left(1 - \frac{1}{a\delta}\right)^{f(t_i)}\right) \quad 1 < i \leq d, \qquad (3)$$

where $f(t_i) = t\prod_{j=1}^{i-1} 1/t_j$.

Equation (2) shows that the correlated-exposing probability is mainly determined by three key parameters: (a) t, the number of compromised tags; (b) δ, the branching factor of the key tree; (c) a, the number of keys belonging to each nonleaf node. Note that if $a = 1$, (2) can also be used to evaluate the security of static tree-based approaches. In Figure 8, we show the theoretical evaluation on the security of SPA in a typical RFID system.

We assume that the system contains 2^{20} tags and the depth of key tree is 20. In the worst case, the adversary A can *simultaneously* compromise t tags at a given time. Then, A immediately starts attacks following the game strategy with challenger C. In addition, we assume there are only T_0 and T_1, which are chosen by C, performing authentication with the reader at this moment. Thus, we can use (2) to compute the correlated-exposing probability for A attacking SPA and static tree-based approaches.

As shown in Figure 8, SPA outperforms static tree-based approaches in defending against compromising attacks. In SPA, although A captures a number of keys shared by some normal tags, those tags are still secure if they update their keys. In contrast, normal tags in static tree-based approaches would be more vulnerable because the keys obtained by A will still be in use. This would ease A's tracking attempts.

In both SPA and static tree-based approaches, the correlated-exposing probability is reduced when enlarging the branching factor δ. This is because enlarging δ leads

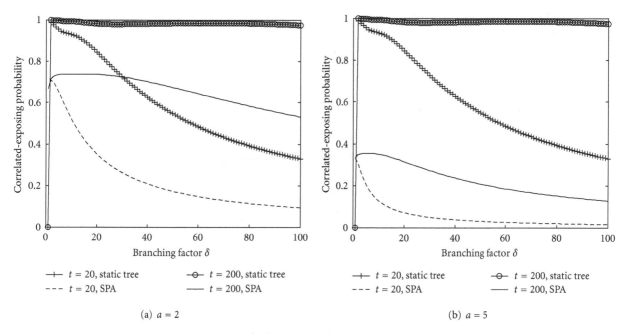

(a) $a = 2$

(b) $a = 5$

FIGURE 8: Defending against the compromising attack.

attackers to capturing fewer keys shared by tags which are not tampered with.

The static tree base approaches are extremely vulnerable to compromising attacks when t is sufficiently large. We find the correlated-exposing probability is close to 1 when $t = 200$ in static tree-based approaches. In this case, enlarging δ does not help much. On the contrary, SPA can decrease the probability by increasing a. The curves of $t = 200$ in Figure 8 show that SPA is more secure under compromising attacks and flexible enough to meet different security concerns.

We here explain why increasing a can enhance the security of SPA. In an RFID system, a part of tags may not be accessed by the reader for a long time. Keys in those tags hereby cannot be updated. The reader must maintain these keys in nonleaf nodes' temporal keys for future use. As discussed in Section 3.2, temporal keys tks store those old keys. The working key k is computed from the temporal keys after these temporal keys have been updated. Therefore, keys of some nonleaf nodes will not be updated if a number of tags are not identified by the reader for a long time. For example, we assume that each nonleaf node has only a single temporal key. If some tags lie in the sub-tree are not accessed by the reader in a period, other tags belong to this node's sub-tree can update keys for only once. That will make the key tree in SPA degenerate into the static tree, thereby alleviate SPA's resilience to compromising attacks. To ease the impact of this problem, we increase the number of temporal keys. We assume that each nonleaf node has one working key k and $a - 1$ temporal keys, $tk_1, \ldots, tk_{a-1}$. Thus, even if a number of tags are not accessed by the reader, keys of other tags in the system can be updated for at least $a - 1$ times. When we enlarge the parameter a, we can enhance the system's capability on resilience to compromising attacks, as shown in Figure 8.

5. Prototype Implementation

In this section, we introduce our experience on SPA prototype implementation. We also evaluate the performance of SPA and compare it with existing private authentication protocols.

5.1. Experiment Setup. We have implemented the SPA protocol on Mantis-series 303 MHz asset tags and Mantis II reader manufactured by RF Code [19]. In terms of its coding, this system is able to support over one trillion tags. A tags' typical transmission range is 300 feet, and the reader can communicate with them at distances of more than 1000 feet depending on the antenna configurations. The back-end database is implemented on the desktop PC with the following configurations: Pentium M 3.2 G dual core CPU, 1 GBytes memory, and 40 G hard disk. We use SHA-1 algorithm as the secure hash function.

In this implementation, the system is able to maintain up to $N = 2^{20}$ tags. For each test, we randomly distribute 40 tags into leaf nodes in the key tree. We perform 1000 independent runs and report the average. We employ a balanced binary tree as the key tree. Each nonleaf node is assigned with two keys, that is, $a = 2$. The length of each key is 64 bit, which is sufficiently long to resist brute-force attacks.

A fundamental concern upon SPA is the latency of key-updating. We use the metric *key-updating Latency* as the time required for the reader to update a tag's keys to evaluate the performance of SPA. On the other hand, the key-updating of SPA should guarantee that the keys are secure enough over their lifetime. We focus on two metrics in the experiments.

(a) Key-Updating Latency. It reflects the computational overhead of key-updating. In SPA, the whole processing

TABLE 1: Experiment settings.

Parameters	Values
δ	2
a	2
d	20
l	64
p	0.1
a_f	10

overhead for an authentication procedure includes two components: *identification* and *key-updating*. Since the static key tree approaches only perform the identification function, we focus more on the computational overhead caused by key-updating of SPA.

(b) Key Security Degree (KSD). It reflects the possibility of keys being obtained when an adversary attacks a RFID system. Let f denote the tag accessing frequency, which means how many tags interact with the reader per second. Let l be the length of a key, let n be the number of updated keys in one key-updating procedure, and let d be the depth of the key tree. We denote p as the probability of an adversary successfully gaining the n keys, and a_f as the attack frequency (i.e., the number of attacks occurred per second). Thus, the key security degree KSD is defined by

$$\text{KSD} = \frac{f \times n \times l \times d}{a_f \times p}. \qquad (4)$$

Because the KSD computed from (4) will be a large value, we use a small real number ε to make the KSD value not too large, where $\varepsilon = 0.0001$ is a system parameter.

KSD reflects the comprehensive ability of a protocol on defending against the active attacks. A higher KSD value represents a more secure protocol. Parameters in our experiments are summarized in Table 1.

5.2. Results. Figure 9 plots the average key-updating latency of SPA. With the increase of the tag accessing frequency, which means how many times a tag is accessed per second, the key-updating latency increases. The processing speed of SHA-1 is 1.73 MByte per second. We find that the latency of key-updating does not exceed 1.7 ms even when the tag accessing frequency approaches 10. Since we construct a tree with the depth of 20 in this experiment, each tag is assigned with 20 keys. Thus, the curve of key-updating is enclosed within two lines: one represents the upper bound (20 keys in a tag are updated) and another represents the lower bound (only one key is updated). The short key-updating latency of SPA enables a reader to support dense access patterns. Due to page limitation, results from other experiments are not reported here.

Figure 10 shows the change of KSD of SPA with different tag access frequencies. The curve of KSD fluctuates when increasing the frequency. In Figure 10, two lines show the upper and lower bounds ($n = 20$ and $n = 1$) of the KSD

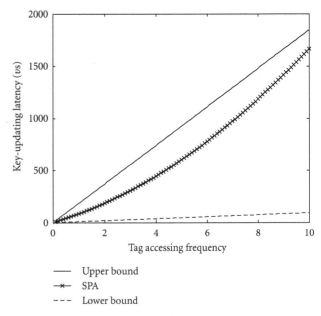

FIGURE 9: Key-updating latency of SPA.

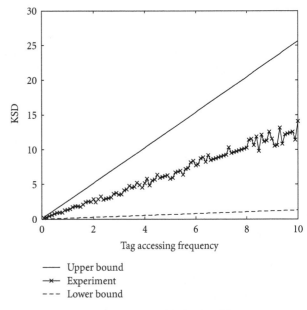

FIGURE 10: Key security degree of SPA.

curve of SPA. We can see that the KSD of SPA increases when enlarging the tag accessing frequency. Clearly, the design of SPA has two advantages. First, tag holders do not need to update the keys of their tags specially. Second, the RFID system is highly secure when tag holders use their tags frequently.

In SPA, the main overhead is caused by SHA-1 computations on the side of R. Therefore, the number of SHA-1 computations reflects the computation overhead of SPA. Figure 11 shows the relationship between the computation overhead and KSD in different tag accessing frequencies. In Figure 11, the y-axis refers to the number of

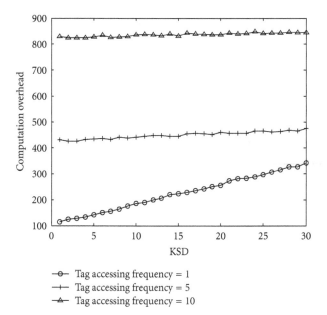

—○— Tag accessing frequency = 1
—+— Tag accessing frequency = 5
—△— Tag accessing frequency = 10

FIGURE 11: Computation overhead versus KSD.

SHA-1 computations. We see that a high tag access frequency results in a smooth curve of overhead. We also find that the computation overhead caused by SPA does not exceed 900 times of SHA-1 even the tag accessing frequency is high, for example, R accessing 10 tags per second, while the PC used in our experiments can perform 86,500 SHA-1 computations per second. It indicates that a significant incensement of KSD only incurs small computation overhead to the system. Hence, SPA is scalable when providing high secure private authentication services.

6. Conclusion

We proposed a privacy-preserving authentication protocol, SPA, to support secure and efficient tag-reader transactions in RFID systems. By using a dynamic key-updating algorithm, SPA enhances the security of existing RFID authentication protocols. SPA is lightweight with high authentication efficiency: a reader can identify a tag within $O(\log N)$ tree walking steps. Compared with previous works, SPA can effectively defend against both passive and active attacks. Through the prototype implementation, we demonstrated that SPA is scalable and practical in large-scale RFID systems.

Acknowledgment

This research was supported by NSFC 60903155 and NSFC 61173171.

References

[1] L. M. Ni, Y. Liu, Y. C. Lau, and A. P. Patil, "LANDMARC: indoor location sensing using active RFID," in *Proceedings of the 1st IEEE International Conference on Pervasive Computing and Communications (PerCom'03)*, pp. 407–415, March 2003.

[2] Y. Li and X. Ding, "Protecting RFID communications in supply chains," in *Proceedings of the 2nd ACM Symposium on Information, Computer and Communications Security (ASI-ACCS'07)*, pp. 234–241, March 2007.

[3] T. Kriplean, E. Welbourne, N. Khoussainova et al., "Physical access control for captured RFID data," *IEEE Pervasive Computing*, vol. 6, no. 4, pp. 48–55, 2007.

[4] C. Qian, H.-L. Ngan, and Y. Liu, "Cardinality estimation for large-scale RFID systems," in *Proceedings of the 6th Annual IEEE International Conference on Pervasive Computing and Communications (PerCom'08)*, pp. 30–39, March 2008.

[5] L. Xiao, Y. Liu, W. Gu, D. Xuan, and X. Liu, "Mutual anonymous overlay multicast," *Journal of Parallel and Distributed Computing*, vol. 66, no. 9, pp. 1205–1216, 2006.

[6] P. Robinson and M. Beigl, "Trust context spaces: an infrastructure for pervasive security in context-aware environments," in *Proceedings of International Conference on Security in Pervasive Computing (SPC'03)*, 2003.

[7] T. Dimitriou, "A secure and efficient RFID protocol that could make big brother (partially) obsolete," in *Proceedings of the 4th Annual IEEE International Conference on Pervasive Computing and Communications (PerCom'06)*, pp. 269–274, March 2006.

[8] D. Molnar and D. Wagner, "Privacy and security in library RFID issues, practices, and architectures," in *Proceedings of the 11th ACM Conference on Computer and Communications Security (CCS'04)*, pp. 210–219, October 2004.

[9] S. A. Weis, S. E. Sarma, R. L. Rivest, and D. W. Engels, "Security and privacy aspects of low-cost radio frequency identification systems," in *Proceedings of International Conference on Security in Pervasive Computing (SPC'03)*, 2003.

[10] A. Juels, "RFID security and privacy: a research survey," *IEEE Journal on Selected Areas in Communications*, vol. 24, no. 2, pp. 381–394, 2006.

[11] D. Molnar, A. Soppera, and D. Wagner, "A scalable, delegatable pseudonym protocol enabling owner-ship transfer of RFID tags," in *Proceedings of the Selected Areas in Cryptography (SAC'05)*, 2005.

[12] M. Ohkubo, K. Suzuki, and S. Kinoshita, "Efficient hash-chain based RFID privacy protection scheme," in *Proceedings of the UbiComp, Workshop Privacy*, 2004.

[13] A. Juels, "Minimalist cryptography for low-cost RFID tags," in *Proceedings of International Conference on Security in Communication Networks (SCN'04)*, 2004.

[14] T. Dimitriou, "A lightweight RFID protocol to protect against traceability and cloning attacks," in *Proceedings of the 1st International Conference on Security and Privacy for Emerging Areas in Communications Networks (SecureComm'05)*, pp. 59–66, September 2005.

[15] G. Avoine and P. Oechslin, "A scalable and provably secure hash-based RFID protocol," in *Proceedings of the 3rd IEEE International Conference on Pervasive Computing and Communications Workshops (PerCom'05)*, pp. 110–114, March 2005.

[16] M. E. Hellman, "A cryptanalytic time-memory trade-off," *IEEE Transactions on Information Theory*, vol. 26, no. 4, pp. 401–406, 1980.

[17] G. Avoine, "Adversarial model for radio frequency identification," Report 2005/049, 2005, Cryptology ePrint Archive.

[18] G. Avoine, E. Dysli, and P. Oechslin, "Reducing time complexity in RFID systems," in *Proceedings of Selected Areas in Cryptography (SAC'05)*, 2005.

[19] RFCode, Inc., http://www.rfcode.com/Solutions/Asset-Management/Products-Overview.html.

12

A Camera Nodes Correlation Model Based on 3D Sensing in Wireless Multimedia Sensor Networks

Chong Han,[1] **Lijuan Sun,**[1,2,3] **Fu Xiao,**[1,2,3,4] **Jian Guo,**[1,2,3] **and Ruchuan Wang**[1,2,3,4]

[1] *College of Computer, Nanjing University of Posts and Telecommunications, Nanjing 210003, China*
[2] *Jiangsu High Technology Research Key Laboratory for Wireless Sensor Networks, Nanjing 210003, China*
[3] *Key Lab of Broadband Wireless Communication and Sensor Network Technology of Ministry of Education, Nanjing University of Posts and Telecommunications, Jiangsu Province, Nanjing 210003, China*
[4] *Provincial Key Laboratory for Computer Information Processing Technology, Soochow University, Suzhou 215006, China*

Correspondence should be addressed to Lijuan Sun, sunlj@njupt.edu.cn

Academic Editor: LiuSheng Huang

In wireless multimedia sensor networks, multiple camera sensor nodes generally are used for gaining enhanced observations of a certain area of interest. This brings on the visual information retrieved from adjacent camera nodes usually exhibits high levels of correlation. In this paper, first, based on the analysis of 3D directional sensing model of camera sensor nodes, a correlation model is proposed by measuring the intersection area of multiple camera nodes' field of views. In this model, there is a asymmetrical relationship of the correlation between two camera nodes. Then, to farthest eliminate the data redundancy and use the node collaboration characteristic of wireless (multimedia) sensor networks, two kinds of cluster structure, camera sensor nodes cluster, and common sensor nodes cluster are established to cooperate on image processing and transmission tasks. A set of experiments are performed to investigate the proposed correlation coefficient. Further simulations based on a sample of monitoring a crossing by three correlative camera nodes show that the proposed network topology and image fusion and transmission scheme released the pressure of camera node greatly and reduce the network energy consumption of communication of the whole network efficiently.

1. Introduction

The integration of low-power wireless networking technologies with inexpensive CMOS cameras and microphones is enabling the development of distributed networked systems referred to as wireless multimedia sensor networks (WMSNs) [1, 2]. The characteristics of WMSNs diverge considerably from traditional network paradigms such as the Internet and even from "scalar" sensor networks. The applications of WMSNs, such as a surveillance sensor network, environmental and industrial monitoring, intelligent traffic congestion control, health-care, and other multimedia digital entrainments, or green city applications, require the sensor network paradigm to be rethought in view of the need for mechanisms to deliver multimedia content with a predetermined level of quality of service (QoS).

Different from conventional sensor networks, WMSNs are characterized by high data rate and directional sensing range on account of multimedia nodes' field of views (FoVs). In a densely deployed WMSN, there exists correlation among the visual information observed by cameras with overlapped FoVs. These differences are calling for new approaches for sensor networking and in particular in network data processing for reduction of data redundancy. So in this paper, aiming at the issue of correlation relationship of multiple cameras, based on the analysis of 3D directional sensing model of camera sensor nodes, we present the correlation model among the camera sensor nodes and propose two kinds of cluster structure, camera sensor nodes cluster and common sensor nodes cluster to cooperate to accomplish image processing and transmission tasks in WMSNs.

The remainder of this paper is organized as follows. Section 2 discusses some previous works on correlation degree of camera nodes which motivated our work. Section 3 presents correlation model for multiple cameras, and the correlation calculate method of multiple camera nodes based on the property of convex is proposed. Section 4 describes correlation-based hierarchical network structure and image processing and transmission scheme. The analysis of the correlation model and performance of the proposed framework are examined in Section 5. Finally conclusions and future work are derived in Section 6.

2. Related Works

There are lots of researches on correlation model of camera sensor nodes based on 2D camera sensing model. In [3], different from conventional sensing models where omnisensing area centers on the sensor node, a directional sensing model of camera sensor nodes is first employed. Meanwhile, the correlation degree of two cameras was defined as the portion of overlapped sensing areas to the entire area of the camera's FoVs. Then two sensors cooperate with each other, image processing scheme based on correlation is proposed. But this scheme is only valid when the sensing directions of the two sensors do not differ very much.

In [4], a spatial correlation model for visual information in WMSNs is proposed. Firstly, a spatial correlation function is derived to describe the correlation characteristics of visual information observed by cameras with overlapped FoVs. Then, by using this spatial correlation model, the correlation characteristics of visual information are obtained at low communication and computation costs. The shortcoming of this spatial correlation model is it just considers the angle between two cameras. But the offset angle of camera, which expresses the area of camera's FoVs, is not investigated, especially, when the offset angle of two cameras is unequivalent. In [5], based on the spatial correlation model put forward in [4], an information-theoretic data compression framework is proposed with the objective to maximize the overall compression of the visual information retrieved by a WMSN.

Papers [6, 7] show how multimedia nodes of a randomly deployed WMSN are categorized in clusters considering the FoVs as the criterion of clustering. If the FoVs of two nodes have a wide common area, sensors are grouped in a cluster since they obtain a similar vision of the monitored area. The established clusters in [6] are disjoint and nonoverlapping while in [7] they overlap each other with common nodes.

Considering the above mentioned, the correlation coefficient, or correlation degree of camera nodes based on overlapped FoVs is an important parameter to effectively divide the monitoring task between two sensors, for example, to calculate the joint entropy of multiple cameras, or to be the criterion of camera node clustering or hibernate redundant nodes, and so forth. And all the above correlation models are based on the cameras' FoVs model which is sector shaped. However, from the human eye's point of view, this simplified 2D FoVs model is reasonable, but it is not very suitable for CCD cameras in monitoring scenario in WMSNs. In practice, the imaging surface of a camera is generally a rectangle, but the shape of the human retina is much closer to a spherical surface. Objects within some range of distances (called depth of field or depth of focus) are in acceptable focus. The field of view of a camera is the portion of scene

space that actually projects onto the retina of the camera. It is not defined by the focal length alone but also depends on the effective area of the retina, for example, the area of film that can be exposed in a photographic camera, or the area of the CCD sensor in a digital camera [8]. So to investigate the 3D perception model of camera node is very necessary.

In [9], since the 2D-based schemes cannot be easily extended to address the coverage issues in 3D directional sensor networks, a 3D directional sensor coverage-control model with tunable orientations is proposed to specify the actual target-detecting scene. Then, address the issue of coverage enhancement by sensors with tunable 3D orientations.

In [10], a 3D wireless multimedia sensor nodes coverage perception model with tunable tilt angle and deviation angle is designed. Through decomposing the 3D space problem to the two aspects of horizontal plane and vertical plane, which reduce the 3D problem to 2D ground. And tilt angle and deviate angle can be adjusted to change nodes' sensing direction, also particle swarm optimization is used to eliminate sensation overlapped area and blind spots, thus ultimate coverage performance of the wireless sensor network can be enhanced. In our prior work [11], based on the 3D wireless multimedia sensor nodes coverage perception model proposed in [10], a FoVs correlation model to describe the correlation characteristics for the images observed by multiple cameras with overlapping FoVs is proposed. Two algorithms, a grid-based and a relative position-based algorithm are devised to calculate the correlation coefficient of two cameras. Eight kinds of relative positions of two cameras's FoVs are shown. Then, a relative position-based approach is designed to calculate the correlation coefficient. The shortcoming of this paper is to use the proposed relative position-based approach, and all areas of cameras's FoVs must be equivalent. This is infeasible in practice.

In this paper, based on the analysis of the 3D directional sensor coverage-control model in [9], we study the correlation characteristics of camera nodes and utilize this correlation to cluster the camera nodes in WMSNs to achieve network energy conservation and prolong network lifetime.

3. Correlation Model for Multiple Cameras

3.1. 3D Sensing Model. In [9], the camera's 3D sensing model is located at a fixed 3D point and sensing direction 3D rotatable PTZ (Pan Tilt Zoom) camera. Figure 1 illustrates that 3D sensing model. This model is denoted by a 5-tuple $(P, \vec{D}, A, \alpha, \beta)$. Where P is the location (x, y, z) of the camera node in 3D space, $\vec{D}$ is the sensing orientation of the camera node, and $\vec{D} = (dx, dy, dz)$ is of unit length, where dx, dy, and dz are the components along x-axis, y-axis, and z-axis, respectively. $\vec{D}$ controls the orientation of the sensor node and can be seen as an angle for the origin of axes. To the original $\vec{D}$ in the actual scene, it is just to control the initial orientation of the camera, and it could be represented by the angle θ. γ is the value of the tilt angle γ; α and β are the horizontal and vertical offset angles of the field of view around $\vec{D}$.

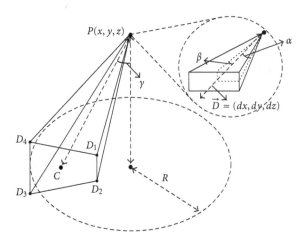

FIGURE 1: The 3D directional sensing model.

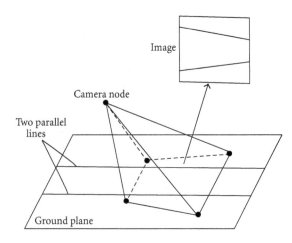

FIGURE 2: The projection of two parallel lines in image.

Through analyzing this camera node 3D sensing model, we can find that the FoVs of wireless camera sensor nodes is trapezium-shaped. Meanwhile, when $\vec{D}$ is represented by the angle θ, based on our priori work [10], the four vertexes in this trapezium can be calculated by:

$$D_1 : (x + d_1 \times \cos(\theta + \alpha), y + d_1 \times \sin(\theta + \alpha)),$$
$$D_2 : (x + d_1 \times \cos(\theta - \alpha), y + d_1 \times \sin(\theta - \alpha)),$$
$$D_3 : (x + d_2 \times \cos(\theta - \alpha), y + d_2 \times \sin(\theta - \alpha)),$$
$$D_4 : (x + d_2 \times \cos(\theta + \alpha), y + d_2 \times \sin(\theta + \alpha)),$$
(1)

where d_1 and d_2 are calculated as

$$d_1 = z \times \tan(\gamma - \beta),$$
$$d_2 = z \times \tan(\gamma + \beta).$$
(2)

In practice, when two parallel lines in the ground plane are taken picture by a camera, the projections of these two parallel lines lying in the image plane will converge on a point in infinity far away. Figure 2 simply illustrates the projection of two parallel lines in the image plane. This is why based on camera 3D sensing model, camera's FoVs is trapezium-shaped.

3.2. Correlation Coefficient. In WMSNs, multiple camera sensors are deployed to provide multiple views, multiple resolutions, and enhanced observations of the environment, meanwhile, they are always deployed in a field of interest, so the cameras' FoVs may overlap with each other. A camera can only observe the objects within its FoV. The observed images from cameras with overlapped FoVs are correlated with each other. For two arbitrary camera sensors C_i and C_j with FoVs F_i and F_j, suppose at a same time, their observed images are X_i and X_j, respectively. X_i and X_j are correlated when F_i and F_j overlap with each other. The definition of correlation coefficient between two cameras is given as below.

Definition 1 (correlation coefficient). Given the sensing areas of camera nodes C_i and C_j with FoVs F_i and F_j as Area(F_i)

and Area(F_i), the correlation degree of X_j to X_i denoted by $\rho_{i,j}$, and the correlation degree of X_i to X_j denoted by ρ_{ji}, respectively are defined as

$$\rho_{ij} = \frac{\text{Area}(F_i) \cap \text{Area}(F_j)}{\text{Area}(F_i)},$$
$$\rho_{ji} = \frac{\text{Area}(F_i) \cap \text{Area}(F_j)}{\text{Area}(F_j)}.$$
(3)

Different from the correlation degree model of two cameras proposed in [3, 4, 6, 11]. In this paper, in most cases, ρ_{ij} is unequal to ρ_{ji} in (3). This is because when a WMSN is initially deployed, in order to gain better surveillance quality of service, lots of coverage-enhancing methods, for example, simulated annealing algorithm [9], particle swarm optimization [10], are used to change sensing orientation and adjust the tilt angle of camera. After network optimization, the area of each camera node's FoVs will be not always equivalent.

From Section 3.1, we know that a 3D space sensor node has trapezium-shaped FoVs in the ground plane. And those four vertexes in trapezium can be calculated by (1). Through this processing, the problem of the overlapping FoVs of two cameras has been formulated as determining the intersection polygon of two polygons in plane geometry. Once the area of the FoV of camera and intersection area of the FoVs of two cameras are calculated, we can get the correlation coefficient ρ of camera C_i and camera C_j in (3). To calculate the overlapping area of two arbitrary camera sensors, the simple and intuitive method is to divide the overall network area into small grids, then check for each grid if its center whether in the FoV of a camera [5] or assuming the sensing area of sensor is composed of discrete points, then examine every point therein and determine if it also falls in others' sensing areas [3]. The time complexity of these two methods is decided by the size of the grid or the number of discrete points. The better precision these two methods pursue, the higher complexity they increase. To remedy these deficiencies, in our priori work [11], a relative position-based approach was proposed to calculate the correlation of

(1) Get the FoVs of two cameras C_i, C_j are F_i, F_j, respectively. V_i and V_j are the sets
  of the four vertices of F_i and F_j, that is, $V_i = \{v_{im} \mid m = 1, 2, 3, 4\}$, $V_j = \{v_{jm} \mid m = 1, 2, 3, 4\}$.
  E_i and E_j are the sets of the four edges of F_i and F_j, that is, $E_i = \{e_{in} \mid n = 1, 2, 3, 4\}$,
  $E_j = \{e_{jn} \mid n = 1, 2, 3, 4\}$;
(2) Initialize the vertex set $V = \phi$, the point of intersection of two edges $v_e = \phi$;
(3) **for** $m = 1$ to 4 **do**
(4)   **if** v_{im} in F_j **then**
(5) $V = V \cup v_{im}$;
(6)   **end**
(7)   **if** v_{jm} in F_i **then**
(8) $V = V \cup v_{jm}$;
(9)   **end**
(10)   **for** $n = 1$ to 4 **do**
(11) $v_e = e_{im} \cap e_{jn}$;
(12)   **if** $v_e \neq \phi$ **then**
(13) $V = V \cup v_e$;
(14)   **end**
(15)   **end**
(16) **end**
(17) $V = \text{Sort}(V)$;
(18) The polygon P constructed by vertex set V is the intersection polygon of F_i and F_j;
(19) **return** $\rho_{i,j} = (\text{Area}(F_i) \cap \text{Area}(F_j))/\text{Area}(F_i)$, $\rho_{j,i} = (\text{Area}(F_i) \cap \text{Area}(F_j))/\text{Area}(F_j)$.

ALGORITHM 1: Correlation coefficient calculation.

multiple camera nodes, but the shortcoming of this approach is all area of cameras's FoVs must be equivalent. In this paper, we extend this approach to various sizes of the FoVs area of camera nodes in the following.

3.3. Correlation Coefficient Algorithm. In a WMSN, when some cameras are deployed and would not move anymore, these cameras are located in the variance height in 3D space, they maybe have different tilt angles γ, horizontal offset angles α, vertical angles β, and orientation of the camera angles θ. The trapezium area size of the camera's FoV is determined by the angle γ, α, β, and the height z of camera nodes. The angle θ just controls the main sensing orientation of the camera. But because every camera's FoV is project in the ground plane trapezium-shaped. As is known, trapezium is a kind of convex polygon, and the intersection of two arbitrary convex polygons still is convex polygon. So we can use the convex polygons knowledge of Computer Geometry to calculate the intersection area of two trapeziums.

Using the property of convex polygon, according to the position to calculate intersection of two trapeziums is feasible. The thought of this correlation coefficient calculate algorithm is as follows: first, judge the four vertices of a trapezium A whether located in another trapezium B. If it is true, add the vertex(s) that locate in B to a vertex set V, vice versa. Then calculate the point of intersection of the four edges in trapezium A with the four edges in trapezium B, respectively. Add the point of intersection to V. Finally, sort this vertex set V by clockwise or counterclockwise order. Now, the polygon constructed by arranged vertex set V is the intersection polygon of trapezium A and trapezium B. Algorithm 1 shows the pseudo code of correlation coefficient

algorithm. From the details of this algorithm, we can obtain it has a processing time complexity of $O(1)$ per camera node.

4. Correlation-Based Clustering

The images observed by cameras with overlapped FoVs are correlated, thus leading to substantial redundancy in the network traffic. To remove such data redundancy, camera nodes can perform intercamera coding with each other by allowing a camera node to encode its image based on the reference of the image from another camera node, so that the coding rate could be reduced. The clustering strategy has been proved to be an effective way to improve network scalability and energy efficiency for sensor networks [12]. This strategy uses the hierarchical concept where the entire network is divided into regions. In many existing algorithms, the metrics for clustering are distance between nodes or node residual energy [13]. In this paper, we aim to construct clusters based on the correlation of cameras so as to minimize the redundancy of network traffic. We divide the entire network into different clustered regions. Each region corresponds to a cluster, in which a group of camera sensors collaboratively perform data processing.

4.1. Network Structure. In WMSNs, the multitier network architecture is recommended [1]. For example, many WMSN testbeds, such as the SensEye [14], adopt multitiered network topology, and it has been shown to improve energy efficiency. In this paper, we further investigate the collaborative visual information compression and transmission scheme in heterogeneous WMSNs. Two types of sensor nodes exist in our network: camera sensor nodes and common sensor nodes.

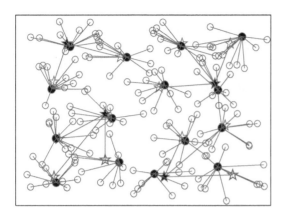

★ Camera cluster head node ☆ Camera node
● Common cluster head node ○ Common node

FIGURE 3: An example of the proposed network clustering architecture.

Camera nodes cluster based on the correlation, and common sensor nodes cluster around each camera node based on shorter distance. So there are two kinds of cluster structure in the network. The network model is illustrated in Figure 3. To construct this multitiered network topology, the following assumptions are made in first.

(1) The overall monitoring area is divided into some key regions, and more than one camera nodes are deployed to monitor a field of interest. The spatially proximal cameras could have highly overlapped FoVs, namely, some camera nodes would have correlation.

(2) There are lots of common sensor nodes randomly deployed around every camera sensor node. And the density of the common sensor nodes is sufficient for guaranteeing that every camera node in the wireless communication link connectivity within the adjacent region to the common sensor nodes is not empty.

(3) All the nodes in the network have a unique ID and the network is time synchronous.

4.2. Clustering Establishment. There are two manners to construct the hierarchical clusters, centralized and distributed. The thinking of the centralized manner is very intuitive. In centralized manner, there are always a central controller. It is sink node in WSNs or WMSNs in general. Sink node provides the full information of the network topology along with the detailed settings (e.g., location, various sensing parameters) for each camera. Sink node based on these information constructs the cluster and broadcasts the result to inform the role of each node.

However, in a large-scale distributed network like WMSN, the centralized operations have limited flexibility and scalability. Moreover, the energy constraint of sensor nodes prohibits network-wide information exchange. So, in this section, we will propose a distributed method that only needs local information exchange to accomplish nodes clustering.

Through network structure proposed in Section 4.1, we know that there are two kinds of clusters structure in the network. One kind is camera nodes cluster. The other kind is common nodes cluster. In the process of establishing the network architecture, we construct the camera node cluster firstly, then build every camera node's common nodes cluster.

In construction of the cluster of camera nodes, one camera node just needs to exchange its sensing parameters, for example, location, tilt angle γ, horizontal offset angles α, vertical angles β, and orientation angle θ to its neighbor camera nodes, which are located in its 1-hop communication range. It is a common assumption that the communication range is at least twice of the sensing range [15, 16], which is d_2 in (2). The details of the camera nodes clustering algorithm are presented in Algorithm 2.

Because one camera node just needs to exchange information with its relevant neighbor camera nodes, for each camera node to construct the cluster, it just needs to calculate the correlation coefficient between it and its neighbor camera nodes instead of all the camera nodes in the whole network. This manner can guarantee that the computational intensity would not increase considerably as the number of cameras goes up.

Once the cluster structure of camera nodes has been established, the next step is to construct the common sensor nodes adjacency cluster around each camera node. In this paper, we call these clusters neighbor clusters. We establish the neighbor cluster of each camera as follows.

(1) Taken a camera node as the center, a certain number of common nodes within this camera node's connective region compose a cluster.

(2) In this cluster, the node with sufficient energy and had best link quality of communicating with station is chosen as cluster head node.

(3) The cluster head broadcasts its ID to the surrounding cluster nodes.

(4) The surrounding nodes in the cluster inform their ID to the cluster head node.

(5) The cluster head node keeps the list of all cluster nodes' ID.

4.3. Network Transmission Scheme. When two kinds of hierarchical clustering structure have been set up already, we discuss the whole network transmission framework in this section.

(1) Based on the network structure proposed in Section 4.1, more than one camera nodes are deployed to monitor a field of interest. The spatially proximal cameras could have highly overlapped FoVs, which is measured by the correlation coefficient. So when the camera nodes cluster established, the common camera nodes send the captured pictures to the camera cluster head node. The camera cluster head node receives and fuses these pictures.

(1) For a group of camera nodes C, $C = \{C_1, C_2, \ldots, C_N\}$, ordered by its (x, y) coordinates;
(2) Get the FoV of each camera node F_i, $F = \{F_1, F_2, \ldots, F_N\}$;
(3) Initialize $i = 1$, correlation degree threshold ε, cluster $X_i = \phi$;
(4) **while** length (C) != 0 **do**
(5) $X_i = X_i \cup C_i$;
(6)   Check the camera nodes which distance with C_i is less than $(d_{i2} + d_{j2})$;
(7)   Add these camera nodes to a set Ct;
(8)   **for** $j = 1$ to length (Ct) **do**
(9)   Calculate $\rho(C_i, Ct_j)$ by Algorithm 1;
(10)   **if** $\rho(C_i, Ct_j) \leq \rho(Ct_j, C_i)$ && $\rho(C_i, Ct_j) \geq \varepsilon \| \rho(C_i, Ct_j) \geq \rho(Ct_j, C_i)$ && $\rho(Ct_j, C_i) > \varepsilon$ **then**
(11)   **if** $Ct_j \in X_{\text{other}}$ **then**
(12) $X_{\text{other}} = X_{\text{other}} \cup Ct_j$;
(13)   **else**
(14) $X_i = X_i \cup Ct_j$;
(15) $C = C - Ct_j$;
(16)   **end**
(17)   **end**
(18)   **end**
(19)   **if** Area(F_k) has the bigest area in X_i **then**
(20) C_k becomes the cluster head in X_i;
(21)   **end**
(22) i++;
(23) **end**
(24) **return** $X_i = \{X_1, X_2, \ldots, X_m\}$.

ALGORITHM 2: Distributed camera nodes clustering.

(2) For energy conservation, the camera cluster head node has no responsibility for compressing and sending the fused pictures to the sink or station. The camera cluster head node just sends the fused picture to the cluster head node of its neighbor cluster.

(3) The common cluster head node receives the picture from the camera cluster head node, then cooperatively compresses the picture with the member of common nodes cluster.

(4) The common cluster head node sends the compressive picture to the sink or station.

(5) In the camera nodes cluster, when the residual energy is less than a threshold, the cluster head of camera cluster will turn to the next camera node, which has sufficient energy and bigger area.

5. Performance Evaluation

In this section, we design some simulations to evaluate the effectiveness of correlation coefficient and the performance of the image transmission scheme we proposed.

5.1. Analysis of the Correlation Coefficient. To investigate the effect of camera's four parameters to correlation coefficient ρ. First, when the locations, α, β, θ of multiple cameras are different and fixed, we increase the value of tilt angel γ gradually to explore the change of ρ.

Figure 4 illustrates that the comparison of correlation coefficients among three cameras, denoted by i, j, k. We can find that the the correlation coefficient of a pair of camera is

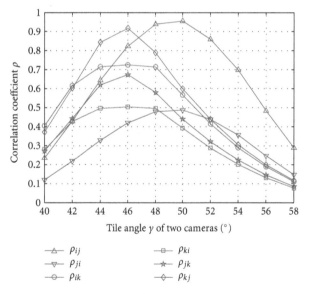

FIGURE 4: The effects of increasing tilt angle γ on ρ.

an asymmetrical relationship. This is because the area of the corresponding two cameras' FoVs is inequal. Meanwhile, the correlation coefficient ρ of a pair of cameras is independent of other pair of cameras, that is, ρ_{ij} (or ρ_{ji}), ρ_{ik} (or ρ_{ki}), and ρ_{jk} (or ρ_{kj}) are irrelevant with each other, but they all have the same variation tendency. As shown in Figure 4, in the beginning, the correlation coefficient ρ increases as the tilt angles γ of these three camera i, camera j, and camera k increase, but when ρ increases to a peak value, subsequently,

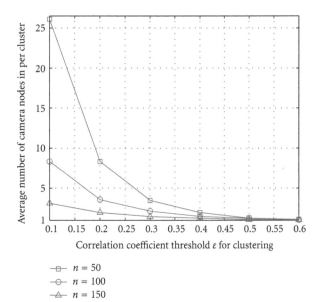

FIGURE 5: The effects of different clustering threshold on average cluster-size.

it would decrease. This is because correlation coefficient ρ denotes the intersection of two cameras' FoVs, and the tilt angel γ increased means that the FoV of camera increasing. Because the locations of these cameras are fixed, to increase the FoV, the overlap will became bigger. So in the beginning, the correlation coefficient ρ increases. But when the FoV of camera becomes very large, the portion of overlapped FoVs in camera's FoV is decreased, so all the curves in Figure 4 are descended eventually.

Like γ, the parameters α, β, and the height z of camera nodes have similarity property to cameras' FoVs, so these parameters have the same effect to ρ, although their influence is kind of moderate.

In Section 4.2, we use the correlation degree threshold ε as a criterion for camera nodes clustering. Next, we discuss the effects of different clustering thresholds on average cluster-size in different numbers of camera nodes in the network. In a square region $S = 100 \times 100 \, \mathrm{m^2}$, we randomly deploy 50, 100, 150 camera nodes, respectively. Based on the uniform distribution model, the camera parameters are setting as follows. The horizontal offset angle is $\alpha \in [30° \ 40°]$. The vertical offset angle is $\beta \in [25° \ 30°]$. The tilt angle is $\gamma \in [40° \ 50°]$. The sensing orientation $\vec{D}$, namely, θ, is taken from $-180°$ to $180°$, and the 3D space height z of camera nodes is taken from 5 to 8. After repeating the experiment for lots of times to take the average value, Figure 5 illustrates that the variety curves of the average cluster-size followed with the different correlation coefficient thresholds ε in three different node densities.

As shown in Figure 5, the higher correlation degree thresholds obviously restrict node memberships and decrease the number of camera nodes per cluster, while lower thresholds increase the area covered by a given cluster at the cost of complexity of coordination. It should be noted

that the situation that signal camera node as a cluster by itself is quite common, even in a very densely deployed network in low correlation degree threshold. This is why in Section 4.1, we assume that every camera node must have a common node cluster around.

5.2. Performance of Network Scheme. We set up a scene to evaluate the network transmission scheme proposed in Section 4.1 as follows. Three cameras are deployed to surveillance an area of interest, for example, a crossing, lots of animals would often pass by. The FoVs of these three cameras are overlapped and by using the Algorithm 2 proposed in Section 4.2. These cameras are in a cluster, which cluster head is camera 2. These three cameras periodicity take photos from their FoVs. At a time, three photos are captured by these cameras. The captured photos are shown in Figure 6. Once the photos have been taken, based on our proposed network scheme, camera 1 and camera 3 would send the pictures to the cluster head node, camera 2, respectively. The cluster head node camera 2 will use stitching technique [17] to roughly fuse the photos, which are received from camera 1, camera 3 and captured by itself. The fused photo by camera 2 is shown in Figure 7. When the photo has fused, the camera 2 will send this photo to the cluster head of its neighbor cluster. This neighbor cluster takes the responsibility to compress and send compressive photo to the sink or station.

Based on this scene, we evaluate the performance of the proposed network transmission scheme in Section 4.3 with comparing without clustering and fusing scheme by energy consumption for communication to transmit these three photos. In Figure 6, the size of photo captured by each camera is $384 \times 512 \times 8$ bit. and in Figure 7, the size of fused photo by camera 2 is $652 \times 397 \times 8$ bit. Without considering the neighbor cluster would compress the photos and reduce the data. According to the energy model for communications in [18], in two schemes, the comparison of whole energy consumption for communication in the network is shown in Figure 8.

From Figure 8, we can see that the whole energy consumption for communication to transmit these three photos by our proposed scheme is obvious less than without clustering scheme. This is very significant in the energy-constrained WMSNs.

Camera node is the key node in the network image transmission in WMSNs. We analyze the energy consumption for communication of the camera node by the following three schemes.

(1) Scheme (A): the camera node directly sends captured photos to the sink or station.

(2) Scheme (B): the camera node sends the captured photos to the neighbor cluster head node, and the neighbor cluster takes the responsibility to compress and send compressive photo to the sink or station.

(3) Scheme (C): the camera node uses the proposed scheme in this paper, to fuse the captured photos and send the fused photos to the neighbor cluster head node.

FIGURE 6: Photos captured by distributed three cameras. (a) Camera 1. (b) Camera 2. (c) Camera 3.

FIGURE 7: Photo fused by the camera cluster head node.

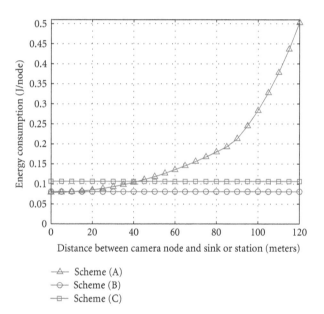

FIGURE 9: Energy consumption for communication of the camera node.

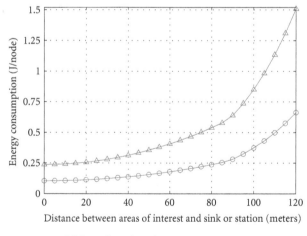

FIGURE 8: Energy consumption for communication in the whole network.

The comparison of energy consumption for communication of camera node in these three schemes is shown in Figure 9. Relative to Scheme (A), in Scheme (B) and Scheme (C), the camera node does not need to send data to the sink or station and abundant energy is saved. In the situation of Scheme (B) and (C), the energy consumption for communication of camera node only is the communication with the neighbor cluster head node. It is unrelated to the distance between camera node and sink or station. This is why the curves for Scheme (B) and Scheme (C) are almost constant in Figure 9. Meanwhile, in Scheme (C), the camera node needs to send the fused photos to the neighbor cluster head node, so its energy consumption for communication is more than camera node in Scheme (B). Although energy consumption of few camera nodes is increased in Scheme (C), the energy consumption in the whole network is greatly reduced. From this point, Scheme (C), the proposed scheme in this paper, is more suitable for image compression and transmission in WMSNs.

6. Conclusions and Future Work

In this paper, the problem of the correlation between camera nodes is investigated. Based on the 3D sensing model of the camera sensor nodes, this problem is reduced to calculate the relative position between camera nodes, and a low complexity and effective distribute method is proposed. Then, using the proposed correlation coefficient, an image fusion and transmission scheme is designed through building network hierarchy structure. A set of experiments are performed to discuss the parameters in 3D camera nodes sensing model influence on the correlation among camera nodes and analyze the perform of the devised network scheme. Simulations demonstrate that the proposed network topology and image fusion and transmission scheme reduce the network energy consumption of communication of the whole network efficiently and save the energy of camera sensor nodes.

Different from the conventional scalar WSNs, the energy consumption of data processing is very important to camera and common sensor nodes in WMSNs. So in our future work, we would consider talking about the energy consumption of data processing to design optimum image processing method to accord with the characteristic of WMSNs.

Acknowledgments

This work is supported in part by the National Natural Science Foundation of China under Grant no. 61003236 and 61171053; the Doctoral Fund of Ministry of Education of China under Grant no. 201132231100002 and 20103223120007; the Natural Science Foundation of Jiangsu under Grant no. BK2011755; the Natural Science Major Program for Colleges and Universities in Jiangsu Province under Grant no. 11KJA520001; the Science & Technology Innovation Fund for Higher Education Institutions of Jiangsu Province under Grant no. CXZZ12_0480; the Priority Academic Program Development of Jiangsu Higher Education Institutions (Information and Communication).

References

[1] I. F. Akyildiz, T. Melodia, and K. R. Chowdhury, "A survey on wireless multimedia sensor networks," *Computer Networks*, vol. 51, no. 4, pp. 921–960, 2007.

[2] B. Bhanu, C. V. Ravishankar, A. K. Roy-Chowdhury, H. Aghajan, and D. Terzopoulos, *Distributed Video Sensor Networks*, Springer, London, UK, 2011.

[3] H. Ma and Y. Liu, "Correlation based video processing in video sensor networks," in *Proceedings of the International Conference on Wireless Networks, Communications and Mobile Computing (WiCOM '05)*, vol. 2, pp. 987–992, Wuhan, China, June 2005.

[4] R. Dai and I. F. Akyildiz, "A spatial correlation model for visual information in wireless multimedia sensor networks," *IEEE Transactions on Multimedia*, vol. 11, no. 6, pp. 1148–1159, 2009.

[5] P. Wang, R. Dai, and I. F. Akyildiz, "Collaborative data compression using clustered source coding for wireless multimedia sensor networks," *IEEE Transactions on Multimedia*, vol. 13, no. 2, pp. 388–401, 2011.

[6] M. Alaei and J. M. Barcelo-Ordinas, "Node clustering based on overlapping FoVs for wireless multimedia sensor networks," in *Proceedings of IEEE Wireless Communications and Networking Conference (WCNC '10)*, Sydney, Australia, April 2010.

[7] M. Alaei and J. M. Barcelo-Ordinas, "MCM: Multi-Cluster-Membership approach for FoV-based cluster formation in Wireless Multimedia Sensor Networks," in *Proceedings of the 6th International Wireless Communications and Mobile Computing Conference (IWCMC '10)*, pp. 1161–1165, Caen, France, July 2010.

[8] D. A. Forsyth and J. Ponce, *Computer Vision: A Modern Approach*, Prentice Hall, 2nd edition, 2011.

[9] H. Ma, X. Zhang, and A. Ming, "A coverage-enhancing method for 3D directional sensor networks," in *Proceedings of the 28th Conference on Computer Communications (INFOCOM '09)*, pp. 2791–2795, Rio de Janerio, Brazil, April 2009.

[10] F. Xiao, L. Sun, R. Wang, and J. Weng, "Coverage-enhancing algorithm for wireless multi-media sensor networks based on threedimensional perception," *Acta Electronic Sinica*, vol. 40, no. 1, pp. 11–18, 2012.

[11] C. Han, L. Sun, F. Xiao, J. Guo, and R. Wang, "FoVs correlation model for wireless multimedia sensor networks based on threedimensional perception," *Advances in Information Sciences and Service Sciences*, vol. 4, no. 3, pp. 27–34, 2012.

[12] W. R. Heinzelman, A. Chandrakasan, and H. Balakrishnan, "Energy-efficient communication protocol for wireless microsensor networks," in *Proceedings of the 33rd Annual Hawaii International Conference on System Siences (HICSS '33)*, pp. 3005–3014, Maui, Hawai, USA, January 2000.

[13] A. A. Abbasi and M. Younis, "A survey on clustering algorithms for wireless sensor networks," *Computer Communications*, vol. 30, no. 14-15, pp. 2826–2841, 2007.

[14] P. Kulkarni, D. Ganesan, P. Shenoy, and Q. Lu, "SensEye: a multi-tier camera sensor network," in *Proceedings of the 13th annual ACM International Conference on Multimedia*, pp. 229–238, Hilton, Singapore, 2005.

[15] X. Wang, G. Xing, Y. Zhang, C. Lu, R. Pless, and C. Gill, "Integrated coverage and connectivity configuration in wireless sensor networks," in *Proceedings of the 1st International Conference on Embedded Networked Sensor Systems (SenSys '03)*, pp. 28–39, Los Angeles, Calif, USA, November 2003.

[16] C. Liu and G. Cao, "Distributed critical location coverage in wireless sensor networks with lifetime constraint," in *Proceedings of IEEE International Conference on Computer Communications (INFOCOM '12)*, pp. 1314–1322, Orlande, Fla, USA, March 2012.

[17] M. Brown and D. G. Lowe, "Automatic panoramic image stitching using invariant features," *International Journal of Computer Vision*, vol. 74, no. 1, pp. 59–73, 2007.

[18] W. B. Heinzelman, *Application-specific protocol architectures for wireless networks [Ph.D. thesis]*, Massachusetts Institute of Technology, 2000.

13

VirtualSense: A Java-Based Open Platform for Ultra-Low-Power Wireless Sensor Nodes

Emanuele Lattanzi and Alessandro Bogliolo

Department of Base Sciences and Fundamentals (DiSBef), University of Urbino, 61029 Urbino, Italy

Correspondence should be addressed to Emanuele Lattanzi, emanuele.lattanzi@uniurb.it

Academic Editor: Yanmin Zhu

Idleness has to be carefully exploited in wireless sensor networks (WSNs) to save power and to accumulate the energy possibly harvested from the environment. State-of-the-art microcontroller units provide a wide range of ultra-low-power inactive modes with sub-millisecond wakeup time that can be effectively used for this purpose. At the same time they are equipped with 16-bit RISC architectures clocked at tens of MHz, which make them powerful enough to run a Java-compatible virtual machine (VM). This makes it possible to bring the benefits of a virtual runtime environment into power-constrained embedded systems. VMs, however, risk to impair the effectiveness of dynamic power management as they are seen as always-active processes by the scheduler of the operating system in spite of the idleness of the threads running on top of them. Avoiding to keep sensor nodes busy when they could be idle is mandatory for the energetic sustainability of WSNs. While most of the tasks of a sensor node are inherently event-driven, the functioning of its hardware-software components is not, so that they require to be redesigned in order to exploit idleness. This paper presents VirtualSense, an open-hardware open-source ultra-low-power reactive wireless sensor module featuring a Java-compatible VM.

1. Introduction

The lifetime of a wireless sensor network (WSN) depends on the capability of its nodes to adapt to time-varying workload conditions by turning off unused components and by dynamically tuning the power-performance tradeoff of the used ones. *Dynamic power management* (DPM) is a wide research field which has brought, on one hand, to the design of power manageable components featuring multiple low-power state and, on the other hand, to the development of advanced DPM strategies to exploit them. DPM is a constrained optimization aimed at meeting the performance requirements imposed by the application at a minimum cost in terms of energy. The main power-saving opportunities come from idle periods, which allow the power manager to take advantage of ultra-low-power inactive modes. Idleness is particularly important in wireless sensor nodes, which spend most of their time waiting for external events or for monitoring requests, and which are often equipped with *energy-harvesting* modules which promise to grant them

an unlimited lifetime [1] as long as their average power consumption is lower than the average harvested power.

State-of-the-art ultra-low-power micro-controller units (MCUs) provide a suitable support to the DPM needs of WSNs, since they feature a wide range of active and inactive power states while also providing enough memory and computational resources to run a virtual machine (VM) on top of a tiny operating system (OS). Virtualization adds to the simplicity and portability of applications for WSNs at the cost of increasing the distance between hardware and software, which might impair the effectiveness of DPM both for the limited control of the underlying hardware offered by the virtual runtime environment, and for the limited visibility of the actual activity offered by the VM. In fact, the VM is usually viewed by the scheduler of the embedded OS as a process which is always active in spite of the possible idleness of its threads. Two solutions have been proposed to address these issues. The first one is provided by *bare-metal* VMs, which runs directly on top of the MCU without any OS [2–4], at the cost of loosing portability. The second one is provided by full-fledged software stacks specifically designed for power manageable sensor nodes in order to make it possible to take DPM decisions directly from the runtime environment and to grant to the OS scheduler full visibility of the idleness of the virtual tasks.

In spite of the availability of ultra-low-power modes provided by the MCU, the effectiveness of DPM risks to be impaired by the paradigm adopted for inter node communication. Although a sensor node is primarily designed to sense a physical quantity and to send a message to the sink to report the measured value, most of the nodes in the network act as routers to relay other nodes' messages towards the sink. While all other activities can be either scheduled or triggered by external interrupts, receiving a message is an asynchronous event which needs to be carefully handled.

This paper presents VirtualSense, an open-hardware open-source platform for the development of ultra-low-power reactive wireless sensor modules featuring a Java-compatible VM. VirtualSense is based on Texas Instruments' MSP430F5418a MCU and on modified versions of Contiki OS [5] and Darjeeling VM [6]. VirtualSense makes directly available from the Java runtime environment all the low-power modes of the underlying MCU. Moreover, it features an event-driven communication library which makes it possible for a Java thread to react to incoming messages without keeping the MCU busy while waiting.

This work provides a comprehensive overview and a detailed description of the results achieved by the VirtualSense project [7] by presenting the VirtualSense platform, by providing a detailed power-state model for it, and by presenting the results of extensive measurements conducted on a working prototype.

1.1. Related Work. Since 1998, the family of UC Berkeley motes, derived from the *Smart Dust* and *COTS Dust* projects, has been a landmark in scientific research on WSNs [8, 9]. In particular the first prototype, called WeC, produced in 1998, was based upon an Atmel AT90LS8553 MCU clocked at 4 MHz and equipped with 512 B of RAM. Based on WeC mote, in 1999 a commercial platform called Rene was produced by Crossbow. Starting from Rene mote, in 2001 Crossbow developed one of the most popular wireless sensor mote called Mica. WeC, Rene, and Mica motes shared the same architecture and the same RFM TR100 radio transceiver (on the 916.5 MHz frequency band), but Mica used the new Atmel 128L MCU equipped with 4 KB of RAM. The Rene project then evolved in several well-known platforms including Mica2, Mica2Dot, and MicaZ. Mica family motes were equipped with different radio transceivers ranging from the Chipcon CC1000, working in the 900 MHz frequency band, for the Mica2 motes to the Texas Instruments CC2420, working in the 2.4 GHz frequency band, installed on the MicaZ mote. In 2005 UC Berkeley developed another popular sensor platform called Telos [10]. Telos was the first mote designed around the extremely low-power Texas Instruments MSP430 MCU family providing low-power modes with a consumption of a few μW. In particular, Telos mote was equipped with the Texas Instruments MSP430F1611 with 10 KB of RAM running

TABLE 1: Main features of existing motes.

Mote name	Arch. [bit]	MCU freq. [MHz]	RAM [kB]	Sleep p. [μW]	RX p. [mW]
WeC	8	4	0.5	65	108
Rene	8	4	0.5	50	108
Mica	16	4	4	48	75
Mica2	16	8	4	48	75
Telos	16	8	10	163	58
Iris	16	16	8	30	65
BTNode	16	8	64	9900	105
TinyNode	16	8	10	18	75
Open-WiSe	32	60	32	6900	131
Opal	32	96	52	21000	105
XYZ	32	57	32	45000	105
iMote	32	12	64	12000	90
VirtualSense	**16**	**25**	**16**	**1.62**	**66**

at 8 MHz in order to minimize power consumption while increasing computational performance. As its predecessors, Telos used the Texas Instruments CC2420 radio transceiver for network communication.

In the last decade a number of wireless sensor nodes have been developed using several MCUs and Radio transceivers ranging from 16 to 32 bit platforms. In particular, in the 16 bit domain we can mention the BTNode [11] developed in 2003 by the Swiss Federal Institute of Technology, the TinyNode [12] developed in 2006 by the École Polytechnique Fédérale de Lausanne (EPFL), and Iris developed in 2006 by Memsic corporation [13]. In the 32 bit domain the most representative motes are Open-Wise [14] from the University of Colima, Opal [15] developed by Autonomous Systems Laboratory of Australia in 2011, iMote [16] and iMote2 [17] from Intel developed in 2003–2006, and XYZ mote developed by UC Berkeley in 2005 [18].

The key features of the motes are summarized in Table 1, which also reports the features of the VirtualSense mote presented in this paper.

Figure 1 provides a graphical representation of the power-performance tradeoff offered by the motes listed in Table 1. Each architecture is represented as a point in a log-log Cartesian plane where performance and power are reported in the x and y axes, respectively. Performance is expressed in terms of computational resources, computed as the product between MCU clock frequency (in MHz) and RAM size (in KB). Consumption is expressed by the average between the power consumption of the deepest sleep state with self-wakeup capabilities, and the consumption of the mote in receiving mode, weighted according to a 2% duty cycle. Power values for VirtualSense are taken from measurements (see Section 6), while all other data are taken from literature. In spite of the arbitrariness of the metrics adopted in Figure 1, they are effective to point out the differences between the existing motes and to evaluate their suitability to run a virtual machine. In particular, the vertical dotted line represents a computational resource threshold

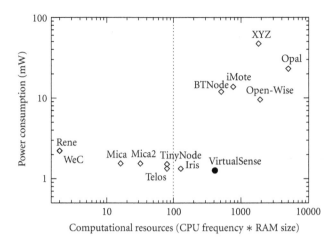

FIGURE 1: Motes comparison.

corresponding to a 10 MHz clock frequency and 10 KB of RAM, which can be regarded as minimum requisites to run a virtual machine on top of a mote. The black dot in the plot represents the positioning of VirtualSense, which provides a performance close to that of 32 bit architectures with an average power consumption lower than 2 mW.

1.2. Organization. The rest of the paper is organized as follows. Section 2 provides a minimum background on power manageable MCUs and on the software stack adopted for the development of VirtualSense. Section 3 presents the HW-SW platform of VirtualSense, outlining the main solutions adopted to address the issues raised by the interaction between the VM and the OS running on top of an ultra-low-power MCU. Section 4 introduces an event-driven communication library which enables the development of high-level communication protocols compatible with DPM. Section 5 outlines the power-state model of VirtualSense, which makes directly available from the Java runtime environment one active state and 7 low-power modes. Section 6 reports the results of extensive measurements conducted in order to characterize the power-state model of the sensor module and to evaluate its energy efficiency. Section 7 concludes the paper.

2. Background

This section provides an overview of the most relevant features of the three main components adopted for the development of VirtualSense, namely: a power manageable MCU, the Contiki OS, and the Darjeeling VM. Moreover, it introduces a power-state diagram to be used to describe the combined behavior of the three components.

2.1. Power Manageable MCU. Ultra-low-power MCUs exploit idleness to switch off power-consuming components in order to save energy. Although different MCUs can differ in the number and in the names of the low-power states they provide, for our purposes we consider a generic MCU to be represented by a power state machine with four categories of

power states, called *Active*, *Standby*, *Sleep*, and *Hibernation*, characterized by the components which are turned off and by the consequent tradeoff between power consumption and wakeup time.

In Active mode the CPU is running and the unit is able to execute tasks without incurring any delay. In Standby mode the CPU is not powered, but the clock system is running and the unit is able to self wakeup by means of timer interrupts. In Sleep mode both the CPU and the clock system are turned off and the unit wakes up only upon external interrupts. In Hibernation even the memory system is turned off, so that there is no data retention. Wakeup can be triggered only by external interrupts and it entails a complete reboot of the CPU.

2.2. Contiki OS. Contiki is an open source real-time OS specifically designed for sensor networks and networked embedded systems [5]. The key features of Contiki OS are: portability, multitasking, memory efficiency, and event-driven organization. Each process in Contiki can schedule its own wakeup and go to sleep without loosing the capability of reacting to external events.

The basic power management mechanism in Contiki exploits the Standby state of the MCU by setting a timer interrupt (namely, `clock`) which periodically turns on the CPU in order to check for elapsed wakeup times. The period of the timer interrupt is a constant (namely, `INTERVAL`) defined at compile time and initialized once and for all during the boot (for Texas Instruments' MSP430 MCUs the period is set at 10 ms). The `INTERVAL` determines the time resolution of the events managed by the OS. Although the CPU can react to asynchronous external interrupts, the OS reacts as if they were aligned with the last timer interrupt.

The inherent event-driven structure of Contiki provides a mean for minimizing the energy overhead caused by periodic wakeup. This is done by making the interrupt handler aware of the next time at which a process has to be resumed in order to go back to sleep without invoking the scheduler in case of premature wakeup.

2.3. Darjeeling VM. Darjeeling is a VM designed for extremely limited devices, specifically targeting wireless sensor networks [6]. Its main advantage stems from the capability of supporting a substantial subset of the Java libraries while running on 8-bit and 16-bit MCUs with at least 10 kbytes of RAM. The size of the bytecode is significantly reduced by means of an offline tool, called *infuser*, which transforms the Java bytecode into a custom bytecode and performs static linking of groups of classes. It is also worth mentioning that the Darjeeling VM provides a garbage collector and supports multithreading.

The VM executes on Contiki as a process which runs together with the OS protothreads implementing the *NET-STACK* communication protocol. The VM scheduler implements a round-robin policy in which each thread is allowed to execute for upto a fixed number of bytecodes before releasing the CPU. Whenever a thread is suspended, the VM waits for the next timer interrupt (possibly yielding resources) before resuming the execution of the next running thread.

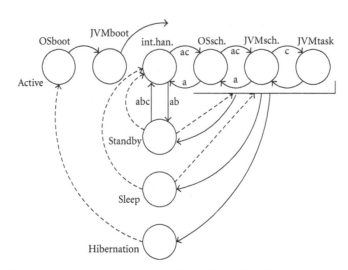

FIGURE 2: Power-state diagram of a generic power manageable MCU running the Darjeeling VM on top of Contiki OS.

2.4. Power State Diagram. Figure 2 shows the power-state diagram of a system running Contiki OS and Darjeeling VM on top of an MCU which provides the four power states introduced in Section 2.1. The Active mode is split into several states to represent the macrosteps required at wakeup to resume the execution of a task on the runtime virtual environment. Dashed arcs represent external interrupts, while solid arcs represent self-events. According to the definition of the low-power states, self-wakeup is enabled only from Standby, while external interrupts are required to wake up from Sleep and Hibernation. It is also worth noticing that a complete boot is required when exiting from Hibernation, while data retention allows execution to resume directly when exiting from Standby and Sleep modes. Transitions represented on the right-hand side of the graph denote the possibility of entering low-power states directly from a code segment and resuming execution from the same point at wakeup at any level of the software stack.

According to the behavior described in Section 2.2, Contiki exploits the Standby state whenever all its running processes are waiting for scheduled timers or external events, but in order to keep control of the elapsed time it sets a periodic timer interrupt which wakes up the CPU every 10 ms. Upon wakeup the interrupt handler evaluates if there are running processes which need to resume execution. If this is the case the control is passed to the scheduler, otherwise the CPU is turned off again soon. As mentioned in Section 2.3, the Darjeeling VM running on Contiki is a process which needs to resume at each timer interrupt in order to check for the status of its threads. If there are no threads ready to resume, the process is suspended until next timer interrupt.

Labels a, b, and c in Figure 2 denote the transitions taken upon a timer interrupt in case of: (a) VM with no tasks to resume, (b) system with no processes to resume, and (c) virtual task to be resumed. Case (c) is the only one which makes the CPU worth to be woken up, while cases (a) and (b) are nothing but an overhead to be periodically paid while in Standby.

Figure 3(A) provides a simplified version of the power state diagram where (a) and (b) are represented as self-loops of the Standby state, while the overhead of the boot is implicitly associated with the wakeup transition from Hibernation, rather than being explicitly represented by the transient states of Figure 2. On the other hand, Standby mode is split into three different states in Figure 3(A) to stress the difference between pure Standby without periodic wakeup, and intermittent Standby with type (a) or type (b) timer interrupts.

A further abstraction is provided in Figure 3(B), where self loops (a) and (b) have disappeared and their power overhead has been directly accounted for in the average power consumption of the corresponding standby states. Since such an overhead depends on the period of the timer interrupt (denoted by T), power states Standby.a and Standby.b represent families of power states, the average power consumption of which depends on the value of T. Because of the default settings of Contiki for the target MCU and of the interaction with the Darjeeling VM, the only low power state which is actually exploited is Standby.a with $T = 10$ ms.

3. VirtualSense Platform

VirtualSense is an open-source open-hardware project. This section outlines both the hardware software solutions adopted in the design of VirtualSense in order to make it possible to fully exploit the power states of Figure 3(B), while running applications on top of the virtual machine.

3.1. Hardware Architecture. VirtualSense is made of ultra-low-power off-the-shelf components in order to keep the overall consumption compatible with state-of-the-art energy harvesters and to enable the fabrication of low-cost motes.

Figure 4 shows the functional block diagram representing the hardware architecture. The core is an MCU belonging to the Texas Instrument MSP430F54xxa family [19]. It communicates through I^{2}C bus with a Microchip

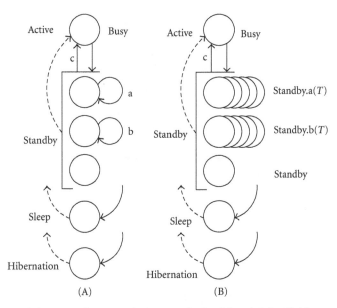

FIGURE 3: Abstract representations of the state diagram of Figure 2 obtained by: (A) implicitly representing transient states as arcs with nonnull transition time and energy (B), removing periodic self-loops, and accounting for the corresponding cost into the power consumption of the corresponding states.

24AA025E48 Extended Unique Identifier [20] and with a Microchip 24AA512 serial 512K EEPROM [21]. The SPI bus is used by the MCU to communicate with a Texas Instruments CC2520 2.4 GHz IEEE 802.15.4 RF transceiver [22] and with an NXP PCF2123 ultra low-power real-time clock/calendar (RTC) [23].

A FTDI FT232R chip provides USB 2.0 communication capabilities and power supply to the sensor node, while a JTAG interface enables on-lab node programming [24]. Finally, 3 ADC channels are used to sample data from sensors. For testing purposes, the prototype was equipped with three representative sensors, namely: a BH1620FVC light sensor [25], an LM19 temperature sensor [26], and an HIH5030 humidity sensor [27].

3.2. Avoiding Periodic Wakeup. Periodic wakeup from Standby is used in the reference architecture outlined in Section 2 to maintain time awareness. The INTERVAL between periodic timer interrupts is also the time resolution in Contiki.

In principle, periodic wakeup could be avoided in a power-managed system as long as an oracle exists to wake up the system right in time to execute useful tasks. The scheduler of the OS has the capability of acting as an omniscient oracle for the self-events scheduled by its processes. Similarly, the scheduler of the VM can act as an oracle for the self-events scheduled by its threads. In the reference architecture, however, neither the OS nor the VM exploits these prediction capabilities, ultimately impairing the energy efficiency of Standby mode. Two changes were made to overcome this limitation.

First, the scheduler of the Darjeeling VM was modified in order to take the time of the next scheduled task (as returned by function dj_vm_schedule()) and

to use it to set an OS timer (namely, &et) and suspend the entire process (by means of PROCESS_YIELD_UNTIL(etimer_expired(&et))). This makes the OS aware of the idleness of the VM, so that premature periodic wakeup can be effectively filtered out by the interrupt handler. Referring to the power state diagram of Figure 3(B), this enables the exploitation of state Standby.b in place of Standby.a.

A second change was implemented in Contiki to make it able to dynamically adjust the INTERVAL of the timer interrupt. An integer slow-down coefficient was used to this purpose in order to maintain compatibility with the 10 ms time resolution of the OS. The interrupt handler was modified accordingly by applying the same coefficient to the timer-interrupt counter to be compared with the time of the next scheduled process. Referring to the diagram of Figure 3(B), the modified version of Contiki provides control of parameter T of Standby states (a) and (b). Moreover, it makes it possible for the OS to set the timer interrupt before entering the Standby mode in order to wake up the processor right in time to execute the next scheduled event, thus avoiding any useless periodic wakeup (state Standby in Figure 3(B)).

The only drawback of slowing down the timer interrupt is the loss of accuracy in the perceived arrival time of external interrupts. In fact, although the MCU is able to react to asynchronous external interrupts regardless of the timer when in Standby mode, timer interrupts are required to update the system clock. This problem will be addressed in Section 3.4.

3.3. Hibernation. The main problem with Hibernation is the lack of data retention, which requires the heap of the VM to be saved in flash and restored at wakeup together with

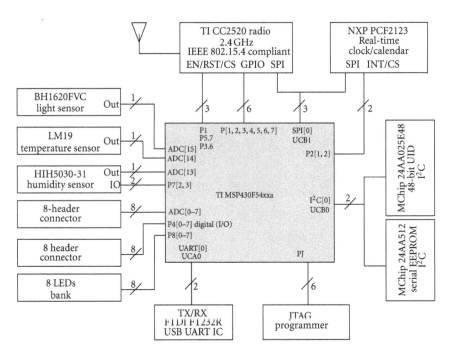

FIGURE 4: Functional block diagram of the VirtualSense hardware platform.

a few external variables, including the base address of the heap. In order to allow hibernation to be possibly triggered by a high-level task running on a thread, the context of the running thread has to be saved in the heap without waiting for a context switch. Moreover, a flag has to be added to the `thread` data structure to recognize the thread which triggered hibernation, while control bytes have to be stored in flash to make sure that the heap is fresh. The control bytes are then used by the `load_machine()` function to decide whether to resume execution from the point of hibernation or to restart the VM process from the `main`. Hibernation process is implemented as a native method, while wakeup from hibernation is directly implemented in the `main` of the VM.

It is worth noticing that the OS is not hibernated, so that it is rebooted at wakeup and the clock needs to be restored in order to make it coherent with the timers of the scheduled self events. Timing issues are discussed in the next subsection.

3.4. Dealing with Time. The low-power states described so far pose timing issues which get worse when moving from Standby to Hibernation. In pure Standby mode, in fact, the timer interrupt is used only to implement right-in-time wakeup, so that it does not provide any information about the actual time at which external interrupts occur. In Sleep mode, the clock system is switched off, so that the MCU is unable to schedule its own wakeup, which can be triggered only by external events which do not provide any information about the time elapsed while the MCU was sleeping. Finally, in Hibernation the RAM is switched off and the OS is rebooted at wakeup, so that even the time at which hibernation was triggered is lost unless it is stored in flash and restored at wakeup.

All these issues can be addressed by exploiting the external RTC available on the VirtualSense platform. The RTC can be used by the MCU both to schedule wakeup calls from the deepest low-power states, and to update the system clock at wakeup. It is worth mentioning that no RTC is required if the MCU is used only to implement bare reactive applications, such as sensor nodes used either to count external events or to give the alarm when specific conditions are detected.

4. Virtual Network Stack

Communication across the radio channel is handled by the `Radio` class of the Darjeeling VM, which makes available a `receive()` method to be invoked by any Java thread waiting for a message. As soon as the method is invoked, the Java thread is suspended by the scheduler of the VM. If there are no other threads ready to execute, the Darjeeling process is suspended as well and rescheduled by the OS at next timer interrupt (i.e., at most after 10 ms). Referring to the state diagram of Figure 2, as long as the message does not arrive, the MCU keeps waking up at each timer interrupt and executing the interrupt handler routine, the OS scheduler, and the VM scheduler before deciding to go back in Standby mode. This is a power-consuming self loop which is labeled with a in Figure 2 and schematically represented by macro state Standby.a(T) in Figure 3(B). No other low-power states can be exploited while waiting for a message.

It is worth noticing that power consumption of Standby.a(T) is several orders of magnitude higher than that of Sleep and Hibernation. Moreover, the wakeup time is larger than 10 ms, so that the MCU would stay always active while waiting for a message unless a longer timer interrupt was set in the modified stack. The minimum timer interrupt

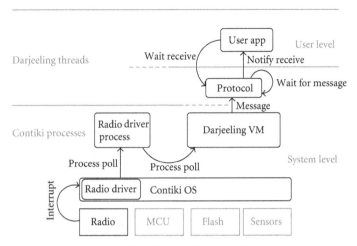

FIGURE 5: VirtualSense software architecture.

which could allow the exploitation of Standby mode is $T = 25$ ms.

The event-driven communication library presented in next section solves this issue by enabling the exploitation of all the low-power states of a power-manageable virtual sensor node waiting for incoming messages.

4.1. VirtualSense Communication. The software architecture of the proposed communication framework is shown in Figure 5, where arrows are used to represent the event chain triggered by the reception of an incoming packet. The figure points out the interactions between user-level and system-level execution flows, as well as those between Contiki processes (namely, `Radio driver process` and `Darjeeling VM`) and Darjeeling threads (namely, `Protocol` and `User app`).

While waiting for an incoming packet all the processes are blocked and they do not consume any computational resource. When a packet is received by the radio device, the `Radio driver` interrupt handler issues a `PROCESS_EVENT_POLL` for the `Radio driver process` which was waiting for it. At this point the scheduler of Contiki wakes up the `Radio driver process` which: takes the packet from the radio device buffer, forwards it to the Contiki network stack, issues a new `PROCESS_EVENT_POLL` for the `Darjeeling VM`, and releases the CPU while waiting for next packet. The CPU is then taken by the `Darjeeling VM` process, which resumes the execution of the `Protocol` thread which was blocked for I/O. The `Protocol` plays the role of consumer by popping the incoming message from the Contiki network stack, which acts as a buffer in the producer-consumer interaction.

It is worth noticing that, in order to make it possible for the `PROCESS_EVENT_POLL` to resume the VM, a new condition has to be added in OR to the `PROCESS_YIELD_UNTIL` instruction introduced in Section 3.2 to suspend the VM (The complete instruction used to suspend the VM becomes `PROCESS_YIELD_UNTIL((etimer_expired(&et)) || ev == PROCESS_EVENT_POLL))`).

The event chain described so far is general enough to enable the implementation of any kind of communication protocol either within the `Protocol` thread or at application level. Depending on the protocol adopted and on its implementation, received packets can either be handled directly by the `Protocol` thread or be forwarded to the `User app` waiting for them.

Sending a packet is much simpler than receiving it: the `User app` which needs to send a message invokes the `send()` method of the `Protocol`, which puts the packet on the Contiki network stack without involving the `Radio driver process`.

In the following we outline the three packages developed to extend the Darjeeling Java libraries in order to support the event chains described above: (i) `javax.virtualsense.radio`, containing the static native methods used to communicate with the radio device; (ii) `javax.virtualsense.network`, making communication primitives available to user-level Java threads; (iii) `javax.virtualsense.concurrent`, providing synchronization primitives. A simplified class diagram is shown in Figure 6.

4.2. Radio Package. The `radio` package contains the `Radio` class (represented in Figure 6) and some other classes used to handle exceptions. The `Radio` class exports static native methods which directly interact with the platform radio driver and with the network stack of Contiki OS: a method to perform radio device configuration and initialization (`init()`), unicast and broadcast send methods (`send()`, and `broadcast()`), a blocking receive methods (`receive()`, and two methods to get the sender and receiver IDs (`getSenderId()` and `getReceiverId()`). All the methods are protected, in order to be used only through the `Protocol` class, which is part of the `network` package.

Unicast and broadcast send methods make use of the Contiki `unicast_conn` and `broadcast_conn` network connections from the `rime` network stack. The `receive()` method suspends the calling Java thread by putting it in a waiting queue and acquires a lock on the radio device

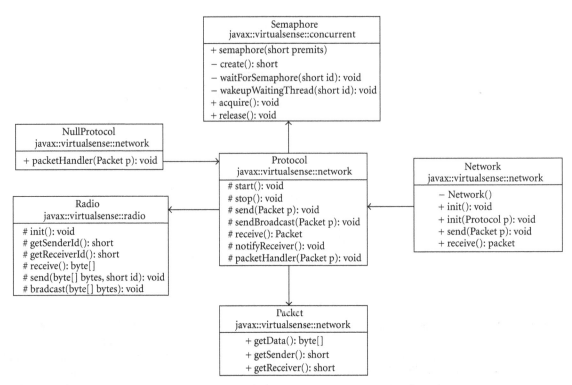

FIGURE 6: VirtualSense communication class diagram. Public methods are denoted means "+,"l while protected and private methods are denoted by "#"and "−,"respectively.

preventing the power manager to shut down the network device. Whenever a radio message is received from the Contiki network stack two different callbacks are activated depending on the nature of the received message: broadcast callback or unicast callback. Both callbacks wake up the suspended Java thread, set the senderId and receiverId attributes, and release the device lock.

4.3. Network Package. The network package acts as a middleware layer which lies between the system level radio package and user-level applications. In particular, this package contains an abstract Protocol class, providing a communication protocol skeleton, and a Network class, providing a public interface to make communication primitives available to user-level threads.

The Network implements the *singleton* pattern, so that it can only be instantiated by means of its init() method, which can be invoked with or without a given protocol (i.e., an instance of a subclass of Protocol. If no protocol is specified, then the NullProtocol is used by default. After network initialization, user level threads can call send() and receive() methods to communicate. These two methods provide a public interface to the corresponding methods of the Protocol class.

Protocol is an abstract class which has to be subclassed in order to implement specific routing strategies. The class maintains as local properties the routing table and the queue of received packets. In order to decouple system-level and user-level packet reception tasks, the Protocol class provides a dedicated thread (instantiated and launched

within the class constructor) which runs a loop containing a call to Radio.receive(). The thread is suspended on this call until a packet is received, as described in Section 4.2. Upon reception of an incoming packet the thread resumes execution and it calls the packetHandler() method, an abstract method that has to be implemented in any Protocol subclass.

Methods receive() and notifyReceiver() provide the means for using the event-driven reception mechanism from user-level threads. To this purpose, an application which needs to receive a packet from the radio device invokes the Network.receive() method which, in turn, calls Protocol.receive() which suspends the calling thread on a counting semaphore. Upon reception of a packet to be forwarded to the waiting application, the Protocol invokes notifyReceiver() to release a permit on the semaphore. From the implementation stand point, the invocation of notifyReceiver() has to be placed inside packetHandler(), which is the method where the actual routing protocol is implemented. The default NullProtocol does nothing but invoking this method to forward to the applications all incoming packets.

4.4. Concurrent Package. The concurrent package provides a robust and efficient way to manage thread synchronization. In particular the Semaphore class implements a standard counting semaphore based on a waiting queue. Any thread waiting for a semaphore permit is suspended by the VM and moved to the semaphore waiting queue. In this way it allows the power manager to shutdown the MCU. As soon as a new permit is available on the semaphore, the waiting thread is woken up by removing it from the waiting queue. Thread suspension and wake up are implemented through native methods `waitForSemaphore()` and `wakeupWaitingThread()`, respectively, which directly interact with the VM scheduler and manage thread displacement.

4.5. MAC Layer. VirtualSense communication relies on Contiki MAC layer [28], which provides a simple duty cycling mechanism to reduce the power consumption of the radio module by keeping it turned off for most of the time without impairing the capability of the node to take part in network communication. This is done by periodically waking up the radio module to sense the channel and wait for incoming packets. In order to relax synchronization constraints, unicast packets are iteratively sent until an ack is received, while broadcast packets are repeatedly sent in a time window large enough to guarantee that they are sensed and received by all the nodes in range.

The current version of Contiki does not support the new Texas Instruments CC2520 radio module, but it provides a driver for its predecessor: the TI CC2420. In order to make it possible for VirtualSense to use the CC2520 (which provides higher energy efficiency, frame filtering capabilities, and low-power reception modes) a specific device driver needed to be developed starting from that of CC2420. The new driver not only exploits all the features of the new radio module, but it also exploits a deeper low-power mode (namely, LPM2 instead of LPM1) for duty-cycling. Since in LPM2 the radio module has no data retention, the driver needs to take care of the reconfiguration of the module at each wakeup.

Although a thorough description of the ContikiMAC protocol is beyond the scope of this paper, extensive experiments will be reported in Section 6.1.3 in order to allow the reader to evaluate the power consumption of the radio module in the different phases of communication.

5. VirtualSense Power-State Model

The changes outlined in the previous subsections enable the full exploitation of the low-power states depicted in Figure 2 and introduce three additional states which correspond to the Standby, Sleep, and Hibernation modes with external RTC. The new low-power states are denoted by suffix ".t" in Figure 7(A). With respect to the corresponding original states the new ones not only provide more accurate timing information, but they also grant the MCU the capability of scheduling its own wakeup from Sleep and Hibernation. This possibility, denoted by the solid arcs exiting from states Sleep.t and Hibernation.t, allows the MCU to exploit the corresponding low power modes even if there are future self events scheduled by the running processes/threads.

Figure 7(B) provides a simplified version of the same power-state model, in which state Standby.a has been removed, and Standby.b has been renamed "Standby.tick". The two changes have been made to point out that the modified software stack of VirtualSense avoids the MCU to

go through the time-consuming self-loop denoted by (a) in Figure 2, and that parameter T used to trigger periodic wakeups from Standby corresponds to the time resolution of the OS. This is the power-state model adopted hereafter to characterize the platform.

To make it possible to develop advanced DPM algorithms while working on top of the virtual machine, a `PowerManager` class has been created which exports methods for adjusting the `INTERVAL` (T) of the timer interrupt and for triggering transitions to any low-power state, possibly specifying the wakeup time and deciding whether to use the external RTC or not.

The frequency and voltage scaling capabilities of the new Texas Instruments MSP430x5xx MCU family [29] have been also exported on top of the Darjeeling VM (by implementing both the native methods and the drivers for Contiki OS) to allow applications to change at runtime the MUC operating frequency. Whenever the operating frequency is changed, the supply voltage of the core is automatically adjusted by the Contiki driver to the minimum voltage compatible with that frequency.

The degrees of freedom provided by the high-level support to frequency scaling add a dimension to the power-state model of VirtualSense which is not represented in Figure 7(B) for the sake of simplicity.

A thorough characterization of the power-state model is provided in next Section, while the effects of voltage and frequency scaling are discussed in Section 6.1.2.

6. Measurements and Results

Extensive experiments were conducted to characterize the power-state model of VirtualSense and to evaluate its energy efficiency in representative situations. To this purpose, synthetic benchmarks were developed and run on top of a VirtualSense mote instrumented in order to make it possible to measure not only the overall consumption of the platform, but also the current drawn by the MCU and by the radio module. This was done by inserting $10\,\Omega$ 1% precision resistors on the V_{cc} lines of each component on the PCB.

Data acquisition and measurements were done by means of a National Instruments NI-DAQmx PCI-6251 16 channels data acquisition board connected to a BNC-2120-shielded connector block [30, 31]. In addition, a National Instruments PXI-4071 digital multimeter was used to characterize the low-power states with sensitivity down to 1 pA [32].

During the experiments the mote under test was powered by means of an NGMO2 Rohde & Schwarz dual-channel power supply serially connected with the PXI-4071 configured as amperometer [33] to capture the total current drawn by the mote.

6.1. Characterization. In order to enable a thorough understanding of the contributions to the overall power consumption of the VirtualSense mote, three sets of experiments were performed: the first set was run to characterize the power state model of Figure 7(B) in fixed working conditions (namely, $V_{cc} = 3\,V$ and MCU clock frequency of 16 MHz) with the radio module in LPM2 (i.e., shutdown);

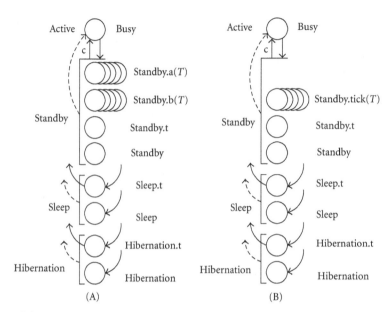

FIGURE 7: (A) State diagram of the power states made available by the solutions outlined in Sections 3 and 4. (B) Power-state model of VirtualSense.

the second set of experiments was used to explore the effects of frequency and voltage scaling; the third set was used to characterize the power consumption of the radio module in receive and transmit modes. All the experiments were performed with a 4 Kbyte heap of the virtual machine.

6.1.1. Power Modes. The characterization of the power modes of the VirtualSense mote was performed by sampling at 100,000 Hz the waveform of the supply current while running a simple benchmark forcing transitions to each low-power mode. The current waveforms were then analyzed in order to single-out the peaks corresponding to shut-down and wakeup transitions. A representative current waveform is reported in the lin-log plot of Figure 8 as provided by the NI-DAQmx. In order to improve the accuracy of the results, the power consumption of the ultra-low-power modes was further measured with the PXI-4071 multimeter while the exact timing of the transitions was determined by instrumenting the benchmarks.

Since the low-power mode denoted by Standby.tick(T) in the power state model of Figure 7(B) represents a family of power states the power consumption of which depends on the length of the ticks used to trigger periodic wakeups, an additional experiment was performed to characterize such a dependence, which is represented in Figure 9. Each point was obtained by setting the tick period (T), by keeping the node in standby for 60 seconds, and by computing the average power consumption. A fitting curve of type $y = c_1/x + c_0$ was then obtained, where coefficients c_0 and c_1 represent, respectively, the power consumption in low-power mode and the energy spent at each periodic wakeup.

Table 2 reports the results obtained with the MCU powered at 3 V and clocked at 16 MHz, using 4 Kbyte for the heap of the VM. For each inactive state 5 parameters are reported: power consumption (Power), wakeup time (WUt),

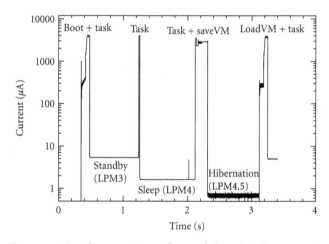

FIGURE 8: Supply current waveform of the VirtualSense mote obtained by forcing transitions to low-power modes.

wakeup energy (WUe), shut-down time (SDt), and shut-down energy (SDe). Since the proposed architecture makes power management available on top of the VM, wakeup costs include the time and energy spent in all the steps required to resume the execution of the running thread. Missing entries in Table 2 refer to transition times lower than 0.01 ms and transition energies lower than 0.01 μJ. The power consumption of state Standby.tick is expressed as a function of the INTERVAL (denoted by T and expressed in seconds) used to trigger periodic timer interrupts. The power consumption of 0.30 μW of the external RTC is explicitly added to all the states which make use of it (namely, Standby.t, Sleep.t, and Hibernation.t) to make it apparent that it can be disabled if such states are not used. The contributions to power consumption of all other

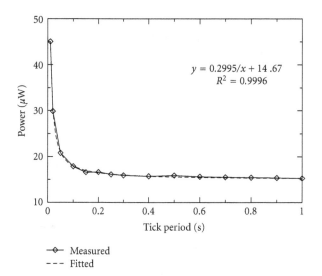

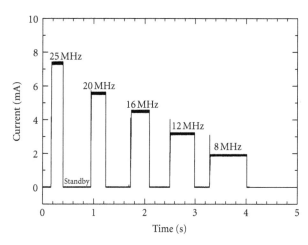

FIGURE 10: Power consumption of the mote while the MCU is executing a CPU-intensive task at different clock frequencies.

FIGURE 9: Power consumption of Standby.tick(T) as a function of tick period T.

TABLE 2: Characterization of the power-state model of a virtualsense mote with the MCU powered at 3 V and clocked at 16 MHz with a 4 kbyte VM heap.

State name	Power [μW]	WUt [ms]	WUe [μJ]	SDt [ms]	SDe [μJ]
Active	13440	n.a.	n.a.	n.a.	n.a.
Standby.tick(T)	14.67 + 0.30/T	23.41	312.72	—	—
Standby.t	14.67 + 0.30	23.41	312.72	—	—
Standby	14.67	23.41	312.72	—	—
Sleep.t	1.32 + 0.30	23.41	312.72	—	—
Sleep	1.32	23.41	312.72	—	—
Hibernation.t	0.36 + 0.30	560	4709.70	78.8	1235.58
Hibernation	0.36	560	4709.70	78.8	1235.58

components installed on the PCB (namely, EEPROM, EUID, and the three on-board sensors) are included in the results.

It is worth noticing that there is a difference between the average power consumption of the three Standby states. For instance, with an INTERVAL of 100 ms, the MCU consumes 17.67 μW in Standby.tick, 14.97 μW in Standby.t, and 14.67 μW in pure Standby mode. Moreover, the power consumption of the external RTC does not impair the energy efficiency of Sleep.t and Hibernation.t modes, their power consumption (of 1.62 μW and 0.66 μW, resp.) being significantly lower than that of the lowest Standby state.

Using for comparison the same MCU running standard releases of Contiki OS and Darjeeling VM, the only inactive state available would have been Standby.a (as defined in Section 2.4) with T = 10 ms. Since the default INTERVAL of Contiki is lower than the time spent to resume the execution of a virtual thread (23.41 ms), power management would have been totally ineffective without the proposed changes.

6.1.2. MCU Voltage and Frequency Scaling. Figure 10 shows the current consumption of the VirtualSense platform

running a benchmark which executes at different clock frequencies a CPU intensive task consisting of 10,000 integer summations. The benchmark makes use of the native methods for DPM provided by VirtualSense to set the clock frequency of the core, execute the task, and go to sleep. The current waveform plotted in Figure 10 clearly shows the power saving obtained by reducing the clock frequency from 25 MHz to 8 MHz, and the corresponding increase in the execution time of the task.

The overall energy spent to execute the task is plotted in Figure 11 as a function of the MCU frequency. The dashed curve (labeled "V_{cc} 3.0 + $V_{scaling}$") is directly obtained from the waveform of Figure 10. The plot clearly shows that the reduction of the operating frequency, combined with the voltage scaling automatically performed by the VirtualSense Contiki driver, provides a benefit in terms of computational energy, in spite of the increased computation time. On the other hand, frequency scaling would be counterproductive in terms of energy if not combined with voltage scaling, as shows by the solid curve in Figure 11.

Two additional curves are shown in Figure 11 for comparison. The dotted line (labeled "V_{cc} 2.4 + $V_{scaling}$") refers to the same experiment conducted by powering the mote at 2.4 V (which is the lowest supply voltage compatible with all clock frequencies) rather than at 3 V. The sizable advantage obtained demonstrates that it is more efficient to reduce the external power supply than relying only on the internal voltage regulator of the MCU. This is further demonstrated by the dot-dashed curve, which refers to a further experiment conducted by manually adjusting the external supply voltage to the minimum value compatible with each frequency level (namely: 2.4 V at 25 Mh, 2.2 V at 20 MHz and 16 MHz, 2.0 V at 12 MHz, and 1.9 V at 8 MHz). The automatic adjustment of the external supply voltage is not supported in the current version of VirtualSense.

6.1.3. Communication Energy. As mentioned in Section 4.5, VirtualSense makes use of Contiki MAC layer for communication. Figures 12 and 13 report the current waveforms of

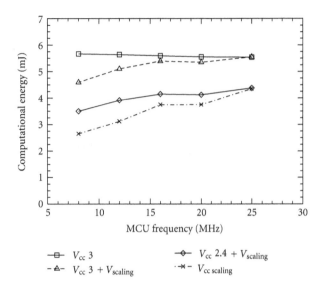

FIGURE 11: Computational energy versus MCU frequency.

the MCU (solid lines) and of the radio module (dotted lines) in the different phases of communication.

Figure 12(a) refers to the case of a channel clear assessment (CCA) without incoming packets. The MCU is woken up by a timer interrupt to run the interrupt handler which wakes up and reconfigures the radio module (the corresponding software overhead is apparent in the plot). According to the ContikiMAC protocol, the radio module then performs the CCA twice, with 1 ms interval in which it goes in LPM1 (rather than in LPM2) in order to avoid further reconfigurations. If nothing is sensed on the channel, the CC2520 goes back to LPM2.

Figure 12(b) refers to the case of a filtered packet. In this case the packet is sensed by the CCA, but it is directly discarded by the frame filter of the radio module upon decoding of the MAC header. This is the case of a unicast packet addressed to another node.

Figure 12(c) refers to the case of a packet which is properly received and then discarded at the MAC layer after having passed the frame filter of the radio module. This may happen, for instance, if the packet is corrupted, or if it was already received. Without frame filtering, this would also happen whenever a nonintended message was received. Hence, the difference in time between cases (c) and (b) provides a measure of the energy efficiency of frame filtering.

Finally, Figure 12(d) shows the additional software overhead which is incurred when the packet is passed up to the application through the protocol stack.

According to the duty cycling mechanism of Contiki-MAC, each packet has to be sent multiple times waiting either for the acknowledge sent back by the receiver (in case of unicast transmission) or for a timeout (in case of broadcast packets). The current waveforms obtained in the two cases are shown in Figures 13(a) and 13(b), respectively. Both of them start with a pattern similar to that of Figure 12(a), corresponding to the timer interrupt and to the channel sensing, with a longer software overhead due

to the preparation of the packet to be sent (the duration appears shorter in the graphs for the different time scale). Then a transmission and a CCA are periodically repeated until one of the two exit conditions (namely, ack or timeout) is met. The CCA is used after each transmission not only to sense for the ACK (in case of unicast packets), but also to sense the channel before repeating the transmission. If a collision is detected, the transmission is aborted straightaway.

6.2. Case Study

6.2.1. Monitoring Task. The energy efficiency offered by the power states of VirtualSense can be evaluated using as a case study a sensor node periodically executing a monitoring task which keeps the CPU busy for 100 milliseconds. Figure 14 provides the average power consumption of the MCU as a function of the monitoring period, plotted in a log-log graph. Each curve refers to a specific power state and reports the average power consumption obtained by spending all the idle time in that state, taking into account transition costs as reported in Table 2. For Standby.tick an INTERVAL of 30 ms was used, while the arrow shows how the corresponding curve would change by reducing the INTERVAL to increase the time resolution of the OS. Sleep and Hibernation states without external RTC are not reported in the graph since they cannot be used in this case because they do not support self-wakeup.

This simple experiment clearly shows the enhanced energy efficiency provided by the deepest low-power states in case of long idle periods, which are typical of sensor-node applications. Moreover, it demonstrates that all the power modes are worth being made available, since none of them outperforms the others in all workload conditions.

6.2.2. High-Level Implementation of a Routing Protocol. This section shows, with a practical example, how to use the Java communication library presented in Section 4.1 to implement a simple routing protocol. Consider as a case study a sensor network programmed to perform a periodic monitoring task: each node in the network senses the target physical quantity once per second and sends the measured value to the sink. The sink is nothing but a sensor node connected to a desktop PC by means of the serial port. All other sensor nodes act also as routers, implementing a self-adapting minimum-path-routing protocol.

The sink collects all the measurements and triggers period updates of the routing tables by sending a broadcast *interest* message (InterestMsg) to the network according to a *directed diffusion* paradigm [34]. The interest contains a progressive counter, called epoch, which is used by the nodes which receive and forward the interest message to verify its freshness. In addition, it contains the number of hops from the sink, which is incremented at each hop to allow sensor nodes to identify the best path. Algorithm 1 reports the Java code of the MinPathProtocol class which extends the Protocol and overrides abstract method packetHandler() to implement the minimum

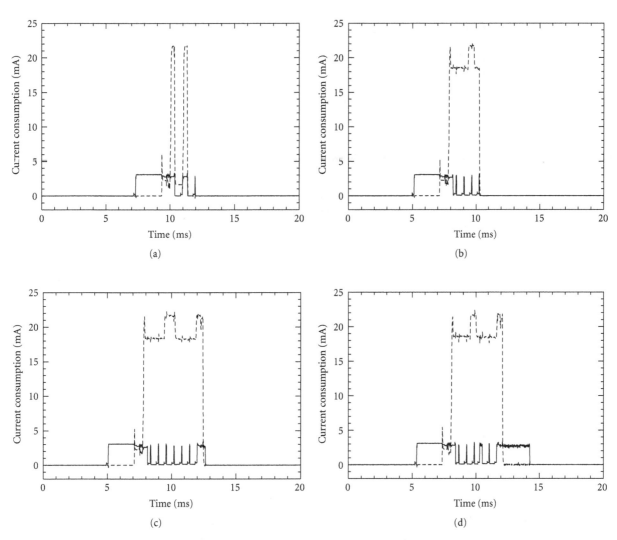

FIGURE 12: Power consumption of MCU (solid line) and radio transceiver (dotted line) during: (a) channel clear assessment, (b) frame filtering, (c) broadcast reception, and (d) broadcast reception and processing.

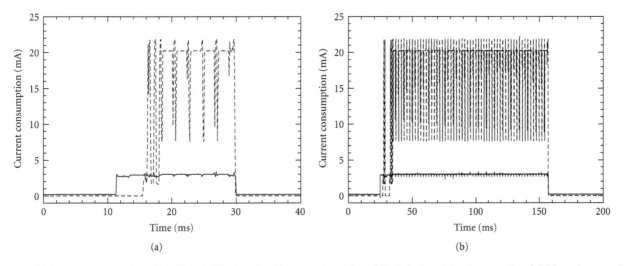

FIGURE 13: Power consumption of MCU (solid line) and radio transceiver (dotted line) during: (a) unicast send and (b) broadcast send.

```
01 import javax.virtualsense.network.*;
02
03 public class MinPathProtocol extends Protocol{
04
05    private short minHops = Short.MAX_VALUE;
06    private short epoch = 0;
07
08    protected void packetHandler(Packet p){
09       if(p instanceof InterestMsg){
10          InterestMsg interest = (InterestMsg)p;
11          if(interest.getEpoch() > this.epoch){
12             this.epoch = interest.getEpoch();
13             super.bestPath = -1;
14             this.minHops = Short.MAX_VALUE;
15          }
16          if(interest.getHops() < this.minHops){
17             this.minHops = interest.getHops();
18             super.bestPath = interest.getSender();
19             interest.setHops(interest.getHops()+1);
20             super.sendBroadcast(interest);
21          }
22       }else if(p instanceof DataMsg) {
23          DataMsg data = (DataMsg)p;
24          if(data.toForward())
25             super.send(data);
26          else
27             super.notifyReceiver();
28       }
29    }//end method
30 }// Tend class
```

ALGORITHM 1: Minimum-path algorithm implementation on top of the VirtualSense communication library.

path directed diffusion algorithm. The actual Java code is reported in place of a more readable pseudocode since the focus is not on the algorithm, but on the API, in order to show how easy it is to implement a communication protocol on top of the VirtualSense communication library.

Whenever a new packet is received, the packet-Handler() checks if it contains an interest message (Algorithm 1, line 09) or a data message (line 22). In case of an interest, its epoch is compared with the previous one (line 11) in order to reset the routing table in case of new epoch (lines 12–14). In the directed diffusion min path protocol the routing table is nothing but the ID of the neighboring node along the best path to the sink. Such an ID is stored in bestPath, which is updated with the ID of the sender of last interest message whenever the number of hops annotated in the message is lower than the current value of minHops (lines 16–19). In this case the interest message is also forwarded (line 20).

Data packets are either to be forwarded to the sink through bestPath (line 25) or to be notified to user-level applications possibly waiting for them (line 27). According to the directed diffusion algorithm sensor nodes never play the role of recipients of data messages. Nevertheless, line 27 has been added in Algorithm 1 as an example of user-level communication.

The proposed architecture was instrumented in order to measure the software overhead introduced by the high-level implementation of the communication protocol. In particular the Contiki and Darjeeling execution times were measured as separate contributions to the reception event-chain starting from the sleep state. Contiki overhead was taken as the time between the reception of a radio interrupt and the corresponding Darjeeling VM process poll. Darjeeling overhead was taken as time between the wake up of Darjeeling VM process and the delivery of the incoming packet to the user-level application. The results obtained at 16 MHz were, respectively, 3.7 ms and 14.4 ms for Contiki and Darjeeling software overheads resulting in a total overhead of 18.1 ms. The software overhead introduced by the proposed Java library in the sending chain was of 3.4 ms.

This example shows how the proposed network library allows the programmer to implement a routing protocol with a few lines of code, enabling the full exploitation of the low-power states of the MCU without impairing the reactivity of the sensor node.

7. Conclusions

VirtualSense is an open-source open-hardware project aimed at the development of ultra-low-power sensor nodes providing a Java-compatible virtual runtime environment which

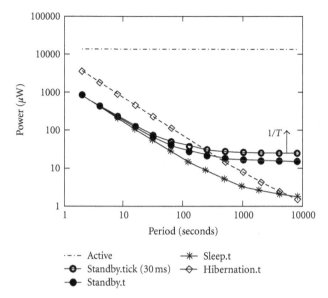

- Active
- Standby.tick (30 ms)
- Standby.t
- Sleep.t
- Hibernation.t

FIGURE 14: Average power consumption of the MCU used to execute a periodic monitoring task which keeps the MCU busy for 100 ms.

makes the power management capabilities of the underlying MCU directly available to high-level application developers. The key issue in this context is how to allow the DPM to fully exploit the idleness of the Java threads in spite of the fact that they run on top of a Java VM which is seen as an always-active process by the OS.

This paper has presented VirtualSense, which implements a solution based on modified versions of Contiki OS and Darjeeling VM, running on top of a Texas Instruments' MSP430F5418a MCU. The implementation details have been outlined and discussed in the paper. Moreover, an event-driven communication library for the Darjeeling VM has been presented which exhibits two distinguishing features: it is general enough to enable the implementation of advanced communication protocols in Java, and it makes it possible for a Java thread to react to incoming messages without keeping the MCU busy while waiting.

A power-state model of VirtualSense has been built and characterized by means of real-world measurements in order to make it possible for a designer to evaluate the suitability of VirtualSense as a platform for the development of WSN applications subject to tight power constraints. Finally, the energy efficiency of VirtualSense has been further analyzed by running representative benchmarks.

The results achieved show that VirtualSense provides a new Pareto-optimal point in the power-performance design space of wireless sensor modules, while also providing the benefit of a Java-compatible virtual runtime environment.

The experiments conducted to characterize the VirtualSense mote pointed out that there is room for further optimizations which are now targeted by specific research tasks within the VirtualSense project. Current work is aimed at: reducing the need for repeated transmissions which is inherent in the duty-cycling mechanism of ContikiMAC; developing a software-controlled power supply module to

enable thorough voltage scaling; segmenting at board-level the power-distribution network in order to make it possible for the MCU to dynamically decide which peripheral components to power.

Acknowledgments

The authors would like to thank Andrea Seraghiti, Massimo Zandri, and NeuNet Cultural Association (http://www.neunet.it/) for their fundamental contribution to the development of the VirtualSense prototype.

References

[1] E. Lattanzi and A. Bogliolo, "WSN design for unlimited lifetime," in Sustainable Energy Harvesting Technologies: Past, Present and Future, Y. K. g Tan, Ed., InTech, 2011.

[2] R. Müller, G. Alonso, and D. Kossmann, "A virtual machine for sensor networks," in Proceedings of the 2nd ACM SIGOPS/EuroSys European Conference on Computer Systems (EuroSys '07), pp. 145–158, prt, March 2007.

[3] D. Simon, C. Cifuentes, D. Cleal, J. Daniels, and D. White, "Java on the bare metal of wireless sensor devices the squawk java virtual machine," in Proceedings of the 2nd International Conference on Virtual Execution Environments (VEE '06), pp. 78–88, June 2006.

[4] P. Levis, D. Gay, and D. Culler, "Active sensor networks," in Proceedings of the 2nd conference on Symposiumon Networked Systems Design & Implementation, vol. 2, pp. 343–356, USENIX Association, 2005.

[5] A. Dunkels, B. Grönvall, and T. Voigt, "Contiki—a lightweight and flexible operating system for tiny networked sensors," in Proceedings of the 29th Annual IEEE International Conference on Local Computer Networks, (LCN '04), pp. 455–462, usa, November 2004.

[6] N. Brouwers, P. Corke, and K. Langendoen, "Darjeeling, a Java compatible virtual machine for microcontrollers," in Proceedings of the ACM/IFIP/USENIX Middleware Conference Companion, pp. 18–23, 2008.

[7] E. Lattanzi and A. Bogliolo, "Ultra-low-power sensor nodes featuring a virtual runtime environment," in Proceedings of the IEEE International Conference on Communications (E2Nets-ICC '12), 2012.

[8] J. M. Kahn, R. H. Katz, and K. S. J. Pister, "Next century challenges: mobile networking for smart dust," in Proceedings of the ACM/IEEE International Conference on Mobile Computing and Networking (ACM/IEEE MobiCom '99), pp. 271–278, 1999.

[9] S. Hollar, COTS dust [M.S. thesis], University of California, Berkeley, Calif, USA, 2002.

[10] J. Polastre, R. Szewczyk, and D. Culler, "Telos: enabling ultra-low power wireless research," in Proceedings of the 4th International Symposium on Information Processing in Sensor Networks, (IPSN '05), pp. 364–369, usa, April 2005.

[11] J. Beutel, O. Kasten, and M. Ringwald, "Poster abstract: BTnodes—a distributed platform for sensor nodes," in Proceedings of the 1st International Conference on Embedded Networked Sensor Systems (SenSys '03), pp. 292–293, November 2003.

[12] H. Dubois-Ferrière, R. Meier, L. Fabre, and P. Metrailler, "TinyNode: a comprehensive platform for wireless sensor network applications," in Proceedings of the 5th International

Conference on Information Processing in Sensor Networks, (IPSN '06), pp. 358–365, April 2006.

[13] "Iris datasheet," http://bullseye.xbow.com:81/Products/Product_pdf_files/Wireless_pdf/IRIS_Datasheet.pdf.

[14] A. Gonzlez, R. Aquino, W. Mata, A. Ochoa, P. Saldaa, and A. Edwards, "Open-wise: a solar powered wireless sensor network platform," *Sensors*, vol. 12, pp. 8204–8217, 2012.

[15] R. Jurdak, K. Klues, B. Kusy, C. Richter, K. Langendoen, and M. Brnig, "Opal: a multiradio platform for high throughput wireless sensor networks," *Proceedings of Embedded Systems Letters*, pp. 121–124, 2011.

[16] L. Nachman, R. Kling, R. Adler, J. Huang, and V. Hummel, "The Intel mote platform: a Bluetooth-based sensor network for industrial monitoring," in *Proceedings of the 4th International Symposium on Information Processing in Sensor Networks, (IPSN '05)*, pp. 437–442, April 2005.

[17] R. Adler, M. Flanigan, J. Huang et al., "Demo abstract: intel mote 2: an advanced platform for demanding sensor network applications," in *Proceedings of the 3rd International Conference on Embedded Networked Sensor Systems (ACM SenSys '05)*, p. 298, 2005.

[18] D. Lymberopoulos and A. Savvides, "XYZ: a motion-enabled, power aware sensor node platform for distributed sensor network applications," in *Proceedings of the 4th International Symposium on Information Processing in Sensor Networks, (IPSN '05)*, pp. 449–454, April 2005.

[19] Texas Instruments MSP430F54xxA Mixed Signal Microcontroller datasheet http://www.ti.com/lit/ds/symlink/msp430f-5418a.pdf.

[20] "Microchip 24AA025E48 Extended Unique Identifier datasheet," http://ww1.microchip.com/downloads/en/DeviceDoc/22124D.pdf.

[21] "Microchip 24AA512 serial 512K EEPROM datasheet," http://ww1.microchip.com/downloads/en/devicedoc/21754e.pdf.

[22] "Texas Instruments CC2520 datasheet," http://www.ti.com/lit/ds/symlink/cc2520.pdf.

[23] "NXP PCF2123 ultra low-power real time clock/calendar datasheet," http://www.nxp.com/documents/data_sheet/PCF-2123.pdf.

[24] "FTDI FT232R datasheet," http://www.ftdichip.com/Support/Documents/DataSheets/ICs/DS_FT232R.pdf.

[25] "BH1620FVC Analog current output ambient light sensor datasheet," http://www.rohm.com/products/databook/sensor/pdf/bh1620fvc-e.pdf.

[26] "Texas Instruments LM19 temperature sensor datasheet," http://www.ti.com/lit/ds/symlink/lm19.pdf.

[27] "HIH-50301 Low Voltage Humidity Sensors datasheet," http://sensing.honeywell.com/index.php/ci_id/49692/la_id/1/document/1/re_id/0.

[28] A. Dunkels, "The ContikiMAC radio duty cycling protocol," Tech. Rep., Swedish Institute of Computer Science, 2011.

[29] Texas Instruments, "MSP430x5xx/MSP430x6xx Family User's Guide," 2012, http://www.ti.com/lit/ug/slau208j/slau208j.pdf.

[30] "National Instruments PC-6251 datasheet," 2012, http://sine.ni.com/nips/cds/print/p/lang/en/nid/14124.

[31] "National Instruments BNC-2120 datasheet," 2012, http://sine.ni.com/nips/cds/view/p/lang/en/nid/10712.

[32] "National Instruments PXI-4071 datasheet," 2012, http://www.ni.com/pdf/products/us/cat_NIPXI4071.pdf.

[33] "Rohde & Schwarz NGMO2 datasheet," 2012, http://www.rohde-schwarz.it/file_1800/ngmo2_21_web-LF.pdf.

[34] C. Intanagonwiwat, R. Govindan, D. Estrin, J. Heidemann, and F. Silva, "Directed diffusion for wireless sensor networking," *IEEE/ACM Transactions on Networking*, vol. 11, no. 1, pp. 2–16, 2003.

14

A Self-Organized and Smart-Adaptive Clustering and Routing Approach for Wireless Sensor Networks

Kyuhong Lee and Heesang Lee

Department of Industrial Engineering, Sungkyunkwan University, Suwon 440-746, Republic of Korea

Correspondence should be addressed to Heesang Lee, leehee@skku.edu

Academic Editor: Yuhang Yang

Efficient energy consumption is a critical factor for the deployment and operation of wireless sensor networks (WSNs). In general, WSNs perform clustering and routing using localized neighbor information only. Therefore, some studies have used self-organized systems and smart mechanisms as research methods. In this paper, we propose a self-organized and smart-adaptive clustering (SOSAC) and routing method, which performs clustering in WSNs, operates the formed clusters in a smart-adaptive way, and performs cluster-based routing. SOSAC is comprised of three mechanisms, which are used to change the fitness value over time, to back up routing information in preparation for any potential breakdown in WSNs, and to adapt to the changes of the number of sensor nodes for a WSN. We compared the performance of the proposed SOSAC with that of a well-known clustering and routing protocol for WSNs. Our computational experiments demonstrate that the network lifetime, energy consumption, and scalability of SOSAC are better than those of the compared method.

1. Introduction

A wireless sensor network (WSN) is an infrastructure composed of wireless sensor nodes, which perform sensing tasks and transmit the data to a base station (BS) that is the final processing node for the WSN. According to the features of the wireless network, WSNs are widely used in dynamic and hazardous regions as well as in many industries including production, logistics, distribution, transportation, and health [1].

WSNs have many characteristics that differ from conventional wireless networks. For example, WSNs have several inherent constraints that are unique to this type of wireless networks [2, 3]. First, a WSN consists of hundreds or thousands of wireless sensor nodes but each node in a WSN is constrained in terms of processing capability and storage capacity. Second, the power device of the sensor node in WSNs cannot be recharged or replaced so that energy efficiency is very important [4].

Routing protocols in a WSN should be developed and proposed with consideration for these unique characteristics. The routing decides the transmission route for a data packet from the sensor node to the final destination BS.

The communication channels of WSNs can be configured through multihop mesh network called "flat routing". In contrast, a "cluster-based routing" method divides a WSN into several clusters. In this cluster-based routing, each cluster is comprised of a "cluster head" (CH) and several "cluster members" (CMs). After formation of the cluster, hierarchical routing is performed, where CMs transmit data packets to its CH, and the CH integrates these data packets and transmits them to the BS directly or via other CHs [2].

Along with the development of communication networks, the routing paradigm has changed from a centralized system to a distributed system due to the demand for better scalability and simple installation. In WSNs, tens or thousands of sensor nodes may be needed to create one network, so when selecting the processor, memory, and power devices, economical devices with limited functions are used [1]. Accordingly, the distributed routing method is used rather than the centralized routing method for WSNs considering the processing ability of the sensor nodes [1]. When distributed processing is used, each sensor node is not allowed to use the information of the entire WSNs and must therefore perform clustering and routing using the localized neighbor information only. When the power device for sensor nodes is not rechargeable or replaceable, it is also important to consider energy efficiency in order to maximize the network lifetime of the sensor nodes by minimizing the energy consumption [4].

Self-organization, which is a further development of distributed processing, is a system that uses local information only through a distributed and peer-to-peer method. Many studies on self-organized systems are being conducted using only local information and simple rules because of the associated advantages such as reduction of overheads in communication traffic, scalability, and robustness. Also, self-organization has been applied to many areas in the wireless network field such as ad-hoc networks, WSNs, wireless LAN, in routing, forming clusters, MAC protocol design, and radio resources management. Some studies have been conducted on self-organization with the features of WSNs [5].

Recently "smart" characteristics of routing have also been suggested in telecommunication networking [6–8]. Here smart means the capability to describe and analyze a situation, taking decisions based on the available data in a predictive or adaptive manner, and thereby performing smart actions.

In this paper, we propose a self-organized and smart-adaptive clustering (SOSAC) and routing method comprised of three mechanisms for a WSN. First, in order to select an appropriate CH, which is the most important factor influencing the clustering performance, two types of performance measure are used. The proposed mechanism adjusts the weights of these two performance measures automatically to reflect the changes in the WSN. Second, the broadcasting range, which is another important factor influencing the performance of clustering in SOSAC, is predetermined as a function of the number of sensor nodes. Third, to overcome problems caused by possible breakdown, damage, or failure of sensor nodes in WSNs, a smart backup mechanism is established to monitor the state of the CH without heavy overhead and to restore the system automatically in the case of such problems.

This paper is organized as follows. Section 2 reviews previous studies on clustering, self-organization, and smart telecommunication networks and their implications for this research. Section 3 presents the radio model that is used and the basic assumptions used in this study. Section 4 explains the process of forming self-organized clusters and routing. Section 5 describes how to operate clustering in a smart-adaptive way by using three proposed mechanisms. In this section, we also compare the performance of the proposed SOSAC with that of another well-known model. The measures for comparison are network lifetime, residual energy after a certain time, and scalability of the model. The last section presents the conclusions of this study and proposes future research directions.

2. Related Works

Grouping sensor nodes into clusters has been widely pursued by the research community in order to achieve the network scalability objective. The objective of clustering is mainly to generate stable clusters in environments with sensor nodes.

In addition to supporting network scalability, clustering has numerous advantages. It can localize the route set up within the cluster and thus reduce the size of the routing table stored at the individual sensor node [3, 9]. Clustering can also conserve communication bandwidth since it limits the scope of intercluster interactions to CHs and avoids redundant exchange of messages among sensor nodes [10]. Moreover, clustering can stabilize the network topology at the level of sensor nodes, and thus cut down on topology maintenance overhead. Sensor nodes are only affected by the connection with their CHs and not by changes at the level of inter-CH tier [11]. The CH can also implement optimized management strategies to further enhance the network operation and prolong the battery life of the individual sensor nodes and the network lifetime [10].

"Self-organization" is defined as the process where a structure or pattern appears in a system without intervention by external directing influences. It organizes through direct interaction in a peer to peer method [5]. The advantages of using the self organized system are as follows [5, 12]. First, one of the most important characteristics of self-organization is the completely distributed control. Each participating system component acts on local decisions, that is, it is not possible to review the current global state and act accordingly. Second, an inherent feature of self-organizing systems is their capability to adapt to changing environmental conditions. This is a direct result of the distributed peer to peer working principle. Third, the robustness of the system prevents any problems due to breakdown, damage, or failure of individual elements. Fourth, scalability protects the system from degradation by increasing the number of individual elements in the system.

Several cluster-based and self-organized protocols for WSNs were studied as follows.

In the LEACH protocol [13], the basic idea is to select sensor nodes randomly as CHs. Random selection of a CH is good for self-organization of the cluster configuration. Cluster configuration is repeated at each round, and the round is divided into two phases: the "set-up phase" and the "steady phase". In the set-up phase, LEACH selects a CH candidate with a threshold for a random number. In this phase, each sensor node compares a random number with the threshold $T(n)$ to elect itself to a CH, and this process is performed independently for each cluster. In the steady phase, the sensor nodes sense environment and transmit data, and the CHs aggregate the data before sending the data to the BS.

LEACH-Energy Distance (LEACH-ED) [14] is another self-organized protocol that is based on LEACH. It uses a different threshold from LEACH. The ratio between the residual energy of a sensor node and the total current energy of all of the sensor nodes in the network is used for the first threshold of LEACH-ED. It also uses the distance threshold as the second threshold. If the distance between a sensor node and an existing CH is less than the distance threshold, the sensor node cannot be elected as a CH.

The hybrid-energy efficient distributed protocol (HEED) [15] selects CHs by combining the residual energy of the sensor and the communication cost for selection of the CH in a WSN. The communication cost is calculated using the average minimum reachability power or the neighbor sensor node degree as the secondary parameter. Once the CH is selected, HEED uses a hierarchical routing protocol with a 3-tier structure, where first each CM transmits data to its CH, second each CH sends data to one special CH by using the breadth-first search tree, and finally the special CH sends all data to the BS.

Robust energy efficient distributed clustering (REED) [16] is a self-organized clustering method which constructs k independent sets of CH overlays on the top of the physical network to achieve fault tolerance. Each sensor must reach at least one CH from each overlay. The method of selection of CH is same as HEED.

Distributed, energy-efficient, and dual-homed clustering (DED) [17] is a self-organized clustering method that achieves fault tolerance by providing an alternative route from sources to the BS. Each regular sensor node has a primary CH and a secondary backup CH. DEED and HEED are the same method for CH selection but use different parameters for the selection.

In telecommunications, although some researchers have studied smart systems for the formation or operation of communication networks, each study has used different methods and different definitions, as shown in the related studies described below.

In traditional networks, passive means were used to send packets or signals to each termination, but active networks have recently been suggested that allow nodes to customize computation on message flowing [18] or a new smart network framework with not only active services but also the concepts of contextawareness and userawareness [19]. In this network, the nodes of the network have the capability to sense, to reason and to be aware of the context and behavior of users, and automatically provide active services to users according to their situation and context knowledge [20].

Stone et al. [21] have suggested a smart network which requires three types of intelligence. First, it is an inference system for collecting information about the user's interaction with the network. Second, it is a framework associated with mobile agents for routing through the network of processing messages and servers. Third, it is a gateway to allow access to the network.

Gelenbe et al. [6, 7] have suggested a cognitive packet network which provides intelligent capabilities for routing and flow control to packets instead of the nodes or protocol in the wired network or wireless ad hoc network. This has enabled the realization of a smart routing system that allows the cognitive packets to find their own route between source and destination in the packet switched networks.

3. Network Modeling

3.1. First Order Ratio Model. A sensor node consumes energy when transmitting and receiving data packets in a WSN. In wireless data transmission, energy consumption is correlated to the data packet size and the distance between the two sensor nodes. Extensive research has been conducted in the area of low-energy radios. Different assumptions about the radio characteristics, including energy dissipation in the transmission and received modes, will change the advantages of different protocols. In our work, we assume the following first-order radio model as our radio energy consumption model.

(i) Transmitting the data packet: a sensor node consumes $\varepsilon_{elec} = 50\,\text{nJ/bit}$ at the transmitter circuitry and $\varepsilon_{amp} = (100\,\text{pJ/bit})/\text{m}^2$ at the amplifier.

(ii) Receiving the data packet: a sensor node consumes $\varepsilon_{elec} = 50\,\text{nJ/bit}$ at the receiver circuitry.

(iii) A k-bit data packet is transmitted from sensor node to sensor node, and d_{ij} is the distance between the two sensor nodes i and j; the energy consumption of sensor node i is given by $T_{ij} = \varepsilon_{elec} \times k + \varepsilon_{amp} \times d_{ij}^2 \times k$.

(iv) The sensor node receives data packet: the energy consumption of sensor node is given by $R_i = \varepsilon_{elec} \times k$.

3.2. Assumptions and Definitions for the Model. We assign the following properties and make the following assumptions for modeling and simulation for the WSN.

(i) The location of all sensor nodes and the BS are fixed.

(ii) The location of the BS (25 m, 150 m) is known in advance in the 50 m * 50 m sensor field.

(iii) The data packet size is 1,000 bits, and signal packet size is 50 bits.

(iv) All sensor nodes have an initial energy of 0.5 J.

(v) Period: in the data transmission phase, a CM creates information sensed by itself into a data packet and transmits this packet to its CH. The CH aggregates the data packets received from its CMs and transmits them to the BS through the intercluster route. A cycle of this process is defined as a "period".

(vi) Round: some number of periods carried out within a data transmission phase can be defined as a "round". In our experiments, we assume that 1 round is made up of 10 periods.

(vii) Network lifetime: the periods until a certain number of sensor nodes drained of its energy can be defined as the "network lifetime".

4. Self-Organized and Smart-Adaptive Clustering (SOSAC): The Proposed Clustering and Routing Protocol

This section explains the procedure of the SOSAC proposed herein. SOSAC decides the CHs every round, and it is comprised of three phases, as set forth in Sections 4.2, 4.3, and 4.4. In Section 4.1, the state of each sensor node of the WSN is explained to help understand the SOSAC operations.

4.1. States of Sensor Nodes. Each sensor node of SOSAC performs its duties while being changed into the following five states depending on the roles. Figure 1 indicates the state transition diagram of SOSAC.

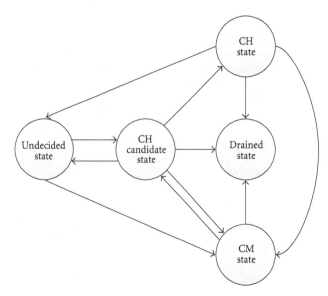

FIGURE 1: Transition diagram of sensor node states.

(i) *Undecided state*: when a sensor node has been scattered first in the sensor field, after a CH has completed its duty, and after a sensor node has dropped out of the node with CH candidate state, the sensor node becomes a node with undecided state. A node with undecided state does not belong to any cluster, yet.

(ii) *CH candidate state*: when the sensor nodes are scattered in the sensor field at period zero, all sensor nodes become a node with CH candidate state. Some of sensor nodes with a CM state also can become nodes with CH candidate state. Only a node with CH candidate state can compete for selection of CHs.

(iii) *CH state*: one node with CH candidate state within a cluster becomes a node with CH state, that is, a CH in that period. As a CH, it collects and aggregates information from its CMs and transfers data packets to other CHs or the BS. Also, a CH decides its nearby nodes as the nodes with CH candidate state for the next round.

(iv) *CM state*: when a CH is decided, all other sensor nodes in the same cluster become nodes with CM state, that is, CMs. A CM periodically sends the sensed information to its CH.

(v) *Drained state*: when a sensor node cannot function anymore because all its energy has been drained or it has broken down, it becomes a node with drained state.

SOCAC is comprised of a clustering phase that forms the clusters, an intercluster routing phase that decides on the transmission route among the CHs, and a data transmission phase that sends/receives the data packets.

Figure 2 indicates the progress of SOSAC in a flowchart.

4.2. Clustering Phase. SOSAC needs a clustering phase for the hierarchical routing. The clustering phase commences if the sensor nodes are scattered first in the sensor field or after the "data transmission phase" has finished. The clustering phase is comprised of three steps: Broadcasting step, CH selection step, and clustering step as shown in Algorithm 1.

4.2.1. Broadcasting Step. When the sensor nodes are scattered in the sensor field at period zero, no sensor node belongs to any cluster, thus all sensor nodes are assumed in the same cluster at period zero. The CHs broadcast a CH-change-signal packet only within the broadcasting range in procedure 2.1 of Algorithm 1 because since a CH was at a good position when it was selected as the CH, it is highly likely that its neighbors are also at good location for being CHs. By limiting the broadcasting range, the overhead of the clustering phase can be reduced because of the proximity of the nodes with the CH candidate state.

4.2.2. CH Selection Step. In procedure 3.2 of Algorithm 1, we update the counter, which is the number of received CH-candidate-signal packets. This counter will be used for calculating the fitness value in procedure 5 of Algorithm 1. A CH-candidate-information-signal packet, which a node with CH candidate state broadcasts in procedure 4.1 of Algorithm 1, contains the energy state of the sending sensor node. Information of the received CH-candidate-signal packets is also used to calculate the fitness value in procedure 5 of Algorithm 1. The CH-candidate-information-signal packets are broadcast within 2*(broadcasting range) for the following reasons. All nodes with the CH candidate state of a cluster must share the neighborhood information with all nodes with CH candidate states within the same cluster. This can be achieved by sending the CH-candidate-information-signal packets within two times of the broadcasting range for

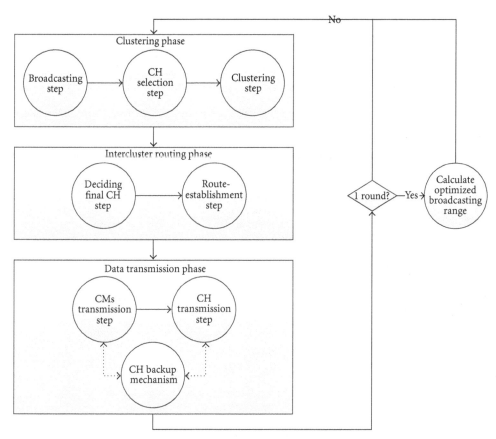

FIGURE 2: Flowchart of SOSAC.

two nodes with the CH candidate state that are farthest away from each other.

4.2.3. Clustering Step. A node with CH state in procedure 8.1 of Algorithm 1 broadcasts a CH-signal packet to the entire sensor field to form its cluster. The sensor nodes in all states except nodes with CH state or nodes with drained state that receive these signal packets select the nearest CH and become a CM of that cluster.

4.3. Intercluster Routing Phase. After the clustering phase, the CHs create an intercluster routing tree and select a CH as the "master CH". Each CH sends packets to the master CH and the master CH transmits the packet to the BS directly. Transmission of data packets through the intercluster routing tree, and its master CH can save energy compared to the direct transmission of data packets from all CHs to the BS.

In the process of creating a tree for intercluster routing, the CHs perform their duties while changing into the following three states depending on the roles.

(i) *Initial state*: if the intercluster routing phase starts, all CHs are initialized as the CHs with initial state. If a CH with initial state receives a route-broadcast-signal packet, it transmits ACK back to the CH that sent the route-broadcast-signal packet to the CH.

(ii) *Route broadcasting state*: after finding the master CH, that CH becomes a CH with route broadcasting state.

The master CH sends route-broadcast-signal packets to CHs with initial state. A CH with initial state that received a route-broadcast-signal packet becomes a CH with route broadcasting state.

(iii) *Route-established state*: the CH with route broadcasting state broadcasts route-broadcast-signal packet to establish an intercluster route and then becomes a CH with route-established state. When all CHs with initial state become CHs with route-established state, all CHs become CHs with route-established state.

Figure 3 indicates the transition diagram of CHs in the intercluster routing phase.

The intercluster routing phase is divided into the deciding master CH step and the route establishment step.

4.3.1. Deciding Master CH Step. The expected residual energy in procedure 1 of Algorithm 2 is the expected remaining energy of each CH, which is calculated as the following.

$$\text{The expected residual energy} = \text{current energy} - \gamma, \quad (1)$$

where γ is the expected consuming energy which sends data packets to BS during the next round. CH broadcasts a CH-expected-residual-energy-signal packet to the whole area of the sensor field in procedure 2.1 of Algorithm 2. We use this simple broadcasting technique because any CH

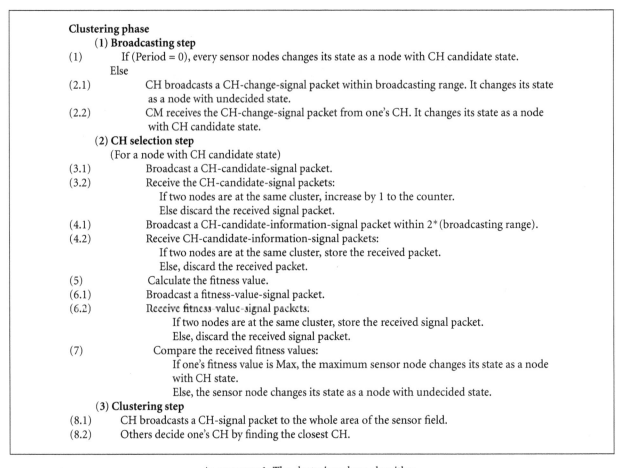

Clustering phase
    (1) Broadcasting step
(1)   If (Period = 0), every sensor nodes changes its state as a node with CH candidate state.
        Else
(2.1)   CH broadcasts a CH-change-signal packet within broadcasting range. It changes its state
            as a node with undecided state.
(2.2)   CM receives the CH-change-signal packet from one's CH. It changes its state as a node
            with CH candidate state.
    (2) CH selection step
        (For a node with CH candidate state)
(3.1)   Broadcast a CH-candidate-signal packet.
(3.2)   Receive the CH-candidate-signal packets:
            If two nodes are at the same cluster, increase by 1 to the counter.
            Else discard the received signal packet.
(4.1)   Broadcast a CH-candidate-information-signal packet within 2*(broadcasting range).
(4.2)   Receive CH-candidate-information-signal packets:
            If two nodes are at the same cluster, store the received packet.
            Else, discard the received packet.
(5)   Calculate the fitness value.
(6.1)   Broadcast a fitness-value-signal packet.
(6.2)   Receive fitness-value-signal packets:
            If two nodes are at the same cluster, store the received signal packet.
            Else, discard the received signal packet.
(7)   Compare the received fitness values:
            If one's fitness value is Max, the maximum sensor node changes its state as a node
            with CH state.
            Else, the sensor node changes its state as a node with undecided state.
    (3) Clustering step
(8.1)   CH broadcasts a CH-signal packet to the whole area of the sensor field.
(8.2)   Others decide one's CH by finding the closest CH.

ALGORITHM 1: The clustering phase algorithm.

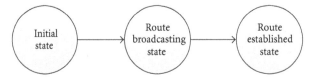

FIGURE 3: Transition diagram of CH states in the intercluster routing phase.

can get energy information for all CHs in the sensor field and compare it with its own energy information since each CH broadcasts CH-expected-residual-energy-signal packets to the whole area of the sensor field. This does not generate a heavy overhead since the signal packets are small and we assume that the sensor field is small (between 50 m * 50 m and 150 m * 150 m) in this study. When the sensor field is very large, we need to modify this intercluster routing procedure by using some flat routing techniques.

4.3.2. Route Establishment Step. A CH with initial state that receives the route-broadcast-signal packets sets the nearest CH with route established state as the first section of its transmission route. The CHs with route broadcasting state broadcast route-broadcast-signal packets in procedure 4 of Algorithm 2. The initial broadcasting range is δ m. (In our

computational implementation, we use δ = 25.) If a CH with initial state receives a route-broadcast-signal packet, it transmits ACK to the CH that sent a route-broadcast-signal packet. If a CH with route broadcasting state does not receive any ACKs during given time interval, it extends the broadcasting range by δm repeatedly until the broadcasting range is wider than (width of the sensor field $*\sqrt{2}$). Within this broadcasting range, if a CH with route broadcasting state does not receive any ACK, it becomes a leaf CH of the intercluster routing tree. This route establishment method yields a spanning tree that includes all CHs. This spanning tree is built as a breadth-first search tree while the CHs exchange the route-broadcast-signal packets and ACKs. While the breadth-first search tree is made, a CH tries to include its neighbor CHs by increasing the broadcasting range δ when the CH does not receive any ACKs, which is a kind of stop-and-wait method.

Intercluster routing phase
    (1) Deciding master CH step
        (For a CH with initial state)
(1)   Calculate expected residual energy.
(2.1)   Broadcast a CH-expected-residual-energy-signal packet to the whole area of the sensor field.
(2.2)   Receive CH-expected-residual-energy-signal packets.
(3)   Compare CH expected residual energy:
               If one's CH expected residual energy is Max, the maximum CH changes its state as
               a CH with route broadcasting state.
    (2) Route establishment step
      While (All CHs with initial state become CHs with route established state)
        (For a CH with route broadcasting state)
(4)   Broadcast a route-broadcast-signal packet within the intercluster broadcasting range. If it receives
            ACK, it changes its state as a CH with route established state.
            If it does not receive any ACK during given time interval, it extends the broadcasting range. If it does
            not receive any ACK within maximum broadcasting range, that CH becomes a leaf CH.
        (For a CH with initial state)
        If it receives route-broadcast-signal packets:
(5)   Find the closest CH that sent route-broadcast-signal packets and establish intercluster route by
            sending ACK to the closest CH. It changes its state as a CH with route broadcasting state.

    End while

ALGORITHM 2: The intercluster routing phase algorithm.

4.4. Data Transmission Phase. Once the clusters and the intercluster routing tree have been created, information sensed by each sensor node is transmitted to the BS using data packets in the data transmission phase. The data transmission phase is divided into 2 steps: CM transmission step and CH transmission step.

In Algorithm 3, a CM transmits data packets, which are created by sensing the surroundings in each period, to its CH. Each CH aggregates the received data packets and transmits the aggregated data packet to the BS through the route that is set in the intercluster routing phase. Sensing and data transmission of each sensor node are repeated during one round.

5. Smart Mechanisms and Computational Experiments of SOSAC

5.1. Smart Mechanisms in SOSAC

5.1.1. Smart Fitness Value Adaptability Mechanism. The most important factor affecting the clustering performance is the CH selection method. SOSAC uses the following fitness comparison procedure to select the appropriate CHs.

First, check the location of each node with CH candidate state for the fitness value. SOSAC uses the number of the received CH-candidate-signal packets to check the appropriateness of the location of a sensor node. In other words, each node with CH candidate state collects information on the locations of some neighboring nodes with CH candidate state (in the same cluster) as the number of received CH-candidate-signal packets and transmits it to the neighboring sensor nodes to compare the number of CH-candidate-signal packets. A CH with many neighboring nodes with

CH candidate state is considered as a good candidate for the CH of a cluster since it is located in the center of the cluster. Accordingly, SOSAC decides on the neighborhood degree fitness of each node with CH candidate state based on the ratio of the number of neighbors of v to the maximum number of neighbors of the cluster where the sensor node belongs to. This fitness value indicates the location appropriateness of the node with CH candidate in the current cluster. We define "neighborhood degree fitness" of a sensor node v that has CH candidate state of the cluster as follows. The "neighborhood degree fitness" consists of the first component of the fitness value.

Neighborhood degree fitness of v

$$= \left(1 + \frac{\text{The number of neighbor of } v}{\text{Max. number of neighbor of cluster}(v)}\right)^{\alpha}, \quad (2)$$

where $\text{cluster}(v)$ is the cluster that sensor node v belongs to, and α is the average ratio of remaining energy to initial energy of $\text{cluster}(v)$.

Second, "energy state fitness" of a node with CH candidate state should be considered as the second component of the fitness value. Since CH consumes more energy than the CMs, SOSAC gives a priority to a node with CH candidate state that has more residual energy. Therefore, the energy state is used as the second component of the fitness value, and we define energy state fitness as follows:

Energy state fitness of v

$$= \left(1 + \frac{\text{residual energy of } v}{\text{Max. residual energy of cluster}(v)}\right)^{1-\alpha}. \quad (3)$$

```
Data transmission phase
    While (1 round)
        (1) CM transmission step
            (For a node with CM state)
(1)             Sense environment.
(2)             Make a data packet.
(3)             Transmit a data packet to its CH.
        (2) CH transmission step
            (For a node with CH state)
(4)             Aggregate received data packets from CMs
(5)             Transmit an aggregated data packet using the established path.
    End while
```

ALGORITHM 3: The data transmission phase algorithm.

Since each component of the two fitness components has values between 1 and 2, the values of the two fitness components are inherently normalized. Also we use α and $1-\alpha$ as exponent parameters, each of which decides the weight of the respective fitness component. A total fitness value can be calculated by adding these two components together as follows.

$$\text{Total fitness value} = \text{neighborhood degree fitness of } \nu$$
$$+ \text{ energy state fitness of } \nu. \tag{4}$$

If the total fitness value is to reflect the state of the networks, then it should be adjusted in a smart way to consider the change in the environment. In the beginning of networking, each sensor node has sufficient residual energy so that the energy state fitness is not very important. Therefore, the neighborhood degree fitness should be weighted more. This can be done by using the suggested total fitness value since the neighborhood degree fitness becomes more important than the energy state fitness as α remains relatively large. As time goes by, however, if the sensor nodes consume more energy, the scarcity of the energy state should be reflected. This can be done by using the suggested total fitness value since the energy state fitness becomes more important than the neighborhood degree fitness as $(1-\alpha)$ becomes large. Hence, SOSAC tries to achieve energy balance by increasing the weight of the energy state fitness.

For SOSAC implementation, we constructed a source code using Visual C++ of Visual Studio 2008 and conducted a computer simulation. The sensor field for the test was 50 m * 50 m in size, and the simulation was carried out under the assumption that 100 sensor nodes with an initial energy of 0.5 J were distributed. The test used the average of the performances of the 10 different sensor distributions in the 50 m * 50 m sensor field.

Figure 4 is an experiment to examine the effects of self-adjusting the weight α of the fitness value in a smart way. We compared the original SOSAC that self-adjusts the weights of the fitness value as time passes with three variations of SOSAC that are given with the fixed weights (0:1, 1:1, 1:0) of the two fitness value components. Here 0:1 means that

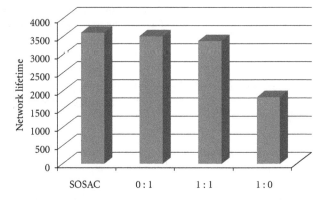

FIGURE 4: Effect of the fitness value with self-adjustment of its weights.

SOSAC uses energy state fitness only, 1:1 that equal weights of two fitness value components are used, and 1:0 that SOSAC uses neighborhood degree fitness only.

In Figure 4, the Y axis indicates the network lifetime and the X axis indicates the ratio of weights. The network lifetime of the automatically adjusted SOSAC is longer than those of the fixed weight (0:1, 1:1, and 1:0) SOSACs. This experiment shows that SOSAC adjusts suitable weights by itself in a smart way rather than providing weight parameters as inputs.

5.1.2. Smart Adjustment of Broadcasting Range. Along with the selection of an appropriate CH in the hierarchical routing, deciding on the number and size of the clusters is one of the important factors that determines the energy consumption of the sensor nodes. In this section, we suggest a method for deciding the appropriate number and size of clusters.

The number of clusters in SOSAC is decided by the broadcasting range of the sensor nodes. As the broadcasting range widens, the number of sensor nodes with CH candidate states, which participate in the election of a CH, increases. Consequently, a large cluster is formed with fewer clusters and CHs. With the fewer CHs, the energy consumption of the CHs for transmitting data packets over a long distance is also reduced. However, because there are more CMs, the CH has to receive more data packets from them. Therefore, the energy consumption is greater when receiving the data packets in a large cluster. On the contrary, if the broadcasting range narrows, the number of clusters and CHs is increased due to the formation of small clusters. With an increasing number of CHs, the energy consumption for receiving is reduced, whereas the energy consumption of the CHs for transmission increases. Therefore, the broadcasting range of SOSAC must be optimized to increase the network lifetime of the WSNs.

Since we can enumerate many values for the broadcasting range of a sensor field in a computer simulation, it is not difficult to optimize the broadcasting range during computer simulation. However, it is impossible for the sensor nodes, which have poor calculation capability, to determine the optimized broadcasting range in real time in the sensor field. Hence we try to find the optimized broadcasting range as the function of the number of sensors that varies from 50 to 250 in the 50 m*50 m sensor field using computer simulations for SOSAC. Hence we make the following predictive formula that calculates the optimized broadcasting range. The formula (5) was made from the following nonlinear regression model that has the adjusted coefficient of determination = 0.977:

$$y = \frac{0.000034x^2 - 0.02783x + 9.677}{\text{an area of sensor field}/2500 \ (50 \text{ m} * 50 \text{ m})}, \quad (5)$$

where y is the broadcasting range(m) and x the number of sensors in the sensor field.

If the sensor nodes sense the number of sensor nodes, an optimal broadcasting range can be adjusted in a smart way using the above formula, and the number of sensor nodes can be computed after the data packets are transmitted in the first round. In other words, respective CHs can determine the number of their CMs using the number of data packets transmitted by their CMs in the first period. This information is transmitted to the master CH through the intercluster routing, and the master CH can determine the number of sensor nodes scattered in the sensor field by summing them. Therefore, in the clustering phase of the first round of SOSAC, clusters are formed in the broadcasting range with the initial value to perform routing. When the first round is over, the master CH calculates an optimized broadcasting range and broadcasts this information to the entire sensor field so that all the sensor nodes can be adjusted in the optimized broadcasting range at the start of the second round.

Figure 5 compares the optimized broadcasting range calculated by an enumerative method without the smart adjustment mechanism with the network lifetime calculated with the smart adjustment mechanism. In Figure 5, the Y axis indicates the network lifetime when 20% of the sensor nodes have become drained in periods, and the X-axis shows five different experimental sizes. Figure 5 shows that the network lifetimes when SOSAC uses an optimized broadcasting range by finding an enumerative method are longer than those when SOSAC uses the smart adjustment mechanism of formula (5). In fact, the smart adjustment of

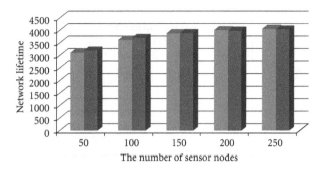

■ Enumerative optimization
■ Smart adjustment

Figure 5: Effect of optimized broadcasting range.

the broadcasting range of formula (5) shows almost identical performance with the enumerative optimum values of the broadcasting range, which cannot be easily implemented in real WSNs. This demonstrates that the smart adjustment mechanism of predictive formula (5), which can be easily implemented in real WSNs, can provided good estimation of the optimal range of broadcasting range.

5.1.3. Smart Backup Mechanism. A WSN can be used in inaccessible and dangerous areas such as battlefields and hazardous regions. Also some of the WSN sensor nodes can be broken down by vicious physical attack or cyber-attack before their energy is used up. Therefore, the robustness of WSNs is important for dealing with potential problems such as breakdown, failure, or attack of the sensor nodes.

When cluster-based routing is used, all information on the clusters may be lost if the sensor nodes in the node with CH state have become drained or failed due to breakdown, failure, or attack. Transmission of the entire network may fail depending on the location of the CH on the tree in the intercluster routing.

In order to avoid these risks, SOSAC has a "smart backup mechanism" that allows all the CMs of each cluster to recognize their CH's states. If a CH losses its function unexpectedly, SOSAC has to select a new CH to minimize the transmission failures in the network. SOSAC can sense all CMs within its cluster range because it has to transmit the data packets that are broadcast by the CH to the CH of the neighboring cluster during intercluster routing. No additional overheads for sensing CHs or CMs are needed because the sensor nodes with CH state can be recognized depending on whether the data packets have been received or not. The smart backup mechanism of SOSAC selects a new CH when the CH has lost its function, and SOSAC needs overheads only to reconnect the network without using failed CHs. The smart backup mechanism is comprised of the following 2 steps: CH reelection step and rejoin intercluster routing tree step.

CH Reelection Step. The CH reelection step is carried out immediately when the CMs recognize a failure of the CH.

CH backup mechanism
    (1) CH re-election step
        If (A node with CM state = TRUE)
(1)   If (CM does not receive a data packet from its CH)
            Changes its state as a node with CH candidate state.
(2.1)   Broadcast a fitness-value-signal packet, within 2*(broadcasting range)
(2.2)   Receive fitness-value-signal packets
            If (Two nodes at the same cluster) store
            Else discard
(2.3)   Compare fitness value
            If (One's fitness value is Max) changes its state as a node with CH state
            Else changes its state as a node with undecided state
(3)   CH broadcasts a CH-signal packet to the whole area sensor field
(4)   Others receive CH-signal packets and set CH
    (2) Re-join intercluster routing tree step
        If (A node with CH state = CH)
        If (Re-elected CH = TRUE)
(5)   Broadcast a re-join-signal packet to the whole area sensor field
        If (Not re-elected CH = TRUE)
(6)   If (Receive re-join-signal packets) re-route establishment.

ALGORITHM 4: The CH backup mechanism algorithm.

In procedure 2.1 of Algorithm 4, the CMs broadcast the fitness values calculated in the previous CH selection step of clustering phase within 2*(broadcasting range) to restore the system as soon as possible when a CH failure occurs. Each CM compares the received fitness values with its own fitness value to select a new CH. The selected CH broadcasts the CH-signal packets (procedure 3). When the CMs receive the CH-signal packets, they select this CH as their new CH (procedure 4).

Rejoin Intercluster Routing Tree Step. All the CMs of the cluster assume that they can obtain information on the neighboring CHs on the intercluster routing tree of their own CH during the clustering step in the clustering phase. The new CH elected in procedures 5 and 6 of Algorithm 4 broadcasts a rejoin-signal packet to its neighboring CHs on the tree to restore the network to a stable state again. The smart backup mechanism of SOSAC is able to restore an unstable network to a stable state by using unused information without incurring additional overhead to the recognition of nodes with CH state.

The smart backup mechanism should be able to restore the network, not only if an error has occurred in the CH, but also if several sensor nodes have lost their functions in a certain concentrated area or sporadic failures of each sensor node in scattered areas. In order to check if the smart backup function works properly, we can conduct two types of experiments. The basic setting for the experiments is the same as the experiment for smart adaptability of the fitness value.

The first experiment observes how long the network is able to maintain itself in the event that all sensor nodes have lost their function to sense any objects within 10 m from a certain point by a physical or cyber error in a certain area. This experiment assumes that the sensor nodes within 10 m

of the center of a coordinate which changes randomly have failed unexpectedly. In order to calculate an average value, we carried out the same experiments 10 times repeatedly and compared the average value with the normal state. To determine the occurrence of errors, we experimented with 3 cases of failure at the 501st, 1001st, and 1501st periods.

Figure 6 indicates that the earlier an error occurs, the shorter the network lifetime is. However, the maximum reduction rate of failure at the 501st period was only 1.8%, which reveals that the smart backup mechanism of SOSAC can cope with external errors in a smart way.

In the second experiment, we tested the result if 5, 10, or 15 sensor nodes stopped their functions sporadically in the WSNs in comparison with the result in the normal state.

Figure 7 implies that the occurrence of sporadic errors barely influenced the network lifetime by using a smart back up mechanism. The results of the two experiments show that the smart backup mechanism of SOSAC is a robust smart mechanism capable of coping with some changes in the external environment.

5.2. Performance Comparison with HEED. In this section, the performance of SOSAC is compared with that of HEED, which is a well-known self-organized clustering and routing method. HEED maintains or improves the network performance by comparing the previous dispersing type methods using the self-organized method. In constructing the source code and simulation for SOSAC and HEED, we used Visual C++ of Visual Studio 2008.

5.2.1. Network Lifetime Comparison. In this experiment, all the cases were compared, ranging from the case in which the network lifetime of the WSN ceases as the energy of the first sensor node is drained to the case in which the network

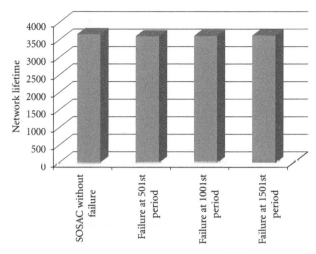

FIGURE 6: Experiment on concentrated failures.

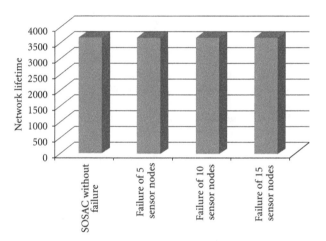

FIGURE 7: Experiment on sporadic failures.

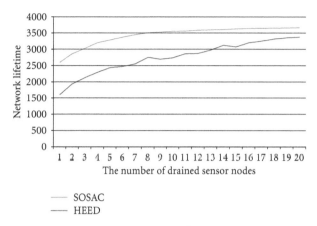

FIGURE 8: Comparison of network lifetime of SOSAC and HEED.

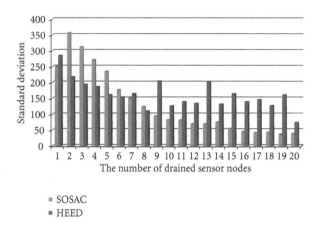

FIGURE 9: Comparison of standard deviations of network lifetimes for SOSAC and HEED.

lifetime of the WSN ceases as the energy of the 20th sensor node is drained.

Figure 8 shows that the network lifetime of SOSAC is between 61.7% (when the 1st sensor node is drained) and 8.5% (when the 20th sensor node is drained) longer than that of HEED. The network lifetimes until 20 sensor nodes had become drained were compared because it is impossible to observe the WSNs normally in the event that over 20% of the sensor nodes lose their functions due to the large vacuum in the sensing function.

We calculated the standard deviations of network lifetimes of SOSAC and HEED in Figure 9. On average, the standard deviation of SOSAC is 18.9% less than that of HEED, indicating that SOSAC shows more uniform performance than HEED.

5.2.2. Residual Energy Comparison. We compared the ratios of the residual energies in the WSNs to the network lifetimes of SOSAC and HEED.

In Figure 10, the Y-axis indicates the ratio of the residual energy in the WSN, and the X-axis indicates the number of drained sensor nodes. Figure 10 shows that the residual energy of SOSAC is between 16.9% and 52.7% shorter than that of HEED. The comparison of the two experiments (Figures 8 and 10) indicates that SOSAC has a longer network lifetime than HEED, and that the sensor nodes of SOSAC consume energy more uniformly than those of HEED when the network lifetime of WSNs ceases. This implies that SOSAC controls certain sensor nodes so as not to consume energy quickly by balancing the energy consumptions of the sensor nodes based on the appropriate fitness value, which gives a relatively long network lifetime.

5.2.3. Scalability Comparison. We compared network lifetimes of SOSAC and HEED for different size sensor fields and different numbers of sensor nodes, while maintaining the same density of sensor nodes. For example, the 100 m * 100 m sensor field with 400 sensor nodes has four times as many as the 50 m * 50 m sensor field that has only 100 sensor nodes. Here the network lifetime of the WSN is defined for the 20% of sensor nodes that are drained.

In Figure 11, the Y axis indicates the network lifetime in periods, and the X axis is the size of the sensor fields. Figure 11 shows that the network lifetime of SOSAC was a maximum of 10.7% and a minimum of 2.2% longer than

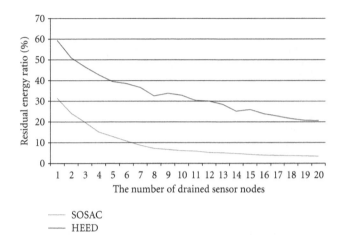

FIGURE 10: Experiment on residual energy ratios of SOSAC and HEED.

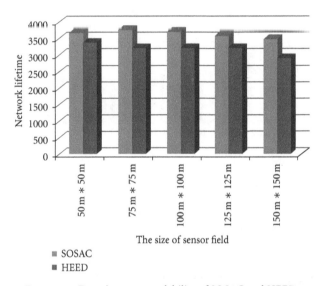

FIGURE 11: Experiment on scalability of SOSAC and HEED.

the network lifetime of HEED in different sensor field sizes and different numbers of sensor nodes. Hence, SOSAC shows good scalability in a smart way, which enables it to form clusters suitable for different sensor field sizes.

6. Conclusion

This paper has proposed a hierarchical clustering and routing model capable of maximizing the network lifetime through the decisionmaking of each sensor node based on local information by adopting a self-organized and smart-adaptive system in the design of the clustering and routing model of a WSN. The proposed method enables the sensor nodes to form clusters without a server or any external assistance, and the subsequent routing is performed based on it. The key advantage of this model is its ability to sense any environmental disturbances such as time changes, number of sensor nodes, and failures of sensor nodes using three smart adaptive mechanisms. The proposed method also

demonstrated superior performance compared to that of an existing self-organized clustering method.

A smart mechanism for WSNs that can cope with diverse changes in the environment needs to be developed in future study. Appropriate research examples are changes in the operation or mobile environment. In addition, research on self-organized and smart-adaptive communication methods for other communication networks holds the promise of valuable results in the near future.

Acknowledgment

This paper is the result of the research with the support of National Research Foundation of Korea (2009-0074081) using the funds from the Ministry of Education, Science and Technology in 2009.

References

[1] J. Yick, B. Mukherjee, and D. Ghosal, "Wireless sensor network survey," *Computer Networks*, vol. 52, no. 12, pp. 2292–2330, 2008.

[2] J. N. Al-Karaki and A. E. Kamal, "Routing techniques in wireless sensor networks: a survey," *IEEE Wireless Communications*, vol. 11, no. 6, pp. 6–28, 2004.

[3] K. Akkaya and M. Younis, "A survey on routing protocols for wireless sensor networks," *Ad Hoc Networks*, vol. 3, no. 3, pp. 325–349, 2005.

[4] S. Mahfoudh and P. Minet, "Survey of energy efficient strategies in wireless ad hoc and sensor networks," in *Proceedings of the 7th International Conference on Networking (ICN '08)*, pp. 1–7, Cancun, Mexico, April 2008.

[5] F. Dressler, *Self-Organization in Sensor and Actor Networks*, WILEY, New York, NY, USA., 2007.

[6] E. Gelenbe, Z. Xu, and E. Seref, "Cognitive packet networks," in *Proceedings of the 11th IEEE International Conference on Tools with Artificial Intelligence (ICTAI '99)*, pp. 47–54, November 1999.

[7] E. Gelenbe, R. Lent, M. Gellman, P. Liu, and P. Su, "CPN and QoS driven smart routing in wired and wireless networks," *Lecture Notes in Computer Science*, vol. 2965, pp. 68–87, 2004.

[8] M. D. Santo, A. Pietrosanto, P. Napoletano, and L. Carrubbo, "Knowledge based service systems," in *System Theory and Service Science: Integrating Three Perspectives in a New Service Agenda*, Social Science Electronic, New York, NY, USA, 2011.

[9] N. Israr and I. U. Awan, "Multilayer cluster based energy efficient routing protocol for wireless sensor networks," *International Journal of Distributed Sensor Networks*, vol. 4, no. 2, pp. 176–193, 2008.

[10] M. Younis, M. Youssef, and K. Arisha, "Energy-aware management for cluster-based sensor networks," *Computer Networks*, vol. 43, no. 5, pp. 649–668, 2003.

[11] Y. T. Hou, Y. Shi, H. D. Sherali, and S. F. Midkiff, "On energy provisioning and relay node placement for wireless sensor networks," *IEEE Transactions on Wireless Communications*, vol. 4, no. 5, pp. 2579–2590, 2005.

[12] C. Prehofer and C. Bettstetter, "Self-organization in communication networks: principles and design paradigms," *IEEE Communications Magazine*, vol. 43, no. 7, pp. 78–85, 2005.

[13] W. R. Heinzelman, A. Chandrakasan, and H. Balakrishnan, "Energy-efficient communication protocol for wireless microsensor networks," in *Proceedings of the 33rd Annual*

Hawaii International Conference on System Siences (HICSS-33), p. 223, January 2000.

[14] Y. Sun and X. Gu, "Clustering routing based maximizing lifetime for wireless sensor networks," *International Journal of Distributed Sensor Networks*, vol. 5, no. 1, p. 88, 2009.

[15] O. Younis and S. Fahmy, "HEED: a hybrid, energy-efficient, distributed clustering approach for ad hoc sensor networks," *IEEE Transactions on Mobile Computing*, vol. 3, no. 4, pp. 366–379, 2004.

[16] O. Younis, S. Fahmy, and P. Santi, "An architecture for robust sensor network communications," *International Journal of Distributed Sensor Networks*, vol. 1, no. 3-4, pp. 305–327, 2005.

[17] M. M. Hasan and J. P. Jue, "Survivable self-organization for prolonged lifetime in wireless sensor networks," *International Journal of Distributed Sensor Networks*, vol. 2011, Article ID 257156, 11 pages, 2011.

[18] D. L. Tennenhouse and D. J. Wetherall, "Towards an active network architecture," in *Proceedings of the Multimedia Computing and Networking (MMCN 96), and Computer Communcation Review*, vol. 26, no. 2, pp. 5–18, April 1996.

[19] E. Amir, S. McCanne, and R. Katz, "An active service framework and its application to real-time multimedia transcoding," *Computer Communication Review*, vol. 28, no. 4, pp. 178–189, 1998.

[20] A. Ren and G. Q. Maguire Jr., "A smart network with active services for wireless context-aware multimedia communications," in *Proceedings of the Wireless Communications and Systems, Emerging Technologies Symposium*, pp. 17.1–17.5, April 1999.

[21] S. Stone, M. Zyda, D. Brutzman, and J. Falby,, "Mobile agents and smart networks for distributed simulations," in *Proceedings of the 14th Workshop on Standards Interoperability of Distributed Simulations*, pp. 909–917, Institute for Simulation and Training, Orlando, Fla, USA, March 1996.

15

Tree-Based Neighbor Discovery in Urban Vehicular Sensor Networks

Heejun Roh and Wonjun Lee

Department of Computer Science and Engineering, Korea University, Seoul 136-701, Republic of Korea

Correspondence should be addressed to Wonjun Lee, wlee@korea.ac.kr

Academic Editor: Junyoung Heo

In urban vehicular sensor networks, vehicles equipped with onboard sensors monitor some area, and the result can be shared to neighbor vehicles to correct their own sensing data. However, due to the frequent change of vehicle topology compared to the wireless sensor network, it is required for a vehicle to discover neighboring vehicles. Therefore, efficient neighbor discovery algorithm should be designed for vehicular sensor networks. In this paper, two efficient tree-based neighbor discovery algorithms in vehicular sensor networks are proposed and analyzed. After suggesting detailed scenario and its system model, we show that the expected value of neighbor discovery delay has different characteristics depending on neighbor discovery algorithms. An interesting observation of our result is that M-binary tree-based neighbor discovery shows better performance than M-ary tree-based neighbor discovery in the parking lot scenario, which is a counterintuitive result. We analyze why such result appears extensively.

1. Introduction

In recent years, wireless sensor networks (WSNs) [1], especially urban vehicular sensor networks [2], have inspired research and industry interests in various applications such as traffic engineering, environment monitoring, and civic and homeland security. A typical sensor network includes hundreds to thousands of sensor nodes, each of which is equipped with various kinds of sensors. In general, sensor nodes have stronger resource constraints than nodes in typical wireless ad hoc network, for example, battery power, memory, computation capability, and communication technology. However, vehicular sensor networks have different characteristics to typical sensor network. First, there is no battery constraint. Therefore, in vehicular sensor networks, communication between vehicles with less delay is one of the most important issues, compared to typical wireless sensor networks.

Especially, since vehicular sensor networks may have no infrastructure controlling the network environment, it is required for vehicles to autoconfigure the environment for establishing a communication network. For example,

if sensor-occupied vehicles arrive at the same area, each vehicle would not know which other vehicles are in its transmission range, implying that the vehicle needs to discover its neighboring vehicles. Since information obtained during the discovery process is required by many network protocols, neighbor discovery of each vehicle in the vehicular sensor network is an important configuration process.

Currently, explicit neighbor discovery may not be performed in typical ad hoc networks [3], a superset of vehicular sensor network. That is, it is assumed that all transmissions are listened to by neighboring nodes in the medium access control layer level. This assumption is not suitable for practical vehicular sensor network implementation, because when many vehicles are in the one-hop transmission range, the delay of neighbor discovery increases dramatically. In addition, the delayed result for neighbor discovery process can be outdated since the neighboring vehicles move too fast to depart the transmission range. Therefore, an efficient neighbor discovery scheme for vehicular sensor networks is required, implying that average delay minimization of neighbor discovery schemes in vehicular sensor networks is an important problem.

Recently, numerous studies on neighbor discovery for wireless networks have been proposed in the literature [4–6]. These studies mainly focus on applications of mobile robot networks, and the IEEE 802.11 network provides robot intercommunication, which is very similar to vehicle-to-vehicle communications in vehicular sensor networks. However, these approaches cannot be applied into the vehicular sensor networks without modification, because if there are many groups of vehicles, the performance of the network may be reduced significantly due to interference and collisions. Furthermore, the network load cannot be controlled by a group of nodes in general [5].

In Santos et al. work [4], an adaptive TDMA protocol for mobile autonomous nodes is proposed. This protocol is an adaptive TDMA protocol with new self-configuration capabilities according to the current number of active group members. This protocol operates over IEEE 802.11 networks in infrastructure and adhoc mode. However, it does not support a dynamic number of nodes. The improved protocol proposed in [5] has dynamic reconfiguration of the TDMA round, which supports changes of the number of nodes. But it is not suitable to assumption, because each node in a group maintains a state machine and the whole member information of the group.

Arai et al. [6] proposed an adaptive reservation-TDMA (AR-TRMA) MAC protocol, which focuses on real-time communication among nodes in a heterogeneous environment by using a reservation mechanism. This protocol supports dynamic time slot allocation schemes during node intercommunication. Furthermore, this protocol considers the packet collision avoidance method in the joining procedure, using the battery voltage level and ID of each node. However, when a packet collision occurs, the protocol uses fixed-size minislots to resolve the collision. This scheme suffers from lack of scalability, because it may not support dynamic situations of vehicular sensor network which include a situation that a large number of nodes and groups move around frequently.

With this motivation, we have studied tree-based neighbor discovery schemes in vehicular sensor networks, which guarantee the discovery of whole neighbors in each leader vehicle. In this study, our objective is to reduce the average delay of tree-based neighbor discovery. According to our study, the delay depends on the tree construction scheme. We focus on M-ary and M-binary tree-based neighbor discovery, because these algorithms have simplicity and optimality, respectively.

In summary, our contributions are twofold. First, we apply tree algorithm variations to neighbor discovery in vehicular sensor networks. To the best of our knowledge, our study is the first work applying tree algorithms to neighbor discovery in vehicular sensor networks. Second, we show that the M-Binary tree-based scheme with optimal M and N is suitable for the neighbor discovery process.

The reminder of this paper proceeds as follows. Our model for sensor-equipped vehicles is described in Section 2. The proposed join schemes are described in Section 3. In Section 4, determining the number of groups in each neighbor discovery process is discussed, and the performance results are also shown. Our conclusion is given in Section 5.

2. System Model

First of all, we explain our system model assumptions. We assume that numerous vehicles are uniformly distributed in a working field (e.g., road), and each vehicle may move freely. Though this assumption is not suitable for some vehicle sensor network applications, many mobile sensor network applications in dense-area monitoring scenario allow this assumption. It is also assumed that the carrier sensing range is twice the transmission range.

In this model, vehicles are classified into leaders and followers. The leader vehicle (LV) is the vehicle managing and controlling a group of vehicles. The other vehicles in the group are called follower vehicles (FVs) or members of the group. A vehicle which is not a follower vehicle and can communicate with a leader vehicle in onehop is called a neighboring vehicle. Note that follower vehicles do not need to identify other vehicles except for the leader vehicle, and a leader vehicle has the number of required vehicles for performing a cooperative sensing task.

A group following a leader vehicle uses TDMA with a channel distinct from the default channel when communication among nongroup members or between a member and nonmember is required. Because the TDMA frame structure guarantees a delay bound and transmission opportunities, each member of the group has a chance to transmit its packet fairly. Figure 1 shows an example of a TDMA frame.

Each of the TDMA frames has several periods: beacon period, joining period, request/leave period, control period, and data period. LV notifies the beginning of a frame by beacon message broadcasting in a beacon period. Acknowledgment of the previous frame is also contained in the beacon message. In a joining period, LV requests its neighbor vehicles to join the group under the number of required vehicles via the proposed schemes. Note that neighboring vehicles which are already joined as follower vehicles do not participate in the joining period. In Figure 1, vehicle A is the follower vehicle which participated in the joining period before, and vehicles B and C are neighboring vehicles which are identified as follower vehicles after the joining period. After joining period, each follower vehicle can request a chance of data transmission or notify the leave itself in request/leave period. LV broadcasts a control message containing the follower vehicles data period schedules during the control period, and each of the follower vehicles can send its own data according to the schedule. This TDMA frame structure can be modified or redesigned given the application scenario and the system requirements.

In this system model, neighbor discovery is performed in the joining period. Depending on the neighbor discovery scheme, the time interval of the joining period may be variable, which causes a significant delay. Therefore, a joining scheme to minimize the total expected delay in the period is required. In this paper, it is called the delay-minimized

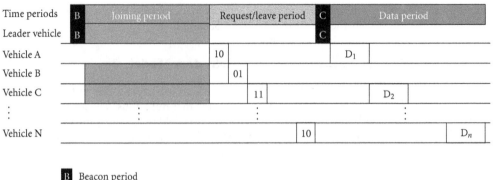

FIGURE 1: An example of TDMA frame structure.

neighbor discovery (DMND), and in the next section, two tree-based DMNDs are discussed.

Generally, the number of neighboring vehicles of LV affects the performance of DMND in our model. Therefore, LV may estimate and use this information to improve the performance. When LV has no follower vehicles, one of the easiest estimation techniques is to use the field size, the transmission range, and the total number of vehicles in the uniformly distributed working field

$$N_{\text{Neighbor}} = \left\lfloor \frac{N_{\text{Tot}} \cdot (\pi \rho_{\text{TX}}^2)}{S_{\text{Field}}} \right\rfloor, \tag{1}$$

where ρ_{TX} is the transmission range of LV, N_{Tot} is the total number of vehicles in the working field, and S_{Field} is the area of the field.

The other method that can be applied to estimate N_{Neighbor} is found in [7], and this can be utilized via the default channel. But further discussion on the estimation method is not considered in this paper.

3. Tree-Based DMNDs

We mainly focus on minimization of the expected delay in order to identify a required number of vehicles from a greater number of neighbor vehicles. The two kinds of tree-based DMNDs proposed are based on various splitting methods. The first one applies M-ary tree splitting for grouping collided vehicles, while the second one combines M-ary and binary tree splitting methods to improve the associated delay performance. The latter requires an algorithm to decide the value of M affecting the performance of the method, and we will derive the optimal $M(M^*)$ which minimizes the average of total delay. Some notations for the description of the proposed DMNDs are as follows. M is used to denote the number of children nodes (branches) in a tree diagram, and N and k are the numbers of neighbor and required vehicles, respectively.

3.1. M-Ary Tree-Based DMND (MT-DMND). In M-ary tree-based DMND, after LV sends a query, which includes the state information of the previous slot, each neighboring

vehicle determines its joining operation using this information. If the state of the previous slot is "C (collision slot)," each of the vehicles which sent an ACK in the slot randomly chooses an integer in the interval $\lfloor 0, M-1 \rfloor$ and concatenates the number onto the end of its ID. Then, if its new ID satisfies the requirements of LV, which is included in the query, the vehicle sends an ACK with its new ID. In case that the state is "S (success slot)," the vehicle which sent an ACK with its ID in the previous slot recognizes itself as a follower vehicle of LV. Each of the other neighboring vehicles that did not send an ACK do send one if its ID satisfies the requirements of LV. If the state is "I (Idle slot)" and the ID of a neighboring vehicle satisfies the requirements of LV, the vehicle sends an ACK with its ID.

On the other hand, in M-ary tree-based DMND, the operation of LV is as follows. First, at the beginning slot of a joining period, LV sends a query requesting an anonymous ID. Then LV waits for a time slot to receive an ACK and recognize the state of the time slot. Based on the state, LV sends another query and waits for a time slot. This procedure repeats until LV identifies k follower vehicles. The policy that LV queries the IDs of neighboring vehicles in the procedure is conceptually similar to "depth-first-search (DFS)" algorithm. When LV recognizes that the state of the previous slot is "C," it concatenates 0 to $M-1$ to the respective queried ID and stacks M IDs into the candidate list. Then it pops an element of the list and sends a query with the element. When the state of the previous slot is "S," it identifies the vehicle which sent the ACK in the previous slot as a follower vehicle. Then it pops an element of the list, and sends a query. When the state of the previous slot is "I," it only pops an element of the list and sends a query. Therefore, LV can construct an M-ary tree by the result of M-ary tree-based DMND, as shown in Figure 2.

3.2. M-Binary Tree-Based DMND (M-BT-DMND). M-binary tree-based DMND is a modification of M-ary tree-based DMND designed to reduce excessive collisions and idle slots. It is based on M-binary tree construction, just as 2-ary tree-based DMND is based on M-ary tree construction. An M-binary tree is a tree that each node has at most 2 nodes, except that the root node has at most M nodes.

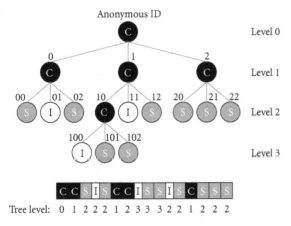

FIGURE 2: The M-ary tree-based DMND (when $M = 3$).

TABLE 1: FHSS System Attributes (Parameters) and Additional Parameters Used to Obtain Numerical Results.

Parameters	Default value
aSlotTime	$50\,\mu s$
DIFS (DCF Interframe Space)	$128\,\mu s$
SIFS (Short Interframe Space)	$28\,\mu s$
MAC Header	272 bits
PHY Header	128 bits
Management frame (w/o payload)	28 bytes
ACK frame	14 bytes
MAC Header	272 bits
MAC Header	272 bits

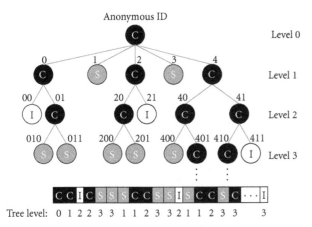

FIGURE 3: The M-binary tree-based DMND (when $M = 5$).

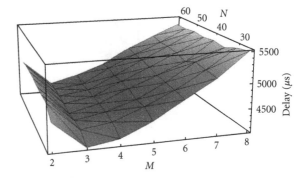

FIGURE 4: Total average delay of M-ary tree-based DMND (MT-DMND) with fixed k ($k = 25$).

Therefore, LV and its neighboring vehicles choose either 0 or 1 for concatenation, except when LV sends a query with an anonymous ID. After LV sends a query with an anonymous ID and a collision slot has occurred, LV and its neighboring vehicles choose an integer in the interval $[0, M - 1]$. Figure 3 shows a typical example of M-binary tree-based DMND. Note that there is no node with only one child, because the "S" and "I" nodes have no children and the "C" node always has 2 or more children. Though further improvement of this scheme can be achieved based on this observation, we do not consider it further due to the complexity of the analysis.

4. Simulation Results

4.1. Simulation Environments. Some simulation experiments were performed to compare DMNDs. To validate each simulation result, we use the values of the IEEE 802.11 FHSS system parameters listed in Table 1 as in [8]. Note that Short Interframe Space (SIFS) is a fixed-size time period between frame transmission used for IEEE 802.11 nodes to detect the correct channel idle. As comparison targets, p-persistent DMNDs [9] with or without query are also simulated. Note that p is optimally chosen by the simulation with the precision of 0.001. We performed 1000 trials for

each scheme, and the delay results are averaged over each scheme for the given (fixed) parameters. In addition, when we use query in a DMND, since success/collision slot needs one query (with 2-bit payloads for 3 slot types), 2 SIFSs, and 1 ACK message (with 32-bit ID), it takes about $532\,\mu s$, while the idle slot that includes one query and one *aSlotTime* takes $388\,\mu s$. It implies that the ratio of the collision slot time to idle slot time equals to 1.371. We denote this ratio to α. α is one of the most important factors in this simulation result, because α determines the overhead ratio in DMNDs. On the other hand, when we do not use query in a DMND, we use *aSlotTime* for the idle slot and $495\,\mu s$ for the success/collision solt, according to [9].

4.2. Optimal Value of M. As mentioned, each of our DMNDs has triple parameters (M, N, k). However, since N is given within the joining period of a frame and k is determined by the task given to LV and the number of follower vehicles identified by LV, M is a tunable parameter in many cases. Therefore, consideration should be given to finding the optimal value of M to minimize the total average delay. Figures 4–7 show the average total delay in case of M-ary and M-binary tree-based DMND with fixed N and k, respectively.

Figure 4 shows the delay of MT-DMND for M and N, where the number of required vehicles for a task, k, is fixed to 25. For a given task and value of M, as shown in the figure,

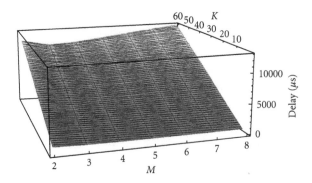

FIGURE 5: Total average delay of M-ary tree-based DMND (MT-DMND) with fixed N ($N = 60$).

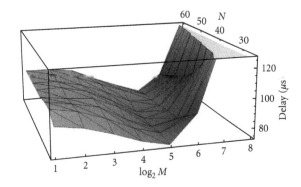

FIGURE 6: Total average delay of M-binary tree-based DMND (M-BT-DMND) with fixed k ($k = 25$).

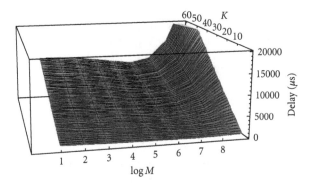

FIGURE 7: Total average delay of M-Binary tree-based DMND (M-BT-DMND) with fixed N ($N = 60$).

the number of neighboring vehicles does not affect the delay. This result is quite different to the depth-first-search (DFS) of M-ary tree. In DFS problem, each node has a distinct key and when a key is given, the objective of this problem is to search the node with the same key. It is popular for DFS to have a time complexity of $O(|N| + |E|)$ where $|N|$ is the number of nodes in the tree and $|E|$ is the number of edges. Therefore, the total delay of DFS can be considered as a linear function of $|N| + |E|$.

However, in case of MT-DMND, the total delay can be calculated approximately. It is not a linear function of $|N| + |E|$ though the procedure is similar to that of DFS. Given

N neighboring vehicles, suppose that LV should identify k follower vehicles with MT-DMND. The total delay of the procedure is denoted by $d_M(N, k)$. We cover only the case that $N \gg k > 1$. In this case, root node is a collision node when this fact is recognized, each vehicle concatenates a random integer $[0, M - 1]$ uniformly to its ID. Assuming a uniform random distribution of integers, M subtrees of the root node have almost the same number of nodes. Then, the following equation is approximately satisfied:

$$d_M(N, k) \approx d_{\text{Coll}} + d\left(\frac{N}{M}, k\right), \qquad (2)$$

where d_{Coll} is the collision delay in the root node.

Because (2) is a recursion formula, we find a number r such that $N/M^r = k$ ($r \geq 1$),

$$d_M(N, k) \approx r \times d_{\text{Coll}} + d_M(k, k)$$
$$= \log_M\left(\frac{N}{k}\right) \times d_{\text{Coll}} + d_M(k, k), \qquad (3)$$

where $d_M(k, k)$ is the total delay of the procedure given k neighboring vehicles and k required follower vehicles.

In this context, for a considerably large k, $\log_M(N/k)$ can be ignored. Therefore, in this case, N has little effect on the total delay of MT-DMND. This is unique characteristic of MT-DMND, which identifies only a fraction of all neighboring vehicles. We can conclude that in MT-DMND, when we choose the value of M, the characteristic of the task is more important than the number of neighboring vehicles.

On the other hand, for a given task (i.e., fixed k), the value of M has a considerable effect on the total delay, as shown in Figure 4. The explanation for this has already been described in the previous section: the number of idle and collision slots is important. If M increases, the number of collision slots decreases. But, if M is very large, the number of idle slots is so large that the delay increases. Therefore, we can determine the optimal value of M by considering the trade-off between the number of collision and idle slots. In the figure, the optimal value of M is 3, since we assume that the value of α in our protocol is 1.371. Note that a different α may lead to a different optimal value of M. Furthermore, it is observed in the figure that when M increases, the effect of the number of idle slots on the total delay is approximately linear.

Figure 5 shows the total average delay of MT-DMND for M and k when the number of neighboring vehicles N is fixed to 60. In this figure, the total delay increases linearly when the number of required vehicles k increases. It shows that if k increases, the respective number of collision and idle slots increases linearly. Especially, the slope of the delay for k is the minimum value in case that M is equal to 3, implying that the optimal value of M is not changed, even though the value of k is changed. Therefore, in M-ary tree-based DMND, the calculation of optimal value of M to minimize delay does not depend on N or k, but depends on the given MAC protocol parameters such as α.

Figures 6 and 7 show the total average delay of M-BT-DMND when k is fixed to 25 and N is fixed to 60, respectively. A comparison of Figures 4 and 6 shows that the

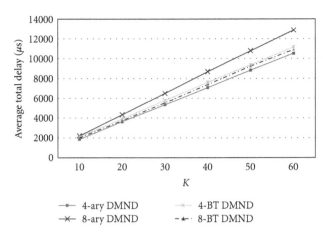

FIGURE 8: Performance comparison of MT-DMND and M-BT-DMND with $M = 4, 8$.

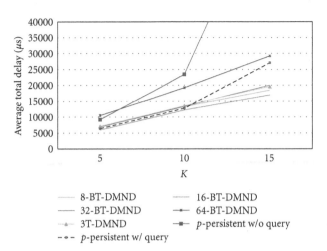

FIGURE 10: Performance comparison of DMNDs with $N = 15$.

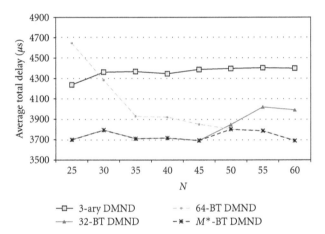

FIGURE 9: Performance comparison of DMNDs with $k = 25$.

number of neighboring vehicles N has a considerable effect on the optimal value of M in M-BT-DMND, compared to the case of MT-DMND. Furthermore, in many cases, M-BT-DMND has a smaller delay than MT-DMND. Therefore, this characteristic is a motivation of M^*-binary tree-based DMND, which is a dynamic version of M-binary tree-based DMND. In the next section, the details of the scheme are discussed.

4.3. Performance Comparison. In this section, we compare DMNDs. First, Figure 8 shows (N is fixed to 60) the average total delay for k, where $M = 4$ and $M = 8$. In this figure, when M is 8, M-BT-DMND has a smaller delay than MT-DMND, but when M is 4, MT-DMND has a smaller delay than M-BT-DMND. This shows that choosing a suitable value of M has a considerable effect on the performance of each scheme. Especially, it justifies the calculation of optimal value of M.

Figure 9 shows the average total delay for N with fixed k ($k = 25$) when each of 3T-DMND, 32-BT-DMND, 64-BT-DMND, M^*-BT-DMND, p-persistent DMND with query, and p-persistent DMND without query is performed,

respectively. M^*-BT-DMND is a dynamic scheme for N that selects the optimal value of M. However, in this simulation, the range of M is given to $\{2, 2^2, 2^3, \ldots, 2^{12}\}$ to reduce its complexity. As shown in this figure, the delay of M^*T-DMND (i.e., 3T-DMND) is generally longer than that of M^*-BT-DMND, and the performance of p-persistent DMND with or without query is worse than tree-based DMNDs. That is, though p is optimally selected, tree-based schemes can show better performance, depending on the system parameters. Furthermore, as we discussed, the optimal value of M in M-BT-DMND depends on N. Therefore, we can conclude that the performance of MT-DMND is stable, while that of M-BT-DMND is dynamic with respect to N. That is if the estimation of N_{Neighbor} is correct, M^*-BT-DMND is more effective than other DMNDs, because it has a smaller delay. But, if the estimation error of N_{Neighbor} is large, MT-DMND may have better performance.

Figure 10 shows the average total delay for k with fixed N ($N = 15$) when each of 3T-DMND, 16-BT-DMND, 32-BT-DMND, 64-BT-DMND, p-persistent DMND with query, and p-persistent DMND without query is performed, respectively. As shown in this figure, when M is similar to N, M-BT-DMND has better performance. However, p-persistent DMND with query may have better performance, when N and k are very small (e.g., $k = 5$). It is similar to the result in [9]. Note that p-persistent DMND without query has the worst performance generally, in both Figure 9 and Figure 10. It is because p-persistent DMND without query experiences too many collision, though p is optimally selected.

5. Conclusion

We have discussed the joining scheme of the TDMA MAC protocol for vehicular sensor networks. This paper proposed two joining schemes for minimizing the total delay of the joining period: MT-DMND and M-BT-DMND. Based on analyses of the proposed DMNDs and p-persistent DMNDs, we found that MT-DMND has better performance when M

is fixed to 3 among MT-DMNDs, while in M-BT-DMND, the optimal value of M depends on the number of neighboring vehicles, N. Furthermore, when we choose M optimally, M-BT-DMND has the best performance than MT-DMND and p-persistent DMNDs. Therefore, when it is hard to estimate the number of neighbors and stability is important, MT-DMND is suitable, while for a small estimation error when quick joining is required, M-BT-DMND with dynamic M calculation is suitable. As a future work, we will study and analyze a scheme to solve the problem that arises from the estimation error.

Acknowledgments

This research was jointly sponsored by MEST, Korea, under WCU (R33-2008-000-10044-0), MEST, Korea under Basic Science Research Program (2011-0012216), MKE/KEIT, Korea under the IT R&D program [KI001810041244, SmartTV 2.0 Software Platform], NRF of Korea under the project of Global Ph.D. Fellowship, and MKE, Korea under ITRC NIPA-2011-(C1090-1121-0008).

References

[1] I. F. Akyildiz, W. Su, Y. Sankarasubramaniam, and E. Cayirci, "A survey on sensor networks," *IEEE Communications Magazine*, vol. 40, no. 8, pp. 102–105, 2002.

[2] U. Lee, B. Zhou, M. Gerla, E. Magistretti, P. Bellavista, and A. Corradi, "Mobeyes: smart mobs for urban monitoring with a vehicular sensor network," *IEEE Wireless Communications*, vol. 13, no. 5, pp. 52–57, 2006.

[3] M. J. McGlynn and S. A. Borbash, "Birthday protocols for low energy deployment and flexible neighbor discovery in ad hoc wireless networks," in *Proceedings of the ACM International Symposium on Mobile Ad Hoc Networking and Computing (MobiHoc '01)*, pp. 137–145, Long Beach, Calif, USA, October 2001.

[4] F. Santos, L. Almeida, P. Pedreiras, and T. Facchinetti, "An adaptive TDMA protocol for soft real-time wireless communication among mobile autonomous agents," in *Proceedings of the Workshop on Architectures for Cooperative Embedded Real-Time Systems (WACERTS '04) in Conjunction with the 25th IEEE International Real-Time Systems Symposium (IEEE RTSS '04)*, Lisbon, Portugal, December 2004.

[5] F. Santos, L. Almeida, and L. S. Lopes, "Self-configuration of an adaptive TDMA wireless communication protocol for teams of mobile robots," in *Proceedings of the 13th IEEE International Conference on Emerging Technologies and Factory Automation (ETFA '08)*, pp. 1197–1204, Hamburg, Germany, September 2008.

[6] J. Arai, A. Koyama, and L. Barolli, "Performance analysis of an adaptive medium access control protocol for robot communication," in *Proceedings of the 11th International Conference on Parallel and Distributed Systems Workshops (ICPADS '05)*, pp. 210–216, Fukuoka, Japan, July 2005.

[7] G. Bianchi and I. Tinnirello, "Kalman filter estimation of the number of competing terminals in an IEEE 802.11 network," in *Proceedings of the 22nd Annual Joint Conference of the IEEE Computer and Communications Societies (INFOCOM '03)*, vol. 2, pp. 844–852, San Francisco, Calif, USA, March 2003.

[8] G. Bianchi, "Performance analysis of the IEEE 802.11 distributed coordination function," *IEEE Journal on Selected Areas in Communications*, vol. 18, no. 3, pp. 535–547, 2000.

[9] K. Kim, H. Roh, and W. Lee, "Minimizing the joining delay for cooperation in mobile robot networks," in *Proceedings of the 2nd IEEE International Conference on Ubiquitous and Future Networks (ICUFN '10)*, pp. 139–144, Jeju Island, Korea, June 2010.

16

Intelligent Analysis for Georeferenced Video Using Context-Based Random Graphs

Jiangfan Feng and Hu Song

College of Computer Science and Technology, Chongqing University of Posts and Telecommunications, Chongqing 400065, China

Correspondence should be addressed to Jiangfan Feng; fengjf@cqupt.edu.cn

Academic Editor: Javier Bajo

Video sensor networks are formed by the joining of heterogeneous sensor nodes, which is frequently reported as video of communication functionally bound to geographical locations. Decomposition of georeferenced video stream presents the expression of video from spatial feature set. Although it has been studied extensively, spatial relations underlying the scenario are not well understood, which are important to understand the semantics of georeferenced video and behavior of elements. Here we propose a method of mapping georeferenced video sequences for geographical scenes and use contextual random graphs to investigate semantic knowledge of georeferenced video, leading to correlation analysis of the target motion elements in the georeferenced video stream. We have used the connections of motion elements, both the correlation and continuity, to present a dynamic structure in time series that reveals clues to the event development of the video stream. Furthermore, we have provided a method for the effective integration of semantic and campaign information. Ultimately, the experimental results show that the provided method offers a better description of georeferenced video elements that cannot be achieved with existing schemes. In addition, it offers a new way of thinking for the semantic description of the georeferenced video scenarios.

1. Introduction

The notion of wireless multimedia sensor networks (WMSNs) is frequently reported as the convergence between the concepts of wireless sensor networks and distributed smart cameras [1]. As a result, an increasing number of video clips is being collected, which has created complex data-handling challenges [2]. Further, some types of video data are naturally tied to geographical locations. For example, video data from traffic monitoring may not contain much meaning without its associated location information. Therefore, most potential applications of a WMSN require the sensor network paradigm to support location-based multimedia services as well as manipulate large scale data at the same time to provide a high quality of experience (QoE), which raises an important issue. How to investigate an intelligent processing method for georeferenced multimedia? Although the question has been extensively addressed theoretically, the method of mapping video sequences to geographical scenes remains to be described. On the other hand, with the growth of geographic information system (GIS) whose major growth area is

the convergence between GIS and multimedia technology, a new paradigm named video-GIS emerged [3–5]. The major researches facing video-GIS are the coding of georeferenced video and the content and types of services that should be provided by georeferenced video. Further improvement of these processes is contingent on deeper understanding of video, as well as improved understanding of the spatial relationship of geographic space. It is due to the necessity of using video-GIS to visualize the relationship between the video analysis methods and the real geographical scene, resulting in georeferenced multimedia intelligent processing method based on context-based random graphs.

Georeferenced video is fundamental process in video-GIS development. Prior research activities on georeferenced video technologies and applications have been conducted. Most of them make use of video and GPS sensors. In [6, 7], Stefanakis and Peterson and Klamma et al. proposed a unified framework for hypermedia and GIS. Pissinou et al. [8] explored topology and direction under the proposed georeferenced video. The work of Hwang et al. and Joo et al. [9, 10] defined the metadata of georeferenced video, which support interoperability between GIS and video images. In the field of georeferenced video search, Liu et al. [11] presented a sensor-enhanced video annotation system, which searches video clips for the appearance of particular objects. Ay et al. proposed the use of geographical properties of videos [12], while Wang gave a method of time-spatial images to extract the basic movement information [13]. Although single media have been studied extensively, its semantics in geographic space are poorly understood. How to determine the spatial relationship of video elements is one of the most important operations on georeferenced video. For instance, a moving video element changes its position, shape, size, speed, and attribute values over time. Understanding the changing process and rules of these attributes is of important significance to the geographical description of the video.

Many techniques for video event recognition have been proposed. As the work on model-driven methodology which has become well established and approached maturity, the most common and popular conceptualization of fusion systems is the SVM model [14, 15]. However, such methodology not only cannot solve the problems, such as multi-instance, diversity, and multimodal, but needs a large number of training samples. Most previous studies to date have used data-driven method [16] which has been carefully designed to signal clear and distinct semantic of the videos [17–21]. In our event recognition application, we observe that some events may share common motion patterns. Though involved in pattern discovery, data-driven method also contributes to social network during pattern discovery [22–25]. These works have showed a high accuracy in the differentiating of video and its semantic extraction frame. However, most multimedia applications are unknown and uncertain, which are extremely difficult to meet the requirements of real-time stream processing.

Previous studies have shown that multimedia intelligent processing method is important to the development of video-GIS and have achieved inspiring progress. However, these solution methods have suffered from the classical ensemble average limitation presented by the analysis of low-level characteristics. Therefore, the spatial data gathered are sometimes inconclusive and, in part, contradictory. These algorithms usually build or learn a model of the target object first and then use it for tracking, without adapting the model to account for the changes in the appearance of the object, for example, large variation of pose or facial expression, or the surroundings, for example, lighting variation. Furthermore, it is assumed that all images are acquired with a stationary camera. Such approach, in our view, is prone to performance instability, and thus it needs to be addressed when building a robust visual tracker.

To overcome these problems, we will begin by looking at some valid models, which are suitable for georeferenced video understanding and behavior analysis. In this paper, we propose a new event recognition framework for consumer videos by leveraging a large amount of videos. As we know, graph structure provides a complex, dynamic, and robust framework for assembling complex relationships involved in the objects [26], which is suitable for our goal. Thus, multiple random behaviors are presented in certain movement,

making the graph structure unsuitable for describing the real video scenario. To circumvent this problem, random graph model has been taken into consideration, which can be seen as a rather simplified model of the evolution of certain communication net [27]. In our research, it could simplify the analysis of the interaction between video objects substantially for revealing the new insight into the relationships between objects and its complex interaction. Our analysis focuses on describing spatial relationships bound to objects using random graph grammar in georeferenced video, developing a scientific analysis of behavior and structured methods of georeferenced video understanding.

2. Preliminary

Surveillance video data is mostly non-ortho image data so that it does not match up with the geography scene vector data using the traditional method. To solve this problem, a mapping method of video scene imaging data to geography scene vector data is adopted in the paper, as showed in Figure 1. Firstly, the virtual viewpoint camera is constructed by the camera interior and exterior parameters. Secondly, geography scene virtual imaging can be gained from geography scene vector data using the process of model transformation, viewpoint transformation, and pruning according to the computer graphics rendering process, with the corresponding relationship between an object in virtual imaging and vector object. Thirdly, the image matching technology based on the features that have invariant character for translation, scale and rotation is used to match the geography scene virtual imaging and video image. Finally, the corresponding relationship between video image and vector data is established using that between an object in virtual imaging and vector object, with the purpose of accomplishing the mapping of video scene to objects in geography scene.

In the following part, we will introduce several preliminary key steps.

2.1. Selection Algorithm of Multicamera Based on Spatial Correlation and Target Priority. Multicamera surveillance system should not only gain detecting and tracking information of motion element of the single camera, but also make the coherent dynamic scene description using all the observations to some extent. Meanwhile, every motion element could be tracked by cameras simultaneously. How to select cameras for tracking a specific target is particularly important in video sensor networks. Based on the spatial correlation [28] and target priority, the paper proposes a selection algorithm of multicamera with task allocation optimized to achieve the automatic selection according to the target priority at each moment.

The algorithm is based on the assumption that a camera with no task carries out the basic single camera tracking which has lower power consumption, and the high-priority task could be preempted when bending. The selection algorithm of multicamera is shown as in Algorithm 1.

The set of images $I = \{I_1, I_2, \ldots, I_N\}$ is observed by these N cameras, and S denotes the set of cameras selected.

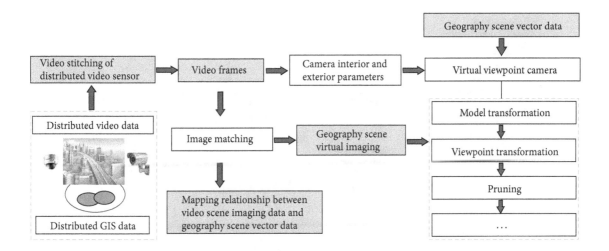

FIGURE 1: Process of the mapping relationship of video scene imaging data to geography scene vector data based on virtual viewpoint.

(1) *begin*
(2) $S = \phi$, $I = \{I_1, I_2, \ldots, I_N\}$, $P_N = P_0$, $\rho(I_i, I_j) = \rho_{ij}$.
(3) *Find* $(I_i, I_j) = \arg \min_{I_i, I_j \in I} \{\rho(I_i, I_j)\}$.
(4) *Add corresponding* I_i, I_j *to* S. $\{$Count $= 2\}$
(5) *for each* $k \in$ Count
(6)   *for each* $(I_{\mathrm{tmp}} \in I$, $I_{\mathrm{tmp}} \notin S)$ *or* $(I_{\mathrm{tmp}} \in I$, $I_{\mathrm{tmp}} \in S, P_{\mathrm{next}} > P_{\mathrm{curr}})$ *do*
(7) $\rho(I_{\mathrm{tmp}}, S) = \max_{I_p \in S} \{\rho(I_{\mathrm{tmp}}, I_p)\}$
(8)   *end for*
(9) $I_{\min} = \arg \min_{I_m \in I, I_m \notin S} \{\rho(I_m, S)\}$.
(10)   *add* $I_{\min}$ *to* S.
(11) *end for*
(12) *return* $S \subseteq \{I_1, I_2, \ldots, I_{\mathrm{Count}}\}$
(13) *end*

ALGORITHM 1: Selection of multicamera based on spatial correlation and target priority.

ρ_{ij} is correlation coefficient of the two images I_i and I_j. The larger the correlation coefficient, the more correlated the two images. In step 6, P denotes the task priority with a default value P_0, which can be marked manually by monitoring person. It assigns cameras to the motion element with high priority and coordinates cameras to track different targets based on spatial correlation and target priority.

2.2. Organization of Video and Location Data.

We have put forward a coding model of video-GIS that is comprised of video and camera's position in conjunction with its view direction and distance. Thus, the location data can be collected automatically by various small sensors to a camera, such as a GPS and a compass (see Figure 2). This eliminates manual work and allows the annotation process to be accurate and scalable. Therefore, we investigate the real-time collection, coding, and integration of video information and GPS information on the SEED-VPM642 platform, and finally we can obtain two different bit-rate location-based streaming media. The lower bit-rate one can be positioned to the wireless network broadcast live, and the higher one can be positioned to the hard disk storage.

In the coding of video-GIS, we need to calculate the three-dimensional coordinate of the video object [29]. As video-GIS coding based on mobile sensor cannot calculate single video frame by three-dimensional control field, the most effective way is using digital map and spatial geometrical relations (see Figure 3).

Therefore, the geometric relationship among GPS, posture sensor, imaging space, and object space should be built. It is assumed that the axis of imaging space x, y, z is parallel with that of object spatial X, Y, Z, respectively. Consider

$$R_G = R_{\mathrm{GPS}}(t) + R_{\mathrm{Att}}(t) \cdot \left[s_G \cdot R_C^{\mathrm{Att}} \cdot r_g^C(t) + r_{\mathrm{GPS}}^C \right]. \quad (1)$$

In detail, R_G is the coordinate vector of point G in the three-dimensional space. The coordinate function of GPS antenna in the given mapping frame is expressed as $R_{\mathrm{GPS}}(t)$. $R_{\mathrm{Att}}(t)$ represents the rotation matrix function while s_G represents the proportional relationship of image frame and object

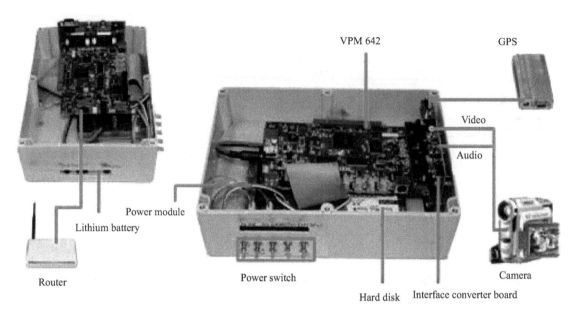

FIGURE 2: Experimental hardware and software to acquire georeferenced video.

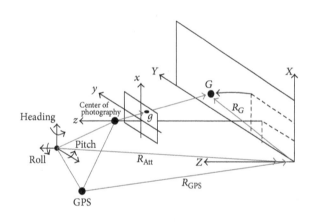

FIGURE 3: Geometry for calibrating multiple sensors.

TABLE 1: Sample of GPS and MIMU.

GPS
UTC 10:12:15 29.564 N 106.585E Alt 213.3 Meters
HPR
Heading 33.4   Pitch 0.5   Roll 1.3

(2) *angle direction elementary information:* including Heading, Pitch, and Roll.

2.3. Digital Map-Based Image Resolution. The features of digital maps are expressed by a two-dimensional plane on the vertical projection of the vector data. From the standpoint of this work, the video image is a raster data expression of the feature in the height direction of the information, and video image can also be expressed as the data format of the dotted line surface after the vector processing. Video images and digital map on the point, the line, and the corresponding expression of the surface can be shown at Table 2.

From the view of technology, we subject map-based image resolution to a three-dimensional measurement challenge and then use single-frame video images and digital map matching to define the changes in three steps. The first step is feature extraction of dense range image, which aims to extract the features of point and line. Under the premise of the full calibration to video frame, we can identify the particular characteristics of extracted target to meet the special requirement. For instance, the corners of building or telegraph pole as a fixed line characteristic for the expression of video image is perpendicular to the target. Once formulated, the second step is to combine the line characteristics into the characteristics of the surface using texture information. The third step is matching with digital map vector data. The contents include a variety of different

spatial. Boresight matrix R_C^{Att} means transformation relation between image frame and main framework of posture sensor. $r_g^C(t)$ represents the vector function of a g point in imaging spatial. And r_{GPS}^C is the excursion of the geometric center of GPS antenna and the camera lens.

For acquiring a more precise spatial locating information, we need to get the GPS information and attitude information generated by a posture sensor at least. Therefore, the spatial locating information is described by the combination of GPS and angle direction elementary (Heading, Pitch, and Roll), which obtained by Micro Inertial Measurement Unit (MIMU), as shown in Table 1.

As shown in Table 1, there are two kinds of the spatial locating information:

(1) *GPS information:* such as UTC time and longitude latitude;

TABLE 2: Correspondence between video images and digital map.

Image → Digital Map		Digital Map → Image	
Map Symbol	Map Object	Map Symbol	Image Object
Point	Point & line	Point	Point & line & Polygon
Line	Point & line & Polygon	Line	Point & line & Polygon
Polygon	Point & line & Polygon	Polygon	Line & Polygon

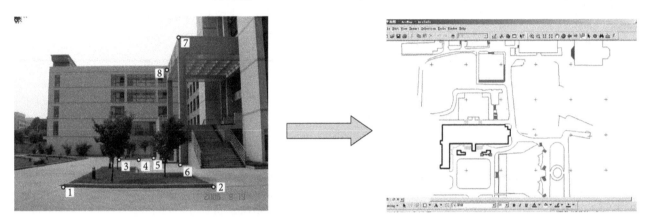

FIGURE 4: Mapping from Image to Digital Map.

matching points, points and lines, a line and a line, and the line and the plane between form and technique, which is shown in Figure 4.

3. Syntactic Structure

3.1. Syntactic Description of Motion Element. Video motion element mainly refers to the entity objects that could be identified clearly in visual and are important in morphology, such as pedestrians in video surveillance. The description methods of motion element are mainly based on color and texture at present, which is difficult to support the definition of motion element, behavior analysis, and behavior understanding. For a better description of the dynamic characteristic of the video motion element, the paper first gives a definition to some related concepts of motion element.

Definition 1. State. The *state* is an abstract of attributes owned by motion element and is a static description of the condition and activity of a motion element at a certain time. *State =* {*Appear, Move, Stop, Disappear*} indicates the basic state of any motion element within the scope of spatial constraint in a georeferenced video stream, including the description information of *Appear, Disappear, Move,* and *Stop.*

(a) Appear. The emerging motion element is newly appear and distinguished from the existing ones in the specific area of geographical boundary, and the state of which is called *Appear.* Then the motion element starts to be detected and tracked. *Appear* instance is regarded as the first instance of motion element.

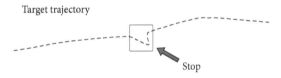

FIGURE 5: The definition of *Stop.*

(b) Disappear. In contrast with the *Appear* state definition, *Disappear* means the state of disappearance in the geographical boundary specific area or the untraceable state within a specific time, which is viewed as the last instance for the state description. *Disappear* state is the signal of canceling motion element detection and tracking.

(c) Stop. Stop S is defined on triple $S = (Area(S), \zeta_{\min}(S), \zeta_{\max}(S))$. Among them, $Area(S)$ means the spatial plane area, and $\zeta_{\min}(S)$ and $\zeta_{\max}(S)$ represent the maximum and minimum time threshold of *Stop,* respectively. And the particular movement or stay that without markedly changed of space coordinate information within a certain region are all viewed as motionless, which is shown in Figure 5.

(d) Move. Within the scope of spatial constraint, *Move M* is a general designation of connecting the other three basic states in a continuous motion process of motion element. An instance of *Move* can be represented as $M = (Appear \mid Stop_k, Stop_{k+1} \mid Disappear)$. By connecting the other three basic state instances, *Move* can form a linear sequence formed through the combination of *Appear, Stop,* and *Disappear.*

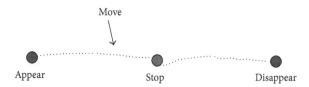

FIGURE 6: *Behavior* state sequence of motion element.

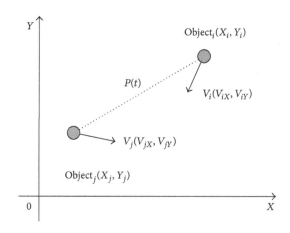

FIGURE 7: A diagram of interaction relation.

Definition 2. Behavior Attribute. Behavior description of a single typical motion element mainly includes spatial location and speed. Spatial location can be defined as *Location(Object)* = (X_i, Y_i, T_i), which means that the spatial location of the motion element *Object* at time point T_i is (X_i, Y_i), and X_i and Y_i represent the horizontal and vertical ordinate values in the two-dimensional plane, respectively. *Speed(Object)* = $\{S_{\text{Value}}, S_{\text{Vector}}, T_i\}$ indicates the motion element *Object* with velocity magnitude S_{Value} and velocity direction S_{Vector} at the time point T_i, among which S_{Vector} is the unit vector in a general planar domain.

Definition 3. Relation. *Relation* is an incidence relation of mutual influence between two motion elements in the same time subspace T. *Relation* = $(Object_i, Object_j, T)$ shows the relationship between motion element $Object_i$ and $Object_j$ in time subspace T which means one-dimensional time coordinates. The measurement of interaction established between the two elements uses probability P, which is dynamic adjustment with the influence of temporal-spatial factor, and $P \in [0, 1]$.

Definition 4. Spatial Relation. *Spatial Relation* includes measuring relation, direction relation, and topological relation. *Spatial Relation SR* = (*Measure, Direction, Topology*). *Measure* indicates the measuring relation among motion element using some measure in measuring space, such as distance. In the same planar reference domain, *Direction* is the equity mutual relationship between source target and reference target.

Definition 5. Visual Feature. In the georeferenced video stream, the visual characters of one motion element, including *color*, *texture*, and *shape*, will be dynamically changed with the time T. Therefore, the changes of visual characters of a motion element within the scope of spatial constraint should be described accurately [30]. And the visual characters mainly include *Color, Texture, Shape,* and *Size.* *Texture* can reflect the structure mode and gray space distribution formed by local pixels in motion element, while the low-level features can clearly define and describe the motion element.

3.2. Behavior and Interaction of Motion Element. In the georeferenced video stream, *Behavior* of the motion element within the specific scope of spatial constraint represents the behavior state sequence, as shown in Figure 6. Let the state set of *Behavior* be a *BehaviorState*, and the typical element is τ with the definition as follows:

$$\tau ::= Appear \mid Move \mid Stop \mid Disappear; \qquad (2)$$

among them, *Appear, Disappear, Move,* and *Stop* indicate the four basic states of motion element, respectively.

As one of the expression forms of motion element in the video stream, *Interaction* represents the mutual influence or joint action caused during the course of the *Relation* of two behavior state instance. The necessary condition for establishing the interaction relationship is the two incidence relation between the two behavior state instances that exist at the same time. It can be defined as five-meshes

$$Interaction = \{Object, BehaviorState, SR, T, Rule\}. \quad (3)$$

Under the influence of temporal subspace T and *spatial relation SR*, *Interaction* is the description of mutual influence between motion element $Object_i$ and $Object_j$. Behavior state of *Object* can be any state instance in the *BehaviorState* collection, and interaction production rule and interaction optimization update rule are involved in *Rule*. Therefore, the measuring of interaction has two influence factors, temporal and spatial factors.

Due to the close correlation of spatial relation at any time point T_{i+1} and former T_i, the spatial relation at T_{i+1} is always closely related to that at former time point T_i. Thus, the spatial relation evolution process among motion elements can be defined as a Markov chain in the temporal subspace T, with its evolution having Markov quality

$$P_T \{G_{t+1} \mid G_t, G_{t-1}, \dots, G_0\} = P_T \{G_{t+1} \mid G_t\}. \quad (4)$$

Meanwhile, the measuring value P of interaction between the two motion element established *Relation* can be computed based on the planar spatial distance *Distance*, velocity magnitude, and direction angle, including the current topology at time point T_t, as shown in Figure 7.

In the georeferenced video stream, the dynamic update function of interaction relation within the scope of spatial constraint is shown as follows:

$$P(t+1)$$
$$= \text{Min}\left[1, \text{Max}\left(0, \sqrt{P^2(t) + \omega(t+1) \times \eta(1-c(t))}\right)\right]. \tag{5}$$

Among them, $P(t)$ represents the interaction relation measuring value between a certain motion element and others, with the range of $P \in [0, 1]$. The higher value indicates the more hospitable relationship. When the interaction is established by behavior state instances, the initial value works as $P(0) = \rho_1 \times Distance(i, j) + \rho_2 \times \theta(i, j)$. $\omega(t)$ indicates the duration of interaction relation with the current state, and the dynamic change of c parameter is shown as follows:

$$c(t+1) = c(t) + a \times \frac{D_{t+1}}{D_t} \times \left(1 - \left|\frac{\omega(t+1)+1}{2} - P(t)\right|\right)$$
$$\times \min[c(t), 1 - c(t)]; \tag{6}$$

$c(t)$ represents a new confidence level while α learning rate. $\min(c, 1 - c)$ ensures parameter $c(t) \in [0, 1]$.

4. Semantics and Formalization of Georeferenced Video

For the accurate description and behavior understanding of motion elements in the georeferenced video stream, the paper proposes an analysis method based on sparse random graphs with the purpose of observing the character evolution with time and presents an indicating and measuring method of video motion element with dynamic topology structure information based on context-sensitive sparse random graph grammar.

4.1. Formalization of Georeferenced Video. Random graph $G = (V, E, \Omega)$ is defined on triple, while the edge set E of graph G with the vertex set V is defined in probabilistic spaces Ω. Consider

$$P(e_{ij} \in E) = P_{ij}, \quad P_{ij} \in (0, 1), \quad \sum P_{ij} = 1. \tag{7}$$

Each edge of random graph G is mutually independent; namely, any two vertexes that established incidence relation connected independently with probability P. As the spatial relation will be dynamically changed during the movement with the time factor, it is necessary to describe the motion state and interaction relationships within specific spatial area using random graph. Context-sensitive sparse random graph grammar can be defined as five-meshes

$$G = (S, V_N, R, \delta, Ch). \tag{8}$$

Among them, S is the root vertex that an initial vertex of semantic event in the georeferenced video stream. There is only one S vertex in the video event sequence. *Vertex* $V_N = \{V_1, V_2, V_3, \ldots\}$ involves all the motion elements emerged in the specific spatial area. R in the formula means the evolution process and rule of random graph G while δ the state transition functions. The cohesion of random subgraph Ch indicates the inner coupling degree of motion element group.

The motion element vertex of random graph can be defined as follows:

$$V_i = (index, Time, State, Location,$$
$$Speed, Interaction, SR, VF). \tag{9}$$

It shows the motion status and interaction information of a motion element V_i labeled index at the time point *Time*. Among them, *Location* and *Speed* represent the position coordinate and the velocity of motion element V_i in the planar area, respectively. *Interaction* is the description of interaction while $SR = (Measure, Direction, Topology)$ the spatial relation existed in the motion element. *Virtual feature VF* shows low-level features information of a motion element including *Color*, *Shape*, and *Size* at the time point *Time*. $State = \{Appear, Move, Stop, Disappear\}$ is the basic state of motion element.

4.2. Evolution Rule. As a posterior method, dynamic process of motion elements in the video stream can be visually described and showed based on sparse random graph. The temporal and spatial evolution model of motion element is able to describe the basic character and dynamic process of spatial relation accurately. The essence of dynamic evolution process of sparse random graph is the continuous transition process of state space in random graphs.

Therefore, the state transition function of sparse random graph can be defined as a mapping relation

$$\delta = \Theta \longrightarrow \Theta. \tag{10}$$

Among them, Θ is the state space of sparse random graph, $\Theta = (d_1, d_2, \ldots, d_n)^T$, and d is a variable in state region.

The dynamic evolution process of sparse random graph includes its character update of motion element vertex V_N, emerging vertex with the *Appear* and *Disappear* behavior states, and the dynamic adjustment of edge set E and interaction relation P of random graphs. For the accurate description of event development process in georeferenced video stream, evolution rule algorithm of sparse random graph is shown in Algorithm 2.

We can get the corresponding dynamic evolution model of sparse random graph using the evolution rule algorithm. Step (2) in the algorithm shows the creating and adding root vertex S, and $G_0 = (V_0, E_0) := (\{S\}, \emptyset)$. Adding a new motion element vertex V_{tmp} in sparse random graph G_{Active} is in step (5) while deleting the vanish vertex V_i and its association edge in step (11). Among them, function $getRestriction(V_j)$ in step (18) and $getAttract(V_j)$ in step (20) indicate whether it can delete or add the edge that vertex V_j associated, respectively. Step (27) accomplishes the dynamic update of interaction relation P in sparse random graph G_{Active}.

Input: sparse random graph G_{Active}, motion element
detection and recognition information;
Output: return G_{Active};
(1) IF $t = 0$ Then
(2)   Create first node S & Add S to V_N;
(3) End IF
(4) While $t \geq 1$ do
(5)   IF $V_{\text{tmp}} \rightarrow$ State Is Equal *Appear* Then
(6)   Find nearest node V_{near};
(7)   Create new edge $E(V_{\text{tmp}}, V_{\text{near}})$;
(8)   Add V_{tmp} to V_N;
(9)   End IF
(10)   For $V_i \in V_N$ do   //Update all Nodes in G_{Active}
(11)   IF $V_i \rightarrow$ State Is Equal *Disappear* Then
(12)   Remove V_i from V_N;
(13)   Delete edge of V_i in G_{Active};
(14)   End IF
(15)   Update V_i;
(16)   End For
(17)   For $V_j \in V_N$ do   //Update all Edges in G_{Active}
(18)   IF *Flag* $\leftarrow$ getRestriction(V_j) Then
(19)   Delete edge of V_j in G_{Active};
(20)   Else IF *Flag* $\leftarrow$ getAttract(V_j) Then
(21)   Add new edge of V_j to G_{Active};
(22)   End IF
(23)   End For
(24)   For $V_k \in V_N$ do   //Update P of Graph in G_{Active}
(25)   IF $V_k \rightarrow$ State Is Equal *Appear* Then
(26) $P \leftarrow P(0)$;
(27)   Else Update other P of G_{Active};
(28)   End IF
(29)   End For
(30) Return G_{Active};

ALGORITHM 2: Evolution rule algorithm of sparse random graph.

4.3. Random Subgraph.

4.3. Random Subgraph. Cohesion of random subgraph refers to the close relation of motion element. To measuring close relation, the paper introduces the concept of structural entropy. As a measuring method of messiness and randomness of the state, structure entropy is related closely to the compactness of random subgraph. The higher the compactness is, the lower the structure entropy value will be.

If vertexes V_i and V_j have close correlation with each other, then $P(V_i, V_j) = P(t)$. Let $N(i) = \sum_{j=1}^{n} P(V_i, V_j)$, associative strength $\xi(i) = N(i)/\sum_{j=1}^{n} N(j)$. The structure entropy of random subgraph is $H = \sum_{i=1}^{n} \xi(i) \ln \xi(i)$, and $\sum_{i=1}^{n} \xi(i) = 1$. Therefore, the Cohesion of random subgraph is $Ch(G') = -\sum_{j=1}^{n} (N(j)/n) \times (\xi(i) \ln \xi(i)/ \ln n)$, with $Ch(G') \subseteq [0, 1]$.

4.4. Early Warning of Video Event. Using the numerical calculation method of interaction relationship, abnormal behavior and emergency in video can be distinguished based on random graph grammar, and the possible special situation can be early warned. There are two different threat levels

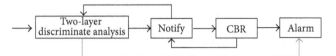

FIGURE 8: Notify and Alarm processing of video event.

generated by video event: notify and alarm, which is shown in Figure 8.

The paper is mainly to detect the unexpected crowd incident and conflict in the massive video events and proposes a novel two-layer discriminate method, which consists of individual attribute layer and group attribute layer. Once occurring video abnormal event, the corresponding real-time status of random graph must be described, which can be expressed as follows.

(1) Individual Attribute Layer. The owned velocity of multiple random graph nodes has modified radically in per unit of time T, and the relevant movement direction has also changed significantly.

Specifically speaking, the detection and selection of variation range or interval of movement attributes in random graph can use sliding window. In the continuous movement attribute value $V = \{V_1, V_2, \ldots, V_n\}$ in time series, V_1 exists before the emergence of V_2, while V_2 exists before V_3. The difference is obtained by the two continuous attribute values. In the paper, the data in the sliding interval ΔT is viewed as the discriminative and forecasting sample, when the continuous difference $D(V_i, V_j, T)$ is larger than the given threshold, and the sliding intervals ΔT is within the max time threshold. Otherwise, recalibrate over the entire sliding intervals for new computation.

(2) Group Attribute Layer. The multiple interaction and distance values among random graph nodes in groups fluctuate greatly, or the multiple numerical variations of interaction relationship in random subgraph are changed significantly. The discriminant analysis of video abnormal event is achieved according to the check whether the change rate of parameter value $\vec{r}$ is greater than the given threshold $pThreh$, as

$$\vec{r} = \frac{dp}{dt} \geq pThreh. \tag{11}$$

Once either circumstance occurred, it must be entering the next notify phase.

When entering the notify discriminative phase, the random subgraph showing diffusion or flocking status makes numerical calculation. Using the computing method of structure entropy value, the corresponding random subgraph status is measured, and the entropy value $Ch(G')$ is viewed as the warning degree of video abnormal behavior and emergency. With regard to different levels of urgency and security, the warning degree $Warning(t)$ is set to different threshold intervals as follows:

$$Warning\,(t) = Ch\left(G'\right) = -\sum_{j=1}^{n} \frac{N\,(j)}{n} \times \frac{\xi\,(i) \ln \xi\,(i)}{\ln n}. \tag{12}$$

The warning degree $Warning(t)$ is divided into three warning threshold intervals in the paper, which are Warning1, Warning2, and Warning3. Specifically, Warning1 indicates the early warning degree, which means that video abnormal event will be occurred in the next unit time and the discriminative module obtains alertness. Warning2 shows the probable warning degree and is the identifying processing transformed into the CBR phase. If the entropy value of random subgraph is greater than the max value of given threshold interval, the CBR discrimination phase works. Based on the video event features, the traditional CBR method is used to further identification. Warning3 expresses the confirmed warning degree, which can enter the Alarm phase of video abnormal event directly without the traditional CBR method.

The discriminate method based on the random graph is defined as graph-based reasoning (GBR) in the paper, while the improved GBR fused with traditional CBR method is GBR-C. The intelligent analysis for different video scenes plays an important role in the real-time detection of video abnormal behaviors and mass incidents. The instantaneous status information of video motion element is integrated with the random graph model and summarizes the random subgraph patterns and behavior rules with a statistical description. In violation of the behavior regularity of common video events, it is a latent exceptional event, and extracts the features of video motion elements involved which are recorded in object layer stream for the efficient retrieval of content-based video.

5. Experiment and Analysis

In order to verify the feasibility and availability of the proposed framework, space information of a motion element is extracted at real-time based on the detection and tracking [31, 32]. According to the dynamic change situation of space semantics, a timing description method using random graph grammar depicts the event development of video stream clearly.

5.1. Interaction Description. Interaction is the mutual incidence relation among motion element. For the accurate description of the dynamic change process of interaction relation, interaction P should be calculated real-time based on the spatial information in experimental video including planar spatial distance, velocity magnitude, and direction angle. And the calculation results of real-time interaction update function $P(t)$ of the video clip trim from frame 550 to frame 685 is shown in Figure 9.

In Figure 9, function P_1 shows a changing trend of increasing first and then decreasing gradually in the video clip. The minimum value of interaction P_1 is at frame 685 with the value 0.11 while the maximum is at frame 586 with the value 0.38. And function P_2 indicates the changing process of two close targets. The minimum value of P_2 is at frame 592 with the value 0.23 while the maximum is at frame 685 with the value 0.79. The increasing planar spatial distance $Distance$ and motion direction variation of two motion elements make the decreasing interaction value. On the contrary, as the planar spatial distance decreases and the duration of interaction continues to increase, interaction value P increases gradually.

The previous results show that it can accurately depict the dynamic varying changes of the interaction relation of video motion elements. However, the accurate depiction is an indispensable premise for the description of the georeferenced video stream.

5.2. Georeferenced Video Stream Description. Based on the richer spatial semantic of motion elements in the georeferenced video stream, we can realize the intelligent parsing of georeferenced video content using context-sensitive sparse random graph grammar. The spatial relationship of motion elements in image space is transformed to that of object space, and the motion status and interaction relation can be depicted using random graph. The continuous transition process of inner state space in random graph is enforced with the dynamic evolution process of sparse random graph.

With the spatial reference data, the sparse random graph evolution processing based on the monitoring target is achieved. And the consecutive people emerged within the video surveillance range are labeled as A, B, C, and D which are shown in Figure 10. As soon as the moving object appears, a new random graph node will express it; when it leaves the surveillance confine, the corresponding node will disappear while the edge set constituted by the interaction that associated with the node is set to null. Using our video test data, the evolutionary process and timing evolving description diagram of the video clip trim from frame 1041 to frame 1712 is shown in Figure 10.

We can see that the timing evolving description diagram can be constructed by the automatic intelligent analysis and calculation of a video clip, and it verifies the correctness and effectiveness of the evolution rule algorithm of sparse random graph. Within the scope of the specific geographical space, the time-varying attributes of random graph nodes are visual displayed, such as behavior state, spatial location, and movement parameter. And the basis recorded information of each video motion element is shown in Algorithm 3.

Among them, the basic information consists of attribute information, spatial location information, and other movement parameter, which are shown in Algorithm 3. The attribute information $State$ indicates the behavior status of the video motion element with succinct expressional number 0, 1, 2 and 3, which are described respectively with the four basic behavior $state \{Appear, Disappear, Move, Stop\}$. And the interaction relationship attribute including the index of two elements, the numerical calculation value of interaction, and the relative spatial directions. The whole structural description of video motion element generated automatically is shown in Figure 11.

The automatically generated file mainly consists of two parts: the configuration data and content data. The movement status information about motion element $Object$ in the georeferenced video stream is described in detail in the content data part while the basic attribute information about testing video clip in configure data part. In the continuous period

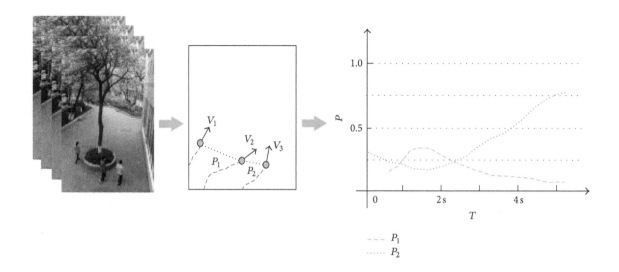

FIGURE 9: Dynamic change process of interaction relation.

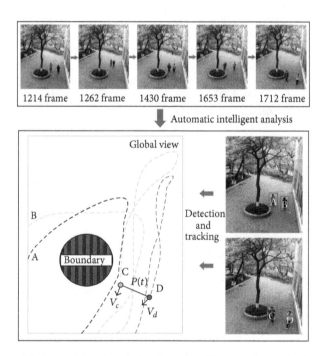

FIGURE 10: Timing evolving description diagram of the georeferenced video stream.

TABLE 3: Three test sample videos.

Test samples	Alarm types	Time (s)	Scenes number
A	Cross-border	372	18
B	Flocking	1423	42
C	Conflict	588	27

of time series, movement status information of each motion element including the behavior state sequence, real-time spatial location information, and the statistical information about interaction relation can be queried directly from the XML file. It also provides a novel simple nonlinear indexing for the understanding and description of video content.

5.3. Performance of Video Event Warning. To validate the proposed early warning method of video abnormal behavior and emergency, we analyzed the performance of various attributes using the video test data which involves a crowd video scene. Experimental analysis mainly contains the real-time warning entropy value of random subgraph, warning degree, and real-time changes of corresponding subgraph node number and

```
<?xml version="1.0" encoding="UTF-8"?>
<SRG>
    <configData>
        <descriptor name="VideoMotionInfo" type="FILE">
            <attribute Medianame="TrackElement_Session_1"></attribute>
            <attribute FrameCount="76283" FPS="30" ></attribute>
            <attribute CamGPS="GPS" UTC="10:12:15" LAT="29.564" LON="106.585"></attribute>
            <attribute CamMIMU="HRP" Heading="33.4" Pitch="0.5" Roll="1.3"></attribute>
        </descriptor>
        <descriptor name="IMGLOCTInfo" type="LOCAT">
            <attribute ReferPoint="0" PixelX="359" PixelY="251" LocatX="582" LocatY="870" ></attribute>
            <attribute ReferPoint="UL" PixelX="184" PixelY="104" LocatX="0" LocatY="0" ></attribute>
            <attribute ReferPoint="UR" PixelX="346" PixelY="142" LocatX="580" LocatY="291" ></attribute>
            <attribute ReferPoint="DL" PixelX="240" PixelY="337" LocatX="289" LocatY="1164" ></attribute>
            <attribute ReferPoint="DR" PixelX="612" PixelY="321" LocatX="1160" LocatY="1162" ></attribute>
        </descriptor>
    </configData>
    <ContentData>
        <object framespan="1:1500">
            <attribute name="MotionElement">
                ...... ......
                <index="17" State="2" frame="302" timeDelay= 302 PixelX="212" PixelY="171"
                    LoctX="160" LoctY="486" DeltX="0.43" DeltY="0.29" Speed="(0.43,0.29)"
                    InteractionNum="1" Interaction="{(18,17, NE, 0.42)}" VF="0" Other="0"/>
                <index="18" State="2" frame="302" timeDelay= 302 PixelX="374" PixelY="259"
                    LoctX="606" LoctY="898" DeltX="0.33" DeltY="0.72" Speed="(0.33,0.72)"
                    InteractionNum="1" Interaction="{(17,18, SW, 0.42)}" VF="0" Other="0"/>
                ...... ......
            </attribute>
        </object>
        <object framespan="1501:3000">
            <attribute name="MotionElement">
                ...... ......
            </attribute>
        </object>
    </ContentData>
</SRG>
```

FIGURE 11: Structural description of video motion feature.

the total graph node number, which are shown, respectively, in Figure 12. And the horizontal axis indicates the video running time with 10 seconds as a scale unit.

As can be seen from the previous illustration, the warning entropy value of real-time random subgraph using the computing method of structure entropy value is due to random fluctuations in Figure 12(a). According to the warning degree of video abnormal behavior and emergency, three different warning threshold intervals are set in our test. And the Warning2 degree occurred between 252 and 270 seconds shown in Figure 12(b). The Warning1 indicates the early warning degree in most of the time, which means that video abnormal event will be emerged. Figure 12(c) shows the real-time nodes number of random subgraph in the video surveillance scope while Figure 12(d) shows the total graph node number.

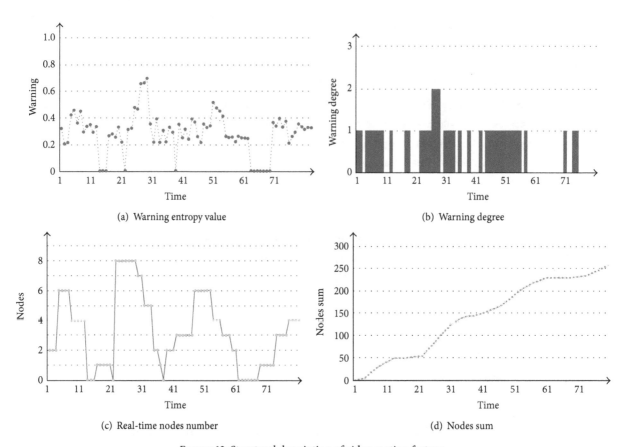

(a) Warning entropy value

(b) Warning degree

(c) Real-time nodes number

(d) Nodes sum

FIGURE 12: Structural description of video motion feature.

```
⟨attribute name="MotionElement"⟩
    ⟨index="63"                                  //Sequence Number
     State="2"                                   //Behavior State
     frame="612"                                 //Current Frame Number
     timeDelay="612"                             //Duration
     PixelX="198" PixelY="211"                   //Image Space Coordinate
     LoctX="45" LoctY="60"                       //Object Space Coordinate
     DeltX="0.85" DeltY="0.24"                   //Relative Distance
     Speed="(0.85, 0.24)"                        //Speed
     InteractionNum="1"                          //Interaction Relationship Number
     Interaction="{(64, 63, NE, 0.51)}"          //Interaction Relationship
                                                 //(Objecti, Objectj, Direction, P(t))

     VF="0"
     Other="0"/⟩
⟨/attribute⟩
```

ALGORITHM 3: Basic information of each video motion element.

5.4. Performance Comparisons of Intelligent Analysis Methods. In this section, we compare the proposed method with other methods, such as the Coarse-Grained SVM, Fine-Grained SVM [15], and MKL [19]. Using the three sample videos (Table 3) which involve some events that contain a group of people interact with each other, we carry out the comparison study. And all the chosen samples are considered as the labeled training data within the target domain.

GBR accomplishes a concise numerical calculation and avoids the problems of computing complexity in the traditional CBR method. In Tables 4, 5, and 6, we compare the performance of GBR, GBR & CBR, with other methods using three different videos.

From Tables 4, 5, and 6, we observe that GBR extends the processing time in a common detection of video event, but the forecasting accuracy of video abnormal behavior and emergency increased significantly with lower computation

TABLE 4: Comparison of crossing sample A with different methods.

Method	Out-Detection	Correct-Detection	Omit-Detection	Time (s)
GBR	20	18	0	0.72
GBR (with CBR)	25	18	0	1.35
Coarse-grained SVM	40	16	2	1.47
Fine-grained SVM	26	15	3	1.21
MKL	30	16	2	1.50

TABLE 5: Comparison of flocking sample B with different methods.

Method	Out-Detection	Correct-Detection	Omit-Detection	Time (s)
GBR	48	35	7	2.74
GBR (with CBR)	51	39	3	4.33
Coarse-grained SVM	90	37	5	5.41
Fine-grained SVM	45	35	7	4.76
MKL	43	36	6	5.53

TABLE 6: Comparison of conflict sample C with different methods.

Method	Out-Detection	Correct-Detection	Omit-Detection	Time(s)
GBR	35	23	4	3.46
GBR (with CBR)	36	24	3	4.17
Coarse-grained SVM	53	24	3	3.90
Fine-grained SVM	37	21	6	3.54
MKL	40	22	5	3.95

and complexity. Therefore, the energy consumption of sensors will be reduced which is consistent with the transmission costs, especially in the nonrecurring flocking emergency with complex video event modeling.

6. Conclusion

In summary, findings from the present study are all based on low-level visual features, which mean that there was a shortage of spatial constraints and coupling analysis with geography environment. It is necessary to establish the relationship between video analysis method and the real geographical scene. A georeferenced video analysis method is proposed based on the context-based random graph. The data are obtained using a wireless network of environmental sensors scattered at the supervising area and a vision sensor monitoring the same geographical area. Experimental results prove that the proposed description method of georeferenced video using random graph is feasible and efficient. Through the intelligent parsing of the georeferenced video data stream, we can get a novel visual description method using random graph which can clearly depict the development clue of video scenes and also offer the possibility to browse the video stream quickly. Meanwhile, random graph can be used as an effective nonlinear indexing for the content-based video indexing and browsing application.

As a future work, we will propose the enhancement of the implemented algorithms with alternative combination rules and the fusion of audio and video to deal with the uncertainty, imprecision, and incompleteness of the underlying information. In addition, large amounts of data should be conducted to set various parameters, such as thresholds, false alarm rates, and fusion weights.

Acknowledgments

The work is supported by the National Natural Science Foundation of China (41101432 and 41201378), the Natural Science Foundation Project of Chongqing (CSTC 2010BB2416), and the Education Science and Technology Foundation of Chongqing (KJ120526).

References

[1] I. F. Akyildiz, T. Melodia, and K. R. Chowdhury, "A survey on wireless multimedia sensor networks," *Computer Networks*, vol. 51, no. 4, pp. 921–960, 2007.

[2] S. A. Ay, R. Zimmermann, and S. H. Kim, "Relevance ranking in georeferenced video search," *Multimedia Systems*, vol. 16, no. 2, pp. 105–125, 2010.

[3] T. Navarrete and J. Blat, "VideoGIS: segmenting and indexing video based on geographic information," in *Proceedings of*

the 5th AGILE Conference on Geographic Information Science, pp. 1–9, April 2002.

[4] C. Larouche, C. Laflamme, R. Lévesque, and R. Denis, "Videography in Canada: georeferenced aerial videography in erosion monitoring," *GIM International*, vol. 16, no. 9, pp. 46–49, 2002.

[5] N. Davies, K. Cheverst, K. Mitchell, and A. Efrat, "Using and determining location in a context-sensitive tour guide," *Computer*, vol. 34, no. 8, pp. 35–41, 2001.

[6] E. Stefanakis and M. Peterson, *Geographic Hypermedia: Concepts and Systems*, Lecture Notes in Geoinformation and Cartography, Springer, 2006.

[7] R. Klamma, M. Spaniol, M. Jarke, Y. Cao, M. Jansen, and G. Toubekis, "A hypermedia afghan sites and monuments database," *Geographic Hypermedia*, pp. 189–209, 2006.

[8] N. Pissinou, I. Radev, and K. Makki, "Spatio-temporal modeling in video and multimedia geographic information systems," *GeoInformatica*, vol. 5, no. 4, pp. 375–409, 2001.

[9] T. H. Hwang, K. H. Choi, I. H. Joo, and J. H. Lee, "MPEG-7 metadata for video-based GIS applications," in *Proceedings of the IEEE International Geoscience and Remote Sensing Symposium (IGARSS '03)*, vol. 6, pp. 3641–3643, July 2003.

[10] I. H. Joo, T. H. Hwang, and K. H. Choi, "Generation of video metadata supporting video-GIS integration," in *Proceedings of the International Conference on Image Processing (ICIP '04)*, vol. 3, pp. 1695–1698, October 2004.

[11] X. Liu, M. Corner, and P. Shenoy, "SEVA: sensor-enhanced video annotation," in *Proceedings of the 13th Annual ACM International Conference on Multimedia*, pp. 618–627, November 2005.

[12] S. A. Ay, R. Zimmermann, and S. H. Kim, "Relevance ranking in georeferenced video search," *Multimedia Systems*, vol. 16, no. 2, pp. 105–125, 2010.

[13] J. Wang and D. Yang, "A traffic parameters extraction method using time-spatial image based on multicameras," *International Journal of Distributed Sensor Networks*, vol. 2013, Article ID 108056, 17 pages, 2013.

[14] C. J. C. Burges, "A tutorial on support vector machines for pattern recognition," *Data Mining and Knowledge Discovery*, vol. 2, no. 2, pp. 121–167, 1998.

[15] Y. Zhuang, Z. Fu, Z. Ye, and F. Wu, "Real-time recognition of explosion scenes based on audio-visual hierarchical model," *Journal of Computer-Aided Design and Computer Graphics*, vol. 16, no. 1, pp. 90–97, 2004.

[16] B. Taskar, P. Abbeel, and D. Koller, "Discriminative probabilistic models for relational data," in *Proceedings of the 18th Conference on Uncertainty in Artificial Intelligence*, pp. 485–492, Morgan Kaufmann, 2002.

[17] C. Wang, L. Zhang, and H. J. Zhang, "Learning to reduce the semantic gap in web image retrieval and annotation," in *Proceedings of the 31st Annual International ACM SIGIR Conference on Research and Development in Information Retrieval*, pp. 355–362, July 2008.

[18] R. Fergus, Y. Weiss, and A. Torralba, "Semi-supervised learning in gigantic image collections," in *Proceedings of the Neural Information Processing Systems*, pp. 522–530, 2009.

[19] G. Mehmet and A. Ethem, "Multiple kernel learning algorithms," *Journal of Machine Learning Research*, vol. 12, pp. 2211–2268, 2011.

[20] J. Liu, J. Luo, and M. Shah, "Recognizing realistic actions from videos "in the Wild"," in *Proceedings of the IEEE Computer Society Conference on Computer Vision and Pattern Recognition Workshops*, pp. 1996–2003, June 2009.

[21] L. Duan, D. Xu, I. Tsang, and J. Luo, "Visual event recognition in videos by learning from web data," *IEEE Transactions on Pattern Analysis and Machine Intelligence*, vol. 34, no. 9, pp. 1667–1680, 2012.

[22] X. Jin, A. Gallagher, L. Cao, J. Luo, and J. Han, "The wisdom of social multimedia: using Flickr for prediction and forecast," in *Proceedings of the 18th ACM International Conference on Multimedia (MM '10)*, pp. 1235–1244, October 2010.

[23] M. Park, J. Luo, R. T. Collins, and Y. Liu, "Beyond GPS: determining the camera viewing direction of a geotagged image," in *Proceedings of the 18th ACM International Conference on Multimedia (MM '10)*, pp. 631–634, October 2010.

[24] L. Cao, J. Luo, A. Gallagher, X. Jin, J. Han, and T. S. Huang, "A worldwide tourism recommendation system based on geotagged web photos," in *Proceedings of the IEEE International Conference on Acoustics, Speech, and Signal Processing (ICASSP '10)*, pp. 2274–2277, March 2010.

[25] E. Gilbert and K. Karahalios, "Predicting tie strength with social media," in *Proceedings of the ACM SIGCHI Conference on Human Factors in Computing Systems*, pp. 211–220, April 2009.

[26] G. Yu, Y. Gu, and Y. B. Bao, "Large scale graph data processing on cloud computing environments," *Chinese Journal of Computers*, vol. 34, no. 10, pp. 1753–1767, 2011.

[27] R. Van Der Hofstad, *Random Evolution in Massive Graphs*, 2013.

[28] R. Dai and I. F. Akyildiz, "A spatial correlation model for visual information in wireless multimedia sensor networks," *IEEE Transactions on Multimedia*, vol. 11, no. 6, pp. 1148–1159, 2009.

[29] F. Jiangfan and S. Hu, "A data coding method of multimedia GIS in limited resource of mobile terminal," *Journal of Information & Computational Science*, vol. 9, no. 18, pp. 5873–5880, 2012.

[30] T. L. Le, M. Thonnat, A. Boucher, and F. Brémond, "Surveillance video indexing and retrieval using object features and semantic events," *International Journal of Pattern Recognition and Artificial Intelligence*, vol. 23, no. 7, pp. 1439–1476, 2009.

[31] T. Zhao and R. Nevatia, "Tracking multiple humans in crowded environment," in *Proceedings of the 2004 IEEE Computer Society Conference on Computer Vision and Pattern Recognition, CVPR 2004*, vol. 2, pp. II406–II413, July 2004.

[32] X. Y. Zhang, X. J. Wu, X. Zhou, X. G. Wang, and Y. Y. Zhang, "Automatic detection and tracking of maneuverable birds in videos," in *Proceedings of the International Conference on Computational Intelligence and Security (CIS '08)*, vol. 1, pp. 185–189, December 2008.

17

Towards Safety from Toxic Gases in Underground Mines Using Wireless Sensor Networks and Ambient Intelligence

Isaac O. Osunmakinde

Semantic Computing Group, School of Computing, College of Science, Engineering and Technology, University of South Africa, (UNISA), P.O. Box 392, Pretoria 0003, South Africa

Correspondence should be addressed to Isaac O. Osunmakinde; osunmakindeio@yahoo.com

Academic Editor: Andrea Acquaviva

The growing number of fatalities among miners caused by toxic gases puts pressure on the mining industry; innovative approaches are required to improve underground miners' health. Toxic gases are very often released in underground mines and cannot easily be detected by human senses. This paper investigates the presence of the inherent types of toxic fumes in critical regions and their suspension and trends in the air and intends to generate knowledge that will assist in preventing miners from contracting diseases. The development of intelligent decision support systems is still in its infancy. Knowledge of how to make them profitable in improving miners' safety is largely lacking. An autonomous remote monitoring framework of wireless sensor networks, which integrates mobile sensing and Ohm's law, coupled with ambient intelligence governing decision-making for miners, is developed. The framework has been investigated in indoor scenarios and successfully deployed for real-life application in an aeronautic engine test cell environment, such as those typically found in underground mines. Useful demonstrations of the system were carried out to provide similar knowledge to safeguard engineers from the inhalation of toxic gases. This provides early warning for safety agents. The system has proven to be suitable for deployment in underground mines.

1. Introduction

Efficient monitoring of concentrations of toxic gases in restricted areas, such as those typically found in mines, is regarded as a problem of special significance by the mining industry [1]. This challenge is significantly greater in an unstructured underground mining environment, such as a stope. A mine stope is formed as a result of repeatedly blasting hard rock from strategic sides with explosives. After mine blasting or other mining activities, such as drilling, construction, and barring, the underground terrains become restricted, unknown, unstructured, and particularly danger-ous owing to the presence of poisonous explosive gases. The mine gases are highly concentrated and toxic, become a threat to both miners' health and the environment, and also limit visibility.

Figure 1 shows an example of a buildup and explosion of toxic gases, such as methane (CH_4), nitrogen dioxide (NO_2), and hydrogen sulphide (H_2S) in an underground mine. The inhalation of an overlooked black damp in mines, which is a mixture of dust, carbon dioxide, and nitrogen [2], gradually overcomes and destroys the body's blood system, which may result in chronic diseases as a consequence of exposure to toxic gases. Research conducted in 2006 revealed a significantly elevated risk of leukaemia among German employees with a long occupational career in underground mines [1]. Several recent references to the incidence of mining-related diseases can be found in [3, 4].

It is therefore worth noting that, after blasting, miners currently have to wait outside the mines for a specified period of time for the poisonous gases/dust to dissipate. The question remains whether the gas/dust disappears completely in the air or merely reduces below that which the human nose can sense before miners enter the unsafe areas. Understanding of the density of the poisonous gases suspended in the air will assist in preventing miners from contracting dreaded diseases and is manifestly a sound basis for improving safety procedures in mines.

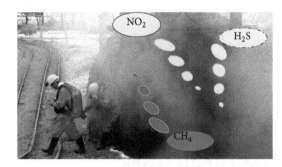

FIGURE 1: A sample underground mine explosion due to the buildup of toxic gases.

Predominant current efforts to monitor gas levels are focused on the use of [5] (i) lag/waiting time, (ii) mining ventilation, (iii) preparedness, and (iv) government regulations and agencies such as the Clean Air Act and Environmental Protection Agency in the USA. These promote activities that reduce air pollution. Each of these practices is successful for some environmental monitoring applications, but they require model intelligence. However, other efforts are being made to combat the problems of toxic fumes, such as the traditional fixed pollution monitoring stations measuring the air quality index, for example, the sophisticated equipment setups in Swansea [6] and in Ohio, USA [7]. They are highly sensitive and well calibrated, but the systems are operated with poor flexibility and expansibility, and the stations are expensive, which could be unaffordable for many developing mines and countries.

We seek a research solution to the deficiencies in the current monitoring approaches, which necessitate real-time sensing and decision-making through a wireless sensor network (WSN). WSNs are characterised by self-organisation, wireless communication, distributed, autonomous, and simple maintenance, which have applications in the research of environmental and underground monitoring systems [8]. This research focuses on making useful decisions on improving safety in restricted areas. The areas contain a roughly dynamic compartment whose sources of toxic gases have to be identified and remotely monitored for safety. Relatively little research has focused on providing methods for knowledge generation in WSNs that can support real-time collaborative decision-making on improving underground safety. The prevailing approaches often use structured query language- (SQL-) like primitives, and events are defined using a subevent list and confidence functions in SQL [9]. However, SQL is not appropriate for describing gas-sensing events in WSNs, as it (i) cannot capture data dependencies and interactions among different sensing scenarios, (ii) does not really support probability models, (iii) is inappropriate in describing complex temporal constraints and data dependencies, (iv) lacks the ability to support collaborative decision-making and triggers, and (v) does not facilitate any global analysis of the gas-sensing event system. In our previous research [10], a Bayesian belief network was used for environmental situation recognition in WSNs. The network was used in offline mode as a main representational structure

of a ubiquitous sensor network, which only uses qualitative analysis for intelligence. However, we believe that crisp values for qualitative knowledge cannot adequately handle the often imprecise sensor readings. In this paper we demonstrate that using both qualitative and quantitative reasoning in real time significantly improves the knowledge generated.

In mining environments, network routing efficiency in WSNs stands out as a pivotal factor [11] beside other research problems. Recently, modelling the complexities of underground tunnel communication systems has been a key focus and has been extensively studied in [12, 13]. Long-distance WSN in [14] was applied in a coal mine by building on an integrated mine network. It was proved that it is suitable for a mine environment. We have studied different existing real-world scenarios where WSNs are being applied. Based on this study we have discovered that there are significant commonalities, but we do not know of any methodology that (i) provides detail of implementation for industry reproducibility and (ii) specifies the best practices that should be used in general, from the level of gas sensing up to decision-making in the case of this restricted area. As recommended in [15], newer frameworks need the extension of technologies to monitor complex toxic situations effectively. A real-time remote monitoring framework of WSNs and ambient intelligence based on temporal statistical methods governing decision-making for miners is developed for bridging the challenging gaps. The major contributions of this paper are as follows:

(i) the development of a reactive remote monitoring framework based on real-time gas sensing, which spans physical layers through application space, by building on mine networks;

(ii) the modelling of the theory in WSNs, Ohm's law, concepts of static and mobile robot sensing, derivations of curvilinear gas calibration equations, and ambient intelligence based on temporal statistical methods;

(iii) the applications to monitor gases remotely in a real-life engine test cell, such as those typically found in underground mines, generating knowledge to improve safety with an assurance of assistance whenever required.

The rest of the paper is arranged as follows: Section 2 presents the background, which includes toxic mine gases, their physiological health effects, and the baseline mine network; Section 3 presents the proposed remote monitoring framework, which includes the sensor publishers, mathematical equations for gas calibration, and the ambient intelligence approach; Section 4 presents two experimental field setups; Section 5 critically presents experimental and comparative evaluations together with benchmarking of our proposed framework. We conclude the paper in Section 6.

2. Background

This section presents toxic mine gases, their physiological health effects, and the baseline mine network. The purpose is to provide the necessary knowledge to understand the requirements of the newly proposed framework fully.

TABLE 1: Common mine gases.

Gases	Properties	Health effects	Concentration in the air
CO_2	Colourless; odourless; heavier than air; acidic taste at high concentrations	At 5%, stimulated respiration; at 7% to 10%, unconsciousness after few minutes of exposure	280–390 ppm
CO	Flammable; colourless; tasteless; odourless; lighter than air	At 200 ppm, slight headache, tiredness, dizziness, nausea after 2 to 3 hrs; at >200 ppm, life threatening after 3 hrs	0-trace ppm
H_2	Colourless; reacts easily with other chemical substances; explosive mixtures are easily formed; lighter than air	High concentration causes oxygen-deficient environment; headaches; ringing in ears; drowsiness; nausea; skin having blue colour	0.5 ppm
CH_4	Colourless; odourless; tasteless; flammable; lighter than air; largest component of fire damp	Asphyxiation, dizziness, headache, and nausea in high concentrations due to displacement of oxygen	1.79–2.0 ppm
NO_2	Reddish-brown colour in high concentrations; acrid or bleach odour; nonflammable; heavier than air	At 1–13 ppm, irritation of nose and throat;≤80 ppm, tightness in chest after 3 to 5 minutes; >80 ppm, pulmonary edema after 30 minutes	0.03 ppm

2.1. Toxic Mine Gases and Physiological Health Effects. Table 1 presents some information about toxic gases commonly found in mine air. The knowledge is extracted from [16]. This information benchmarks our intelligence system to guide the early warning triggers.

2.2. Baseline Mine Network for Remote Monitoring. The integrated mine network proposed in [23] is intended for use as a baseline to connect with the proposed framework. The integrated mine network is composed of optical fibre as the main network through the shaft and uses WSNs in the roadway where monitoring is needed. The WSNs also connect other networks via gateway nodes, realising information interaction of aboveground and underground networks, as shown in Figure 2. The benefits of this mine network are as follows: (1) full usage of the existing network in the mine, which implies low maintenance, (2) no need for a WSN to lay lines for communication and power, which makes it more flexible, (3) sensor nodes that could be positioned optionally and compactly, making it possible to monitor stopes and any other areas in the mine, and (4) expandability of the network even when nodes and roadways are modified, making it convenient to monitor moving robot sensing in underground mines.

In our approach, the network is intended for deploying the sensing nodes to identify toxic gases and sense what is happening underground. The inclusion of fibre-optic cabling through the shaft alleviates the challenges of no network coverage in underground tunnel regions. The fibre-optic cable communicates to a server or data-logger aboveground, which stores sensor readings for forward transmission to the Internet or network space, as used in Figure 3.

3. Proposed Remote Monitoring Gas Sensing Framework

This section introduces the new reactive framework in Figure 3 for remotely monitoring toxic gases in restricted

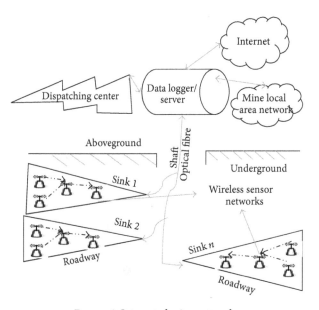

FIGURE 2: Integrated mine network.

areas, such as those typically found in underground mines. It uses the WSN and ambient intelligence technology by building on Figure 2. The goal of this framework is to guide the monitoring of toxic gases in restricted areas through a set of well-defined nodes in its entire real-time system. As shown, the reactive system is divided into three major nodes: sensor publishers in Section 3.1, gas calibration in Section 3.2, and intelligent decision support system (DSS) nodes in Section 3.3. We expect the benefits of this framework to be numerous: (i) mobile robot sensing balancing between maximising the detection rate of gases and minimising the number of missed detections/unit areas, (ii) the timely detection and early warning of many common problems such as failing sensors, toxic fume levels hazardous to health in various regions, and potential gas explosions, (iii) an intelligent goal-directed decision-making process, (iv) an increase

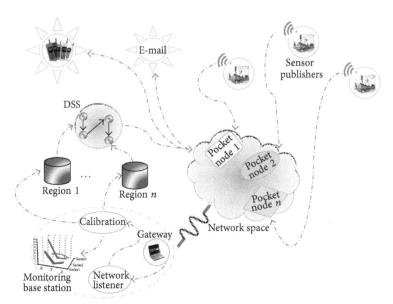

FIGURE 3: New remote gas monitoring framework.

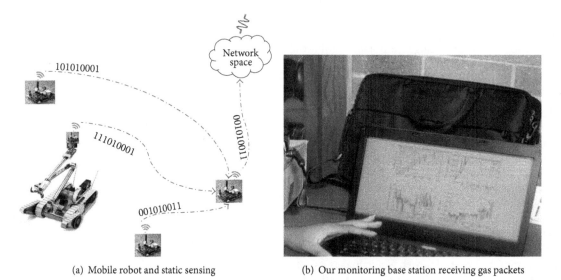

(a) Mobile robot and static sensing   (b) Our monitoring base station receiving gas packets

FIGURE 4: Mobile robot and static sensing publishing gas packets to the gateway for integration into Figure 3.

in coordination between the different working nodes on the framework, thanks to a clear division of responsibilities, and (v) the reproducibility of knowledge gathered from real-world WSN applications.

3.1. Sensor Publisher Nodes-Physical Layer. The sensor publishers, implemented as shown at the top right of Figure 3, collect gas data from different regions of an environment, which is necessary to understand the concentrations of the gases being monitored fully. This physical layer consists of an exhaustive design of the framework, which could include mobile sensing, shown in Figure 4(a). This is expatiated in the following.

Static and mobile robot sensing nodes provide an electronic "nose" on board, which includes an SD card slot and GPRS capabilities for sending an sms, and come in different communication flavours of Zigbee using the Xbee protocol.

Zigbee can operate on line-of-sight or use the direct-sequence spread spectrum to penetrate barriers. The node uses a lithium battery, which can be recharged through a dedicated socket by a solar panel, allows extra sensors and GPS on board, and can transmit over a distance of 75 m. Low-level software programming is embedded onto different board circuitry, enabling wireless communication. Tagging each sensor board at this physical layer enables localisation of the source of various toxic gases, thereby making concurrent gas publishing onto the network space identifiable in Figure 4(b) as separate packet voltage (v) values. Thus, the network space aligns our framework with the integrated mine network, where the network space represents the Internet.

3.2. Mathematical Equations for Gas Calibration Nodes-Middle Layer. Every sensor used in gas measurement can be characterised by a specific response function or calibration equation relating the sensor output voltage (V) to a gas concentration normally measured in parts per million (ppm). The goal of this middle layer is to input the voltage and empirically generate the ppm that subsequent nodes in Figure 3 use. The raw gas measurements captured over the sensors are usually in millivolts (mV), and they are converted to V, obviously by dividing by 1,000. This needs to be converted back to the resistance of the sensor using Ohm's law [24] in

$$R_s = \frac{V}{I} = \frac{V}{V_s/R_l} \implies \frac{V * R_l}{V_s},\qquad(1)$$

where R_s is the resistance of the sensor, V is the voltage supplied, I is the current over the sensor, R_l is the constant load resistance, and V_s is the voltage over the sensor. When a sensor remains without power for a prolonged period of time, it possibly shows an unstable output. This stability is regained after many consecutive cycles of power supply with a defined R_l over the sensor, leading the resistance of the sensor to

$$\implies R_s = \frac{V * R_l}{(V_s - R_l)}.\qquad(2)$$

More information and the values of R_l and V can be found in gas datasheets in [25]. Therefore calibration of the gas sensors involves two steps, which are (i) deriving base resistance (zero point) and (ii) span calibration. Since there is no established standard that defines zero air, a good reference point can be an office area where air may be considered fresh. The sensors used here are relative; no device gives the same reading for a certain concentration of gas, but the relationship between the readings for a particular sensor for different concentrations of readings is constant. About ten readings could be experimentally taken in fresh air and averaged to give the calibration point (R_0) of the gas sensor. For the span calibration, subsequent readings using (2) will be compared to R_0 to form a ratio R_s/R_0. The calibration node collects mathematical equations (3)–(9) and autonomously finds a well-fitted model for translating the ratio to corresponding ppm, depending on the known nature of the behaviour of the gas being measured and the measurement process itself. This process minimises any sensor inaccuracies by regulating the reliability of its readings.

The linear regression model is expressed in (3) as

$$\hat{y} = m * r + c,\qquad(3)$$

where

$$m = \frac{\left(n\sum xy - \sum x \sum y\right)}{\left(n\sum x^2 - \left(\sum x\right)^2\right)},\qquad(4)$$

$$c = \overline{y} - m * \overline{x},$$

$\hat{y}$ is the estimated ppm, r is the ratio, and x and y are known volts and ppm. The goodness of fit of the model is examined using the Pearson correlation coefficient, R, in

$$R = 1 - \frac{\sum_i \left((x_i - \overline{x})(y_i - \overline{y})\right)}{\sqrt{\left(\sum_i (x_i - \overline{x})^2\right)\left(\sum_i (y_i - \overline{y})^2\right)}}.\qquad(5)$$

If x and y are linearly correlated, R would be strongly close to +1 or −1, then the system selects (4) for the calibration. Otherwise, any of the four curvilinear models in (6)–(9) is selected, depending on the highest value of R:

Power series:

$$y = ax^b,\qquad(6)$$

Logarithmic:

$$y = \ln\left(ax^b\right),\qquad(7)$$

Exponential:

$$y = ae^{\alpha x},\qquad(8)$$

Polynomial:

$$y = ax^2 - bx + \beta.\qquad(9)$$

Parameters a, b, α, and β are estimated by linearising equations (6)–(9), which can be found in [26]. In the present case, the system selected is (i) power series for calibrating gases CO, NO_2, H_2, CH_4, and NH_3, (ii) polynomial model for calibrating H_2S, and (iii) exponential for calibrating CO_2.

3.3. Ambient Intelligence Node for Decision Support System-Application Layer. Sensors are generally believed to be imprecise and not completely accurate even after the calibration process. To increase our confidence in the presence of uncertainty in toxic gas sensing, an intelligent DSS for reasoning over some periods of time is needed, as shown in Figure 3. One of the important tasks in our remote gas monitoring is sending early warning to safety officers through the real-time intelligence node based on temporal statistical models for reasoning on the imprecise gas sensor readings and allowing users interaction through the theory of situation awareness (SA) [10, 27]. We prefer the theory and the models because of ease in the interpretation of results, fast execution time, and scalability for large multidimensional data sets.

The objective of the SA was to guide safety officers through the decision-making process by detecting hidden patterns in the data captured over the WSN and revealing *what is happening, why it is happening* to the environment, *what can be done* to avoid unwanted behaviour, and *what will happen next.* In consolidating SA, we construct the temporal statistical mean, median, mode, standard deviation, and skewness in Table 2 for describing the situation of the toxic gases, while chi-square inference based on contingency table analyses relationships between parameters in multiple regions over time.

As the toxic gases are observed over time, the statistical models change dynamically in values describing the location and variability of situations based on what is intended to be known in the regions observed. Since skewness measures the shapes of distributions, it characterises the degree of asymmetry of a distribution around its mean [28]. This means that, when skewness > 0 or < 0, the gas concentrations are clustered on one side, and when skewness = 0, they are distributed normally.

TABLE 2: Temporal statistical methods used in real time.

Temporal statistical methods	Their models
Mean ($\overline{x}_t$) and standard deviation (SD_t)	$\overline{x}_t = \dfrac{1}{n}\sum_{i=1}^{n} x_i;$ $SD_t = \sqrt{\dfrac{1}{n-1}\sum_{i=1}^{n}(x-\overline{x})^2}$
Skewness (S_t)	$S_t = \dfrac{\sum_{i=1}^{n}(x_i - \overline{x})^3}{(n-1)s^3}$

For analysing the relationships between gases, the following five stages are required: (i) a contingency table, which is a frequency between two or more variables, is first constructed, while independence between the variables is conducted by computing the expected values from the observed values using (10); (ii) a chi square test and degree of freedom are then computed as shown in (11) and (12), respectively; (iii) a temporal probability (p_t) representing the degree of independence is computed using an χ^2 distribution function as shown in (13); (iv) an inference on the relationship is made by comparing the p_t with a significant level often set at 5%; and (v) if $p_t < 0.05$, the two variables thus have a relationship, otherwise no relationship can be concluded in the contingency table as follows:

$$e_{ij} = \frac{\sum_i o_{ij} * \sum_j o_{ij}}{\sum_i \sum_j o_{ij}}, \tag{10}$$

$$\chi_t^{2} = \sum_i \sum_j \frac{\left(o_{ij} - e_{ij}\right)^2}{e_{ij}}, \tag{11}$$

$$df_t = (\text{total rows} - 1) * (\text{total columns} - 1), \tag{12}$$

$$p_t = \chi^2 \text{DIST}\left(\chi^2, df\right). \tag{13}$$

It is believed that the theory of SA and the temporal statistics can significantly minimise the number of false positives, as they combine qualitative and quantitative reasoning. To the best of our knowledge, no previous work on applying decision-making to gas monitoring has considered the effects of both theories on the accuracy of early warning. The contribution of this phase is an integration of the set of calibrated gases from multiple zones and building the temporal statistical models for real-time decision-making. The output of the ambient system is the provision of accurate early warning for each zone, taking into account cell phone and E-mail communication with the safety officers.

4. Experimental Field Setups

Hypothesis 1. Mobile sensing will not track the variability of gas concentration in air as well as static sensing over WSNs indoors.

(a) Static gas sensing

(b) Mobile gas sensing

FIGURE 5: (a) Static sensing node 1 on a filing cabinet in an aerated office, 5 metres away from the monitoring station. (b) Sensing node 2 on a mobile pioneer robot at the printing and network server section, 10 metres and two doors (barriers) away from the monitoring station.

FIGURE 6: A mechanical engine test cell, over 20 metres and four walls (barriers) away from Figure 4(b).

In other words, it might not be necessary to implement mobile and static gas sensing over WSN indoors if it is known ahead of time that an environmental volume of air cannot be polluted beyond absorbable levels. To test the hypothesis, it is necessary first to establish different fields' setups, such as Figure 5(a) showing a cross-ventilation area and Figure 5(b) with no free flow of fresh air.

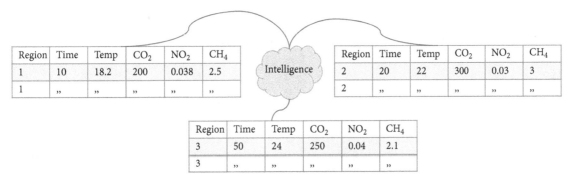

FIGURE 7: Sample gases data model and the ambient intelligence.

Hypothesis 2. The performance of remote monitoring of gases in restricted areas over WSNs is not correlated to its performance in areas such as those typically found in underground mines.

An underground mine can be modelled in a more or less detailed fashion as a restricted area. For a mine consisting of multiple features such as wall barriers, the features would ideally need to be modelled separately. A real-life setup in two aeronautic mechanical engine test cells with dimensions $800 \, \text{m}^3$ and $650 \, \text{m}^3$ was used to test this hypothesis. Although it will not be able to reveal whether more accurate setups give better results in all cases, it will allow us to observe the effects of wall barriers encountered during transmission of gas packets outside the enclosed test cell, such as those typically found in underground mines. The good news is that our demonstrator does not rely only on line-of-sight for transmission, but also uses a direct-sequence spread spectrum to penetrate the barriers.

To assess the readiness of our system for underground mine deployment in terms of sensing some toxic gases and localising their sources, the following objectives are set: (i) performing ambient measurements assessing temperature, CO_2, NO_2, and CH_4 buildup or distributions, (ii) getting a feel for the gas flow, (iii) picking up other possible fumes, and (iv) responding to environmental activities/events in the cell. Because of confidentiality in industries, the real-life engine test cell is presented as shown in Figure 6. A sensor node R_1 is located high up, close to the inlet, where fresh air enters the cell, a sensor node R_2 is located at the basement in front of the engine, and a sensor node R_5 is located behind the engine close to the air extractor, while the base monitoring station is outside the cell.

5. Experimental Results and Evaluations

From the ambient measurements, the six variables captured are quantitative data types where *temperature* is the warmness of the region measured in degrees Celsius (°C), and *region* values are in integers, while gases CO_2, CH_4, and NO_2 are in ppm. The time step on the x-axis of Figures 8 and 9 is in seconds, and the interval between two time step units was set to 40 seconds. The last time step 80 on the figures implies that the sampling time or observations in the test cell took about

one hour. The data model used in these experiments is in the form shown in Figure 7.

Hypothesis 1 (indoor environments). The static and mobile sensor nodes in Figure 5 capture the concentration of gases in the air, publish a stream of gases in voltages over the WSN onto a gateway subscription, and calibrate it into ppm, as shown in Figure 4(b).

5.1. Situation Awareness for Indoors-Qualitative Reasoning. The objective here is to assess the qualitative performance of the static sensing in a ventilated environment with the region 1 results shown over time in Figure 8(a), which exhibits noticeable differences when compared to the mobile sensing in an enclosed environment with region 2 results in Figure 8(b). In particular, the SA questioning paradigm in the following guides the safety officers through a decision-making process.

Decision-Making: Sample Qualitative Reasoning at Time Step 90.

Q_1: *What is happening?*

A_1: CH_4 concentration and temperature seem slightly higher in R_2 than R_1; higher instability of CO_2 in R_1 than R_2; slightly more NO_2 concentration in R_1 than R_2.

Q_2: *Why is it happening?*

A_2: Higher fresh air and noise dilution in R_1 than R_2; suspicious clearer spikes in R_2 due to steady mobility and of course machines in R_2 generate more heat.

Q_3: *What can we do about it?*

A_3: Unwanted behaviours could be avoided if detonation of explosives is avoided, and machines are serviced regularly.

Q_4: *What will happen next?*

A_4: Since the concentrations approximately revolve around the acceptable values shown in Table 1, the two regions seem relatively safe to health.

Hypothesis 1 states that mobile sensing will not track the variability of gas concentration in air as well as static sensing over WSNs indoors. The qualitative results, however, show

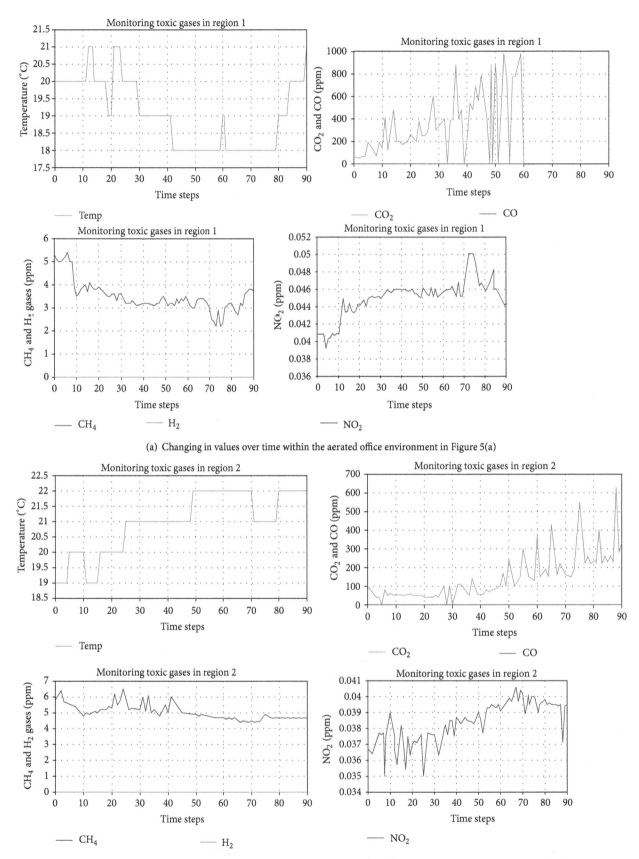

(a) Changing in values over time within the aerated office environment in Figure 5(a)

(b) Changing in values over time within an enclosed indoors area of printing environment in Figure 5(b)

FIGURE 8: (i) Temperature at the top left-hand corners, (ii) CO_2 and CO expected at the top right-hand corners, (iii) CH_4 and H_2 expected at the bottom left-hand corners, and (iv) NO_2 at the bottom right-hand corners of (a) and (b).

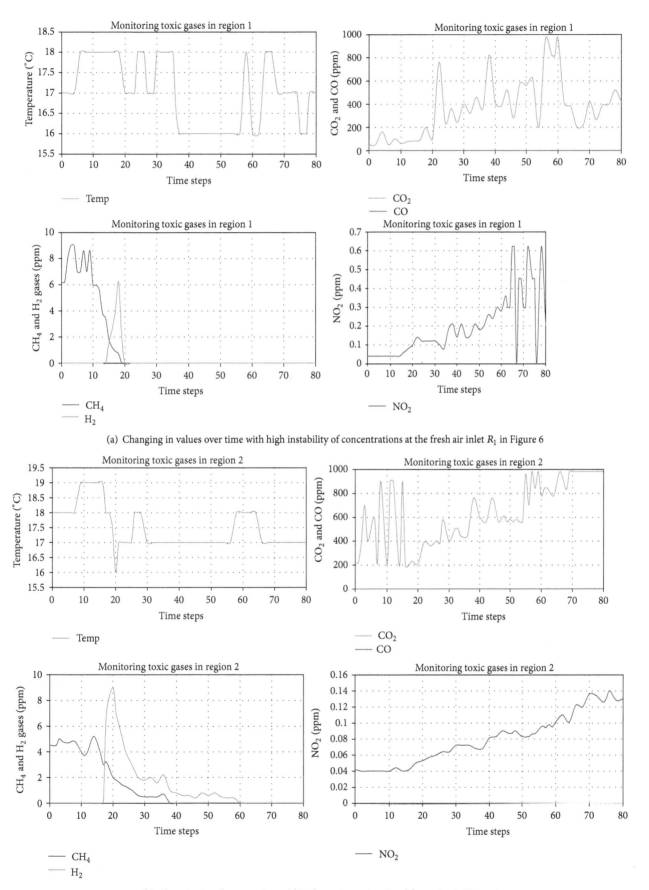

(a) Changing in values over time with high instability of concentrations at the fresh air inlet R_1 in Figure 6

(b) Changing in values over time within the testing region R_2 of the engine in Figure 6

FIGURE 9: Continued.

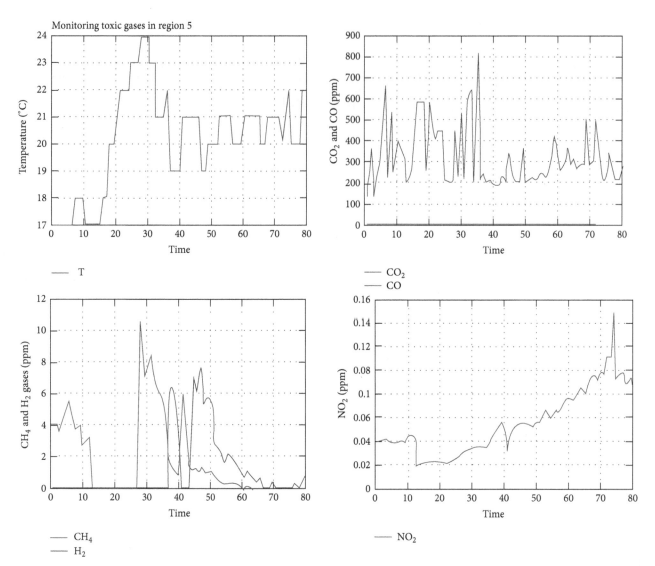

(c) Changing in values over time at the air extractor region R_5 shown in Figure 6

FIGURE 9: (i) Temperature at the top left-hand corners, (ii) CO_2 and CO expected at the top right-hand corners, (iii) CH_4 and H_2 expected at the bottom left-hand corners, and (iv) NO_2 at the bottom right-hand corners of (a), (b), and (c).

that it is not the case, implying that mobile sensing accurately captures the dynamism in region 2, as well as static sensing does in region 1.

Hypothesis 2 (mechanical engine field test cell).

5.2. Situation Awareness of Engine Test Cell-Qualitative Reasoning. The objective here is to access the qualitative performance of a restricted engine test cell for an underground mine. The underlying objectives are to assess (i) temperature and get a feel for its flow, (ii) CO_2 and NO_2 buildup, and (iii) other possible fumes.

Decision-Making: Sample Qualitative Reasoning at Time Step 80.

Q$_1$: *What is happening?*

A$_1$: From R_1–R_5, at time step 80, NO_2 reduces from 0.5 to 0.08, CO_2 from 400 to 300 ppm, though the engine emits more CO_2 in R_2; H_2 fumes were detected in the cell around time step 20, but disappeared over time with CH_4; temperature gradually increases across R_1–R_5.

Q$_2$: *Why is it happening?*

A$_2$: The air extractor proves effective, as the concentration drops towards the outlet R_5; an event with fire took place at step 20, giving rise to H_2 fumes.

Q$_3$: *What can we do about it?*

A$_3$: The air extractor must be maintained and declared effectively before testing any engine.

Q$_4$: *What will happen next?*

TABLE 3: Quantitative results of region 1 shown in Figure 9(a).

$t_0 \cdots T_{80}$	Temp	CO_2	NO_2	CH_4	H_2
Mean	17.02889	369.2593	0.208272	1.301235	0.223457
Standard error	0.09528	24.97194	0.017473	0.299694	0.097962
Median	17	360	0.18	0	0
Mode	16	50	0.04	0	0
Standard deviation	0.857524	224.7475	0.157256	2.697244	0.881656
Skewness	−0.09152	0.917227	1.269842	1.814768	3.777197
$\chi^2 = 397.37$			df = 340		Prob. = 0.0173

A_4: Staying away from R_2 is recommended in view of too high CO_2 concentration, though the entire test cell seems safe to engineers.

5.3. Situation Awareness of Engine Test Cell-Quantitative Reasoning. From the real-time monitoring of the engine test cell, we specifically assess the quantitative performance of our ambient intelligence approach to consolidate the qualitative reasoning ranging from the use of temporal statistics to finding dependencies between parameters. We set and implemented five research questions in the following. These assist in sending early warning whenever hazardous observations are made over time, as indicated in Figure 6. We want to know the following over time.

q_1: *What is the level of health safety in each of the three regions in the engine test cell?*

q_2: *What concentrations of the gases are commonly sensed in most regions?*

q_3: *At what temperature levels are the gases' concentrations being sensed?*

q_4: *Are there any interesting events that could be picked up from the gases' distributions?*

q_5: *Is there any relationship between CH_4 concentrations and the temperature of the region?*

Having implemented the temporal statistical models, the results obtained at time step 80 in Tables 2–4 provide answers to the research questions and substantiate the qualitative results reflected in Figure 9. It can be noted that all observed results are quite accurate from a general standpoint, as most standard errors compared to the mean values are less than 5% in all regions.

An interesting observation that can be made from the engine test cell is that the air extractor inlet (R_1) and outlet (R_5) are working perfectly. The reason for this is that the average of most of the gases suspended in air is more in R_2, but lower in regions R_1 and R_5. In Table 3, R_1 is largely safe when the mean values are compared to the normal gases' values in Table 1. In Table 4, region 2 is where the engine is run; the system becomes aware of the emission of more CO_2, that is, increasing concentration to 900 ppm, making it unsafe, unlike other gases. For the outlet in R_5, however, Table 5 shows a quick reduction in CO_2 to 300 ppm, making the region safe, as it is for other gases. This answers question q_1 and autonomously sends an sms to safety agents.

At the 80th time step, concentrations commonly sensed in regions R_1, R_2, and R_5 are shown on the modal rows, within temperature = 16°C, 17°C, and 21°C, respectively. The temperature reveals the direction of heat flow. The tables show that CH_4 and H_2 are rarely found in the cell, while NO_2 is constantly low. It is concluded that enough noise is present at the inlet in region 1 with a low 50 ppm concentration of CO_2 compared with other regions. This answers questions q_2 and q_3 and autonomously sends a message to the mobile phones of the safety agents.

The values of skewness in the three tables are greater or less than 0, showing clearly that events took place in the engine test cell: (i) three safety agents opened a door into/out of the cell, and (ii) a fire was ignited from a nozzle for tracing wind direction in the cell, leading to the detection of H_2 gas in the process. This actually correlates with the results in Figure 9 and answers question q_4.

Since the degrees of independence or probability (of X^2 in R_1 and R_2) < 0.05, it implies that there is a relationship between CH_4 and temperature. However, there may not be a relationship between them in region 3, since the probability (= 0.9606) > 0.05. It reveals that a higher temperature reflects a high CH_4 concentration and vice versa. This interestingly conforms to the properties of CH_4 shown in Table 1. This answers question q_5.

There are diverse discoveries of knowledge that the system could reveal, but our main questions q_n are needed in order to focus on the hypotheses. Hypothesis 2 states that the performance of remote monitoring of gases in restricted areas, such as the engine test cell, over WSNs is not correlated to its performance in areas such as those typically found in underground mines. These experiments, however, showed that this is not the case, implying that they are correlated.

5.4. Benchmarking Our Quantitative Reasoning with Publicly Available Observations and Methods. One of the ways to substantiate the reliability of our demonstrator is to benchmark its quantitative reasoning with publicly available air observations and methods. The Texas commission on environmental air quality captures hourly data collected, in particular, in the CPS Pecan Valley C678, Heritage Middle School C622, and Calaveras Lake C59 regions of San Antonio metropolitan area, USA, in [29]. The information is updated hourly, and it is officially certified by the technical staff. The air gas pollutants considered in this study are CO, SO_2, and NO_2, with different temperatures in an apparent one-hour

TABLE 4: Quantitative results of region 2 shown in Figure 9(b).

$t_0 \cdots T_{80}$	Temp	CO_2	NO_2	CH_4	H_2
Mean	17.50074	612.9259	0.080642	1.230864	1.033333
Standard error	0.077014	32.35313	0.003432	0.194949	0.212597
Median	17	581	0.08	0.1	0
Mode	17	999	0.04	0	0
Standard deviation	0.693128	291.1782	0.03089	1.75454	1.913374
Skewness	0.985312	0.023658	0.225995	1.176821	2.465437
$\chi^2 = 696.99$		df = 312		Prob. $= 2.00E - 31$	

TABLE 5: Quantitative results of region 5 shown in Figure 9(c).

$t_0 \cdots T_{80}$	Temp	CO_2	NO_2	CH_4	H_2
Mean	20.17654	359.8519	0.06537	2.447654	1.174074
Standard error	0.214816	15.80476	0.011157	0.285151	0.214534
Median	20.9	340	0.046	2.2	0
Mode	21	299	0.04	0	0
Standard deviation	1.933344	142.2428	0.100415	2.566361	1.930806
Skewness	−0.27947	0.982282	8.174952	0.706862	1.569931
$\chi^2 = 802.87$		df = 875		Prob. $= 0.9606$	

time lag in the data. The sample data for August 25, 2012, was integrated into our temporal statistical models implemented in a Python distributed programming environment.

The temporal quantitative results obtained at time step 23 pm in Table 6 provide answers to most of the research questions, especially question q_1 on the level of health safety in the metropolitan area, which the Texas commission provides for benchmarking. An interesting observation that can be made from the area is that the average of most of the gases suspended in air is fairly higher in the Heritage Middle School C622 and Calaveras Lake C59 regions, but lower in the CPS Pecan Valley C678 region. In Table 6, our temporal quantitative reasoning shows that the top region (CPS Pecan) is *fairly safe* when the mean values of the gases are compared to the acceptable values in air, except for NO_2, which is 1.896 ppm. In the middle region in Table 6, the mean values of SO_2 and NO_2 gases increase to concentrations of 2.608 ppm and 1.658 ppm, respectively, making it manageable or *fairly unsafe*, except CO, which is within the acceptable range. For the bottom region, however, Table 6 shows relatively more NO_2 with 1.642 ppm, making the region *fairly unsafe/manageable*, though other gases are not recorded. Although our early warning decision to the safety agents is very meticulous, one can see that our quantitative reasoning on the level of health safety is well correlated with the Texas air quality index (AQI) decisions. This answers the main question q_1, which benchmarks the two methods and shows the reliability of our approach.

5.5. Comparative Evaluations of the Proposed Framework with Other Related Methods. The evaluation of the contribution to mine safety using our proposed framework indicates that it is similar to the contributions derived from the related methods. A comparison of the related methods and the proposed framework is summarised in Table 7. The comparison and application of the related methods and the proposed framework to achieve mine safety and monitoring of toxic gases in particular show that our approach is comparatively complementary and building on the related baseline methods with regard to the following aspects.

(a) Methodology: (i) the proposed system is a reactive remote monitoring framework developed for real-time gas sensing, which spans physical layers through application space; (ii) the modelling of the theory in WSNs, Ohm's law, concepts of static and mobile robot sensing, and derivations of curvilinear gas calibration equations are intended to achieve autonomy; (iii) our approach implements distributed sensors more cheaply than the big sophisticated sensors, which could be laborious to set up or expensive for developing mines/countries. Thus, every methodology in Table 7 is obviously driven by the problem focus.

(b) Decision support system: (i) integrating intelligent DSS with distributed WSN for remotely monitoring toxic gases builds on the baseline produced by the related methods; (ii) the ambient intelligence, based on temporal statistical methods governing decision-making for miners, works well with both qualitative as well as quantitative parameters; (iii) this decision-making technique is comparatively easy to use, as it is lighter than using computationally time-consuming algorithms that could be heavy weight, affecting our real-time system with time lag.

(c) Field work: (i) our approach monitors gases remotely in a real-life engine test cell, such as those typically found in underground mines, generating knowledge to improve safety with an assurance of assistance

TABLE 6: Benchmarking our approach with USA San Antonio metropolitan regions and its AQI method determining the health safety status.

Regions	12:00⋯23:00	Temp	CO	SO$_2$	NO$_2$	Our approach	Texas AQI
	Mean	82.820833	0.291667	0.020833	1.895833		
	Standard error	1.185525	0.005763	0.020833	0.129726		
	Median	82.05	0.3	0	1.95		
CPS Pecan Valley c678	Mode	77	0.3	0	2	Fairly safe	Good
	Standard deviation	5.807864	0.028233	0.102062	0.635527		
	Kurtosis	−1.002790	9.123966	24	−0.701763		
	Skewness	0.368065	−3.219960	4.898979	0.265184		
	Mean	83.545833	0.4	2.608333	1.658333		
	Standard error	1.112332	$2.31498E-17$	0.859725	0.441297		
	Median	82.65	0.4	0.2	0.6		
Heritage Middle School	Mode	77.1	0.4	0	0	Fairly unsafe	Moderate
	Standard deviation	5.449290	$1.1341E-16$	4.211776	2.161907		
	Kurtosis	−0.947188	−2.190476	3.683374	2.008987		
	Skewness	0.473571	−1.067940	1.889303	1.575467		
	Mean	84.35	0	0	1.641667		
	Standard error	1.448200	0	0	0.124516		
	Median	83.5	0	0	1.45		
Calaveras Lake C59	Mode	78.5	0	0	1.5	Fairly unsafe	Moderate
	Standard deviation	7.094701	0	0	0.610001		
	Kurtosis	−0.903842	0	0	1.366540		
	Skewness	0.464159	0	0	1.440687		

whenever required; (ii) knowledge of how to implement DSS and WSN approaches and how to make them profitable in improving miners' safety is demonstrated; (iii) the proposed model not only assists mine management/companies in doing simulations like most related methods, but has also done real-life field work indoors and in an aeronautic engine test cell, similar to those typically found in underground mines.

6. Concluding Remarks

The study on remote monitoring of toxic gases targeting underground mines has analysed various aspects of using a WSN, SA, and temporal statistical models as ambient intelligence in an attempt to effect autonomous decision-making in real time. Some of the main conclusions that can be drawn from the experiments and analysis are as follows.

(i) Every implementation node in our framework functions as well as the pioneer robot when all its parameters are configured appropriately.

(ii) The experiments confirmed some of the claims discovered in the literature survey about toxic gases, Ohm's law, statistical methods, the theory of SA, and direct correlation of the properties of the engine test cell and underground mines.

(iii) Even the simple ambient intelligence proposed, based on the temporal statistics, provides better results

than common qualitative decision-making through consolidation.

(iv) The chosen gas calibration equations may have considerable effects on the accuracy of the ppm results.

(v) It is assumed that the robot navigates moderately to add extra airflow to the sensing node as it perceives higher evident peaks.

While working on the research project, a number of possible variations on the experiments were considered, yet not implemented. These are listed here as topics for future research:

(i) detecting redundant sensor nodes and optimal sensor placement;

(ii) autonomous determination of battery lifetime and remotely hibernating battery power;

(iii) noise removal and alternative decision-making models;

(iv) integrating Figures 2 and 3 to improve safety in underground mines.

The approach of defining hypotheses before performing experiments has advanced researchers' knowledge in an intriguing approach to studying problems and their potential solutions. Thus, this is a directed research project affecting lives by improving health safety and therefore ready for deployment in underground mines.

TABLE 7: Comparative evaluations of mine safety methods for toxic gases.

Related work	Problem focus/objective	Methodology	Results	DSS	Field work
Minming et al. 2009 [17]	Data aggregation modelling	(i) Directed diffusion (ii) Geographical information metrics	Addresses: data redundancy and transmission delay	N/A	(i) N/A (ii) Simulation
Yuan et al. 2009 [18]	High energy consumption in long-distance roadway	Uneven fixed cluster and mixed routing	Good network lifetime and connectivity	N/A	(i) N/A (ii) Simulation
Niu et al. 2007 [19]	Design WSN for mine safety monitoring	Overhearing-based adaptive data collecting scheme	Reduces traffic and control overheads	N/A	Real-life test
Shao et al. 2008 [20]	Safety monitoring system of mine	Ad hoc technology	Design of physical, MAC, and network layers	Manual	Not specified
Wu et al. 2010 [21]	Network deployment and multihop routing patterns	BRIT (bounce routing in tunnels) algorithm	Hybrid signal propagation model in three-dimensional underground tunnels	N/A	(i) N/A (ii) Simulation
Government practices [22]	Monitoring toxic gases	(a) Trainings (b) Ventilation (c) Lag time (d) Big sensors	Laborious and inaccurate	Manual	Reallife
Proposed system model	Decision-making in monitoring toxic gases	(i) Distributed portable sensors (ii) Calibration algorithm (iii) Regression models (iv) Ohm's law (v) Static and mobile sensing and phones	(i) Satisfactory (ii) Real-time and remote monitoring	(i) Autonomous (ii) Ambient intelligence (iii) Temporal statistical models	(i) Real-life test (ii) Aeronautic engine test cell (iii) Indoors

Acknowledgments

The author gratefully acknowledges resources and financial support made available by the University of South Africa (UNISA) and the Council for Scientific and Industrial Research (CSIR), South Africa.

References

[1] M. Möhner, M. Lindtner, H. Otten, and H. G. Gille, "Leukemia and exposure to ionizing radiation among German uranium miners," *American Journal of Industrial Medicine*, vol. 49, no. 4, pp. 238–248, 2006.

[2] M. C. Betournary, "Underground mining and its surface effects," Interstate Technical Group on Abandoned Underground Mines Fourth Biennial Abandoned Underground Mine Workshop, Report MMSL 02-021, 2010.

[3] M. Kreuzer, L. Walsh, M. Schnelzer, A. Tschense, and B. Grosche, "Radon and risk of extrapulmonary cancers: results of the German uranium miners' cohort study, 1960–2003," *British Journal of Cancer*, vol. 99, no. 11, pp. 1946–1953, 2008.

[4] MHSC, http://www.mhsc.org.za/

[5] R. S. Conti, Fire-fighting resources and fire preparedness for underground coal mines, National Institute for Occupational Safety and Health Pittsburgh Research Laboratory, 1994.

[6] Swansea Station, http://www.swansea.airqualitydata.com/cgi-bin/faqs.cgi?1009.

[7] Ohio Station, http://www.nytimes.com/2006/09/27/us/27steub-enville.html.

[8] E. R. Musaloiu, A. Terzis, K. Szlavecz, A. Szalay, J. Cogan, and J. Gray, "Life under your feet: a wireless soil ecology sensor network," in *Proceedings of the 3rd IEEE Conference on Embedded Networked Sensors (EmNetS '06)*, 2006.

[9] S. Li, S. H. Son, and J. A. Stankovic, "Event detection services using data service middleware in distributed sensor networks," in *Proceedings of the 2nd International Conference on Information Processing in Sensor Networks (IPSN '03)*, pp. 502–517, Springer, Berlin, Heidelberg, 2003.

[10] A. B. Bagula, I. Osunmakinde, and M. Zennaro, "On the relevance of using Bayesian belief networks in wireless sensor networks situation recognition," *Sensors*, vol. 10, no. 12, pp. 11001–11020, 2010.

[11] T. Melodia, M. C. Vuran, and D. Pompili, "The state-of-the-art in cross-layer design for wireless sensor networks," in *Wireless System/Network Architect*, M. Cesana and L. Fratta, Eds., vol. 3883 of *Lecture Notes in Computer Science*, pp. 78–92, Springer, Heidelberg, Germany, 2006.

[12] M. G. D. Benedetto and G. Giancola, *Understanding Ultra Wideband Radio Fundamentals*, Prentice Hall, Upper Saddle River, NJ, USA, 2004.

[13] M. Z. Win and R. A. Scholtz, "Ultra-wide bandwidth time-hopping spread-spectrum impulse radio for wireless multiple-access communications," *IEEE Transactions on Communications*, vol. 48, no. 4, pp. 679–691, 2000.

[14] Y. Yuan, Z. Shen, W. Quan-Fu, and S. Pei, "Long distance wireless sensor networks applied in coal mine," *Journal Procedia Earth and Planetary Science*, vol. 1, pp. 1461–1467, 2009.

[15] K. R. Rogers, S. L. Harper, and G. Robertson, "Screening for toxic industrial chemicals using semipermeable membrane devices with rapid toxicity assays," *Analytica Chimica Acta*, vol. 543, no. 1-2, pp. 229–235, 2005.

[16] Inspectapedia, http://inspectapedia.com/hazmat/Environment_Building.php.

[17] T. Minming, N. Jieru, W. Hu, and L. Xiaowen, "A data aggregation model for underground wireless sensor network," in *Proceedings of the WRI World Congress on Computer Science and Information Engineering (CSIE '09)*, vol. 1, pp. 344–348, April 2009.

[18] Y. Yuan, Z. Shen, W. Quan-Fu, and S. Pei, "Long distance wireless sensor networks applied in coal mine," *Journal of Procedia Earth and Planetary Science*, vol. 1, no. 1, pp. 1461–1467, 2009.

[19] X. Niu, X. Huang, Z. Zhao, Y. Zhang, C. Huang, and L. Cui, "The design and evaluation of a wireless sensor network for mine safety monitoring," in *Proceedings of the 50th Annual IEEE Global Telecommunications Conference (GLOBECOM '07)*, pp. 1291–1295, November 2007.

[20] Q. L. Shao, Z. X. Zhang, and Z. C. Zhang, "Research on safety monitoring system of mine based on ad hoc technology," in *Proceedings of the International Conference on Information Management, Innovation Management and Industrial Engineering (ICIII '08)*, vol. 2, pp. 450–453, December 2008.

[21] D. Wu, L. Bao, and R. Li, "A holistic approach to wireless sensor network routing in underground tunnel environments," *Journal of Computer Communications*, vol. 33, no. 13, pp. 1566–1573, 2010.

[22] Centers for Disease Control and Prevention, Atlanta, USA, http://www.cdc.gov/niosh/mining/topics/Ventilation.html.

[23] R. Lin, Z. Wang, and Y. Sun, "Wireless sensor networks solutions for real time monitoring of nuclear power plant," in *Proceedings of the 5th World Congress on Intelligent Control and Automation (WCICA '04)*, pp. 3663–3667, June 2004.

[24] J. Hashem, T. Liu, Z. Liang, and J. Ye, "Using Ohm's law to calibrate a picoammeter to 0.4 pico-ampere precision," *American Journal of Undergraduate Research*, vol. 10, no. 1, 9 pages, 2011.

[25] http://www.libelium.com/products, http://www.futurlec.com/Gas_Sensors.shtml.

[26] C. Sophocleous and R. J. Wiltshire, "On linearizing systems of diffusion equations," *Journal of Symmetry, Integrability and Geometry*, vol. 2, article 004, 11 pages, 2006.

[27] M. R. Endsley, "Theoretical underpinnings of situation awareness: a critical review," in *Situation Awareness Analysis and Measurement*, M. R. Endsley and D. J. Garland, Eds., LEA, Mahwah, NJ, USA, 2000.

[28] N. Maxwell, *Data Matters: Conceptual Statistics for a Random World*, Key College, Emeryville, Calif, USA, 2004.

[29] Texas Commission on Environmental Air Pollution Data Quality, USA, http://www.tceq.texas.gov/airquality/monops/hourly_data.html.

Permissions

The contributors of this book come from diverse backgrounds, making this book a truly international effort. This book will bring forth new frontiers with its revolutionizing research information and detailed analysis of the nascent developments around the world.

We would like to thank all the contributing authors for lending their expertise to make the book truly unique. They have played a crucial role in the development of this book. Without their invaluable contributions this book wouldn't have been possible. They have made vital efforts to compile up to date information on the varied aspects of this subject to make this book a valuable addition to the collection of many professionals and students.

This book was conceptualized with the vision of imparting up-to-date information and advanced data in this field. To ensure the same, a matchless editorial board was set up. Every individual on the board went through rigorous rounds of assessment to prove their worth. After which they invested a large part of their time researching and compiling the most relevant data for our readers. Conferences and sessions were held from time to time between the editorial board and the contributing authors to present the data in the most comprehensible form. The editorial team has worked tirelessly to provide valuable and valid information to help people across the globe.

Every chapter published in this book has been scrutinized by our experts. Their significance has been extensively debated. The topics covered herein carry significant findings which will fuel the growth of the discipline. They may even be implemented as practical applications or may be referred to as a beginning point for another development. Chapters in this book were first published by Hindawi Publishing Corporation; hereby published with permission under the Creative Commons Attribution License or equivalent.

The editorial board has been involved in producing this book since its inception. They have spent rigorous hours researching and exploring the diverse topics which have resulted in the successful publishing of this book. They have passed on their knowledge of decades through this book. To expedite this challenging task, the publisher supported the team at every step. A small team of assistant editors was also appointed to further simplify the editing procedure and attain best results for the readers.

Our editorial team has been hand-picked from every corner of the world. Their multi-ethnicity adds dynamic inputs to the discussions which result in innovative outcomes. These outcomes are then further discussed with the researchers and contributors who give their valuable feedback and opinion regarding the same. The feedback is then collaborated with the researches and they are edited in a comprehensive manner to aid the understanding of the subject.

Apart from the editorial board, the designing team has also invested a significant amount of their time in understanding the subject and creating the most relevant covers. They scrutinized every image to scout for the most suitable representation of the subject and create an appropriate cover for the book.

The publishing team has been involved in this book since its early stages. They were actively engaged in every process, be it collecting the data, connecting with the contributors or procuring relevant information. The team has been an ardent support to the editorial, designing and production team. Their endless efforts to recruit the best for this project, has resulted in the accomplishment of this book. They are a veteran in the field of academics and their pool of knowledge is as vast as their experience in printing. Their expertise and guidance has proved useful at every step. Their uncompromising quality standards have made this book an exceptional effort. Their encouragement from time to time has been an inspiration for everyone.

The publisher and the editorial board hope that this book will prove to be a valuable piece of knowledge for researchers, students, practitioners and scholars across the globe.

List of Contributors

Mario Collotta, Gianfranco Scatà and Giovanni Pau
Facoltà di Ingegneria, Architettura e delle Scienze Motorie, Università degli Studi di Enna—Kore Cittadella Universitaria, 94100 Enna, Italy

Di Wu and Yan Ling
School of Computer Science and Engineering, Dalian University of Technology, Dalian 116023, China

Hongsong Zhu
State Key Laboratory of Information Security, Institute of Information Engineering, Chinese Academy of Sciences, Beijing 100093, China

Jie Liang
School of Engineering Science, Simon Fraser University, Burnaby, BC, Canada V5A1S6

Thomas A. Wettergren and Russell Costa
Naval Undersea Warfare Center, 1176 Howell Street, Newport, RI 02841, USA

Xiaopei Lu, Dezun Dong and Xiangke Liao
College of Computer Science, National University of Defense Technology, Hunan 410073, China

Haigang Gong and Lingfei Yu
School of Computer Science and Engineering, University of Electronic Science and Technology of China, Chengdu 611731, China

Peng Zhu
Department of Information Management, School of Economics and Management, Nanjing University of Science and Technology, 200 Xiao Ling Wei Street, Nanjing 210094, China

Fei Jia
Division of Education Affairs, Nanjing Forest Police College, Nanjing 210046, China

Wazir Zada Khan and Mohammed Naufal Bin Mohammed Saad
Electrical and Electronic Engineering Department, Universiti Teknologi PETRONAS, Bandar Seri Iskandar, 31750 Tronoh, Perak, Malaysia

Mohammed Y. Aalsalem
School of Computer Science & Information System, Jazan University, Jazan 45142, Saudi Arabia

Yang Xiang
School of Information Technology, Deakin University, 221 Burwood Highway, Burwood, Melbourne, VIC 3125, Australia

Million Mafuta
Electronic and Electrical Engineering Department, University of Strathclyde, Royal College Building, 204 George Street, Glasgow G1 1XW, UK
Electrical Engineering Department, University of Malawi-The Polytechnic, Chichiri, Blantyre, Malawi

Graham Ault
Electronic and Electrical Engineering Department, University of Strathclyde, Royal College Building, 204 George Street, Glasgow G1 1XW, UK

Harry Gombachika and Timothy Chadza
Electrical Engineering Department, University of Malawi-The Polytechnic, Chichiri, Blantyre, Malawi

Marco Zennaro
T/ICT4D Laboratory, The Abdus Salam International Centre for Theoretical Physics, Strada Costiera, 11-34151 Trieste, Italy

Antoine Bagula
ISAT Laboratory, University of Cape Town, 18 University Avenue, Rhodes Gift, Cape Town 7707, South Africa

Hui Zhao and Jinqi Zhu
School of Computer Science and Engineering, University of Electronic Science and Technology of China, Chengdu, Sichuan 611731, China

Dahlila Putri Dahnil, Yaswant Prasad Singh, and Chin Kuan Ho
Faculty of Computing and Informatics, Persiaran Multimedia, 63100 Cyberjaya, Selangor, Malaysia

Li Lu
School of Computer Science and Engineering, University of Electronic Science and Technology of China, Chengdu 611731, China

Jinsong Han
School of Electronic and Information Engineering, Xi'an Jiao tong University, Xi'an 710049, China

Lei Hu
State Key Laboratory of Information Security, Chinese Academy of Sciences, Beijing 100049, China

Lionel M. Ni
Department of Computer Science and Engineering, Hong Kong University of Science and Technology, Hong Kong, China

Chong Han
College of Computer, Nanjing University of Posts and Telecommunications, Nanjing 210003, China

Lijuan Sun and Jian Guo
College of Computer, Nanjing University of Posts and Telecommunications, Nanjing 210003, China
Jiangsu High Technology Research Key Laboratory for Wireless Sensor Networks, Nanjing 210003, China
Key Lab of Broadband Wireless Communication and Sensor Network Technology of Ministry of Education, Nanjing University of Posts and Telecommunications, Jiangsu Province, Nanjing 210003, China

Fu Xiao and RuchuanWang
College of Computer, Nanjing University of Posts and Telecommunications, Nanjing 210003, China
Jiangsu High Technology Research Key Laboratory for Wireless Sensor Networks, Nanjing 210003, China
Key Lab of Broadband Wireless Communication and Sensor Network Technology of Ministry of Education, Nanjing University of Posts and Telecommunications, Jiangsu Province, Nanjing 210003, China
Provincial Key Laboratory for Computer Information Processing Technology, Soochow University, Suzhou 215006, China

Emanuele Lattanzi and Alessandro Bogliolo
Department of Base Sciences and Fundamentals (DiSBef), University of Urbino, 61029 Urbino, Italy

Kyuhong Lee and Heesang Lee
Department of Industrial Engineering, Sungkyunkwan University, Suwon 440-746, Republic of Korea

Heejun Roh and Wonjun Lee
Department of Computer Science and Engineering, Korea University, Seoul 136-701, Republic of Korea

Jiangfan Feng and Hu Song
College of Computer Science and Technology, Chongqing University of Posts and Telecommunications, Chongqing 400065, China

Isaac O. Osunmakinde
Semantic Computing Group, School of Computing, College of Science, Engineering and Technology, University of South Africa, (UNISA), P.O. Box 392, Pretoria 0003, South Africa

Printed in the USA
CPSIA information can be obtained
at www.ICGtesting.com
JSHW051438221024
72173JS00006B/1511